Bible
Speaks
today

T0335124

the message of

EXODUS

Series editors:
Alec Motyer (OT)
John Stott (NT)
Derek Tidball (Bible Themes)

the message of
EXODUS
The days of our pilgrimage
Revised edition

Alec Motyer

INTER-VARSITY PRESS
36 Causton Street, London SW1P 4ST, England
Email: ivp@ivpbooks.com
Website: www.ivpbooks.com

First published 2005
This edition published 2021

British Library Cataloguing-in-Publication Data
A catalogue record for this book is available from the British Library.

ISBN 978–1–78974–294–7
eBook ISBN 978–1–78359–645–4

Set in 9.5/13pt Karmina
Typeset in Great Britain by CRB Associates, Potterhanworth, Lincolnshire
Printed and bound in Great Britain by Ashford Colour Press Ltd, Gosport, Hampshire

Produced on paper from sustainable sources.

Inter-Varsity Press publishes Christian books that are true to the Bible and that communicate the gospel, develop discipleship and strengthen the church for its mission in the world.

IVP originated within the Inter-Varsity Fellowship, now the Universities and Colleges Christian Fellowship, a student movement connecting Christian Unions in universities and colleges throughout Great Britain, and a member movement of the International Fellowship of Evangelical Students. Website: www.uccf.org.uk. That historic association is maintained, and all senior IVP staff and committee members subscribe to the UCCF Basis of Faith.

To
Peter and Sally Salmon
Maurice and Jean Bell
Audrey Whitaker
and in memory of Harold Whitaker

Contents

Bible Speaks today

GENERAL PREFACE

The Bible Speaks Today describes three series of expositions, based on the books of the Old and New Testaments, and on Bible themes that run through the whole of Scripture. Each series is characterized by a threefold ideal:

- to expound the biblical text with accuracy
- to relate it to contemporary life, and
- to be readable.

These books are, therefore, not 'commentaries', for the commentary seeks rather to elucidate the text than to apply it, and tends to be a work rather of reference than of literature. Nor, on the other hand, do they contain the kinds of 'sermons' that attempt to be contemporary and readable without taking Scripture seriously enough. The contributors to The Bible Speaks Today series are all united in their convictions that God still speaks through what he has spoken, and that nothing is more necessary for the life, health and growth of Christians than that they should hear what the Spirit is saying to them through his ancient – yet ever modern – Word.

ALEC MOTYER
JOHN STOTT
DEREK TIDBALL
Series editors

Author's preface

This book began its life in 1974 when the Keswick Convention invited me to prepare the morning Bible expositions – with an additional request for something from the Old Testament – and I elected to undertake Exodus. The work alerted me all over again to the richness and importance of the book, and the attempt to compress forty chapters into four hours got me interested in its structure. By 1985 it was my happiness to have become minister at Christ Church, Westbourne, Bournemouth, and the large Wednesday morning gathering there offered an opportunity for a less restricted return to Exodus.

More recently, the memory of those twenty or thirty studies prompted the thought of writing them up into a book. I also remembered the marvellous help Susan Rebis had been in the early 1990s when I wrote *The Prophecy of Isaiah*. She agreed to undertake the task of putting my transcribed tapes into a properly edited and suitably literary form – for usually (and always in the case of one as prone to adjectives and adverbs and as repetitious as I am) there is nothing uglier or less readable than the spoken word on paper! Our first intention was that Susan would work on the tapes while I found a way of inserting in and around them some of the huge heap of additional notes on Exodus gathered in the intervening fifteen years. This neat plan just would not work, and in the event, everything has been written all over again, with all the fresh material added, only this time Susan has been the presiding genius over my written work, gently removing the adjectives and adverbs, making all sorts of needless sentences and repetitions disappear, and giving to the book whatever helpful, readable and stylish qualities it may possess. I owe her an immense debt – and you, the reader, owe her even more!

In addition, as has always been my experience when associated with IVP, a whole line of people, known and unnamed, has lined up to help me. In prospect of undertaking Exodus, I was greatly encouraged on my way by Colin Duriez, and, after his departure, I owe more than I can say to the kindness, leadership and advice of Philip Duce. I wrote in the preface to another book that no-one could possibly feel more cared for, or in safer hands, than those who achieve publication with IVP. This remains true, and I am happy to express my gratitude.

My first request is that this book be read with an open Bible alongside, for the best benefits will be reaped by patient reading which takes time to look up cross-references. Where the structure of a section or passage is given in diagram form, please work through it, point by point, before going on to read what is written about it.

Reference must be made here to the number of footnotes attached to this study of Exodus. Not everything important to the understanding of Exodus can be accommodated in an expository treatment, where the emphasis is on the emerging message, and so the footnotes are offered in the hope that they will give students and preachers access to this additional material. From time to time the footnotes threatened to swamp the page! In these cases, they have been moved to become additional notes attached to the chapter in question.

Cassuto says about his extensive commentary that 'we shall not cite the various interpretations [but] content ourselves with expounding the simple meaning of the text in the manner we deem correct'. This is the case here too, indeed it has to be so, for neither ability nor space would permit a comprehensive review and critique of what all the commentaries say. I have chosen, for example, not to give any sort of extensive introduction to the documentary analysis of the Pentateuch and Exodus into the famous J, E, D and P strands. It would, however, be an absurd 'head-in-the-sand' attitude to ignore totally an understanding of Exodus that has been so hugely influential. For myself, I have to confess that the documentary theory has never commanded my adherence or seemed to me the most helpful or natural way of approach. I plead for the tolerance of those who think otherwise. I have occasionally offered extra comments in the notes where it seems that this method particularly lacks coherence, evidence or persuasiveness.

Other commentaries will have to be consulted on this and many other questions, and I have provided a list of books I have used, which taken as a whole will be found reasonably comprehensive. The concern of this book, as of the whole Bible Speaks Today series, is 'The Message of Exodus', what it testifies of the Bible's God, in what ways it points to the Lord Jesus Christ and heralds him in advance, and how it bears, within the unity of the Bible, on the nature and life of the people of God, their redemption, obedience, security and inheritance.

Now that this particular bout of study on Exodus is finished, I shall miss it greatly: the sheer joy of engaging with its message; its frequently stately, sometimes earthy and businesslike, and always beautiful Hebrew; and its uplifting revelation of the Lord God in his power and patience, tenderness and redemption, and in his inflexible insistence on honouring his word and keeping his promises. In their history as recorded here, our early brothers, sisters and parents in the Israel of God found him in turn to be their covenant-keeping Redeemer in slavery, the Angel of the Lord, their divine companion in pilgrimage, and the Holy One indwelling their camp and sharing their lot. He is still unchangeably the same.

ALEC MOTYER

Chief abbreviations

BDB	*A Hebrew and English Lexicon of the Old Testament*, F. Brown, S. R. Driver and C. A. Briggs (OUP, 1906)
ESV	The English Standard Version of the Bible (2001)
GK	*Gesenius' Hebrew Grammar*, ed. E. Kautzsch (Oxford, 1910)
JSOT	*Journal for the Study of the Old Testament*
KB	*Lexicon in Veteris Testamenti Libros*, L. Koehler and W. Baumgartner (Brill, 1958)
KJV	The Authorized (King James) Version of the Bible (1611)
LXX	The Septuagint (ancient Greek translation of the Old Testament)
NASB	The New American Standard Bible (2020)
NBC	*The New Bible Commentary*, ed. D. Guthrie, J. A. Motyer, A. M. Stibbs and D. J. Wiseman (IVP, 1970)
NBC(21)	*The New Bible Commentary, 21st Century Edition*, ed. D. A. Carson, R. T. France, J. A. Motyer and G. J. Wenham (IVP, 1994)
NBD	*The New Bible Dictionary*, ed. I. H. Marshall, A. R. Millard, J. I. Packer and D. J. Wiseman (IVP, 1996)
NIV	The New International Version of the Bible (1973, 1978, 1984, 2011)
NKJV	The New King James Version of the Bible (1982)
RV	The English Revised Version of the Bible (1884)
TB	*Tyndale Bulletin*
TOTC	Tyndale Old Testament Commentary
TWOT	*Theological Wordbook of the Old Testament*, ed. R. L. Harris, G. L. Archer and B. K. Waltke (Moody, 1980)

Select bibliography

This list includes works referred to in the notes by the author's surname, with title or volume number where appropriate, and recommended further reading.

Begg, A., *Pathway to Freedom: How God's Laws Guide Our Lives* (Moody, 2003).

Bentley, M., *Travelling Homeward: Exodus Simply Explained* (Evangelical Press, 1999).

Buber, M., *Moses* (Oxford, c.1944).

Cassuto, U., *A Commentary on the Book of Exodus* (Magnes, 1967).

Charles, R. H., *The Decalogue* (Clark, 1923).

Childs, B., *Exodus*, Old Testament Library (SCM, 1974).

Coates, C. A., *An Outline of the Book of Exodus* (Morrish, c.1920).

Cole, R. A., *Exodus*, TOTC (IVP, 1973).

Currid, J. D., *Exodus*, 2 vols. (Evangelical Press, 2000, 2001).

Davidman, J., *Smoke on the Mountain* (Hodder, 1963).

Davies, G., *Israel in Egypt* (JSOT Press, 1992).

Davies, G. H., *Exodus*, Torch Bible Commentaries (SCM, 1967).

Dennett, E., *Typical Teachings of Exodus* (Rouse, 1895).

Dray, S., *Exodus*, Crossway Bible Guide (IVP, 1993).

Dunnam, M. D., *Exodus*, Communicator's Commentary (Word, 1987).

Durham, J. I., *Exodus*, Word Biblical Commentary (Word, 1987).

Ellison, H. L., *Exodus*, Daily Study Bible (St Andrew, 1982).

Enns, P., *Exodus*, The New Application Commentary (Zondervan, 2000).

Fretheim, T. E., *Exodus*, Interpretation (John Knox, 1991).

Gispen, W. H., *Exodus*, Bible Student's Commentary (Zondervan, 1982).

Gooding, D. W., *The Account of the Tabernacle* (Cambridge, 1959).

——, *How to Teach the Tabernacle* (Everday, 1977).

Herbert, G., *When Israel Came out of Egypt* (SCM, 1961).

Hyatt, J. P., *Exodus*, The New Century Bible (Oliphants, 1971).

Kaiser, W. C., *Exodus*, Expositor's Bible Commentary (Zondervan, 1990).

Mackay, J. L., *Exodus*, Mentor Commentary (Christian Focus, 2001).

Mackintosh, C. H., *Notes on the Book of Exodus* (Morrish, 1832).

Moberly, R. W. L., *At the Mountain of God* (JSOT Press, 1983).

——, *The Old Testament of the Old Testament* (Fortress, 1992).

Motyer, J. A., *Isaiah*, TOTC (IVP, 1999).

——, *Look to the Rock* (IVP, 2000).

——, *The Prophecy of Isaiah* (IVP, 1993).

——, *The Revelation of the Divine Name* (Tyndale Press, 1959).

Murphy, J. G., *A Critical and Exegetical Commentary on the Book of Exodus* (1866, repr. Klock, 1979).

Nielsen, E., *The Ten Commandments in New Perspective* (SCM, 1968).

Noth, M., *Exodus*, Old Testament Library (SCM, 1962).

Poythress, V. S., *The Shadow of Christ in the Law of Moses* (P&R, 1991).

Rainsford, M., *The Tabernacle in the Wilderness* (Hodder, 1897).

Ramm, B. L., *His Way Out: A Fresh Look at Exodus* (Regal, 1974).

Stamm, J. J., and M. E. Andrew, *The Ten Commandments in Recent Research* (SCM, 1967).

White, F. H., *Christ in the Tabernacle* (Partridge, 1875).

Notes

The divine name

The Lord God has a personal name (just as we have 'Christian names'). This name came prominently to the fore in Exodus when the Lord revealed its significance to Moses (3:13–15; 6:2–8). It is usually pronounced Yahweh, but English translations have in general followed an ancient scruple by representing it as 'the LORD'. In this book, 'the Lord' always refers to Yahweh, and, frequently enough, the divine name itself is used.

Hebrew verbs

The root form of a verb is indicated by the square-root sign, √.

Verse numbers

Sometimes versification in the Hebrew original differs from the English. Where this is so the Hebrew reference is added in brackets, [ ].

Bible quotations and versions

For the most part, quotations are taken from the New International Version, in keeping with the policy of the series. Some may be found to come from the ESV, NKJV and other versions, or to be freshly translated from the Hebrew.

Introduction

Abraham and his ever-expanding family were uniquely favoured people. He had known the call of God (Gen. 12:1), and the divine promise of innumerable descendants and of a land to live in (Gen. 17:5, 8). His family, too, enjoyed this favoured spiritual status with its good earthly prospects (Gen. 17:7–8).

At the opening of the book of Exodus, Abraham himself was, of course, long dead (Gen. 25:8), and his family, now organized under the names of the twelve sons of Abraham's grandson Jacob, was resident in Egypt. Over the years it had expanded considerably and enjoyed the good life under the patronage of Joseph, Pharaoh's deputy (Gen. 41:39–46). With the death of Joseph and a change of government, however, the good times were over (Exod. 1:6, 8). The Egyptian authorities had become pathologically nervous about this increase in the immigrant population and determined first on a policy of persecution and then ethnic cleansing and genocide (1:9–11, 22).

What had become, then, we might ask ourselves, of Israel's uniqueness, their favoured position before God, the promises made to Abraham and the prospect of their own land?

1. Abram and the forecast of history (Gen. 15:13)

When the Lord promised the land of Canaan to Abram and his descendants (Gen. 15:7), every part of it was already occupied by other peoples. It would not have been consistent with the righteousness of God if he had simply taken this land from its rightful inhabitants and given it to someone else. We read, therefore, that the Lord proposed to give the Canaanite nations a four-hundred-year probation period, and only if they failed that

1

probation would their land pass out of their possession (Gen. 15:16). In the fullness of time the ousting of the Canaanites was accomplished by Joshua and his troops, and although we recoil, as surely we must, from the horrendous judgment then inflicted on the Canaanites (e.g. Josh. 6:21), we must, nevertheless, be sure to see it in the light of its Genesis background and say that the Judge of all the earth has done right (Gen. 18:25). A genuine, even generous, probation had been allowed, but four hundred years saw only a steady decline into atrocious corruption, until the knife of the divine surgeon was the only recourse. Thus far the providence of God can be seen to be working along the lines of his perfect justice.

Genesis 15:13 also forecasts the future of Israel with, surely to our astonishment, four hundred years of exile, including oppression and servitude. Neither in Genesis nor elsewhere in the Bible is this prolonged adversity explained. There is never any suggestion that this banishment to Egypt was because of sin – indeed, sin does not feature as a factor in Israel's consciousness until the episode of the golden calf in chapter 32. At a later date the holy anger of the Lord deprived his people of the Promised Land and banished them to Babylon (e.g. 2 Kgs 21:10–15), but nothing like this is said about their sojourn in Egypt.

Was it, then, a case of 'just the way the cookie crumbles'? Earthly life is, after all, a chancy affair, and although it would indeed have been 'nice' if Israel could have awaited its inheritance in security and prosperity, that was not the way it worked out. Without a Bible to teach us, what other view could we take but this? With the Bible, however, the idea that 'history' is simply the lucky or unlucky spin of the wheel is ruled out. It is always first and foremost 'his story', and what happened in Israel's case was all deliberate and part of a greater plan. Once before, the Lord had stepped in to rescue Abram from Egypt, where he had gone without permission (Gen. 12:10–20), and on another occasion he had expressly forbidden Isaac to take the Egyptian road (Gen. 26:1–2), but Abraham's grandson Jacob had been specifically directed to take his whole entourage and move southwards to Egypt, even though what ultimately lay ahead was slavery (Gen. 46:1–4).

2. A real mystery

The Bible will not allow us to say that Jacob 'got his guidance wrong', though that might well seem a logical deduction from the way events panned out. The opposite is in fact true, for Jacob went to Egypt by the will and word of God, with loving assurances that he would see his long-lost son Joseph and with promises of coming greatness and future restoration ringing in his ears (Gen. 46:1–4). Furthermore, he went into a situation where the grace of God had anticipated his needs by sending Joseph ahead (Gen. 50:20; Ps. 105:17–23). He had, however, also embarked on a journey that led eventually to slavery, suffering and the attempted extinction of his descendants (Exod. 1:8–14, 22), and during those long, long years of distress heaven above them remained silent. Even when the promise of rescue was finally fulfilled (Exod. 12:40–42), no explanation was ever offered of the years of pain and loss.

This is the mystery of the divine government of history, whether on a national, domestic or individual level: the great and loving God is in control, and because he is truly sovereign he works out his purposes in his way, not ours (Isa. 55:8). He offers no explanations, but grants his people a sufficient insight into his ways, his character, his intentions and his changeless faithfulness so that, however dark the day, they can live by faith and be sustained by hope.

3. The covenant God

The particular revelation of the divine character that spans from Genesis into Exodus is expressed by the idea of the covenant. In its typical biblical use, covenant means 'promise' and in particular a promise that does not need to be made but which arises from the free decision and will of the promise-maker, and which is bestowed without merit, deserving or bargaining on the part of the recipient.

It was in this way that the Lord made his covenant with Abram (Gen. 17): the promise was personal (5), domestic (6), spiritual (7) and territorial (8). It was 'sealed' to Abraham by the sign of circumcision (10–11) so that ever after he was literally a 'marked man', the man to whom the Lord had made his covenanted promises and who carried the sign and proof of it in his own body.

Genesis 17:1–2 needs to be guarded from misunderstanding as it might be taken to mean, 'If you walk before me and be blameless, then I will make my covenant with you.' This would make the covenant appear as a divine response to Abram's commitment, even a reward for the perfection of his 'walk'. This cannot be so because the covenant between God and Abraham had already been formally inaugurated many years before (Gen.

15:18). Also, the wording in Genesis 17:2 does not express the idea of inauguration but rather confirmation. A literal translation would be, 'and I will place my covenant', an expression which signifies the covenant coming into active operation as the stated relationship between its maker and its recipient. Abraham's life of fellowship with the Lord was not the precondition of the covenant but rather the response by which he entered into the promised blessings. From beginning to end, God's covenant relationship with his people is based on his grace and not their merits.

4. The mainspring of Exodus

The covenant is the mainspring from which the action of Exodus flows. In 1:8–22 we enter in various ways into the miseries of Israel in Egypt, but at 2:23 we reach the point where their groaning became praying: (lit.) 'they groaned because of their slavery and screamed aloud, and their cry for help rose up to God, and God heard and God remembered his covenant with Abraham'.

The whole story of Exodus is a covenant narrative. The God who pledged himself to Abraham and his descendants remained the faithful God. He had made promises and intended to honour them, and when his moment came, honour them he did. He claimed Israel as his own (4:22), brought them out of Egyptian bondage (12:41–42), succoured and cared for them as a loving covenant God would all through the long wilderness years (Deut. 8:2–4), and finally gave them the land which, centuries before, he had pledged to their fathers (Gen. 15:7; 26:3; 28:13; Josh. 21:43–45).

Did the suffering people sustain themselves by remembering these promises through the darkness of slavery? We do not know. That part of their story is not recorded. What we do see, however, from the first chapter of Exodus and the nervousness of the Egyptians, is that the Hebrews had managed somehow to retain their separate identity. We also learn that when Moses came to them in the name of the God of their fathers and of the Lord (3:13–14; 4:31), he was welcomed by them as one speaking of a God they knew.

5. Exodus in the Bible
a. The divine name and the blood of the lamb

The covenant theme, of course, binds Exodus into the whole Bible, and leads directly to the teaching of the Lord Jesus and beyond (cf. 24:8 with

Luke 22:20, and 29:42–46 with Rev. 21:3). At the heart of the Exodus covenant action of God two great events come together: the name of the Lord
is brought into new focus (3:13–15; 6:2–8) and the blood of the lamb is
placed at the heart of the covenant sacrifice of the Passover (12:13). Both
of these will concern us in detail later but require a brief preliminary
glance here.

i. The divine name

The Bible describes the Lord as *'ĕlōhîm*, 'God'. This Hebrew noun is plural
and probably points to the being in question possessing the full and total
range of divine attributes. This is what is called a 'plural of amplitude' or
'fullness'. The singular noun *'ēl* appears to point to the one who rightly
owns and enjoys supernal transcendence, 'God' in the essence of deity.
The Bible also uses *'ēl* as a component in various titles, each encapsulating
something distinct about this transcendent God. For example, *'ēl-šadday*
('God Almighty', Gen. 17:1) and *'ēl-'ôlam* ('the Eternal God', Gen. 21:33).[1]

While there are many titles for God, there is only one name in the sense
of his personal name, and this name, represented in Hebrew by the four
consonants yhwh, was almost certainly pronounced Yahweh.[2] Moses
expected to be asked about this on his return to Egypt (3:13–15), and it was
in this name that he couched his foundational teaching. 'Yahweh' is
specifically the God of the exodus, the Redeemer (6:6), Giver of the law
(20:2) and the one who indwelt his people in the tabernacle (29:46).

ii. The lamb

The name Yahweh resounds throughout the whole of the account of
the Passover: it is the Lord who ordains the sacrifice; the Passover is the
Lord's Passover; the Lord is redeemer, deliverer, law-giver and judge, and
the people are the Lord's people. Just as the inauguration of the Abrahamic
covenant required sacrifice (Gen. 15:9–18), so the Exodus account binds

---

[1] See Motyer, *Name*, pp. 24ff.

[2] From the third century BC onwards, in order to avoid the possibility of blasphemy, there was a growing reluctance to utter the divine name, and various evasive synonyms were used to refer to God, such as
'the Power' or 'Heaven'. When reading or reciting Scripture the word *'ădōnāy*, 'Lord', was substituted for the
Tetragrammaton, yhwh. In the sixth century AD it became necessary to provide a system of vowel signs in
order to vocalize the Hebrew Bible for those unfamiliar with traditional pronunciation, and the vowel signs
of *'ădōnāy* were superimposed on the Tetragrammaton to remind the reader not to attempt to pronounce the
unutterable divine name. Christian scholars of the sixteenth century misunderstood this device and fused
the consonants yhwh with the vowels of *'ădōnāy* to give the impossible hybrid form of Jehovah, which is
meaningless in Hebrew. In most English Bibles yhwh is represented by using small capital letters as 'the Lord'.

into one the covenant-working of God, the fresh focus on his name and the blood of the Passover lamb, whose death is seen in propitiatory and substitutionary terms.

iii. The name and the lamb in the New Testament

All this anticipates the double focus that we find in the New Testament. When the Lord Jesus Christ came to the waters of his baptism, he brought to us the first ever plain revelation of the Holy Trinity: the Father who addressed his beloved Son, the Son for whom the heavens were opened, and the Holy Spirit in visible gentleness as a dove descending upon him. It was as if a divine hand had suddenly adjusted the focus of a film projector and the multiplex revelation of the one God throughout the Old Testament sharpened and consolidated into the vision of the three who are one, the one who is three.[3] This is especially the emphasis in Matthew (3:13–17), Mark (1:9–11) and Luke (3:21–22). John's Gospel does not describe the baptismal event itself but has John the Baptist making it known that for him Jesus had been validated as Messiah and Son of God by the descent and abiding of the Holy Spirit (John 1:31–34), proclaiming this Jesus as 'the Lamb of God'. Indeed, the title 'Lamb' is the bracket around John the Baptist's whole reference to the Lord's baptism (John 1:29, 35–36).

Thus, the point at which Exodus gives its 'new beginning' to the Old Testament matches the point at which the New Testament begins its distinctive testimony: the divine name, Yahweh, is the personal name of the Holy Trinity, and the Passover lamb is Jesus, the Son of God.

b. The two sons of God

The matching of Old and New Testaments around the Exodus theme can be pursued a little further. Exodus, right at the start, announces that the currently enslaved and oppressed Israel is none other than 'my firstborn son' (4:22). This, too, is where Matthew's Gospel begins. The son of David, son of Abraham, son of Mary is also 'my Son, whom I love; with him I am well pleased' (Matt. 1:1, 16; 3:17). Yet Jesus' life, like the existence of Israel, was threatened by the contemporary political authorities, and, like them,

---

[3] In the Old Testament the one God (cf. Deut. 6:4) is cumulatively revealed as the 'Lord of Hosts', the one who is within himself the concentration of every potentiality and power. His oneness can be compared to that of the tabernacle, which although it was made of a multitude of distinct parts was nevertheless a perfectly united single whole: it became 'one' (Exod. 26:11; 36:13). The revelation of the New Testament allows us to see the multiplicity and unity of God as the Holy Trinity. The God of the Old Testament is, therefore, not God the Father but the Holy Trinity incognito.

he even made the journey into and out of Egypt (Matt. 2:13–15). He too was subjected to adversity and satanic opposition (Matt. 4:1–11).

It is instructive to note other parallels. Just as Israel left Egypt and came to the Red Sea (Exod. 14), Matthew immediately follows the account of Jesus' return from Egypt (the only reference he makes to the boyhood of Jesus) with his coming to the Jordan for baptism (Matt. 2:23; 3:1). Just as Israel emerged from the Red Sea to go into the wilderness (Exod. 15:22), so Jesus went from the waters of baptism into the wilderness (Matt. 4:1). Israel experienced in turn absence of water and food (Exod. 15:23; 16:3), as did Jesus during his first temptation (Matt. 4:1–4). Israel came to the place where they put the Lord to the test (Exod. 17:2), something that Jesus refused to do in his second temptation (Matt. 4:7). Israel arrived at Mount Sinai (Exod. 19) where, promptly, they turned from the Lord to worship an idol (Exod. 32:1–6), whereas, by contrast, looking on all the kingdoms of the world from a 'very high mountain' Jesus insisted that only the Lord is to be worshipped (Matt. 4:8–10).[4] In other words, Exodus is the story of the son of God who stands in need of salvation, failing at every point of life and even of privilege; Matthew tells of the Son of God who brings salvation (Matt. 1:21), perfect and righteous at every point and in every circumstance and test.

6. The significance of Exodus

The point of all this is to underline the importance of Exodus in the Bible. It is as significant a turning point or new beginning as is Matthew at the start of the New Testament. To go no further than recall its revelation of the divine name or its story of the blood of the lamb is at once to give it the same place in the Old Testament that the coming of Jesus and the cross of Calvary hold in the New. It begins the normative Old Testament (and biblical) revelation of God's way of salvation; it underlines the nature of God as holy and of humankind as sinners; it explains the meaning of blood and sacrifice; it is a book of the grace which reaches down from heaven and of the law which teaches redeemed sinners to live in heavenly terms. While some of these great biblical truths are foreshadowed in

---

4 The other side of the parallel between Exodus and Matthew is that despite Israel's sin, when they came to Mount Sinai, God himself descended to reveal his word (Exod. 19:18–19). Jesus too took his place on a mountain, not as Israel awaiting the word of God, nor as the mediator Moses, ascending and descending, but as God come to teach his people (Matt. 5:1).

Genesis, Exodus pulls them all together, giving them a shape and definition that the rest of the Bible will not alter. Under the simplest of forms, and by many a fascinating story, Exodus reveals fundamental truth and is, in fact, one of the Bible's great building blocks.

7. The shapes of Exodus

a. Telling the story

Exodus contains many different types of literature but in essence it is a planned exercise in storytelling.[5] As such it falls into three parts, most easily seen if the book is set out as a diagram, and best appreciated if the book is read through as a whole following this outline:

Part 1: Israel in Egypt: the Saviour (1:1 – 13:16)
   a. The Lord's hidden providence (1:1 – 2:22)
   b. Yahweh revealed (2:22 – 6:13)
   c. The saving Lord (6:14 – 13:16)

Part 2: Israel at Sinai: the Companion (13:17 – 24:11)
   a. The Lord's public providences (13:17 – 17:16)
   b. Yahweh revealed (18:1 – 23:33)
   c. The covenant Lord (24:1–11)

Part 3: Israel around the tabernacle: the Indweller (24:12 – 40:38)
   a. The Lord's provision (24:12 – 31:18)
   b. Yahweh revealed (32:1 – 34:35)
   c. The indwelling Lord (35:1 – 40:38)

The titles given in the third section of each part summarize a central aspect of the revelation of God in Exodus. The hidden yet active God of the opening stories (1:20) suddenly 'intervenes', delivering (3:7–8) and redeeming (6:6). The explanatory note that he 'remembered his covenant'

---

[5] Many will be aware that specialist study of Exodus has long busied itself with uncovering supposed earlier 'documents' behind the text as we have it. The aridity of this approach and the lack of certainty that accompanies it are now being increasingly recognized. Barry Webb perfectly expresses a different and more productive approach in his study of Judges, one of, in the words of J. P. U. Lilley, seeking to see it as 'a literary work starting from the assumptions of authorship', i.e. as a unified work of literary art (B. Webb, *The Book of Judges: An Integrated Reading* [Sheffield, 1987], p. 29). That is certainly the intention of the present work on Exodus.

(2:24) flowers in the covenant ceremony of 24:1–11. He had indeed brought his people to himself, as he said he would (6:6), and the description that he carried them 'on eagles' wings' (19:4) was no mere hyperbole for he had shown himself as their companion God and their provider in all the vicissitudes of the wilderness trek from Egypt to Sinai (13:17 – 17:16). This companionate relationship is then given its final Old Testament form in the provision and meaning of the tabernacle, which, as 29:42–46 explains, was Yahweh's deliberate purpose behind the whole exodus undertaking, to be their indwelling God.

b. The God of fiery holiness

Fire is a pervasive motif in Exodus, playing a significant part in each division of the book.[6] Throughout the Bible 'fire' signifies the active holiness of God, holiness not as, so to speak, merely a 'passive' attribute but as the active, menacing hostility of a holy God to everything that offends his holiness. Genesis does not dwell on this, but it pervades Exodus, where God's first revelation of himself to Moses is in the un-approachable burning bush (3:1–5). Simple as the story is, it contains elements basic to Exodus: the Lord's holiness is unapproachable (3:5a), yet the Lord himself declares, indeed makes simple, the terms on which the unworthy can come before him (3:5b). In so many ways this is, in fact, the theme of the whole book.

In the first part of Exodus, the holy God is, inexplicably, not the foe but the friend, the deliverer, of Israel. In the second part, the fire of the holy God is resident in the great pillar which was the constant guide-companion (13:21–22) and timely protection (14:19) of the people, as well as being the sign of the presence of the unapproachable, 'dangerous' God on Sinai (19:11–18). Finally, in the third part, the pillar of cloud and fire, the reality of Sinai, comes to rest on the tabernacle right at the heart of Israel's camp (40:34–38). In a word, Exodus cannot be described simply as the book of the holiness of the Lord, nor simply as the book of the presence of the Lord, but as the book of the holy God present in all his holiness at the heart of his people's life, their provident saviour and friend, who

---

[6] All who know him recognize David Gooding as a master of biblical analysis, as demonstrated in e.g. *According to Luke* (IVP, 1987) and *True to the Faith: The Acts of the Apostles* (Hodder, 1990). David Gooding has been my kind friend, not only lending me books but also generously sharing with me some of his own thoughts about Exodus. It is to him that I owe these observations about the 'fire' theme, and I count it a privilege to acknowledge my indebtedness for this and for so much more.

makes provision whereby they, in all their unworthiness, may live safely with him.

c. The great central truth

The book of Exodus has been composed with great artistry. It opens with a slave people building cities for Pharaoh (1:11) and ends with the same people, now liberated, building a tent-dwelling for their God (35 – 40). It tells of the lamb of God (12:1–12) but relates how the same people who sheltered under the blood of the lamb turned to make and worship a golden calf (32:1–6). It is a book of the grace of the God who first saves (1 – 12), then accompanies (13 – 17) and finally indwells (29:42–46) his people. And at its centre lie the Bible's fundamental truths of grace and law (19 – 24).

Exodus has, in fact, a 'chiastic' plan, whereby its opening sections (A[1], B[1], C[1]) are balanced by its closing sections (C[2], B[2], A[2]) either side of a middle section (D), which contains the central thought of the whole book.

> A[1] Building for Pharaoh (1 – 5)
> > B[1] The lamb of God (6 – 12)
> > > C[1] The companion God (13 – 18)
> > > > D The grace of God and the law of God (19 – 24)
> > > C[2] The indwelling God (25 – 31)
> > B[2] The golden calf (32 – 34)
> A[2] Building for God (35 – 40)

There, so to say, in a nutshell, is the whole sweep and thrust of Exodus and the whole story of salvation. According to A[1,2], the Lord's redemptive work and plan bring us out of servitude to the world into his service and indwelling presence (cf. 1 Cor. 3:16; 6:19); B[1,2] reveals the wonder of the way of salvation and the dire reality of disloyalty and defection; C[1,2] shows the beauty and practical efficacy of the presence of the Lord; and in D we see the priority of God's saving grace and the responsive life of obedience.

Exodus 1:1 – 2:10

1. Days of darkness

The title of this chapter comes from an old hymn, 'I Will Sing the Wondrous Story' by F. H. Rowley. It is a hymn of great realism, spiritual and circumstantial, and its words, even if slightly antique for today's taste, catch exactly the national and personal plight of the Israelites[1] in Egypt:

> Days of darkness still come o'er me;
> Sorrow's path I oft may tread

So indeed it was! After its fashion, the Bible narrative does not itemize the dark sufferings the people endured. We are never told all we might want to know, but only what we need to know, and the narrator apparently considered that the words 'slave masters . . . oppress them with forced labour . . . worked them ruthlessly' (1:11–13) were quite enough to sketch in the picture. Beyond that public oppression, however, lay agonizing depths of private and domestic grief (22). 'Darkness' and 'sorrow' unbounded!

1. The people of God and their inscrutable God

And these were the people of God. That is the point where the mystery deepens. Exodus takes the trouble to assure us of the family tree of these

---

[1] The expression 'Israelite[s]' occurs only twice in Genesis (32:32; 36:31); it appears about 125 times in Exodus. This indicates that while Exodus makes a new beginning, it is careful to establish links with Genesis. The list of names in 1:2–5 is identical with Gen. 35:23–26 and preserves the same characteristic grouping of Jacob's sons under the names of their respective mothers.

sufferers (1:1–5). Their ancestry to Jacob and doubtless the story of Genesis 46:1–4 had been told down the generations: they were where they were by divine command, under divine promise, awaiting divine intervention. Of these things, however, they saw no outward sign. Heaven above was as silent as earth around was threatening. And before we allow the thought to arise that all this happened long ago, we need to ask why Paul thought it necessary to teach the disciples of Lystra, Iconium and Antioch that 'We must go through many hardships to enter the kingdom of God' (Acts 14:22), or why Peter addressed the church as 'God's elect, exiles' or 'foreigners' (1 Pet. 1:1; 2:11). Experience without explanation, adversity without purpose, hostility without protection – that is how life will always appear for the earthly people of God.

2. Living in the shadows

What a tale of suffering these verses actually tell. 'Days of darkness . . . Sorrow's path' indeed for our ancestors in Egypt! There was general hardship as slave masters were put *over them to oppress them* (11). The word *oppress* means 'to bring them low', 'to beat down'. The tale continues in verses 13 and 14: the Egyptians made Israel into slaves and *worked them ruthlessly*. This is an unusual word which is used only five times in the Bible and signifies the imposition of general hardship and ruthlessness of behaviour.[2]

In addition to all this there came a further frightful and cutting hardship: the murder of the children. Pharaoh told the Hebrew midwives that *When you are helping the Hebrew women during childbirth . . . if you see that the baby is a boy, kill him; but if it is a girl, let her live* (16). The NIV translation differs from the Hebrew original by replacing 'son' and 'daughter' with 'boy' and 'girl'. Parents discover this distinction when they have a baby. Immediately after the birth there comes the moving and tender element of relationship when the baby becomes so much more than just a boy or a girl: it is a son or a daughter. So, it was not just boys and girls who were being killed or kept alive, it was sons and daughters, and we get a glimpse of the personal anguish this caused.

---

[2] Cf. Lev. 25:43, 46, 53; Ezek. 34:4. The word is *pārek*, and its parent verb, which is not found in the Bible, can be traced in cognate languages meaning 'to display violence'.

The weight of opposition ranged against the people of God was enormous. Pharaoh wanted to bring about a genocide, and therefore he did the logical thing by trying to kill all the male babies. When this failed, he mobilized the whole force of the land of Egypt against the Hebrews (22): Pharaoh at the top, his people living cheek by jowl with the people of God, who were spread throughout the land,[3] and finally the river god itself. All the power of Egypt, all the power of the enemy – royal, popular, supernatural. Days of darkness indeed!

3. Help arising from unexpected places

Ranged against the might of Pharaoh and his slave masters was a series of seemingly insignificant women.[4] First of all, there were the two midwives, Shiphrah and Puah, whose names have gone down in Scripture because of their heroic faith.[5] Then there was the resolute Jochebed, Moses' mother, who loved her baby, the third of her children. She seems also to have recognized something special about him, which made it even more unbearable to think of throwing him into the river, or allowing anybody else to do it (2:2).[6] So, at what terrifying risk to herself we are not told, she hid the little one and, when necessity drove, obeyed the letter but not the spirit of Pharaoh's edict. She did actually commit her child into the devouring mouth of the river god, the Nile, but only to find that there was, on her side, a power over all the power of the enemy (cf. Luke 10:19; 1 John 4:4).

---

[3] The reference in 1:6 to the fact that the Israelites were *fruitful*, had *multiplied greatly* and *become exceedingly numerous* is meant to alert us to the fact that God had been faithful to his covenant promises and was at work on his people's behalf (cf. Gen. 12:1; 17:2). We can see it as we read from Genesis into Exodus, but did the people of the time also understand their extraordinary fruitfulness in this way? We are not told, but there are sufficient indications that the ancestral traditions were known and were being passed from generation to generation: e.g. Moses' anticipation that the people would want to know the nature of the God who had spoken to him, the pervasive references to 'the God of your fathers' (e.g. 3:13) and the people's lack of surprise when Moses told them that the Lord was going to take them out.

[4] There is a wealth of irony running through these opening chapters. Here, e.g., for all his 'greatness', Pharaoh is left unnamed, while the midwives (whom he regarded as mere tools of his policy) are remembered individually. This is Exodus's perception of who is important and who is not!

[5] There must have been more midwives. These two are named as representatives or leaders of the rest. We read in verse 20 that God *was kind* to the midwives because of their actions. Their reply to Pharaoh was certainly evasive (19), but their explanation must have had an element of truth in it for it to have been accepted without question. God did not bless their 'economy' with the truth but their resolute standing for what was right.

[6] When Moses is described as *a fine child* (Heb. *ṭôb*), does it mean anything more than in his mother's eyes he was a 'beautiful baby'? The LXX translates *ṭôb* with *asteios*, 'nice, charming' (repeated in Acts 7:20 and Heb. 11:23), which does not help on this point. Fretheim's association of it with God noting his creation as 'good' is a bit far-fetched for so common a word.

Then there was Miriam, that resourceful girl! Imagine noticing so acutely how Pharaoh's daughter's face changed when she looked at the baby, and realizing so intuitively that behind the royal countenance there was a compassionate heart – and then to have the audacity to bring the baby's mother into the equation as his nurse. What a turnaround! Far from this Hebrew baby being killed by the will of the royal house, his rescuer emerged from the royal house, and his own mother was actually paid to bring him up as a prince of Egypt!

Finally, there was Pharaoh's daughter herself, who was much more than a 'minor miracle'. Out of the core of the genocidal royal family came this precious person, a tender-hearted princess. Her father could, apparently without pity, consign 'sons' to the Nile and 'daughters' to slavery, but his own daughter had not inherited his personality. She had a maternal heart, eyes easily moved to tears, feeling for the feelings of others, and Moses, as we shall discover, grew up to be like his adoptive mother, a tender-hearted, compassionate man.

4. Bare bones, rich nourishment

These, then, are the bare bones of a great story. It is a story to delight in, showing how the weak and powerless of the world overcame the strong and mighty; a story to horrify because of the terrible suffering it portrays; and a story to encourage because of the sure, providential care of God. It is, however, more than anything, a story to puzzle, because the people to whom these dreadful things happened were the people of God. We are forced to ask ourselves why those whom God had chosen and to whom he had made his covenant promises should have had to suffer like this.

Whatever else Exodus may say to us, this is where it starts – with the suffering of God's people. The opening verses, where the people are known by name and individually numbered, point back to the impeccable line of descent of the Israelites in Egypt, leaving us in no doubt that they were God's chosen people (1:1–5). We also know from Genesis 46:1–4 that they were where they were by divine command, under divine promise and awaiting divine intervention.[7] In the meantime, they had no certificate of

---

[7] The Bible allows us to speak of God 'intervening' as part of the way it sees things from the human perspective (e.g. Exod. 2:24 represents God as, so to speak, suddenly waking up to the realities of the situation). Many commentators note that 1:7 'reflects' the purpose of God in Adam (Gen. 1:28; 9:1) as well as the promise of God to Abram (Gen. 12:1–3). This gives us a sense of the ceaseless work of God, both in creation and in his

immunity to pain and hardship. With first the death of Joseph and then the accession of a king who neither knew about Joseph's special status nor recognized any obligations to his descendants, they were exposed to the full blast of worldly opposition.

5. The twelve tribes of God's church: light for dark days

So, Exodus begins to speak to us in our situation. James addressed his letter to 'the twelve tribes scattered among the nations' (Jas 1:1) and in doing so parallels Exodus, for we – the church of Jesus Christ – are the tribes of God's people dispersed in the world. The corollary of this is that the Exodus people are our ancestors. Like them, we find ourselves exposed to days of darkness, and we ask the inevitable question, 'Why?'

We would like some 'spelling out' of the situation which would satisfy our need for logic. Very often, of course, suffering is totally logical – by our sinfulness we bring suffering on our own heads, we 'ask for it' and sometimes we get it. In such circumstances we might go on to question whether the actual apportionment of suffering is 'fair', but, nevertheless, the nexus between crime and punishment remains plain enough. The Bible never, however, says that Israel was sent to Egypt as a punishment or that their sinfulness cried out to heaven for this, or any, requital. The Egyptian experience belongs to a different league.

6. Light in the darkness

It is not God's way to explain himself other than to record in his Word for our learning that 'my thoughts are not your thoughts, neither are your ways my ways' (Isa. 55:8), so the biblical account provides us with no pat answers to our questions, but it does provide us with a framework and context within which we can begin to make sense of the days of darkness which have ever been the lot of God's people throughout history. If we look at the Genesis record of God's dealings with his people up to their arrival

---

particular plans for the family of Abraham. Fretheim puts the matter well: 'God's intentions in creation are being realised in this family . . . in tune with [his] creatorial purposes' (p. 25; the whole section pp. 24–26 is important). God's redemptive work is, therefore, not accurately seen in 'interventionist' terms. That is merely how it looks to the human observer. He is the ever-present, ever-active Creator (John 5:17), and his work in creation provides a basis for his work in redemption; his work in redemption fulfils his work in creation.

in Egypt, we will find that it throws light on subsequent events and enables us to see God's hand at work from beginning to end. We see him working out his own schemes in his own way, on his own scale, to his own time plan and according to his own wisdom, and we find the assurance that, although the days were dark, it was all right, it was all planned and it will all be well.

a. Everything was all right

Genesis 46:1–4 recounts the sensitive moment when Jacob was about to lead his family down into the land of Egypt. At that juncture he needed and received a word from God: 'I am God, the God of your father . . . Do not be afraid to go down to Egypt, for I will make you into a great nation there. I will go down to Egypt with you.' If ever the thought occurred to the Israelites that all their troubles must have meant that they had taken a wrong turning and were outside the will of God, this would have reassured them that it was not the case. Everything was all right. God had led them down into the land of Egypt – in fact, he had accompanied them there. Plainly, this does not make anything easy, but it does make it right.

b. Everything was planned

Furthermore, if we turn back to Genesis 15, we find another light that plays on the opening scenes of Exodus – it was all planned. Their experiences may have come as a surprise to the people of God,[8] but if this was the case, then it was because – as we might put it – they were not reading their Bibles! Genesis 15 contains the very clear promise to Abram that God would give him the land in which he was then but a resident alien – but not yet. There would be an intervening period during which 'for four hundred years your descendants will be strangers in a country not their own and . . . they will be enslaved and ill-treated there' (Gen. 15:13). The day of darkness was all part of God's plan to bless the descendants of Abraham – a long day, no doubt, and longer to live through than merely to say or read about.

---

[8] Earthly sufferings may well have taken Israel by surprise (as they do us), but they come as no surprise to the Lord. The Egyptian experience was all anticipated in Gen. 15:13. Ramm observes that 'God works in the pushes and pulls of history, even though we who live in the midst of history and cannot see the end from the beginning have no way of detecting his work' (p. 8).

c. It will all be well

Verse 14 of Genesis 15 goes on to make plain that not only was everything just as God had planned it, but it would all come out right in the end, for 'I will punish the nation they serve as slaves, and afterwards they will come out with great possessions'. The day of deliverance would eventually dawn when the time of darkness would end and the people would emerge from their enslavement with great wealth. Genesis 46:4 also speaks of the certain and sure end to the long period of suffering: 'I will go down to Egypt with you, and I will surely bring you back again.' In each half of that sentence the pronoun 'I' should be emphasized. The people were living under a personal divine undertaking. All would be well.

Stephen claimed at his trial that Moses 'received living words to pass on to us' (Acts 7:38), and his words apply just as much to us as to his first-century audience. The gap of thousands of years between the Lord's word to Moses and Stephen and on to our possession of Holy Scripture means nothing. There is a contemporary reality about the word of God, so that when we read Exodus we are not just learning of the past, we are learning for the present. This is a living word for us. The people of God – we – are still the twelve-tribe-unity scattered in the world, subject to the world's pressures, enduring the world's hardships, suffering the world's sorrows. We would like an answer to our question 'Why?', but God does not come down to explain himself. Experiences without explanations – that is what the first chapter of Exodus is all about. Our only comfort is that God comes to us in the day of darkness and lovingly reassures us that 'It is all right, it is all planned and it will all be well.'

7. God behind the scenes

The next two lines of the 'Days of darkness' hymn,

> But my Saviour still is with me;
> By his guiding hand I'm led

are important and relevant. In the middle of the day of darkness there is this as well: secret and ceaseless care. The people of God are never 'merely' gripped in life's circumstances, they are always gripped in the hand of God (John 10:28–29). We can trace the evidence for this in the supernatural preservation of the Israelites during their suffering in Egypt.

The facts are quite illogical given the circumstances. Pharaoh had set his sights on totally destroying the people of God, and, as a totalitarian ruler, he set the whole machinery of government and the weight of popular feeling in motion against the Hebrews.[9] But far from being crushed by all this we read that *the more they* [the Hebrews] *were oppressed, the more they multiplied and spread* (1:12). This is so much against what 'should' have happened that we can account for it only by saying that there must be some other factor at work that ensured that the people were not at the mercy of circumstances. Here we can see evidence of a secret and ceaseless care whereby the Israelites not only were preserved in life but, against all the opposition that was heaped upon them, they went on increasing, flourishing and expanding.[10] When the midwives refused to kill the babies, God was there watching and working with them (20). In the midst of the darkness is this indication that God was 'in it' with his people, caring for them and blessing them through the actions of these brave and faithful women.

There is a deliberate contrast between verses 10 and 12 which says it all. Pharaoh's actions were all taken (lit.) 'lest they multiply', but the resulting reality was 'so they multiplied'. The same verb expresses the mind of the would-be destroyer and the mind of God, so that in the outcome the measure of oppression became the measure of multiplication. All through the days of darkness, there is just that one gleam of light, but behind that one gleam of light stood the God of secret and ceaseless care.

In chapter 2 we discover that it was not just the people as a whole who were in the hand of God, but that his providence covered the individual as well. Chapter 1 ends by saying, *Pharaoh gave this order to all his people: 'Every Hebrew boy* [lit. son] *that is born you must throw into the Nile, but let every girl* [lit. daughter] *live.'* Chapter 2 opens with just such a son, born under the edict of death: *Now a man of the tribe of Levi married a Levite woman, and she became pregnant and gave birth to a son.* With the help

---

[9] Pharaoh tried various methods to deal with the Israelites: political shrewdness (1:10; in Durham's translation, 'let us out smart them'), force (11), secret manipulation (15) and, finally, popular feeling and ruthlessness (22). Popular feeling about the large and growing immigrant population is expressed by the verb *qûṣ* (12; cf. Gen. 27:46; Num. 21:5; 22:3; Isa. 7:16). It suggests 'pathological dread', 'sick with worry'. It would seem, therefore, that Pharaoh anticipated no difficulty in mobilizing his people for genocide. This background prepares for the final, dreadful divine judgment visited upon the Egyptians (12:30). Cf. Mackay: 'the guilt of complicity is spread throughout all the Egyptians . . . all will be involved in the judgmental catastrophe' (p. 44). Note also that the Pharaoh who targeted 'sons' (22) brought about the death of Egypt's sons (11:4–6).

[10] There was still an abundance of males at the time of the exodus (12:37), so the plan for the slaughter of the baby boys cannot have been very successful.

of hindsight, we know that Moses was special, but at this stage in the story he was just a case in point, an example of the fact that everywhere among the Hebrews little boys were being born, and that all the weight of the Egyptian power ranged against them was being frustrated by the Lord's care for the individuals of his people. Not, we would suppose, in every case, but in more cases than that of Moses, the Lord's gracious power was proving itself against all the power of the enemy.

The whole of 1:22 – 2:22 is typical of the thoughtful, artistic way that much of Exodus is written. Embedded within the structure we see the pervasive hand of God turning events to his purposes. We see also the irony of the situation: Pharaoh's plan of genocide included the preservation of daughters but, as things turned out, it was daughters who were its downfall.

A^1 Sons destined for slaughter: the people under threat (1:22)

    B^1 Marriage: Moses' parents (2:1)

        C Key daughters

           Levi's daughter and the baby Moses (2:1–3)

           Jochebed's daughter and the infant Moses (2:4–9)

           Pharaoh's daughter and the growth of Moses (2:10)

           Jethro's daughters and Moses' safety (2:11–20)

    B^2 Marriage: Moses and Zipporah (2:21)

A^2 A son born in safety: the people continue (2:22)

8. Individuals in the hand of God

We can see Moses, therefore, as an example of the fact that in Egypt individuals were just as surely in God's hand and under his secret and ceaseless care as were the whole people. Moses was threatened by the king, the people and the river, but what happened? Moses' mother took her son, put him in a little boat and set it down in the shallows of the Nile, and the river was foiled of its prey, and in the process a great god of Egypt was defeated.[11]

It was not just the river but also the royal house that was subordinated to God's overruling providence. The very same royal house which had

---

[11] The proper name 'Nile' is not used in 2:3. Instead we have the semi-technical term for the great river of Egypt, *yĕ'ōr*.

decreed death was made the instrument of life when *Pharaoh's daughter went down to the Nile to bathe* (2:5). She came from a savage and heartless royal family, capable of an edict of genocide, of commanding that babies should be thrown into the river, and yet she was a girl with a tender, maternal heart. As she was walking along the riverbank she saw the little basket among the reeds and when it was opened, there was the baby. *He was crying, and she felt sorry for him* (6). She did not react as her father would have done by saying, 'A Hebrew boy! Throw it in the river!' No, she felt sorry. How God in his providence cares for his people. He subjects all the power of the enemy to his own power.

So, the river cannot capture its prey, and even Pharaoh's house is changed from destroyer to saviour, but what about the people who were so hostile to their Hebrew neighbours, the third strand in the hierarchy of power in 1:22? They too were prevented from carrying out the death sentence on the baby Moses. When Miriam secured Moses' mother as his nurse, the baby came under a powerful royal protection that no-one could challenge (7–9). We can well imagine Moses' mother carrying the baby out and about and being met in the street with, 'That's a lovely little girl you have there, Mrs Amram' (because, of course, sons would not be out on public view), and being able to reply, 'Oh, no, this is my son, Moses.' 'Well then, hadn't you better keep him hidden?' would have been the obvious response. 'Certainly not!' she could say with confidence. 'He's the adopted son of Pharaoh's daughter. They can't touch him.'

9. So . . . for us?

Pharaoh left the God of the Hebrews out of his reckoning; that was his big mistake, and it can be ours too. There is something very basic in us that needs life to be logical and is restless and resentful when we cannot see adversity fulfilling some purpose. Our faith needs to mature if it is to survive the days of darkness that will inevitably come upon us. The first two chapters of Exodus teach us three qualities of such a faith.

First, it is a trustful faith and rests in the knowledge that underpinning everything that happens to us there is a secret, undeclared providence always at work, always providing, always purposeful, always on the side of the people of God (cf. Rom. 8:28). With such a faith our experience will be, one way or another, like that of our Hebrew ancestors who 'the more they were oppressed, the more they multiplied'.

Second, it is an expectant faith. In the Bible angels do not grow wings nor glow with supernatural light. That is reserved for Christmas cards! They often come in very ordinary guises (cf. Heb. 13:2) – God's agents in God's place at God's time. Like the midwives to whom Pharaoh turned to support his programme of ethnic cleansing, only to find that they were pre-committed to a very different policy for which they were prepared to 'stand up and be counted'! Four hundred years before, Abraham's expectancy of faith had affirmed 'The LORD Will Provide' (Gen. 22:14), and so he does.

Third, it is a patient faith. Four hundred years is easier to look back on – and to say quickly – than to live through. Nevertheless, the Lord had promised, 'I will go down to Egypt with you, and I will surely bring you back again' (Gen. 46:4), and the divine promise-keeper works out his moral government of the world with perfect justice (Gen. 15:16), endless patience (2 Pet. 3:9, 15) and according to his own timetable. Hebrews 6:12 sums up the lessons of the Egyptian sojourn – and indeed the experience of many more in the Bible than those to whom it directly refers – when it insists that it is 'through faith and patience' that we inherit the promises of God.

Exodus 2:11–25

2. The turning point

We have now taken the story of the days of darkness to the time of the birth of Moses. Hindsight tells us that this was a decisive event in the fortunes of God's people in Egypt, but those suffering under that harsh regime did not recognize it as such, and indeed, were not to know it for many a long day yet.

1. Long, dark years

How many years are covered by the words *after Moses had grown up* (11)? The Bible tells us that this was a period of forty years but reveals virtually nothing of their content. Indeed, all we do know comes from the brief New Testament comment that Moses was educated in all the wisdom of Egypt (Acts 7:21–22). Beyond that, we know that he went on to spend forty years in the land of Midian. But forty years take a long time in passing, and it was forty further years of darkness for his fellow Israelites in Egypt. A whole new generation grew from the expectancy of youth to the disappointment of old age while Moses was in Midian, and God seemed to do nothing. They were born into slavery, they grew up in slavery, they moved towards death in slavery, and the days of darkness still continued.

2. No quick fixes

There is no way in which we can read this story and say there is a quick or easy way out of, or even through, the sufferings and difficulties of this life. Indeed, even when Moses came back from Midian, the way was still hard.

There was a contest with Pharaoh (chapters 5–11), which for the most part meant defeat and delay, and even though the Lord finally triumphed over the Egyptians, the immediate outcome of one divine visitation after another was that Pharaoh hardened his heart, and the bondage became if anything worse than it had been before (5:7–8).

As for the people themselves, when Moses first intervened on their behalf, they did not at all appreciate that God was doing anything for them (14; cf. Acts 7:24–25), nor could they see any sign of a dawning light in the years of his absence. Even, indeed, when Moses returned from Midian, it seemed only to be a false dawn without any realistic hope of the full light of day (cf. 4:31 with 5:21).

Hymn writers sometimes allow themselves to exercise poetic licence and to oversimplify the realities of life, and in doing so step beyond what Scripture permits. Take for example the words

> Not a shadow can rise,
>> not a cloud in the skies,
> but his smile quickly drives it away.[1]

Presumably, the words express what must have been true for the writer at the moment of writing, but they are certainly not capable of being generalized over the whole of everyone's life. To the contrary, however, the book of Exodus makes us face the prevailing and continuing of the darkness which is often a part of our experience, while at the same time lifting the corner of the dark curtain to tell us that there is also another story going on – that the people who walk in darkness are on their way to the great light (cf. Isa. 9:2). The Lord is in the process of bringing his people out of darkness.

We always naturally want simple, quick solutions, the equivalent of instant coffee in spiritual reality! Occasionally the Lord will satisfy that desire, but for the most part he does not, and, like the Exodus people, we face the demand for persevering in faithfulness and patience awaiting the coming day.

3. The false dawn: Moses the failure (2:11–22)

Even a cursory glance reveals that this passage is a story of failure and of a chronic loss of self-belief. It is all the more striking when we see it against

---

[1] J. H. Sammis, 'When We Walk with the Lord'.

the background of what we learn about Moses himself. He had so much going for him.

a. His position

Verse 11 tells us that Moses *went out* (i.e. from the palace) in order to go among his own people. He had grown to adult years as the son of Pharaoh's daughter, a prince of Egypt, with the riches of Egypt at his disposal (Heb. 11:26). Who could blame him if he thought that all he had to do was lift his little finger and Egyptians and Hebrews alike would come running? At the same time, who can fail to admire him, in that he set out to exploit his position, not for himself but on behalf of his oppressed fellow Israelites? Furthermore, Moses was no effete palace darling (cf. Matt. 11:8). He was if anything all too resolute, resourceful, brave and effective in action. But position, commitment and courage are not enough.

b. His vocation

Acts 7:25 tells us that when Moses killed the Egyptian, he was acting in obedience to a divine vocation as he understood it. He saw himself as God's appointed deliverer. This New Testament comment in no way contradicts anything in Exodus here, but rather runs along the grain of the narrative. The references in verse 11 to *his own people* (lit. 'brothers') and in 3:6 to 'the God of your father', taken at face value, show that Moses was brought up in the wisdom of Israel as well as that of Egypt (cf. Heb. 11:25). He knew who he was, where he had originated and what he believed. This was what prompted him to act – but it was not enough.

c. His good-hearted concern

There was something in Moses which could not stand idly by and watch the weak being downtrodden. It made his blood boil to see an Egyptian striking a Hebrew (11). Maybe, for all we know, nationalism came into the picture, but this played no part in his intervention on behalf of one Hebrew striking another (13), and even less in his gratuitous intervention on behalf of the girls at the well (16–17). This is all evidence of Moses' good character, inherited perhaps from a biological mother who could not bear to consign her son to the river and an adoptive mother whose heart was melted by a baby's tears. Tender-hearted concern was his, both by nature and by nurture, and he could have had no better preparation for the work that still lay ahead when the recalcitrance and ingratitude of the people he led tested his compassion to the limit, yet without breaking it (e.g. 32:32).

Moses was so plainly the right man for what lay ahead in the will of God. The unaided human mind might say that with this inheritance and upbringing, Moses had just the qualifications God was looking for. The scripturally instructed mind sees in Moses a working of grace whereby the Lord brought into being exactly the man he required (cf. Jer. 1:4–5). It is those whom he has trained to be fishermen that he calls to be fishers of men and women (Mark 1:16–17). Putting the matter personally, whatever the Lord may call any of us to, we may rest assured that his gracious preparation has made us exactly right for the task. But, as we see in the young Moses, not even a wonderfully tender heart was enough.

4. Further delay

Humanly speaking, when Moses took the law into his own hands, he put the day of deliverance further back. Of course, from the divine point of view there is no disorder in the Lord's programme. For one thing, Moses, as we shall see, had himself still so much to learn in the school of divine discipline. Nevertheless, humanly speaking, when Moses bustled onto the scene, he put the divine programme back forty years.

First, his murder of the Egyptian slave master was foolish (12). Getting rid of an individual Egyptian here or there was not going to disturb the smooth waters of the whole regime. It was a totally impractical way to go about liberating the people of God. Second, his attempt to settle the dispute between the two Hebrews served only to antagonize them (14). Moses found himself in the dilemma that all through history has beset the would-be liberator: as soon as he or she tries to free people by force, the would-be liberator begins to antagonize those who need help. They very rightly and logically round on him or her and say, 'We have seen enough of killing; why should we trust another killer? We have far too many people with swords in their hands. We do not need another one.' Third, Moses' action was doomed from the start. He thought he could conceal the murder (12), but his crime was discovered, and *When Pharaoh heard of this, he tried to kill Moses* (15). How could Moses, no matter how 'highly regarded' he was in Egypt (11:3), single-handedly tackle and overthrow all the power of Pharaoh upon his throne? The thing was a nonsense from the start.

5. Gone but not forgotten (2:15–22)

Moses left himself with no option but to take to his heels. His fellow Israelites did not want another killer-prince, and Pharaoh would brook no rival, so Egypt was no longer Moses' safe haven. Anywhere beyond the long reach of the arm of Pharaoh's law would do, and Moses chose Midian (15).[2]

Traumatic though it must have been, the experience did not, to begin with, change Moses. Still unable to see the oppression of the weak and do nothing about it, Moses impetuously put himself at considerable risk over a dispute about water rights (16–17). (Since pretty girls were involved, we might ask ourselves if this too is a window into Moses' character!) This time, however, unlike the previous episode, forceful intervention won him friends, indeed a home and family of his own (20–21). No comment is offered about this, but we cannot be wrong to discern the hidden hand of God.

Maybe the most important initial lesson for Moses (and us) from his flight to Midian was that the Lord still loved and cared for him in the midst of his mistakes and failures (cf. 1 Kgs 19:3–8). Moses, who, humanly speaking, had 'messed the whole thing up', found safety, home and family awaiting him, made ready by a gracious but yet undeclared providence.

Moses was not forgotten, but he did change. He was content to stay where he was, and when his son was born he chose a name that represented how he felt about his situation – *I have become a foreigner in a foreign land* (21–22). He had obviously buried the ambitions that had previously motivated him and seems to have 'come to the end of himself' and accepted the nonentity and proper obscurity of a failure. God, of course, had different intentions.

6. False starts and true beginnings

If we look at 2:11 – 3:10 we find four obvious sections: Moses' life in Egypt (2:11–15a); his settlement in Midian (2:15b–22); God's 'sudden remembrance' (2:23–25); and God's self-revelation to Moses (3:1–10). The first two sections are all about Moses – in verses 11–15a there are sixteen verbs,

---

[2] We do not know exactly where this was, as is so often the case with biblical locations, but it is likely to have been somewhere to the east of the Gulf of Aqaba. The biblical writers are more often interested in the 'what' rather than the 'where', and G. H. Davies makes the important point that in fleeing to Midian 'Moses fled from one branch of Abraham's family to another' (Gen. 25:1–2).

and Moses is the grammatical subject of fourteen of them. In the second two sections, however, the action passes into the hands of God: it is he who 'intervenes' (24–25), and it is he who intrudes so abruptly, so disruptively, into the even tenor of Moses' adopted role of shepherd (3:1–10). Thereby hangs a tale indeed!

It is not common for biblical narrative to draw lessons or stop to make moral comments.[3] Yet the point to be made here and the conclusion to be drawn is obvious: in the work of God mere human effort, however well intentioned, committed or influential, results in failure. The only way forward is (speaking reverently) to 'mobilize God' on our side. Seen in this light, 2:11–22 may be called 'the way of failure', and, by contrast, 2:23–25 bring us into 'the place of effectiveness'.

7. In a nutshell

The concluding verses of the sections are worth noting. At the end of the first, Moses' naming of his son in line with his sense of alien status is a sad comment on the mission that failed (2:22). The Moses who burst with such triumphalism onto the scene of oppression as would-be deliverer is now a self-exiled resident alien. At the end of the second we have hints of a new beginning (2:25). There is here a balanced contrast with 2:11. Previously, Moses went out and *watched* (lit. 'looked upon') the needs of Israel but achieved only a disaster; now *God looked on the Israelites.*[4] What had taken place to bring about this shift from failure to effectiveness?

8. The groan and the cry

There is a place of effectiveness in the work of God. We have seen that Moses, by depending solely on his own strength, made a hash of things and even postponed the hour of deliverance. By contrast, we can now learn that there is a factor which brings about the real hour of deliverance.

It is often said that time is a 'great healer', but time proved to be no healer for the people of God in Egypt. *During that long period* (lit. 'those many days') while Moses was in Midian the plight of the children of Israel

---

[3] Cf. Joseph's own words in Gen. 39:9 and the historian's comment in 2 Sam. 11:27.

[4] *Watched* in verse 11 and *looked on* in verse 25 both represent the ordinary Hebrew verb 'to see' (√rāʾâ). The fact that in verse 11 it is used with an indirect object (governed by the preposition bĕ) and in verse 25 with a direct object makes little difference to the meaning.

remained the same and they still *groaned in their slavery* (23). Sometimes when leadership passes into new hands many changes come in its wake, but such political upheaval was no solution for the Israelites; their oppression continued despite the death of the king who had initiated it. We might ask if the movement of thought from 'died' to 'groaned' suggests that perhaps they had hoped the new reign might bring relief? But if so, they were doomed to disappointment.[5] They had a new king, but still the old sorrows.

What was it then that made all the difference for the people of God? The wording of verse 23b is important: they (lit.) 'moaned . . . shrieked . . . their call for help' (NIV *groaned . . . cried out . . . cry for help*). All three are well-used words, and the first two may be synonymous and simply there for emphasis.[6] If, however, a difference is intended, the first suggests the burdensomeness of their lives and the second its hurtfulness. It is the third word, *their cry for help*,[7] that marks the change. They 'moaned' (a natural, spontaneous reaction to trouble), they 'shrieked' (a natural, spontaneous reaction to affliction), and God, sensitively aware of their distress, heard their inarticulate groans (24). The decisive moment came, however, when the inarticulate moaning and crying-out became a prayer and their *cry for help . . . went up to God* (cf. 3:7).

Where time brought no relief and political change brought no improvement, prayer made the difference. If, as we said, when considered from a human standpoint, Moses' precipitate action put back the moment of deliverance, then we must equally also say that when prayer was made, deliverance dawned (cf. Dan. 9:23). The prayer of the people of God is the beginning of their deliverance because prayer brings God into the situation. The chapter ends with the highly significant declaration of God's response to his people's prayer: *God heard . . . God looked on [saw] . . . and was concerned [knew]* (24–25).[8]

So God *heard* (i.e. the people had caught his undivided attention), he *saw* (i.e. he reviewed the situation in which his people found themselves)

---

[5] 4:19 is possibly the only suggestion that new hope had come with the new pharaoh and that it was now safe for Moses to return and even that things were about to get easier for his people. Could it be that the late pharaoh had an obsessive hatred of Moses which made him especially spiteful to Moses' compatriots?

[6] They 'moaned' (√'*ānah*) and 'shrieked, cried out in horror or terror' (√*zā'aq*). In this and the following verse the people's misery is evident in the heaping up of 'hardship' words – 'groaned', 'cried out', 'cry for help' and 'service' (NIV *slavery*).

[7] *Cry for help* is the noun *šaw'â* from √*šāwa'*. It is used in this sense both as a noun (e.g. 2 Sam. 22:7; Pss 34:15[16]; 145:19) and as a verb (e.g. Ps. 18:6[7], 41[42]; Isa. 58:9).

[8] This is echoed in the next chapter, where God says, 'I have indeed seen . . . I have heard . . . I am concerned [know] . . . So I have come down' (3:7–8).

and, having reviewed it, he *knew*. The verb 'to know' is, of course, first of all, the registering of the facts (cf. Gen. 18:21), but it often goes beyond this. In the Old Testament, 'knowing' someone also implies actively entering into an intimate relationship with that person, just as, in another setting, the Hebrew says that Adam 'knew' his wife: in other words, he entered into the deepest, most personal intimacy of mutual knowledge two humans can experience (Gen. 4:1).[9] Similarly, when Psalm 1:6 says (lit.), 'God knows the way of the righteous', it means he registers how they are and then maintains an intimate and knowledgeable relationship with them as they go through life (NIV 'watches over [them]').[10] His knowledge of how we are placed, how we feel, what it is like to be us, is not a remote or merely objective acquaintance with the facts. It involves a 'coming down', a knowing companionship – indeed, a transforming intention. This is made apparent in Exodus 3:7–8, where God says, 'I am concerned about [know] their suffering. So I have come down.'

It was prayer that made all the difference, even though there was no immediate change. That horrible dark curtain of suffering still hung over the people of God, Moses was still in Midian, and there was no gleam of heavenly light or discernible declaration from God that their prayer had been heard. The Israelites in Egypt had no public declaration from God that their prayer had been heard; they were still walking in darkness and seeing no light (cf. Isa. 50:10). We, however, see a different picture because the Lord uses his Word to lift the corner of the curtain for us. We are able to see what they could not: that when the prayer was made, the prayer was heard; the grim realities of the situation were registered, and God entered into fellowship with his people in their need and came down to deliver them. This is a straightforward demonstration of the effectiveness of prayer as echoed in Daniel 9:23, 'As soon as you began to pray, a word went out' (or 'an answer was given'; cf. Jer. 33:1–3).[11] It was prayer that made all the difference.

---

[9] 'Knew' is sadly lost in the NIV's choice of 'made love to', just as here in Exodus the NIV evaporates it into 'was concerned about' (cf. NKJV 'acknowledged'; ESV 'knew'). The NIV's translators apparently thought 'to know' in Gen. 4:1 was a euphemism for having sexual intercourse, as though the Bible were afraid to call a spade a spade. It is, however, not a euphemism but a definition of what marital sexual union *is*. 'To know' is retained, as we would expect, in the NKJV and restored in the ESV.

[10] In Exod. 2:23–25 there is quite an emphasis on the spiritual status of the intercessors. They are (lit.) 'the sons of Israel' and those to whom the covenant with Abraham, Isaac and Jacob applies. God always sees and knows us in our spiritual reality and position within his purposes of grace and redemption.

[11] There is a striking illustration of this in Luke 1:13. The coming Messiah's forerunner was predicted by the prophet Malachi (Mal. 4:5) and his timing fixed on the divine calendar (Gal. 4:4), but it is nevertheless portrayed as coming about in answer to prayer.

9. Voicing our needs

The prayer that the people made gave voice to their needs.[12] It was not wordless groaning, nor some non-specific petition. They *groaned in* [lit. because of] *their slavery*, and their 'call for help' came up to God *because of their slavery* (23). The repetition of the phrase *because of their slavery* is important: their need gave rise to their prayer, and their need commended their prayer.

Prayer is our opportunity to bring our needs to God, and we should feel free to do so. The grounds on which we can approach God in prayer are multifaceted. We can come to him, for example, and say, 'Lord, I make this request because you have made a promise.' An example of this is when parents plead on behalf of their children on the basis of Genesis 17:7 or Acts 2:39. Since he has promised, we may ask. Or, again, we can come to him and ask for something in the 'name of Jesus' (cf. John 14:13–14; 15:16); that is to say, we pray to the Father as those who are united by faith with his Son.[13] The greatness of God's love for us as individuals is, however, perhaps most strikingly seen in this: that we can appeal to him simply because we are in need. In Egypt the people's 'cry for help' was heard because of their need, *because of their slavery*. The need of the people of God is in itself an appeal and a ground of prayer. The need prompts the prayer, and the need also commends the prayer to our loving heavenly Father. Such is God's love for us.

10. Earthly prayer, heavenly purpose

There is another truth here about prayer. Prayer reflects our needs, but it also promotes the purposes of God. This is a great mystery because, as the Bible teaches, God's purposes are fixed and indeed inflexible. He, as we say, knows the end from the beginning – and, we might add, all points in between. Where is there room, then, for our prayers to operate and 'make a difference'? Nowhere is this problem highlighted more than in Exodus 2:24, where the point at issue is God's faithfulness to his covenant, for his

---

[12] Cf. Ps. 142:1[2] (lit.) 'with my voice I cry . . . with my voice I seek [his] grace', i.e. the 'cry' was put into words, something that is not apparent in the NIV's choice of 'aloud'.

[13] We come into the Father's presence through our one divine mediator, the Lord Jesus, and, to the best of our ability, we request those things which match his revealed nature (i.e. his 'name') and which he would himself ask if he were placed where we are.

covenant is his solemn pledge to be God perpetually to his people (e.g. Gen. 17:1–7). Surely he can be left, without our help, to attend to this on his own. Surely in this matter of his central providential care and saving plans for his people he needs no prompting. Yet the Bible says that we must pray. Jesus commands us to pray, not only about things that might seem to be within our province, but also about matters fixed within the purposes of God (e.g. Matt. 24:20). We are to pray for no other reason than that God hears and answers prayer.

Here in Exodus, in that delightfully human way that the Bible speaks to us about God, we have a perfect example of this truth. It says in verse 24 that *God heard their groaning* and *remembered his covenant*. This is the way in which he is represented to us, but, of course, we know that it is impossible for God to forget: he never forgets his people nor the word that he has pledged, his covenant (Deut. 4:31; Isa. 49:15). Yet here he is represented as though he woke up one morning, the phone rang, and when he picked it up he heard the voice of his people in Egypt saying, 'We're in such a pickle', and the Lord said to himself, 'By George, I'd quite forgotten about them.' Of course it did not happen like that, but God is represented as though his elbow needed jogging and our prayer did the trick. Thus we learn what a marvellous and potent thing his people's prayer is.

The prayers of the people of God have such a key role to play that the Bible can make it clear only by speaking of it in terms we can understand. It therefore depicts the unforgetting God as though he were capable of forgetting, and our prayers as having the marvellous effect of causing him to remember. Our prayers are so effective, and so delightful in his ears, that God condescends to accommodate his eternal, sovereign, providential working to what we can understand, as though to say, 'Oh, thank you for reminding me.'[14]

Effective and potent though prayer is, events are still held within the framework of God's timetable. This is why it says that *he remembered his covenant with Abraham, with Isaac and with Jacob* (24). The example of the long-dead patriarchs is a call to patience and to waiting. God works to his own timescale, and he expects his people to wait for him and to wait with him. We who know the end of the Exodus story could well ask why it was forty years before Moses came back. To this perfectly natural and

---

[14] See B. Ramm, *The Christian View of Science and Scripture* (Paternoster, 1955), pp. 61–62 for some helpful comments.

understandable question no answer is given (cf. Acts 1:6–7). The Lord expects his believing people to wait for him with patience.

11. Divine moral providence

Once again here, the Bible lifts the curtain just a little bit, and we have an indication that the apparent delay in the Israelites' deliverance had something to do with God's moral providence at work in the wider arena of world events.

When the people of God were finally brought out of Egypt, two other nations were going to suffer dreadful divine judgment: the Egyptians at the start of the journey as the Israelites went out of slavery, and the Canaanites at the end as they entered the Promised Land (12:30; Josh. 6:21; 10:40). The former suffered the judgment of God as his people went out of the land; the latter suffered the judgment of God as his people came into the land. Both nations were given a time of probation: that of the Canaanites is foretold in Genesis 15:16 and that of the Egyptians is recounted in Exodus 7 – 12. We cannot but cower back from these records of divine visitation. We rightly say, how dreadful are the judgments of God! But he is 'the Judge of all the earth', and he does what is 'right' (Gen. 18:25), never inflicting what is not due, and blending his central care of his people into his total management of the world in righteousness. So why was Moses forty years in returning to Egypt? Because Egypt was not yet ripe for its final time of probation and the Amorites were not yet ripe for their appointed judgment. More than that, however, Moses was not yet ripe to be a leader. Those years in Midian were to be important years of training for him.

Additional notes

The framework of Moses' life is drawn from a variety of Scripture passages. Acts 7:23 says he was forty years old when he left Egypt for Midian (Exod. 2:11), and Acts 7:30 records he spent forty years in Midian, making him eighty when he returned to Egypt (Exod. 7:7), and he then led Israel in the wilderness for another forty years (Num. 14:34; Deut. 8:2). This fits with Deuteronomy, which says he was 120 years old when he died (Deut. 34:7). The neat parcelling of Moses' life into three blocks of forty years suggests deliberate patterning, and Currid (vol. 1, p. 75) notes that forty is frequently a period of testing in the Bible (e.g. Gen. 7:17; 1 Sam. 17:16). This is not, of course, to question the Bible's veracity but to take into account an allowable symbolic use of numbers and to suggest that Scripture may be more interested here in the quality of Moses' life than its chronological span – certainly every part of his life was a time of testing par excellence. The comment in Deut. 34:7 on Moses' exceptional vitality despite his great age suggests that the numbers are likely to be correct.

Exodus 3:1–10

3. Old Moses . . . new Moses

1. The mountain of God

The induction of Moses to be the great leader and deliverer he became began with his encounter with the Lord at Horeb, *the mountain of God* (1).[1] Mountains, especially Horeb, or Sinai as it is also known in the Old Testament,[2] figure largely in the spiritual history of Moses. Horeb makes its first appearance in the story here as the mountain of conversion or new beginnings, and in chapters 19 to 34 it is the mountain of revelation, the place of Moses' seven ascents (19:3, 8, 20; 20:21; 24:15; 32:31; 34:4). Beyond Horeb lies Mount Pisgah, which could be called Moses' mountain of disappointment, as it was from there that he viewed the land he had been forbidden to enter (Deut. 34:1). Then, in the distant future, there is the place of Jesus' transfiguration, Moses' mountain of homecoming (Matt. 17:1–3).

This first visit to Horeb can allowably be called Moses' moment of conversion. C. S. Lewis described himself at what he recorded as his moment of conversion as a 'most reluctant' convert,[3] but, as we shall see, there was certainly no more reluctant convert than Moses. Yet God's meeting with him at Horeb was indeed that radical and life-changing

---

[1] Opinion is divided as to whether Horeb is here called *the mountain of God* because it was already a revered religious site or whether the title is being used proleptically, i.e. reflecting a later accepted usage (cf. saying 'The Queen was born in 1926' and meaning 'a baby who later became queen'). Jethro was, after all, a 'priest of Midian' (2:16), and the mountain could have been sacred to the Midianite religion.

[2] The Old Testament seems to use Horeb or Sinai for the general area, the mountain range, and the specific mountain itself. A convenient summary of specialist opinion can be found in the article on Sinai in *NBD* (pp. 1109ff.).

[3] C. S. Lewis, *Surprised by Joy* (Fontana, 1959), p. 182.

experience which a true conversion is. The new Moses may have been slow to emerge into the light of day, but that can also be the hallmark of a deep and lasting change of heart. With beautiful simplicity, John 1:12 teaches that the moment we place our faith in the Lord Jesus Christ there is an eternal and irreversible change as we 'become children of God'. This results in spiritual illumination as our eyes are opened, personal re-orientation from darkness to light, transference of kingdom membership from Satan to God, forgiveness of sins and an eternal inheritance (Acts 26:18). This fundamental change of heart which occurs when someone turns to the Lord was just as true under the old covenant as it is under the new and, then as now, must prove its reality by progressive transformation of character and conduct. As Moses the man emerges to take centre stage in the mighty events Exodus records, we shall be able to trace in him some of that development and maturing, but it all started here when Moses found himself confronted by the holy and living God.

2. A map of the Exodus terrain

We have already noted something of the artistry with which the book of Exodus as a whole is composed.[4] This same attention to structure is discernible in the book's individual sections, as here in 2:23 to 4:31.

A[1] Israel in Egypt: the new divine initiative revealed (2:23–25)
        Two verbs of grief: groaned, cried out
        Four verbs of divine reaction: heard, remembered,
        saw ('looked on'), knew ('was concerned about')
    B[1] The Lord and Moses: revelation and commission (3:1–10)
           The sufficiency of the Lord
    B[2] Moses and the Lord: hesitation and obedience (3:11 – 4:28)
           The inadequacy of Moses
A[2] Israel in Egypt: the new divine initiative believed (4:29–31)
        Two verbs of the Lord's intervention: visited ('was concerned
        about'), saw ('had seen')
        Four verbs of response: believed, heard, bowed, worshipped[5]

---

[4] See Introduction.

[5] The literary device of *inclusio* (using the same words or ideas as brackets around a passage to indicate its coherence) is evident here in the use of the verbs 'heard' and 'saw' in A[1] and[2].

3. The Lord takes centre stage

Forty years on (Acts 7:30) and Moses was still a shepherd. The Hebrew of 3:1 involves a verbal form which stresses continuance,[6] fully endorsing the use of the word 'still' and justifying the statement that 'God is not in our kind of hurry'.[7] This does not indicate any delaying or dithering on God's part. He wanted a shepherd for his people (Ps. 77:20[21]), so his chosen man had to learn how to look after someone else's sheep! In other words, Moses too had his period of probation and of undeclared discipline and training. Did he know that the hand of God was secretly shaping his destiny? If he did, he does not tell us so, but he certainly had to learn the lesson of being faithful in the ordinary humdrum routine of everyday life. This casts its own light on the desire of Jesus that we be found 'trustworthy' in small matters (Luke 19:17; cf. Luke 16:10; 1 Cor. 4:2). When God's moment came, however, Moses' patient management of Jethro's flock took him to the right place at the right time. For suddenly he was confronted by God himself. Such is the wonder and exactness of divine providence.

4. God appears in the burning bush

a. The angel of the Lord

Exodus describes Moses' encounter with God as *the angel of the* LORD appearing to him. When we look at the other references to 'the angel of the LORD' or 'the angel of God', we find that he is someone very special indeed. A. B. Davidson puts it this way: 'This Angel is not a created angel – He is Jehovah Himself in manifestation . . . identical with Jehovah, although also different.' Angels in general, writes Davidson, can represent one aspect or another of the divine nature but 'in the Angel of the Lord He is fully present'.[8] Malachi 3:1 is a case in point, where 'the LORD [*ʾādôn*, the Sovereign]' and 'the messenger/angel of the covenant' are in

---

[6] A periphrastic verb involving a participle ('shepherding') and the verb 'to be'.

[7] A. P. Baker in an unpublished lecture.

[8] A. B. Davidson, *The Theology of the Old Testament* (T&T Clark, 1904). E. Jacob sees the angel as 'the double of Yahweh' (*Theology of the Old Testament* [Hodder & Stoughton, 1958], p. 77). G. A. F. Knight calls the angel an 'alter ego of God himself' (*A Christian Theology of the Old Testament* [SCM, 1959], p. 78). J. Pedersen says the personalities of Yahweh and his angel are 'merged into one another', yet the angel is 'an independent divine personality' (*Israel III & IV* [Oxford University Press, 1953], p. 496). See also W. C. Kaiser, *Toward an Old Testament Theology* (Zondervan, 1978), p. 85, and the references under 'Angel' in Kaiser's index.

apposition: literally, 'Suddenly, the Lord whom you seek, the angel of the covenant whom you desire, will come to his temple. Behold! He is coming! The LORD [YHWH] of hosts has said it!' The coming of the angel is the coming of Yahweh in all his sovereignty, yet Yahweh announces the coming of the angel as though speaking of someone else. All this is amply borne out in the references to 'the angel of the LORD' throughout the Old Testament.[9]

We see in the account of the burning bush that it is by means of his angel that the Lord comes among people (2) and that when the angel comes, the Lord himself is present (4).[10] In Exodus the angel figures as the Lord, present and protecting (14:19). He is to be reverentially accorded full divine honours because the divine 'Name' (the whole revealed nature of God) is in him (23:20–23). In 33:1–2 the angel is revealed as the merciful 'accommodation' or 'condescension' of God, whereby the Lord can be present among a sinful people when, were he to go with them himself, his presence would consume them. We can put it this way: the angel suffers no reduction or adjustment of his full deity, yet he is that mode of deity whereby the holy God can keep company with sinners.

There is only one other in the Bible who is both identical with and yet distinct from the Lord. One who, without abandoning the full essence and prerogatives of deity or diminishing the divine holiness, is able to accommodate himself to the company of sinners and who, while affirming the wrath of God, is yet a supreme display of his outreaching mercy. Such indeed, is the angel of the Lord as revealed in the Old Testament, and, consequently, Barton Payne rightly does not hesitate to say these 'revelations of the unique Angel . . . can be appreciated only when understood as a pre-incarnate appearance of Jesus Christ'.[11]

b. Holy fire . . . fiery holiness

When the angel of the Lord came to Moses, he clothed himself *in flames of fire from within a bush* (2),[12] and this linking of fire with God's presence

---

[9] Among the many references to angels, 'the angel of the LORD', by this and other titles accorded him, stands out as a unique personage (Gen. 16:7; 21:17; 22:11; 31:11; 48:16; Exod. 13:19–22; 23:20–23; 32:34; Judg. 2:1; 6:11; 13:3; Isa. 63:9; Hos. 12:4 [cf. Gen. 32:24–30]; Zech. 1 – 6 [e.g. 1:12; 3:6–10]).

[10] We can see this in the fact that the person in the bush is referred to as 'the angel of the LORD', 'the LORD' and 'God'.

[11] J. B. Payne, *The Theology of the Old Testament* (Zondervan, 1962), p. 170.

[12] 'As a flame of fire' is a more idiomatic translation, and seen in this way fire is a continuing theological theme throughout the Bible starting with Gen. 3:24; cf. Exod. 19:18; 40:38; Lev. 9:24; Deut. 4:11, 36; 5:5; 2 Kgs 1:10; Ps. 97:3; Isa. 31:9; Jer. 21:12; Zech. 2:5; Matt. 3:11; Acts 2:3; 2 Thess. 1:7; Heb. 12:18, 29.

recurs throughout Exodus (13:21; 14:19; 19:18; 33:10; 40:38). The first occurrence of the symbol of fire in a covenant setting can be found in Genesis when God made his covenant with Abram and signified his presence as (lit.) 'an oven [with] smoke and a flashing of fire' (Gen. 15:17). The picture here is of the portable earthenware oven of the nomad, which when filled with combustible material would heat the pot to the temperature required for cooking. During this process, the oven vented a mass of smoke and flame. The symbolism is not explained in Genesis, but Exodus reveals that the fire stands for the presence of the holy God and the smoke for the gracious veiling of that holiness when he comes among humans. The fire and smoke of Abram's cooking pot reaches its full expression in the towering flames and smoke of Sinai (19:18), the pillar of cloud and fire that was Israel's guard and guide during their wilderness wandering (13:21–22), and the outward and visible sign of the Lord's presence in the tabernacle among his people (40:38).

So, what is this 'holiness'? Why is it linked with fire? Can the dilemma whereby God both summons Moses (4) and warns him not to come near (5) be solved?

i. Holiness

There is some debate as to whether the foundational meaning of the word 'holy' is '[unapproachable] brightness' (cf. 1 Tim. 6:16) or 'separateness, distinctness'.[13] While we must guard against introducing any mere idea of God being 'different' because that would beg the question, 'Different *from* what?', 'separateness' seems to offer the best hope of bringing together all that the Bible says about the Holy One. The idea of separateness has a positive rather than negative connotation in that the holy being is seen as belonging in its own distinctive sphere, with its own distinctive characteristics, and, in the case of the Lord, as unique (cf. Exod. 15:11; Pss 71:19; 86:8; 113:4–6; Isa. 40:25).

The understanding of holiness as separateness can be illustrated by human examples. When, for example, Jeremiah is spoken of as being sanctified from birth, it means that God set him apart not *from* the world, but *for* himself and for the task of prophesying (Jer. 1:5). Even more telling is the use of [lit.] 'holy woman' to describe the girl whom Judah treated negligently as a common prostitute (Gen. 38:21). She was not a prostitute

---

13   See Motyer, *Look to the Rock*, p. 207.

as we understand the word but a temple servant who took part in rituals at the Baal shrine that involved sexual acts. She could, therefore, be called 'holy' because she had been set apart for the god she served, behaved in ways acceptable to that god, and was supposed to belong to the divine sphere of reality. The fact that the God of Israel forbade such service (Deut. 23:17) shows that the kind of holiness he both embodies and requires is of a different kind, being pure, moral and ethical. The actual revelation of this, however, lies further on in Exodus and in the Bible as a whole.

ii. The imagery of fire

There are many examples in the Old Testament of people going in fear of their lives because they have met God, stood before him or seen him (e.g. Judg. 6:22–23; 13:21–22), and Exodus 33:20 shows that this fear was not groundless. The scene is set, and in so many ways the meaning is fixed, by Genesis 3:24. In a word, there is that in the nature of God which banishes and endangers sinners. To put it like this is, of course, to import terminology which runs beyond what Genesis actually says, but not in any way to do violence to its ideas. For, though Genesis 3 reveals humankind falling into sin, it does not speak of 'sin', and while it reveals the Creator as holy, it does not use the word 'holy' of him.[14] Even here in Exodus, holiness is implied of the Lord rather than stated, but the implication is unmistakable.

In Genesis 3, Adam and Eve were wilfully disobedient. To them this seemed a comparatively minor matter, leaving them at liberty to remain, albeit in hiding, within the garden (v. 8), but to the Lord God it was not so. Their disregard of his command required banishment from the garden (v. 23), and involved danger and the impossibility of ever returning (v. 24). We are standing on the same ground in Exodus 3:2–5. While the verses do not say that the Lord is holy, they imply that holiness is where the Lord is, and unassisted humankind cannot approach him.

Holiness endangers the sinner because the holiness of the Lord is not a passive attribute but an active force, embracing all that conforms to it (Ps. 24:3–4) and destroying all that offends (1 Sam. 6:19–20). The trepidation humans feel before the Lord is not, therefore, the trembling of the lowly before the Almighty or the created before the Creator, but the fear of sinners endangered by holiness (Isa. 6:3–5). The biblical symbol of this

---

[14] Gen. 2:3 is the only reference to holiness in Genesis. Yet, Bible in hand, who can read the first eleven chapters of the book (to go no further) without standing in awe of the holy God?

perilous force of holiness is fire, and it pervades the book of Exodus. In particular, fire is the bracket (or '*inclusio*') which provides a framework around the central narrative of Exodus. It starts with the fire in the bush (3:2) and ends with the fire on the mountain (19:18), and in each case the fire is linked with the separateness of the divine and the exclusion of the human as endangered.

This was the starting place for Moses as 'servant of the Lord', as it is indeed for all true and effective service. For 'unless we have been on our knees, more or less in tears, because of the holiness of God, we have not begun'.[15]

iii. Approaching God

Fortunately, exclusion is not the last word on the subject, for out of his blazing holiness the Lord calls to Moses and commands him to remove his sandals (5). Mackay may be correct in thinking that this symbolized putting aside all that had been in contact with the 'defilement' of earth.[16] The idea is appealing, but it is not the simplest, and may not be the best, way to understand what passed between the Lord and Moses. The Lord's command signifies, first, his desire that Moses should be enabled to remain standing on 'holy ground', and, second, the conditions necessary for that to take place. It would appear that God desires us to be in his presence, but the question 'Who may ascend the mountain of the LORD? Who may stand in his holy place?' (Ps. 24:3) comes naturally to us. It would exhaust all our human wisdom to attempt to fashion a reply according to our notions of fitness, and we would remain excluded until he told us how to come to him.

There is a striking simplicity and accessibility in what the Lord directs: take off your shoes! The principles enunciated here remain constant throughout the Bible, even though the forms change. In the full Mosaic system, acceptance was through the atoning power of the divinely provided sacrifices (Lev. 17:11). These sacrifices point forward to the Christ who suffered, 'the righteous for the unrighteous, to bring you to God' (1 Pet. 3:18), whose blood opened the way into 'the Most Holy Place' (Heb. 10:19), and through whom we 'have access to the Father by one Spirit' (Eph. 2:18). The point, therefore, of Moses taking off his shoes is a lesson

---

[15] A. P. Baker, unpublished lecture, Trinity College, Bristol.

[16] Cf. Cassuto, 'Do not tread on this ground with your travel-stained sandals.'

in simple obedience: we should bow humbly to whatever God may require of us, rejoicing in the simplicity and effectiveness of his provision as he admits us to his presence.

5. The unchanging God

It was during the encounter with the awesome and holy angel of the Lord that Moses learned what his life mission was to be. The task set before him by God was to *bring my people the Israelites out of Egypt* (10), a task of unparalleled magnitude and difficulty in which he would have to face demands never experienced before. For Moses to know that those who had sought his life were dead (4:19) was, presumably, some comfort, but it also meant that he was not returning to what he had known before. With the old rulers dead, the past was in large measure gone. What would he find? Whom would he face? And, as far as Israel was concerned, his forty-year absence would have seen the end of the senior generation under whom he had grown up, and its replacement with others whom he did not know and who did not know him. It was, in fact, 'flying blind'. Again, he was to be one man against a superpower – and he was already a proven failure at the task.

Moses may have viewed returning to an unknown situation in Egypt with trepidation, but he was immediately reassured that, whatever else had changed, one thing remained the same – the God who spoke to him out of the burning bush was *the God of your father, the God of Abraham, the God of Isaac and the God of Jacob* (6).[17] It also served to remind him of his own membership of the covenant community.

Bible history tells us nothing of Moses' father, save that his name was Amram (6:20), and it is striking, therefore, that the Lord stirred Moses' memory to recall not his mother, with her godly and memorable resoluteness, but the one in whom Moses must have seen an even more sterling example of faith and of knowledge of God shared in the home.[18] Of course, we are not made privy to Moses' thoughts at this point, but would we be miles off the mark in wondering if the thought rose unbidden that the God who was enough for Amram in those frightful days of persecution would

---

[17] Durham (p. 31) is sensibly insistent on the correctness of the singular 'your father', referring to Amram, for 'despite the various (and unjustified) attempts to make it plural . . . [the singular] connects the speaking deity with the faith of Moses' family'.

[18] The faith of both of Moses' parents is commended in the list in Heb. 11:23.

also be enough for himself? We need not, however, spend time wondering if our surmise is correct because behind Amram lay the known characters and histories of Abraham, Isaac and Jacob, and it is mainly to these that the attention of Moses was called. Something in the experience of each of them was relevant to Moses as he faced the uncertain future.

In response to the call of God, Abraham left everything behind and set out for an unknown destination (Gen. 12:1; Heb. 11:8); Isaac faced the impossible odds of death itself and experienced a God who did indeed provide and whose promises could be trusted (Gen. 22:1–14; Heb. 11:17–20); and Jacob discovered the folly of living by his wits when he should have been trusting the promises of God (cf. Gen. 27 with 25:23).

It was by his identification with these three that the God who called Moses wanted to be known. They were such complex characters that much more could be said of each of them, but enough has been said to suggest the relevance of 'the God of Abraham, Isaac and Jacob' to Moses and his needs. God had not changed from what he had been to the patriarchs in those far-off days. He was still the God who calls into the unknown, overcomes impossible odds to keep his promises, and bothers with those who have tried and failed, and, certainly in the case of Jacob, is the God who can take the unpromising material of our lives and transform it.

Furthermore, the miracle that Moses saw of a *bush . . . on fire* that *did not burn up* must have had an impact on him (2). Here was a flame nourished by its own life, needing no external fuel to feed it, a truly living flame. It was an important element in the Lord's self-revelation to Moses, for it was what he used in the first instance to capture Moses' attention. The essence of this revelation is that Yahweh is the living God, a self-maintaining, self-sufficient reality that does not need to draw vitality from outside.

If the flame symbolized the presence of God, should Moses have seen the bush as a symbol of himself? The juxtaposition of the transcendent God in all his holiness and vitality and the ordinary, earthly bush[19] is a powerful metaphor for the indwelling, transforming presence of God with his people. This is the implication of his words to Moses. First, there is the sensitive feeling which makes the Lord aware of Israel's plight and the

---

[19] The Hebrew word, *sĕneh*, is completely non-specific and is found only here and in Deut. 33:16. As with all biblical locations, it is not the place as such that is important but what happens there.

graciousness which prompts him to identify with them in their need: *I have indeed seen the misery of my people in Egypt . . . So I have come down to rescue them* (7–8). Second, although he could have delivered Israel by the mere exercise of his personal presence and power, it was God's choice to do it through a chosen emissary (*So now, go*, 10), whom he would accompany on the mission (*I will be with you*, 12).[20] It is always so. No-one who goes at the behest of God ever goes alone. The 'I' who accompanies is the God of Abraham, Isaac and Jacob, the God also of Moses.

Additional notes

3:1 Moses led his flock 'behind/after' (Heb. *'aḥar*), NIV *far side*. This can also mean 'west' (as Hyatt, Cole) and indicates that for that day's pasturage Moses chose the western end of his range. Cassuto prefers to translate it 'led his flock in search of pasture'. The Hebrew for 'desert' (*midbār*) is versatile. According to W. J. Martin (lecturing at Tyndale House, Cambridge, in the 1950s), we should think of it as 'the open space between conurbations', rather like our 'green belt'. It does not necessarily mean the howling wilderness of Deut. 8:15.

---

[20] God says he has *come down to rescue them* (8) and at the same time sends Moses to accomplish the task (10). To go at God's bidding is to join the winning side from the start, for we are participating in what he has already committed himself to do. The imperative behind *bring my people . . . out* (10) is an example of the Hebrew idiom of 'certain consequence', used when an outcome is so certain that it may be commanded to happen.

Exodus 3:11 – 7:7

4. A sneak preview

God bothered with Moses. That, in itself, is a marvellous truth, amply borne out as we look back from the vantage point of 3:1–2. As we peep behind the scenes, we can see a secret providence at work governing the fortunes of Israel as a people – countering adversity of circumstances (1:12a), foiling royal schemes (1:17), bringing help from humanly impossible quarters (2:6) and turning the place of enmity into the place of shelter (2:10). We can also see this same careful providence in the case of Moses as an individual – all evidence that in both the general and the specific things of life God is working his purposes out. He never ceases to work, he never forgets, and nothing can foil his working or cancel out his promises.

1. Let Bible history speak

The stories in the early part of Exodus speak to us in our times of greatest and most urgent need, when we are tempted to say, 'God has forsaken . . . God has forgotten . . . Why are things like this? . . . There is no purpose in it', and so on. Exodus quietly reminds us that the contrary is true: God has not forsaken us, he has not forgotten us and our need, and, despite appearances, his promises and purposes remain firm and their fulfilment is on the way. Habakkuk, indeed, was right:

> The vision awaits its appointed time;
>   it hastens to the end – it will not lie.

If it seems slow, wait for it;
> it will surely come; it will not delay.

(Hab. 2:3, ESV)

2. Moses' chronic insecurities

As chapter 3 opens we find Moses simply getting on with the daily occupation in which he had been settled now for forty years, the shepherd of another man's flock. He did not know, as we do, that, by this humdrum existence, the Lord was training him for a life work in which he would shepherd the Lord's own sheep (Ps. 77:20[21]). So it was, then, that eventually in the context of daily faithfulness in very little things (cf. Luke 19:17) the Lord opened Moses' eyes to a heavenly vision: a flame of fire in the midst of a bush burning by its own energy and not by consuming the bush, representing the ever-living God, who is life in himself and who needs no outside sustenance but exists by his own eternal energy, Israel's ancestral God, unchanged and unchanging. The immediate effect of the vision and its startling movement of thought from what God will do (3:8–9) to what he has in mind for Moses to do (3:10) was to rouse in Moses all manner of doubts and insecurity (3:11 – 4:17).

A detailed discussion of this will concern us in the next chapter, but there is a most important lesson to be learned from standing back and viewing the whole picture. The fact of the matter is that Moses needed tons of reassurance. He was chronically uncertain about himself. That episode in Egypt all those years ago (2:11–17) must have really knocked the stuffing out of him. All the old bounce was gone, and the man who was now not the prince of Egypt but the shepherd of Midian needed crowds of reassurance, tender loving care and hand-holding. This is the way his conversation with the Lord went:

'Who am I?' (3:11)
'What shall I tell them?' (3:13)
'What if they do not believe me?' (4:1)
'I have never been eloquent' (4:10)
'Please send someone else' (4:13)

We can feel Moses' almost overwhelming insecurity. How uncertain he was! First, there is his sense of personal inadequacy (3:11). Is this the same man who once thought he could solve everything by simply making his presence felt? It is, but his self-confidence has been deflated by the experience of failure and the forty long years of relegation which followed. Then there is his desperate attempt to plead ignorance and incompetence (3:13), and lack of the personal stature and authority that would command attention and commend the message (4:1) and of any natural abilities that would suit him to the task (4:10). Finally, he came to that place where we too so often find ourselves and said, 'Here am I; send someone else' (4:13).

3. The Lord of the insecure

If Moses lives in our memories as the towering leader of Israel in deliverance and pilgrimage, it is well to remember where he started – insecure, uncertain, unprepared, unworthy and un-almost-everything-else! It is also well to remember how patiently the Lord took him at point after point and ministered reassurance to him.[1] Again, we are not here pausing on details, but simply observing the flow of the narrative.

A^1 I am not the person you need: unfitness (3:11)

  B^1 I have not the necessary gift: knowledge (3:13)

    C I have not the required effectiveness (4:1)

  B^2 I have not the necessary gift: eloquence (4:10)

A^2 I am not the person you need: unwillingness (4:13)

Notes

What are we to make of the literary artistry and balance evident in Moses' demurrals? The most obvious answer is that behind Moses' statement of his difficulties there is the ordering mind of the Spirit of God imposing his own shape on what was destined to become part of Holy Scripture. Alternatively, we may transfer the Spirit's inspiring role to the writer who crafted into this form what he learned from Moses. Durham says that

---

[1] Fretheim makes Moses in some sense a contributor to God's plans. He notes (correctly) that 'God treats the dialogue with Moses with integrity', but goes on to say that God 'honors [Moses'] insights as important ingredients for the shaping of the task' (pp. 52–53). This latter point is not so. Moses does not contribute 'insights'. All he does is moan about his inadequacy and unwillingness. Rather, the dialogue reveals with what gentleness the irreversible sovereignty of God works. He gets his own way not by bulldozing Moses into the ground but by nursing him along. Fretheim goes so far as to say that God 'needs' Moses, with the implication that he adjusts his plans and requirements so as to secure Moses as his partner. On the contrary, God, according to the words of the old prayer, 'declares his almighty power most chiefly by showing mercy and pity'.

documentary criticism finds here 'an amalgam of EJ source material' but notes that the passage has 'a unity superseding that of either narrative [i.e. J or E] in its original form . . . forged into a single sequence [which is] nothing short of brilliant' (pp. 36–37). This seems to be just another way of saying that the 'documentary hypothesis' requires J and E to be here, but that without that hypothesis no-one would ever think of finding them.

In this way we can see a rounded statement of Moses' perception of the difficulties that faced him in the task the Lord had proposed for him. Any one of them could well have seemed a decisive argument against pursuing his candidature any further, but that is not the Sovereign's way. With gentle – and, as we read it, persuasive – patience, every one of the 'problems' was solved. Yes, but in what way?

4. Where are you looking?

If we look at Moses after his return to Egypt and his first conferences with Israel (4:30–31) and Pharaoh (5:1–5), we find him unchanged in abilities, reactions or feelings from the man we met at the outset (6:12). Here is someone who had failed yet again. The result of Moses' efforts was that Pharaoh made things even worse for the people (5:7–11), and Israel wanted no more to do with him (5:19–21). He emerged from this bruising experience with no confidence for the task and no hope of success coming his way. In other words, the Lord had not solved Moses' problems by changing Moses either inwardly, in feelings or temperament, or outwardly, in effectiveness. The whole intent of the Lord had been in an entirely different direction.

In reply to Moses' qualms, the Lord, in effect, said to him – and this is reflected throughout 3:11 – 4:17 – 'But what about me? Are you taking me into account? Where are your eyes fixed?' The Lord did not take away – or even promise to take away – Moses' nervousness, or impart boldness to him. He did, however, call him to a position of trust. Consequently, the proposed solutions to Moses' problems involved him resting in the Lord's presence (3:12), bearing simple testimony to the Lord's revelation of truth about himself (3:14), doing what God commanded on the assumption that God himself would produce the results (4:8–9), receiving the Lord's help to overcome inadequacies, expecting abilities to match needs (4:11–12) and trusting the Lord's promise that help was on its way (4:14). God proved himself to be trustworthy in the event, but in prospect Moses was called to 'the obedience of faith' without seeing any actual change in himself or his situation. We can put it another way. When Moses was faced with his vocation to 'bring my people the Israelites out of Egypt' (3:10), his reaction was, 'I can't, therefore I won't.' The Lord sought to bring him to the point where he would say instead, 'I can't, but *he* can, therefore I will.' That is the obedience of faith: doing the will of God because he will always do what he has willed; trusting the promises of God because he will always keep his word; acting on the assumption of divine provision because he will never fail to provide.

5. Don't go out before you come in

The whole sequence from 3:1 – 12:36 follows an important pattern:

A¹ **Vision (3:1–10)**

The Lord confronts Moses and draws him into a personal meeting

> B¹ **Reassurance and commencement (3:11 – 4:31)**
>
> Moses, commissioned in 3:10, is nourished in divine promises and returns to Egypt
>
> > C¹ **Failure (5:1–21)**
> >
> > Initially accepted by Israel (4:31), Moses tackles Pharaoh, but with the result that he is rejected both by Pharaoh (5:1–20) and by Israel (5:21)

A² **Vision (5:22 – 6:8)**

Moses brings his grief to the Lord. His commission is renewed in the context of further revelation of the Lord and his intent

> B² **Reassurance (6:9 – 7:7)**
>
> Failing to convince Israel (6:9), Moses doubts the value of a further approach to Pharaoh (6:10–13). The Lord renews his promises (especially 6:28 – 7:7)
>
> > C² **Success (7:8 – 12:36)**
> >
> > Perseveringly, Moses battles with Pharaoh amid signal acts of God until (e.g. 12:41) he leads Israel out of Egypt

Probably the really big question arising out of this pattern is whether there is some key factor at work to transform the failure of C¹ into the success of C². Why did vision (A¹) and reassurance (B¹) lead to failure in one instance but then to success in another? There must surely be some crucial principle of Christian service, of the service of God, to be shared with us here. There is, but it must wait until we study the details of chapters 5 and 7. The other, equally important, matter to notice is that before Moses ventured out into his ministry (chapter 5) or returned to the fray (7:6), he was first drawn into the presence of the Lord (3:1ff.; 5:22ff.).

This is particularly noticeable when Moses 'hit rock bottom' after his initial failure (5:22–23). The Lord did not turn snappy with Moses and say, 'I've given you a vision of myself as the God of eternal life and power. Whatever more can you possibly want?' Rather, how marvellously gentle he was with his failing servant! Moses had to admit, 'Lord, absolutely nothing has happened. Things are worse than they were before I came', but the divine rejoinder was not to rebuke or mock but simply to say, 'Come and have another look at me. Let me tell you again who I am. I am Yahweh. Let me remind you who I am. Let me reassure you all over again' (6:2–5).

What is it, then, that leads to true Christian service? What we have here is not the whole answer because there is still the vital ingredient which will emerge in chapters 5 and 7. Nevertheless, Exodus is very clear about where true Christian service begins. It begins in the presence of the Lord. The Lord said to Moses, 'I am sending you to Pharaoh' (3:10), but before he sent him out he brought him in and let him stand in his presence and commune with his God. The biblical preparation for service is always that we be found in the presence of the Lord.

We could follow this principle right through the Bible. Why was John the Baptist in the wilderness until he appeared publicly to Israel (Luke 1:80)? Why did Paul go away into Arabia before he ventured into missionary service (Gal. 1:17)? Why did the Lord Jesus spend forty days in the wilderness pondering the book of Deuteronomy (Matt. 4:1–11)? Why did Isaiah, as he looked forward to the perfect service rendered by the perfect Servant of the Lord (Isa. 50:5–9), first reveal that Servant in a 'morning by morning' private interview with the Lord (Isa. 50:4)? There is a principle involved. Before we go out we must come in, and so we see how the Lord brought Moses into the secret place of communion with himself prior to sending him out to Israel and Pharaoh. The Lord has a training school. He says, 'Come into my presence.' Satan will, of course, always seek to reverse that procedure, reminding us all the time of the needs of the world and of the desperate necessity to get on with the work. The Lord, however, is saying, 'Just wait a bit. I'm not in your sort of hurry. Come and linger in my presence.' Satan says, 'No, think of the needy world. There are souls to be saved', because he wants us to go out onto the battlefield unarmed. He does not mind one bit if we go out to the Lord's battles, provided that we have no hope of winning when we get there! But the Lord says, 'No, come and stand with me for a bit. Come and listen to me.' Service begins in the presence of the Lord, spending time alone with God.

6. The Lord, before whom I stand

Elijah was destined for a work every bit as demanding as that given to Moses, facing and outfacing a murderous king and an even more murderous queen, but he went to stand before the earthly king as one who had already taken his stand before the heavenly King (1 Kgs 17:1; 18:15).

Moses used his time alone with God to unload all his hang-ups. And in this too he is our example, for there is nothing we cannot bring to the Lord when we have him to ourselves. We are left with the feeling that Moses was an extraordinary person for God to want to use, a person with all those insecurities, weaknesses and inadequacies, so defensive and unwilling. But we are reminded, nevertheless, that there is nothing we cannot say to the Lord or share with him – we can even come to him and say, 'Lord, I don't want to.' For when we come into his presence, we have him to ourselves and he has us to himself, and that is the place where true service begins.

Exodus 3:11–22

5. The God who is sufficient

It would seem that we can never lose, but only gain immeasurably, by being honest with God. It is foolish, of course, to try to hide from the one who sees everything (Heb. 4:13) – although we do! The message that comes to us from Moses, as he responded to God at the burning bush, is that honesty is the best policy and that there is nothing we cannot say to God, no problem we cannot bring. Moses was almost frighteningly frank about himself, but how beautifully at each point his frankness opened a door to floods of divine patience, understanding, promise and provision.

1. What? Me? (3:11–12)

Moses' first problem was his sense of personal inadequacy, the 'What? Me?' syndrome. Moses said, 'Who am I?' and the Lord replied, 'But I . . .' Notice the Lord's graciousness here in not trying to deny Moses' inadequacy. How differently we react to one another. Somebody comes to us and says, 'I'm not really up to it', and we immediately and thoughtlessly reply, 'Of course you are!' That is not the way the Lord dealt with Moses – or the way he deals with us. He does not sweep the difficulties we feel aside. Moses said, 'Lord, I'm not adequate', and the Lord said, 'No, but I am!' He accepted Moses' self-estimate and graciously promised his presence as adequate for the inadequate man. He neither said to him, 'Of course you're adequate', denying Moses' feelings, nor did he say to him, 'It doesn't matter.' He accepted Moses' sense of inadequacy as one of the facts of the situation, but then countered it by the adequacy of his own presence.

This is so important that it is worth trying to put it another way. Moses' position was, 'Look, I'm not up to the job. You shouldn't have picked me.' The Lord's reply was, 'Of course you are not up to the job. I knew that when I chose you for it. The point is not your ability, but mine!' Moses' 'I' of incapacity is balanced by the Lord's 'I' of ability. In a nutshell, that is how matters stand – and not just for Moses, but for always and in every situation of divine choice and call. The Lord does not call us because of our adequacy, nor is his presence conditional upon us becoming adequate; it is rather promised to those who are inadequate. When we say, 'But I'm not adequate', the Lord says, 'You needn't tell me, but I will be with you.'[1]

Furthermore, the Lord's reaction was not to promise to make Moses adequate, somehow to transform him into someone who was up to the task. (Although that is what he did do as time went on.) What he did promise was the sufficiency of his own presence. In other words, he called Moses to a position of faith – to go into this work not expecting to be a different man but expecting a sufficient God. He met Moses' inadequacy with the pledge of his own sufficiency and called Moses to believe the promises and to demonstrate the obedience of faith.

2. The sign (3:12)

In the Old Testament signs fulfil two purposes. In some circumstances they can serve as present persuaders. The signs in 4:1–9 are like that, designed to persuade those who saw them that Moses had indeed been sent by the Lord (cf. Deut. 13:1–2; Judg. 6:17; 1 Sam. 14:10; Isa. 7:11; 38:22). At other times they are future ratifications or confirmations of something said or done earlier, as, for example, when the signs which Saul experienced (1 Sam. 10:1–7) ratified the word Samuel had earlier spoken about kingship (cf. 1 Sam. 2:34; Isa. 7:14; 38:22). The flow of verse 12 is forward-looking, suggesting that the sign will act as a future ratification. Once the people have been delivered, they will come to Sinai and worship God there, and this will confirm to Moses that the Lord did indeed send him.[2]

---

[1] Cf. Judg. 6:15; Jer. 1:6. Mackay comments, 'It does not matter who you are . . . What matters is that God has called you . . . not who Moses was . . . but who was with Moses' (p. 74). On 'with you', cf. Gen. 31:3; 46:3–4; Josh. 1:4–5; Ps. 46:7[8]; Jer. 1:8; Acts 18:10.

[2] Some prefer to think that the burning bush is the sign referred to. It was indeed a sign of God's presence and could, therefore, have confirmed to Moses the reality of his call.

What purpose would this subsequent confirmation serve? If Moses had entertained doubts as Pharaoh's opposition grew more and more obdurate, then the appearance of a confirmatory sign would have been very welcome. But once Sinai was in sight, why would he then have needed reassuring? This, in fact, is the nub of the matter. As Cassuto points out, the prediction that the Israelites would worship God *on this mountain* (12) was a cause for wonder because Mount Horeb was not situated on the direct road from Egypt to Canaan. Indeed, when Pharaoh saw the direction the people were taking, he exclaimed, 'They are wandering in the land; the wilderness has shut them in' (14:3, ESV), and the people themselves later gave vent to disquiet about the route they were taking, saying, 'You have brought us out into this desert to starve this entire assembly to death' (16:3). Even Moses himself could not have failed to notice the difference between the expected 'land flowing with milk and honey' (3:8) which was the goal to which he had been called and the aridity of the actual landscape into which he was leading the people.

When, therefore, the Lord spoke of 'worshipping on this mountain', Moses must have been astonished, and he must have lived to be grateful for this anticipatory word of the Lord and the sign to which it was leading. In spite of every appearance to the contrary, he could be confident that all was well and going according to plan. Had not the Lord told him it would be so? Thus, standing in the presence of the Lord and listening to the word of the Lord, Moses was being prepared both to withstand coming shocks and also to reassure the people when they were overtaken by what would otherwise be to them an inexplicable turn of events.[3]

3. 'But I wouldn't know what to say!' (3:13–22)

Moses' second problem was his lack of knowledge: *Suppose I go to the Israelites and say to them, 'The God of your fathers has sent me to you,' and they ask me, 'What is his name?' Then what shall I tell them?* (13). This is a very ordinary, common problem, and one we ourselves often echo when we think of speaking out about the Lord Jesus or taking a public stand on some current issue. It is comforting to know that Moses was there before us. He envisaged himself going into Egypt, announcing to the people that

---

[3] It is worth noting that in *the sign to you, you* is singular and refers to Moses. In *you will worship, you* is plural and refers to the people as a whole. Thus, even in the terminology used by God there is further reassurance to the self-doubting Moses who can be confident of success even before he sets out for Egypt.

he had been sent by *the God of your fathers*, and then being asked the most extraordinary question, *What is his name?* Notice that he was not asking what God's name is, but was expecting Israel to ask him the 'name' of the God of Abraham, Isaac and Jacob.[4]

a. What news and what proof?

What were the people really asking for when they wanted to know God's 'name'? In the Bible, names often had a serious significance, and in the case of the Lord his 'name' was his 'story'; it summed up who he was and what he wanted to make known about himself.[5] In other words, asking Moses for God's 'name' was a shorthand way of saying, 'What revelation of God do you bring?'[6] It was in these terms that the Lord met and answered the question Moses expected to be asked.

It is intriguing, and though unprovable not too fantastic, to wonder if the name Yahweh was a closely guarded secret among the Hebrews in Egypt and could, therefore, have been used as a proof of veracity if anyone claimed to come in the name of Israel's God (cf. Deut. 13:1). This would explain why Moses expected the question about the name, why he would not have been able to answer it, and why without it there would have been no progress with his mission. A claim to have received a word from God carries no weight unless tested and found to be valid (cf. 1 Thess. 5:20–21; 1 John 4:1), and the test of a secret name would have been determinative.

b. 'I AM WHO I AM' (3:14)

Whatever conclusions we come to regarding the reason for the question about the name of the ancestral God, the fact is that the question was raised, and the Lord graciously condescended to answer it. Just as Moses

---

[4] Why did Moses think that he would be asked this question? Why should the Israelites have thought that the time had come to find a hitherto unknown name for the God of their fathers or even to imagine that such a name existed? Their current knowledge of him seems to have been rich enough to have supported all that was to happen to them at the exodus (Gen. 46:1–4; Exod. 6:2–3). So why should they ask after his name? Durham (p. 37) makes a neat contrast by saying Moses' first question was 'Who am I?' and his second was 'Who are you?', but this is not what happened. He goes on to say that if Moses was satisfied with the designation 'the God of Abraham . . .', then why should he think it would not satisfy Israel? Fretheim says that the name would establish Moses' credentials but does not say how (p. 63). Other commentators do not deal with the question at all. The point cannot be emphasized too much that Moses was not seeking information for his own satisfaction but in order that he might answer a question that he foresaw being asked. For whatever reason, he envisaged Israel in Egypt making this enquiry.

[5] Cf. Motyer, 'Name', in *NBD*, pp. 799–802.

[6] Tolkien's character Treebeard speaks of his name in this way: 'My name is growing all the time, and I've lived a very long, long time; so my name is like a story. Real names tell you the story of the things they belong to' (J. R. R. Tolkien, *The Lord of the Rings* [HarperCollins, 1991], p. 454).

was made to stand in the presence of the living God as the foundation of everything that was to follow, so Israel must (through Moses) meet with God in his word as the starting point of their liberation.

The God of Abraham, Isaac and Jacob was a God of many titles and one single name. At last Moses was to be allowed to supplement what had been missing in Genesis: 'Yahweh' ('the LORD')[7] would no longer be a mere form of address but would tell its own story about the divine nature and do so in a way immediately relevant, endlessly satisfying and bafflingly enigmatic – the famous *I AM WHO I AM*!

i. The God ever-present, ever-active, interventionist for good

The link between the divine name and the Hebrew verb 'to be' is the plainest feature of this passage. This is what Durham calls the 'is-ness' of the God of Israel. In every place, at every point in time, in every circumstance or need, he 'is'. Unlike Greek, which uses different verbs to express either existence or active presence, Hebrew has only one verb for both meanings, √*hāyâ*, but unquestionably this verb leans strongly in the direction of 'active presence'. The old hymn by J. L. Black which proclaimed 'God is here, and that to bless us' caught the sense exactly. The presence of this God is not, therefore, a bare 'is' but a living force, vital and personal. In no situation is he an ornamental extra; in every situation he is the key active ingredient.

We can feel the surging force of this by looking at verse 12 where, in reply to Moses' sense of inadequacy, there is the simple and sufficient 'I will be with you' or 'I am with you', as if the divine name had been announced even before the question of verse 13 was asked. Does God just mean that he is omnipresent? Certainly not. Rather, it is that where Moses was inadequate, there was a more than sufficient makeweight in the living, omnicompetent God; where Moses was weak, almighty power would be at work. The God of the flame that needed no outside nourishing, bursting with his own superabundant vitality, would be there – and not because he had been invited or called upon but by his own will in

---

[7] A huge difference of opinion has arisen over the matter of the divine name (for a more detailed treatment see the comments on 6:2–3). Most specialists take the view that this was the first time that the name, usually vocalized as Yahweh, was revealed. They then develop different theories to explain how it could have been used in Genesis before the time of Moses. While Moberly, *Old Testament,* offers a serious and carefully considered alternative view, I still hold the opinion that what was happening here was not the disclosure of a new name as such but the revelation of the meaning or 'story' of a name known from earliest times (cf. Gen. 4:26) and throughout the period of the patriarchs. See Motyer, *Name.*

fulfilment of his own nature as the God whose name is *I AM* and who allows his people to know him as 'He is' (the third-person verb, Yahweh, *the LORD*, 15).

ii. The ever-independent, sovereign God

The construction *I AM WHO I AM* finds an instructive parallel in Exodus 33:19, 'I will have mercy on whom I will have mercy, and I will have compassion on whom I will have compassion.'[8] If we invert these phrases we will catch their force better: 'On whom I will have mercy, I will have mercy . . .' In other words, 'I bestow my grace exactly and only where I choose.' The same applies here: 'It rests solely with me when and where and with whom I make my presence felt.'

Moses was given an all-embracing assurance in verse 12, 'I will be with you', but he had yet to learn that there are things which comply with the presence of the Lord and things which alienate him. His presence as such is guaranteed, but the enjoyment and realization of that presence is another matter. When Moses returned to Egypt, he promptly gained the consent of Israel to his mission (4:30–31) and went forthwith to Pharaoh (5:1). The immediate result was harder labour (5:6–8), beatings (5:13–14) and a wedge of alienation between Israel and Moses (5:20–21), so that Moses 'returned to the LORD' (5:22) with the bitter complaint that things had only got worse and that the use of the divine name had meant nothing (5:23). So what went wrong? Nothing went wrong, except in Moses' expectations. By revealing himself as *I AM WHO I AM* the Lord had in effect said, 'Yes, I have committed myself to you to be actively present with you, but I am not at your unfettered disposal. My active presence is mine and mine alone to exercise as and when and under what conditions I choose.'

In chapter 5 and again in chapter 7 we will learn the secret that to know God by name is a wondrous revelation and a great privilege, but the name itself is also a warning that God remains God. Lightness, careless irreverence, thoughtlessness or bland assumption before him will not do.

iii. The inexhaustible God

I AM WHO I AM is without doubt an enigmatic statement and conceals at least as much as it tells. It is an open-ended assertion of divine sufficiency:

---

[8] The Hebrew offers a closer parallel than appears in the English, needing as it does the use of 'to whom' etc. – *'ehyeh 'ăšer 'ehyeh* (3:14) and *wĕḥannōtî 'et- 'ăšer 'āḥōn wĕriḥamtî 'et- 'ăšer 'ăraḥēm*.

'Whatever circumstance may arise, I will be there and I will be sufficient.' The understanding of the divine name accords with the opening promise of the section (12), but it also means that no matter how much of himself the Lord is now revealing to Moses, he is also (so to speak) keeping himself in reserve. There is an endless abundance yet to be explored and experienced. There is no way in which our emerging needs in ever-changing circumstances and demands can 'catch him out', prove him inadequate or reach the end of his resources and competencies. We live under the 'umbrella' of 'the unsearchable riches of Christ' (Eph. 3:8, ESV). In the same spirit Jesus says, 'No one knows the Son except the Father, and no one knows the Father except the Son' (Matt. 11:27), and Paul says, 'no one knows the thoughts of God except the Spirit of God' (1 Cor. 2:11).

c. Comprehensive revelation

Exodus 3:13–22 falls into three easily recognizable broad sections. It starts with Moses and the Lord (13–14), then there is Moses and Israel (15–17) and finally Moses and Egypt (18–22). Within this overall movement, however, lies a richly detailed revelation of God's nature.

i. The God of self-revelation (3:14–15)

Right through the Bible the distinguishing mark of God's earthly people is their knowledge of a self-consistent God who speaks by his word and allows them to know his unchanging name. This was so even when there was only Adam: the hallmark upon his life was that he possessed the word of God to obey, and his privilege as the tenant of the garden was conditional upon living by that word (Gen. 2:15–17). Again, what distinguished Abraham and the patriarchs from their Canaanite contemporaries was not that they were emigrants from Mesopotamia but that they were in Canaan because God had spoken to them and made them his word-bearers. In the New Testament period, Paul in his second letter to Timothy defines the church as the possessor, student and preacher of the God-breathed Scriptures (2 Tim. 1:13–14; 2:14–15; 3:14–17; 4:2). He does not think in terms of structures, however venerable, nor does he expect fresh revelation of further truth. The distinguishing mark of the church is that it is the trustee of the given word. This was how it was for Moses. He was sent to Egypt as the bearer of the divine word, the understanding of the name which God had spoken to him.

ii. The changeless and caring God (3:16)

A recurring title of God in the Old Testament is *the God of Abraham, Isaac and Jacob*. The familiarity of this can blind us to the fact that centuries had passed between Abraham and Moses. Vast changes of time, place and fortune had befallen Abraham's descendants, and he must have seemed to them a bygone figure lost in the mists of antiquity. But by faith they could grasp the changelessness of the God who had spoken to Abraham and who still cared for his people.

This is reflected in the key Exodus verb √*pāqad*, translated in verse 16 and elsewhere in the NIV as *watched over* but traditionally represented by 'I have visited' (e.g. NKJV). This verb is very versatile and branches out in many directions from its foundational meaning of 'visit, inspect'. It is used of David reviewing his troops (2 Sam. 18:1), of a shepherd inspecting his flock (Job 5:24) and of the Lord coming to the relief of the childless Sarah (Gen. 21:1) and famine-struck Israel (Ruth 1:6). It also has a darker side, for when the Lord 'visits' he may find what outrages him and demands judgment (e.g. Exod. 32:34). The present verse matches the expectations of Genesis 50:24 and represents the Lord as the God who comes to the aid of his people, who is aware of and sensitive to individual and national needs, inspecting, caring and providing.

iii. The promise-keeping God (3:17)

The promise referred to in verse 17 reveals a God of deliverance, inheritance and good providence. It is two-sided: the people are to be both 'brought out of' and 'taken into', although this emphasis is possibly a shade more prominent in the Hebrew than appears in translation (cf. Deut. 6:23). The Lord had in mind both sides of this promise. As we have seen, he offered no explanation to Abram for the coming enslavement of his family, but he did predict their liberation and had in mind the gift of the land of Canaan as soon as it could justifiably be taken from its existing owners (Gen. 15:7, 13–16). Therefore, he did not here promise deliverance as an end in itself, but only deliverance coupled with inheritance. The Lord is a God who can both rectify the past and open the door to a blessed future. For, as he says later in not dissimilar circumstances, 'I know the plans I have for you . . . plans to prosper you and not to harm you, plans to give you hope and a future' (Jer. 29:11).

iv. The God of foreknowledge and patience (3:18–19)

At the beginning of verse 19 the pronoun 'I' is emphatic and could be reflected by saying, 'But I know full well.' Moses did not know what lay ahead, nor did Pharaoh, for all that he would try to manipulate the future, but nothing was hidden from the Lord. He set a programme before Moses, even to the extent of putting words into his mouth, for the messenger of the Lord is meant to be a mouthpiece of the word of the Lord. The Lord knew how both Israel and Pharaoh would react. The fact that Pharaoh could resist the Lord's hand in verse 19 but submitted to it in verse 20 lies within the doctrine (and problem) of divine providence.[9] The Lord does not put forth all his mighty power at once. His ways with sinners are patient and probationary, as if he were advancing by trial and error. He will never overwhelm the sinner before full opportunity has been given for repentance and amendment of life. When final judgment falls, it must be plainly and palpably just. Just as the Lord waited centuries while the Amorites were on probation (Gen. 15:16), so the almighty *hand* did not judge Pharaoh before the right time. The God of providence is so very long suffering (2 Pet. 3:9, 15).

v. The God of power and sufficient resource (3:20)

The movement of thought from the apparent failure of the *mighty hand* in verse 19 would lead us to expect an array of adjectives of power to accompany the successful *hand* in verse 20. If the *mighty hand* was insufficient, would there not be need of a 'super-mighty, omnipotent hand'? No, just *my hand*! It was mercy and kindly providence and a longing for repentance that allowed the power of Pharaoh to prevail for so long against such displays of divine displeasure (cf. 1 Tim. 2:4). The overthrow of even the greatest power in the world, however, needs no special effort on the Lord's part – it is enough that his hand has unfettered operation.

vi. The God of victory and of transformation (3:21–22)

It is not just that the Lord has power over all the power of the enemy, but even people's hearts are his to sway, direct, change and command. In chapter 1 we saw how the Egyptians' feelings towards the Israelites

---

[9] Many commentators find difficulty with the fact that verse 19 seems to say that the Lord's *hand* will not succeed, whereas verse 20 says that it will. There is no objective justification for emending the text to get over this problem, as the NIV does. Durham's translation is more acceptable: 'not even under pressure of a strong hand', or, more literally, 'will not let you go. Indeed not! In spite of a mighty hand.'

changed first to fear and then to loathing (1:9, 12), and it is against this background that we must now see the transformation sketched in verses 21–22 and fulfilled in 12:35–36. It was this wealth that later would provide for the beauty and richness of the tabernacle (chapter 25 onwards). The Lord brought about a transformation of relationships (21a), conditions (21b–22a) and status (22b) whereby the hated became the favoured, slaves were enriched and the erstwhile victims triumphed over their erstwhile masters.[10]

4. Rich revelation, but only a start

Throughout this section we have seen some of the riches embraced by the divine name: a God for all seasons, all eventualities, all tasks, all needs. But even the least awareness of what the rest of Exodus contains – not to mention the rest of the Bible – reminds us that under each of these headings there is much, much more yet to come. God has so much more to reveal of himself, his care, his faithfulness to his word, his loving patience, his power and might. The divine name is the name of the inexhaustible God.

Additional note

3:20 *Wonders:* the verb is √*pālā'*. For the indicative (niphal), cf. Gen. 18:14; Ps. 118:23; Zech. 8:6. For the participle niphal (as in the present case), cf. Exod. 34:10; Ps. 40:5[6]. The noun is *pele'*; cf. Ps. 77:14[15]; Isa. 9:6[5]. For the broader meaning of 'beyond the ordinary/out of the ordinary', cf. 2 Sam. 1:26. The plagues are called *signs* ('ôt, 7.3; 8:23; 10:1), pointers to some significant truth or explanation; *wonders* and 'miracles' (*môpēt*, 7:3, 9), marvels causing the onlooker to 'stop in his or her tracks'; and *acts of judgment* (*mišpāṭ*, 7:4), decisions reached authoritatively, in this case by the Lord.

---

[10] At this point Cassuto (p. 44) calls attention to Deut. 15:13–14 where, according to the Lord's law, slaves who have completed their term of servitude were to be provided for by their former masters on their departure, and says, 'The heavenly court saw to it that the requirements of law and justice were carried out.' Mackay prefers the less telling motif of 'a triumphant army laden down with booty' (p. 83).

Exodus 4:1–17

6. The God who is able

All the way through chapters 3 and 4 the Lord has done far more talking than Moses, which suggests the genuineness of Moses' negative feelings about himself – he was very far from 'protesting too much'! The simple statements of inadequacy (3:11), inability (3:13), ineffectiveness (4:1), incompetence (4:10) and grudging submission (4:13) were enough. To Moses they were self-evident, even axiomatic, but in each case the Lord gave a lengthy and detailed reply.

1. Words before deeds

The fact that the Lord replies to Moses at such length has an importance that goes beyond showing his determination to have the man he has chosen, though, of course, it does that too. It bears importantly on the matter of how the Lord reveals himself; in particular, how his words precede his deeds. In the two replies considered so far, what an array of truths about the Lord, his divine nature and capacities, his intentions towards Israel and Egypt, and his foreknowledge of the course of history, are revealed. So far he had *done* nothing but he had *said* a very great deal. The God of the Bible is a God of words before deeds, a God of verbal revelation, who speaks and then acts to confirm what he has said.[1] The Bible is

---

[1] The view that the Bible primarily records the acts of God and the subsequent interpretation of those acts by authorized individuals has an impressive history. It can be studied in G. E. Wright, *The God Who Acts* (SCM, 1952) or, at a more philosophic and demanding level, in W. Temple, *Nature, Man and God* (Macmillan, 1940, pp. 315ff.). Temple coined the telling formula that there are no revealed truths, only truths of revelation, i.e. truths (hopefully) arising from the (correct) interpretation of what God has done. For a critique of this view, see J. A. Motyer, *Look to the Rock* (IVP, 1996), pp. 81–88.

not first and foremost the book of the acts of God, which people at the time and later sought to interpret as best they could. Rather, it is the book of the words of God.[2] Amid all that he said, the Lord also revealed to chosen agents (like Moses) what he proposed to do, and what his coming actions would mean. Like the later prophets, Moses was made 'wise before the event', not left to scrabble around to find meaning in something that had already happened.

2. They will not believe me (4:1–9)

The third of Moses' objections and yet another area in which he felt inadequate was his certainty that his mission to Israel, should he go on it, would prove ineffective. He knew himself to be the sort of person no-one would believe! And he is surely on stronger ground here than with his previous protestations, for forty years ago he had tried and failed to deliver Israel (2:11–15). The passing years had not relieved him of that sense of failure, and he speaks like a thoroughly discredited person.

Once again, the Lord took Moses at the level of his own self-appraisal, but this time he answered him with three actions for him to perform, involving a rod that became a snake (2–5), a hand that became leprous (6–7) and the Nile water that became blood (8–9). We might well ask what on earth we are to make of this small collection. They are recorded without comment in Exodus, and their subsequent performance is given only the briefest possible notice (30), so that we have scarcely any pointers to help us understand them.

a. Signs and wonders

The first thing we can note, however, is that they are called *signs* ('ôt, 8–9; cf. 3:12) and 'wonders' (môpēt, 21; cf. 7:3, 9). These two words are often used together in the Old Testament (e.g. Deut. 13:1[2]). The distinction between them, as is so often the case with near synonyms, must not be overpressed, but in a broad sense a 'wonder' is something that halts people in their tracks, making them stop and stare, and a 'sign' points beyond itself to something else. A 'wonder' is meant to catch our attention; a 'sign'

---

[2] See e.g. J. W. Wenham, *Christ and the Bible* (IVP, 1972); J. I. Packer, 'Contemporary Views of Revelation', in C. F. H. Henry, *Revelation and the Bible* (Tyndale, 1959); J. I. Packer, *God Has Spoken* (Hodder & Stoughton, 1979); W. A. Grudem, 'Scripture's Self-Attestation', in D. A. Carson and J. D. Woodbridge (eds), *Scripture and Truth* (Baker, 1992).

is meant to engage our minds. A 'wonder' astonishes; a 'sign' instructs.[3] Plainly, a rod turning into a snake and back again, a hand becoming leprous and then healthy again, and water becoming blood are quite rightly called 'wonders', but as 'signs' what are they pointing to? What truth do they illustrate or confirm?

We do not know what sort of sign or wonder the false prophet of Deuteronomy 13:1[2] might have performed to validate the message, but possibly it was the same sort of supernatural conjuring that Simon practised later in Samaria (Acts 8:9). The Lord's signs, however, are always meaningful illustrations and not just clever tricks (e.g. Gen. 9:12; 17:11; Isa. 20:3). Even if the three signs here were primarily a way of authenticating Moses' claims to have been sent by God, the likelihood is that they were also pointers to deeper truths. Since the Bible does not explain them, we can assume that they must have had a plain meaning for those who saw them performed, and do our best to understand them in their original context.

b. Watch out, Egypt!

The three signs that were given to Moses involved factors common in Egyptian religion and life – a snake, leprosy and the Nile. The kings of Egypt wore crowns adorned with the uraeus, a cobra with raised hood threatening Egypt's enemies. The cobra crown was also associated with the sun god Ra, the 'Living King', who, when united with Amon, was the most powerful deity in Egypt.[4] Victory over the serpent was, therefore, a comprehensive motif for challenging and overthrowing the central realities of Egyptian religion and sovereignty, and thus, by this sign, Egypt's power, whether divine or royal, is shown to be under the Lord's sovereign sway. Moses may well have fled from it in the past, but by obedience he can also subdue it.

Cassuto associates the sign of the leprous hand with the prevalence of leprosy in Egypt, where it was reckoned incurable. Certainly, in the Old Testament, Egypt was held to be notoriously unhealthy, and possibly leprosy would have been taken as an apt symbol of this.[5] Like Egypt's

---

[3] The burning bush is a good example of a 'wonder' (3:3).

[4] See M. Bunson, *The Encyclopedia of Ancient Egypt* (Gramercy, 1991), pp. 225, 226, 274. Durham remarks that 'widely in the ancient Near East the serpent was [a] symbol of wisdom, fertility and healing. In Egypt in particular serpents were worshipped' (p. 44). In *Riddles of the Sphinx* (Sutton, 1998, pp. 164–165), Paul Jordan notes that the uraeus united the pharaoh with the sun god and pointed to his divinity as king.

[5] Cf. Exod. 15:26; Deut. 28:27, 60. In the Bible 'leprosy' was a general term for various skin diseases and could well have been used to represent the afflictions listed here.

power, Egypt's contagion was subject to the Lord, either to inflict or to cleanse.

The third sign, the corruption of the Nile, struck at the very heart of Egypt's existence. It is estimated that the Nile basin received as much as 30 feet of mud in the river's annual inundation, making it 'the black land' in contrast to 'the red land' of the surrounding desert. Every year the Nile waters washed, cleansed, renewed and increased Egypt's soil and were the reason for Egypt's famed fertility and so her great wealth and power. The Nile also abounded in fish and fowl.

> The river was endless in its bounty, and the people sang its praises continually . . . [It] was 'the Father of Life' . . . 'the Mother of All' . . . the manifestation of the god HAPI, the divine spirit that unceasingly blessed the land.[6]

To threaten and destroy the Nile was to destroy Egypt itself – and this, too, the Lord showed he could do.

c. A word to Moses

As loudly as the signs were to speak to Egypt, they spoke also to Moses, the man who in the past had fled from difficulty (2:15), settled for obscurity (2:21; 3:1) and backed away from challenging situations (3:11). Taking the serpent by the tail may well have been the bravest thing he had ever done (4). Not only was he overcoming his natural terror, but he was taking the most dangerous of all actions and making himself vulnerable to the danger he feared – for seizing the tail left the deadly head of the creature free to strike. But he did it as an act of obedience to the Lord's word and saw a 'sign' that the path of obedience is the path of victory. The Lord is the God of transforming power. He can take the ordinary (the staff) and make it the deadly (the snake), but he can also make the deadly subordinate to the person of obedient faith.

Our discussion of the signs has sought to move them out of the realm of mere conjuring tricks or marvels into the realm of meaningful, persuasive acts. The second sign is different from the other two in that Moses is, so to speak, required to deal not with things external to himself – water and snakes – but with realities within his own body and

---

[6] Bunson, *Encyclopedia of Ancient Egypt*, pp. 189–190. Cf. Isa. 19:5–15.

person. The hand that emerged from contact with his hidden flesh (6, lit. 'Put your hand into your bosom') was leprous. If anything could be said to sum up Moses' unworthiness before God and his unfitness for divine service, this outbreak of leprosy did. Moses' low estimation of his qualification for divine service had all been true, but the Lord made him go lower still and discover a contagion within himself. This was so that the Lord could make the very place of contagion the place of renewal and restoration. The old Moses could become the new Moses, not imprisoned by what he had been, and indeed still was (7). The power of the Lord is a power of regeneration, making people new.

The sign of the pollution of the Nile (9) adds that the Lord is the God of victory over all the power of the enemy. The Nile as the concentrated symbol of the life and vitality of Egypt *was* Egypt summed up in one word, but a single person, Moses, in all his acknowledged weaknesses, fears, inabilities and hesitancies, could overmaster Egypt by acting in obedience to the Lord's word.

The Lord is Lord of power – to transform (2–5), to renew (6–7) and to conquer (8–9) – and obedience is the channel through which all this power flows. In terms of resources, what Moses had in his hand looked pathetically inadequate, but the Lord could make it more than sufficient (2–5). In terms of fitness for the task, Moses was the source of his own contagion, but the Lord could make the foul not only clean but the source of cleanness (6–7). In terms of opposition, Moses against the superpower looked like a foregone conclusion, but the Lord was more than a match for the enemy (8–9). Moses acting alone had no hope of taking on the might of Egypt, but when he obeyed the word of God, he mobilized the power and resources of God and the expected outcome was totally transformed.

3. I am slow of speech (4:10)

How patient the Lord is. As soon as he replied to Moses on one point, Moses continued working his way down his shopping list. So, even after the demonstration of divine abilities in the three signs, we come to Moses' last objection, *I am slow of speech and tongue.*

The persistence of gentle patience

Moses' final attempt to avoid what God wanted him to do (see pp. 45–46 above) received a double reply. First, there is the fundamental response from the Lord that he is the Creator God, able to give gifts or to make good deficiencies (11–12), and second, there is his providential response of sending the eloquent Aaron to act as Moses' mouthpiece (14b–16). The second solution in no way negates or modifies the divine sovereignty implicit in the first. Neither Moses' incompetence (10) nor Aaron's competence (14b) is the decisive factor, but the Lord's masterful presence. He remains in control throughout, for when he points to his own all-sufficiency as Creator he immediately follows it with the promise to Moses, *I will help you speak and will teach you what to say* (12),[7] and when he appoints the vocal Aaron and defines the individual roles of Moses and his brother, it is undergirded by the promise that *I will help both of you speak and will teach you what to do* (15).[8] The Lord provides but he does not abdicate; the promise of his personal presence and help, his truth and his direction remain unchanged.

The question very properly arises whether, by providing Aaron, the Lord was opting for 'second best' – that is, that Moses acting alone was his first and best choice, but since he could not have it, he adapted his plans to accommodate Moses' infirmities and conscripted Aaron into the proposal. The answer is both yes and no. Yes, in the sense that divine mercy takes note of our weaknesses and makes provision for them; no, in the sense that 'I the Lord do not change' (Mal. 3:6) and whatever he does is always his first and best intention. He does not deal in second bests, for himself or for us. We see a particularly striking example of this in the way kingship was instituted in Israel (1 Sam. 8 – 10). On the one hand, giving the people a king was a concession to their weakness of faith (1 Sam. 12:10–12), but, on the other hand, as the royal messianic theme develops in the Bible, it becomes plain that kingship and the coming perfect king was, in fact, always the Lord's best intention for his people. It can be stated as a principle that the Lord always bestows his intended blessing in such a way as to expose our weakness and to magnify his grace. Thus, Aaron came on the scene as an antidote to the weakness of Moses' faith, but as the place of Aaron in the rest of Exodus and in Israel's religion shows, he was no divine afterthought but an essential part of the Lord's plan.

---

[7] Lit. 'I will myself be with your [sing.] mouth and will teach you [sing.].'

[8] Lit. 'I will myself be with your mouth and with his mouth. I will teach you [plural] what you [plural] are to do.'

The point is of some importance for our comfort. Many Christians can look back with sorrow either to some signal refusal to obey the Lord's will or, more broadly, to those many smaller refusals which make our lives second rate. Is everything then irretrievably 'second best'? Not if we know the Lord as the Bible reveals him. He is not (as C. S. Lewis says somewhere in one of his science fiction novels) a twig to be trodden underfoot or a leaf to be blown off course. The mercy of God understands our weakness and meets us in our frailties; the sovereign magnificence of God fulfils his own purposes without adjustment or alteration – from beginning to end.

When Moses addresses God here (10), he uses *Lord*, not the Tetragrammaton but the Hebrew noun *'ăḏōnāy* meaning 'sovereign, master, lord'. In a way that is both sad and understandable, Moses appeals to the Sovereign One – a title implying 'You can do anything and everything you wish' – but goes on to make his own inabilities the determinative factor. This is a theological version of having your cake and eating it if ever there was one!

If the Lord is truly sovereign over all things, then the only reasonable response is to trust him; it is his omnipotence that matters, not our incompetence. In his reply to Moses it is as though God says, 'Look, you call me "Sovereign". Can you not believe what you say? I am the Sovereign God. Why do you talk to me about gifts that you have or have not got? I *made* the mouth. I can either give or withhold any and every gift at will.' If we can say that the Lord introduced Moses to the tenderness of God at 3:11–12 – and he did – then he introduced him to the majesty of God at 4:11–12. Gladly we enter into his tenderness – his patience, his perseverance, his deliverance. Can we not also enter into his greatness? When he calls, is he not great enough for the task he gives? Of course, he is – but in consequence his next word to Moses is, *Now go* (12). As the Sovereign, he is inflexible. He took Moses seriously and did not deny his sense of inadequacy, but he made him face realistically the sort of God he professed to believe in. Does Moses believe in a great God – the Sovereign God which the title he uses implies? If he does, 'Well then, go.' Do not refuse to go because you are what you are, but go because he is what he is.

It has to be said that in the final stages of the dialogue the Lord lost patience with Moses, and no wonder. But, we need to ask, what was there about Moses' reply in verse 13 which proved, so to speak, to be the last straw? His words were deliberately vague, (lit.) 'Send by whose hand you will send', and most commentators (e.g. Cassuto) understand Moses to mean 'Send by anyone else you wish.' This outright, if vaguely expressed, refusal on Moses' part could well account for the Lord's anger but it imparts a meaning to the Hebrew that is not justified. It would be more suitable to the deliberate vagueness of the construction to understand Moses simply to say, 'Oh, have it your own way!' or 'Oh, do what you want!' – not a vaguely expressed refusal but the grudging acquiescence of a beaten man.

If this is a correct interpretation, it is one that speaks with the full weight of the Bible behind it, for the life to which the Bible calls us is one of obedience and trust, and the Lord is outraged if we return a flat or a concealed 'No' to his will. As we will see ever more clearly as we make our way through Exodus, the primary mark – the hallmark – of the people of God is obedience to his word.[9] The Lord looks for trust, loves to be trusted, reacts against the withholding of trust, and assures his people that the way of trust is the way of life.[10] This fits in exceedingly well with the thrust of the whole episode of Moses 'call', for in response to the variety of stated needs, whether in Moses himself or in the task to which he was being sent, the Lord just offered himself. He did not alter Moses' self-awareness so that he 'felt' competent; he did not undertake to change circumstances or suggest that the task was, after all, easier than it looked. He did not even guarantee immediate success or urge Moses to 'think positively' and not be so defeatist. No, he offered nothing but that he himself is the accompanying Lord (3:12), self-revealing (3:13–15), promise-making (3:16–17), victorious (3:18–20), transforming (3:21–22), superior to every foe and every opposing factor (4:1–9), the creator (4:10–11) and provider (4:14–16). The 'call' really consists of nothing more than the Lord asking Moses, 'Do you trust me? Will you go simply trusting me?' And, of course, the evidence of that trust will be obedience, the obedience that arises from and rests on faith.

4. Gentle determination

At point after point Moses had been frank about his faults. Humanly speaking, any one of them would have been sufficient to disqualify him.

---

[9] Note how Isaiah singles out obedience as the primary mark of the perfect servant in 50:4–5. Cf. John 4:34; 8:29.

[10] See Job 13:15; Pss 20:7[8]; 44:6[7]; 61:4; 78:21–22; 118:8; Isa. 30:2; 31:1; Jer. 17:5–7; Hos. 10:13b–15; cf. Matt. 8:10–12; 14:31.

Cumulatively, they made his candidature absurd. Yet this was the man the Lord had chosen and called, and other considerations are beside the point (cf. Isa. 55:8). The Lord was not to be deflected but responded to Moses at every point of confessed need. We see here that what is referred to as 'the perseverance of the saints' is in fact the perseverance of the Lord with those he has called. Moses persisted in enumerating all his disqualifying factors but the Lord, with gentle determination, went on countering them until, in silent acquiescence if not yet in hearty commitment, Moses gave up – a reluctant conscript, indeed, but nonetheless one enrolled and commissioned.

Surely it should be enough for us that God has pledged to be with us, that he has given us a whole book whereby we may know his name and his nature and can share it? That he is the God who takes up the ordinary and makes it a living force, who cancels the iniquity and contagion of our hearts with a new nature, and has power over all the power of the enemy? That he is Sovereign and bestows gifts according to his will for his work? In a word, it should be sufficient for our peace of mind and obedience that we recognize him as God.

But even in his anger, see how beautifully merciful the Lord is to Moses – *What about your brother, Aaron the Levite? I know he can speak well. He is already on his way to meet you, and he will be glad to see you* (14). Even in his anger he remembers mercy, as if to say, 'Well, Moses, if you need a prop, I have a prop already on its way for you. If you need Aaron to help you in the way of faith, then you shall have him. It has already been taken care of.' The Lord knows our needs before we ask (Matt. 6:8). And even when what we ask is a manifestation of distrust, he still bothers with us and provides for our needs. He is trustworthy, he ought to be trusted and he longs to be trusted. This beautiful God is our God for ever and ever.

Additional notes

4:13 S. R. Driver says that the construction here (involving the same verb on either side of a relative pronoun either stated or understood) 'deliberately caters for vagueness . . . where either the means or the desire to be more explicit does not exist' (*Notes on the Hebrew Text of the Books of Samuel* [OUP, 1890], p. 146, on 1 Sam. 23:13). See also S. R. Driver, *Hebrew Tenses* (OUP, 1892), p. 38.

Exod. 16:23 is a good place to study the way the *idem per idem* construction works. There, 'what you bake, bake; what you boil, boil' means 'Do what you want. Cook whatever you like in any way you like.' So here, a better translation would be, 'Do what you want. Send whomever you wish.'

4:13–17 Durham says 'it is very likely that the Aaron verses represent a subsequent layer inserted into the narrative . . . a later pro-Aaron campaign', but notes candidly that documentary analysis fails to agree which 'source' the verses belong to – Fohrer says 'E', Hyatt says 'J' – but most consider verses 13–17 'secondary' (pp. 48–49). I find myself baffled how anyone could find the reference to Aaron 'confusing the sequence . . . a kind of postscript', as Durham claims to do. The verses read smoothly and fit in a natural progression as the Lord's mercy deals with Moses.

Exodus 4:14–28

7. Interlude: into the arena

Up to this point Moses had been alone in private conversation with God, and so, as in many other instances in the Bible, we know about it only because Moses himself revealed it. Now, however, he was about to come out of the secret place, first to return to Jethro (18), then to meet Aaron (27) and finally to confront Israel (29) and Pharaoh (5:1).

Referring to these verses as an 'interlude' is not meant to suggest that they are either an intrusion or even a pause in the narrative. The provision of Aaron as a spokesman is continuous with the Lord's patient replies to Moses' objections, and the promise made in verse 14 is fulfilled in verse 27; the return to seek Jethro's consent (18–30) is something required by both courtesy and custom; and, though the events of verses 24–26 take us by surprise, they happened on the journey to Egypt which began in verses 19–20. To describe all this as an 'interlude' simply calls attention to the fact that it falls between the commissioning of Moses (3:1 – 4:17) and the start of the main action of his ministry (4:30).

Besides this, the passage offers itself as a self-contained unit, marked off by the *inclusio* of the promise of Aaron as a colleague (14–16) and the humanly 'undesigned coincidence' of the arrival of Aaron on the scene (27). We shall discuss this further later. Within this *inclusio* there are three sections: first, the *providence* of God in having Aaron already to hand to meet Moses' need (14–17); second, the *guidance* of God, who prompted Moses when the moment of his fateful journey had arrived (18–23); and third, the *law* of God as a serious factor in the life of the commissioned servant (24–26).

1. Providence: the God who anticipates (4:14–17)

'Providence' means 'foresight', and in relation to God this includes both his foreknowledge of what will happen and his preparation beforehand of whatever will meet the needs of his people as they arise.[1] Packer describes divine providence as 'the unceasing activity of the Creator whereby, in overflowing bounty and goodwill . . . he upholds his creatures in ordered existence'.[2] Thus, in the present instance Aaron is not a 'miraculous' divine intervention but a provision long since prepared with the necessary gifts and now emerging from the shadows by divine prompting (27). The Lord does not say that he will now see to it that Aaron has the necessary gift of eloquence, but that Aaron, born actually three years before Moses (7:7), *can speak well* (14), as if this was a natural endowment which the Lord just happened to have noticed! The whole story of Aaron here (14, 27) makes him a striking example of the 'anticipatory providence'[3] of God: born before Moses, grown to adult life with the necessary gift which was recognized and developed, and now setting out from Egypt before Moses left Midian, so that they might meet 'at the mountain of God' (27). We shall come across many other anticipatory providences in Exodus – for example, the rock, part of creation itself and waiting from time immemorial to meet the needs of the thirsty people (17:1–7) – but possibly none are clearer or more kindly and condescendingly thought out beforehand than the meeting between Moses and his older brother.

a. Help as need arises: the God who speaks (4:15–16)

The first truth here, then, is that the Lord's forethought anticipates our needs. The onset of any given need may take us totally by surprise, but nothing takes him by surprise. He has been there already. In Moses' case, the quiet course of his life was disrupted by the intrusion of an unexpected, overwhelming task, but for that too the Lord had his answer long since at the ready. It is told of an early explorer in a remote part of Mongolia where allegedly no human foot had trodden, coming upon a hitherto

---

[1] See the articles on 'Providence' in W. A. Elwell (ed.), *The Evangelical Dictionary of Theology* (Baker, 2001), T. D. Alexander and B. S. Rosner (eds.), *The New Dictionary of Biblical Theology* (IVP, 2000), and especially *NBD*.

[2] *NBD*, p. 979.

[3] I first heard the phrase 'anticipatory providence' from Alan Stibbs, at the time vice principal of Oak Hill Theological College, in a sermon on Exod. 15:22–26. Anything good that I may write on that passage comes from Stibbs's sermon.

uncatalogued flower and gathering his companions around to say, 'Look! God has been here!' Whether this tale is true or not, it serves to illustrate how God anticipates everything that happens to us; he is always there first.

b. The given word

God is also always present to provide. Moses had already confessed his ignorance (3:13), but he must have been aware that his needs in this area ran deeper than simply the name of God. Would not we, placed as he was, be harassed by the broader issues of our lack of knowledge? Every aspect of his calling and every contact he would subsequently make are summed up in the question, 'But what shall I say?' For this need too the Lord promised a provision, the supply of his word as the need arose: *I will help both of you speak and will teach you what to do* (15).

This is a very revealing and significant promise. Both here and in the identical promise in 6:28 – 7:2, the giving of the divine word to Moses is couched in terms that will later define the relationship between the speaking prophets and the inspiring Lord. This is understandable since Moses was to become the standard for all prophets and prophecy (Deut. 34:10). In the present case a 'chain of command' is set up. Moses is given the part of God (16b; cf. 7:1), and he is to 'put words in [Aaron's] mouth' (cf. Num. 22:28; 23:16; Deut. 18:18; 2 Sam. 14:3). Since the mouth is the organ of speech and verbalization, this cannot mean merely that Moses was to indicate the general tenor of what Aaron was to say, but rather was to pass on the precise words to be used.[4] Indeed the Hebrew makes this meaning unmistakable with (lit.) 'you shall put the words in his mouth'. This 'verbal inspiration' is how the Lord will subsequently work with those whom he chooses to be his prophets. It enables them to say exactly what God himself would have said had he chosen to speak directly in his own person. The words that the prophets use, while typical of their own personal vocabulary and style of speech, are nevertheless the very words God himself imparts. The New Testament registers the same claim for the apostolic word (1 Cor. 2:12–13) and ultimately for the whole of Scripture (2 Tim. 3:14–17; 2 Pet. 1:16–21). The privilege that was given here for Moses' comfort and reassurance is ours whenever we open our Bibles. The

---

[4] Cf. Num. 12:8, where 'face to face' is literally 'mouth to mouth' and indicates thoughts put into words, expressed and shared; and the vivid picture of Baruch taking down Jeremiah's dictation (Jer. 36:4, 6, 17–18, 27, 32).

same teaching Lord (15) who superintended the donation of the words (to Moses' mouth) and their transmission (by Aaron's mouth) was the teacher also of the apostles (John 14:26) and, by implication, is ours too when we come to his written Word.

c. The token of the presence: the God who reassures

We must not overlook the mention of the staff in verse 17 or defer its consideration until we reach verse 20. It is deliberately referred to here in order to hold together all the promises of God under which Moses was to launch out into his terrifying task, and shows how the God of providence had anticipated and prepared for all his needs (14). The God of the word will give the words Moses will need (15–16), and the God of power will even put himself into the hand of Moses for the tasks ahead, saying, 'and *this staff* [Heb. emph.] you shall take in your hand, by which you shall do the signs'.

We would be right off beam if we were to think of the staff in terms of a magic wand. Moses never used the staff (which we have presumably already met as his shepherd's staff in 4:2) in a magical way but, apart from 17:9, always by divine command.[5] In other words, the staff was not independently effective but operated as a sign of the Lord's presence and power. As the covenant signs of the rainbow (Gen. 9:9–17) and circumcision (Gen. 17:1–10), because they were bearers of the promises of God, excited and invited God's covenant people to respond in faith and obedience, so the staff assured Moses of the Lord's presence in power and prompted him to action, believing that the Lord would prove to be as good as his word. The contemporary covenant signs of baptism and the Lord's Supper exercise the same function.

2. Waiting for guidance: the God who tends and cares (4:18–23)

This is the second of the three sections into which our present passage falls. In it we move from considering the provision the Lord made for his

---

[5] In 7:9–13 and 8:5[1] the staff is spoken of as Aaron's, but thereafter it is Moses who uses it, including the disastrous unauthorized usage recorded in Num. 20 (Exod. 9:23; 10:13; 14:16; 17:9; Num. 20:8). The movement from Aaron to Moses at 'centre stage' reflects Moses' own growth in personal confidence from the timorous and inarticulate man of Exodus chapter 3 to the assured orator of Deuteronomy. His early need of Aaron gradually evaporated, as was right and proper.

servants, to noting his careful guiding, prompting and preparing of them for the service that lay ahead. The present verses contain the following material:

A¹ The decision to return to Egypt (18)
  B¹ Divine prompting and reassurance (19)
A² The journey begun (20)
  B² Divine preparation for the future (21–23)

This is all perfectly understandable as a coherent narrative, both historically and in domestic and psychological terms.[6] Naturally, as an example to us of proper courtesy, Moses put his request to leave to the head of the family (18) and did so in a way that Jethro could most easily accept. To have announced that he had been called to bring Israel out of Egypt would surely have been a recipe for colossal family misunderstanding and even argument, possibly prompting Jethro's incredulity and certainly exciting his fears for his daughter and grandsons. Courteous discretion within the bounds of truth is an enviable grace.[7] Moses, therefore, observed what will later become the Lord's commandment to honour father and mother and also 'domesticated' his return to Egypt by a choice illustration of truth, courtesy (recognition of Jethro's headship) and consideration (allaying Jethro's alarm) combined.

Even after the great decision, however, Moses did not cease to be his hesitant self. We can hardly say often enough that conversion and commitment do not necessarily alter temperament – in fact, they rarely, if ever, do! The naturally introvert or melancholic becomes a converted (but not altered) introvert or melancholic. It is correct, therefore, to read between the lines of verses 18–19 and hear Moses' alarmed thought, 'What *have* I done?' The Lord graciously comforted and assured him and pointed ahead to what was to take place. Verse 19 opens in Hebrew with the conjunction *waw*, which is most frequently taken to be equivalent to

---

[6] Durham's comment (p. 54) that verses 18–31 constitute 'one of the loosest sequences in the entire book of Exodus' is hard to understand. The passage is episodic, that is to say, it brings together significant moments in this period of Moses' life and tells us what we need to know, rather than all we might wish to know, about them. The fact that it consists of discrete events – approaching Jethro (18), preparing for the journey (20), words from the Lord (19, 21–23) and the attack (24–26) – is typical of all biblical historical narration, and the whole is a coherent portrayal.

[7] Fretheim's view that Moses' reference to seeing if his family were still alive is yet another attempt to circumvent his call – 'if they are now all dead, there is no call to heed' – sounds unimaginative (p. 76). Saul knew how much to tell his uncle and how much to hold back (1 Sam. 10:16).

'and' but can also be used, as here, to represent 'for' and introduce an explanation, 'for [NIV *Now*] the Lord had said'.[8] Moses' approach to Jethro was thus eased by a word from the Lord. The major task of extricating Israel from Egyptian oppression must have weighed heavily on Moses' mind, but the immediate fear of arrest, imprisonment and execution could be dismissed. That danger at least belonged to the past. Thus, the Lord superintended the obedience of his servant and, by his word, soothed his anxieties and fears. Sadly, in keeping with the Old Testament pattern, we are not told how such a word of the Lord came, but we do know that in our case the written Word of God lies to hand, imposing on us the responsible joy of keeping our lives, fears and would-be obedience under its gentle care.

Once he had started on the road back to Egypt, Moses would naturally have begun to think his way imaginatively into what lay ahead and have asked himself questions like, 'How shall I go about this task? What must I do first? What have I let myself in for? What, indeed, am I to say?' It is important to note that Moses actively took the steps open to him to face the future, for we are told that he *took the staff of God in his hand* (20). This, as we have already seen, was a visible way of arming himself with the power of God, assuring himself that the Almighty God was with him and reminding himself of the convincing signs that would win him acceptance. In other words, he did not go into the arena unprotected or unprepared. It is incumbent also on us, in the words of George Duffield, Jr, to 'Put on the gospel armour, / Each piece put on with prayer.'[9]

a. Understanding the future (4:21–23)

As part of the continuing picture of superintending guidance and care, God met with Moses in the course of his journey, and his word covered three elements of what was to come: Moses' part (*perform . . . all the wonders*, 21a), the Lord's part (*I will harden*, 21b) and the issue at stake (*my firstborn son . . . your firstborn son*, 22–23). Paul's word that 'it is required that those who have been given a trust must prove faithful' (1 Cor. 4:2)

---

[8] This particular idiom, where the conjunction introduces an explanation, is called the *waw explicativum* and is very common. I think this is the easiest understanding of verse 19, but to take it as following on from verse 18 is also instructive. In speaking to Jethro Moses had 'burnt his boats', and he was now committed to a return to Egypt. It was just at this moment that all his inner uncertainties came flooding back. He had made life easier for Jethro by talking about visiting his relatives, but his own mind was filled with the dire thought of facing his foes with their legitimate charges against him.

[9] From 'Stand Up, Stand Up for Jesus', which is based on Eph. 6:10–18. Cf. Rom. 13:11–14; 1 Thess. 5:8.

springs to mind in this context. All that was required of Moses was that he do what he had been told to do, which is another way of saying that it was up to the Lord to perform the work (3:8) and that he would do so in his own way (cf. Judg. 7:7), with Moses fitting into the divine scheme as instructed. Hence the reminder to *perform . . . all the wonders*. Did it seem pathetically silly to Moses to face the world's superpower by throwing down a staff, displaying and curing a leprous hand and turning water into blood? His was not to reason why! The Lord always gives his Holy Spirit to those who obey him (Acts 5:32). What were earlier called 'signs' are here *wonders*, striking indications that a different power was at work, and Moses must publicly side with that power in a life of 'simply obeying'.

We will defer the matter of Pharaoh's heart for future treatment; save only to say here that, of course, 'the Judge of all the earth' always does 'right' (Gen. 18:25). There can, therefore, be no injustice or unfairness – or anything else questionable – in this exercise of heart-hardening. The Bible believes in a God who is really and truly God. Not a sparrow falls to the ground without him (Matt. 10:29–30); the 'chance' roll of the dice is under his control (Prov. 16:33); the fluctuations of the human heart are in his hand in both welcome and unwelcome ways (Pss 4:7; 105:25); it is his to recreate (Ps. 51:10[12]), to direct (Ps. 119:36) and to restrain (Ps. 141:4); and the heart that knows him is his gift (Jer. 24:7), as is the 'new heart' (Ezek. 36:26). The old prayer says rightly that 'the hearts of kings are in thy rule and governance, and thou dost dispose and turn them as seems best to thy godly wisdom'.[10] And, we might add, 'thy godly justice'. As is its custom, the Bible takes us beyond secondary causes to the great first cause, the Creator God, who rules all things in heaven and earth (Ps. 103:19; Dan. 4:25–26). Our fundamental position as the Lord's people is not to know how to work the system, the secondary causes, but how to walk with God, how to mobilize his power on our side, how to enjoy his unbroken favour and how to face life in faith. It is a far more serious matter to fall out of the power of God than to fall into the power of Satan. But he who is our God is God of all the earth, and no matter how central and supremely important it was to deliver Israel from Egypt, the moral government of the universe was not forgotten and Pharaoh's heart was kept within the divine sights to receive its just due at this crisis hour.

---

[10] From the service of the Lord's Supper in the Book of Common Prayer.

b. The love that permeates justice: the God who is Father

These verses are a broad, not an itemized, vision of the future, designed not to fill in the calendar but to prepare and assure Moses. They offer a carefully crafted review:

A¹ The Lord and Moses: equipping – *Perform . . . the wonders* (21a)
   B¹ The Lord and Pharaoh: judging – *I will harden* (21b)
A² The Lord and Israel: claiming – *My firstborn son* (22)
   B² The Lord and Pharaoh: punishing – *I will kill* (23)

The ideas of Israel as the Lord's son and of the Lord as Israel's father are both used very sparingly in the Old Testament.[11] Mackay may be right in noting a hesitancy here lest the relationship be developed in pagan directions, implying a quasi-physical 'begetting' on the part of God and a derivative quasi-deity of his children. Be that as it may, it is certainly true that the father–son relationship is largely reserved for the New Testament, another example of the cumulative revelation which marks the Bible. Here in Exodus, however, Israel is for the first time called the Lord's son. This is important, for it shows that the relationship is not one of 'natural' descent but had a beginning in history and is contemporary with the Lord's acts of deliverance and redemption (Exod. 6:6). It is, therefore, a matter of divine decision, selection and election (cf. Eph. 1:3–6; Jas 1:18). The grace of salvation initiates and bestows the grace of adoption (John 1:12; Gal. 4:4–7). In Exodus this work of salvation was done at the Passover (Exod. 12) and, as we shall see, it was there that sonship and salvation were indissolubly linked. It was the Lord's firstborn who was kept safe, under the blood of the lamb, on the night that Pharaoh's firstborn perished.[12] If Moses was awed by the hardness and opposition that awaited him (21b), he ought to have been enthralled that the end of the matter was just as surely guaranteed (23). For Moses' future (any more than ours) was not a haphazard conglomeration of 'events' nor a chance sequence of 'one thing

---

[11] In the Old Testament, sonship is used in connection with supernatural beings (Gen. 6:2, 4; Job 1:6; 2:1; 38:7; Pss 29:1; 89:6[7]), Israel (Deut. 14:1; 32:5, 20; Ps. 82:6; Isa. 1:2, 4; 30:1, 9; Jer. 3:14, 22; 4:22; 31:20) and the Davidic king (2 Sam. 7:14; 1 Chr. 17:13; 22:10; 28:6; Ps. 2:7). For references to divine fatherhood in the Old Testament see Deut. 32:6; 2 Sam. 7:14; Ps. 89:26[27]; Isa. 63:16; 64:8; Jer. 3:4, 19; 31:9; Mal. 1:6; 2:10.

[12] In Exod. 12 it is important, as we have seen, to underline the corporate sonship of all Israel, a reality to which 4:22 has alerted us. Nevertheless, it is also true that had any Israelite flouted the Passover regulations it would have been at the expense of the singular, firstborn son of that family. In this sense, verses like Num. 8:16–17 note that the literal firstborn was the special object of divine salvation on Passover night and was purchased by the Lord to belong to himself (cf. Exod. 13:12–16).

after another'.[13] Moses' future, like ours, was known by God and under his control (*I will*, 21b, 23b) and guaranteed to eventuate in salvation (cf. Acts 14:22; Rev. 7:13–15).

3. Obedience is primary: the God of insistent law (4:24–26)

This is the third 'movement' in the concerto of Moses' progress into the arena, and it is different from the other two. They ministered to our comfort and reassurance, showing how the Lord's gracious providence never lets us out of his sight (14–17) and his careful superintendence guides us in his way (18–23), so that we can rest in his care and stay alert for his promptings. The third movement, however, summons us to vigilance in order that we might be diligent in meeting his requirements.

We come, then, to the extraordinary incident in verses 24–26.[14] This most remarkable and seemingly odd story is written for our learning like the rest of Scripture, and there is a truth to be harvested from it. A more literal translation will help us:

> And on the road, at the lodging,[15] the Lord met him and sought to put him to death. And Zipporah took a flint and cut the foreskin of her son and made it touch his feet.[16] And she said, 'Indeed a bridegroom of bloods are you to me!' And he let him alone. It was then that she said, 'A bridegroom of bloods', referring to the circumcision.

---

[13] It is told that when British Prime Minister Harold Macmillan was asked what caused most difficulties in his premiership, he replied, 'Events, madam, events.' Life looks like that – the onset, often the buffetings, of the unexpected. This passage encourages us by its revelation that events are foreknown and in the hand of God (cf. 1 Cor. 10:13).

[14] These verses have been subject to many interpretations, and the commentaries must be consulted. What follows above is no more than one person's best effort to grasp their meaning and application. Many take the episode to mean that Moses had not himself been circumcised and that Zipporah, by identifying him with her son's circumcision, secured his safety. Josh. 5:9 calls uncircumcision 'the reproach of Egypt', and it seems that Moses must be rid of this disgrace before he engages in his mission. Fretheim suggests an interesting comparison with Gen. 32, where the Lord stopped Jacob in his tracks. Just as none can enter the Promised Land without divine permission, so none can engage in the work of God without obeying the command of God.

[15] Hebrew often uses the definite article where English would use the indefinite. Here, for example, it has 'the lodging', but this does not mean there was only one but rather 'at the lodging where he met him'. We would say 'a lodging'.

[16] The Hebrew does not say whose feet, but to make the blood touch the feet of the boy who had been circumcised would hardly make sense. It was, therefore, an act of identifying the incapacitated Moses with what Zipporah had done.

First, then, we discern God's opposition to Moses in verse 24: *the Lord met Moses and was about to kill him.* Probably, it seemed at first sight to Zipporah that Moses was suffering a seizure or some other illness that had every appearance of being fatal. Presently, however, she realized that its cause was not physical but spiritual, and not demonic but divine.[17] The Bible carefully avoids the two extremes of saying that every sickness is an oppression from God or that no sickness is an oppression from God. We must face every illness and ailment with the upward look and the question, 'Lord, what is in this as between you and me?' Somehow, in the present instance it was given to Zipporah to know that the problem was that their son had never been circumcised. In other words, at the heart of Moses' family there was an offence against the will and word of God, who had commanded that Abraham, the covenant man, mark himself out by the sign of circumcision as the one to whom the promises of the covenant had been made. God had further commanded that the sign be given to Abraham's infant sons in token that the covenant was between 'me and you and your descendants' (Gen. 17:7; Acts 2:39). We do not know why Moses had disobeyed, but what we do know is this: that the Lord in effect said to him, 'You cannot go on in my service until you are right with me.' Zipporah saw what the problem was but, since circumcision should have been the father's act (Gen. 17:23–27; 21:4), she took the blood of circumcision and touched Moses with it, thereby associating him with what had been done. And suddenly all was well, and the crisis was over.

Second, we come to Zipporah's greeting to Moses. As Moses, now plainly better, opened his eyes and looked at his wife, she greeted him with a loving cry as though to say, 'Moses, you're back with me! You're my bridegroom and husband all over again. Instead of taking you from me, God has given you back to me because of the blood of circumcision. My bridegroom of blood!' This gives us a very lovely insight into Zipporah and her love for Moses, that she should greet him when he came back, as it were, from the dead, with such a glad cry, 'It's just as if we have got married all over again and you are my bridegroom once more.' A marriage threatened with termination was renewed, and Zipporah's understanding and resolute action had brought Moses back into the way of obedience.

---

[17] Cf. the occasions in Gen. 12:17 and 20:17 where God used illness as a warning and where it was understood as such.

a. A serious warning

Seen in this light, a strange, unexpected event becomes an important story. Isaiah exhorts, 'Be pure, you who carry the articles of the LORD's house' (Isa. 52:11), and through Jeremiah the Lord declares (lit.), 'If you take forth the precious from the vile, you shall be as my mouth' (Jer. 15:19). There has to be a sifting in our lives, an abandonment of 'the vile' and a recognition of 'the precious', if we are to be the mouthpieces of the Lord, and this was what, in essence, the Lord came to Moses in his lodging to say.

b. Circumcision: the sign of grace

What precisely was Moses' failure? Fundamentally, that God had given a command and he had not obeyed. Sadly, Moses did not learn the lesson, and in the end an equally obvious lapse in obedience cost him entry to Canaan (Num. 20:7–12). The Lord treats obedience with a seriousness that is in marked contrast to our casual and self-excusing ways.

Like all the covenant signs, circumcision signifies, on God's side, the gift and sealing of his promises, and, on our side, the marking out of those to whom the promises apply. The rainbow expressed divine promises to Noah (Gen. 9:11–17), and Noah, seeing and understanding it, embraced the promises as and when the need arose. To Abram, God made promises of personal transformation, family development, spiritual security and territorial possession (Gen. 17:4–8). This was the Lord's covenant undertaking, and the sign of the covenant, the seal of the promises, was circumcision. This was to be the mark distinguishing Abram and his family as those to whom the promises had been made and summoning them to life under the grace which the promises expressed. Covenant signs express covenant promises to covenant people.

Did all this not matter to Moses? Did he not need the assurance of personal transformation, family prosperity, spiritual security and territorial possession? Why, they were the very things he needed more than anything else in his hazardous enterprise. But he had overlooked them as if promises had not been made, and as if he could afford to ignore them. This is why disobedience is such a serious matter: it is acting as if we had no need of God, his grace and his pledges. In other words, it is nothing short of a sort of enacted atheism.

c. Armoured for the fight

Only by returning to the way of obedience could Moses continue to walk in the way of service. The divine assault was really an exceedingly kind work of grace. Taking his first steps back towards Egypt, Moses was fortified by the providence of God (the promise of Aaron, 14–16), equipped with and assured of the power of God (the staff, 17), directed and comforted by the word of God (19, 21–23) and brought within the embrace of the promises of God (the assault and the circumcision, 24–26).

Additional notes

4:14 Commentators often ask why Aaron is so precisely called *the Levite* in verse 14, and indeed why Moses' levitical ancestry is thought worthy of mention in 2:1, but the Bible offers no clues. The subsequent significance of the tribe of Levi (cf. Exod. 32:26–29; Num. 8:5–26; Mal. 2:4–9) could have prompted a proleptic reference in 2:1, but here *the Levite* seems to suggest a contemporary title or function. We know little or nothing of the social or religious organization of Israel in Egypt, but it must have existed and maybe the tribe of Levi were functionaries within it. Levi is associated with the verb meaning 'linked, attached' (√*lāwâ*; cf. Gen. 29:34), and so Cassuto finds a play on words here. The suggestion, though it is not developed by Cassuto, is that *the Levite* is equivalent to 'the associate *par excellence*' (p. 50).

4:24–26 Readers of the KJV will need to beware of the rendering 'a bloody husband', which, inevitably, seems to cast some sort of slur over Moses and Zipporah's marriage. The word translated *bridegroom* is *ḥātān*, which basically means 'relative by marriage' and always needs to be translated according to context. Either 'husband' or 'bridegroom' suits here. The plural of the noun *blood* is used for either 'blood guilt' or 'shed blood', and the latter suits the flowing blood of the circumcision wound here.

The noun *circumcision* (*mûlōt*) is plural. Since it occurs only here, we have no means of knowing if it was a noun customarily used in the plural (as e.g. 'trousers' in English) or if it was being used deliberately as a plural of intensification or greatness – 'with reference to this notable circumcision' (notable because it was the saving of Moses' life).

Some commentators suggest that neither Moses nor his son had been circumcised. To touch Moses with the blood was, therefore, to make him party to a rite he had not experienced. Those who adopt this view usually assume that the word *feet* is being used euphemistically for the genitals (cf. Isa. 7:20 [lit.] 'the hair of the feet', NIV 'private parts'). When we recall that Moses spent his first three months with his Hebrew parents (2:2), it is virtually impossible that he had not been circumcised (cf. Gen. 17:10–12). The documentary view of the Pentateuch usually discounts the possibility that Gen. 17 records the institution of circumcision, but unless we set out to rewrite the Bible that is precisely what it does.

Exodus 4:29 – 7:7

8. Yes . . . No . . . Why? . . . Now

In order to come to terms with this rather long section, it will be best to start by, so to speak, drawing a map. There are two main divisions: 4:29 – 5:21, which tells the story of Moses' arrival in Egypt with Aaron, his initial success with Israel and his subsequent failure with both Pharaoh and Israel; and 5:22 – 7:7, which relates how the disconsolate Moses brought his unexpected, to him at least, failure back to the Lord, received divine redirection and learned the lesson of his earlier mistake.

1. Moses arrives in Egypt (4:29 – 5:21)

a. Failure

Though we can isolate the two sections in this way – indeed, though we must do so if we are to be faithful to the artistry of Exodus – each one is individually shaped to tell its own story. It is helpful to read 4:29 – 5:21 following this outline:

> A^1 Moses and Aaron accepted by Israel (4:29–31)
>> B^1 Fruitless appeal to Pharaoh: refusal to recognize the Lord (5:1–5)
>>> C The new and harsher regime (5:6–14)
>>>> a^1 Oppressive conditions (5:7–8)
>>>>> b Aimed at distracting attention from the word of God (5:9)
>>>> a^2 Physical affliction (5:10–14)
>> B^2 Fruitless appeal to Pharaoh: refusal to allow worship of the Lord (5:15–18)
> A^2 Moses and Aaron rejected by Israel (5:19–21)

b. Expectations

The only person to be satisfied by results in this section was Pharaoh – and he had yet to discover that he had been entertaining entirely the wrong expectations. As for Moses and Israel, however, nothing had turned out as they had expected. If ever a man crept off with his tail between his legs it was the Moses of 5:22–23. He certainly had not expected the savage deterioration of Israel's fortunes which his arrival provoked. Indeed, to the contrary, their first reaction could only have quickened his sense that victory might after all have been easily won (4:31). And surely both Israel's initial exhilaration and their subsequent strong revulsion (5:21) are so very natural and understandable. Most of us have been there. Moses was to ask the question 'Why?' about his failure (5:22), and we too must try to penetrate behind Israel's reactions and ask, why did they collapse so soon and so easily after their first flush of enthusiasm on learning that the Lord was 'on the move'?

c. Faith and conflict

When the Lord Jesus listed differing responses to the 'seed' which is the word of God, he included those who, when they hear the word, 'at once receive it with joy. But since they have no root, they last only a short time. When trouble or persecution comes because of the word, they quickly fall away' (Mark 4:16–17). The principle which our Lord enunciates here is that there is no such thing as an untested faith, and this concept runs through the Bible. Writing to the Thessalonians, Paul notes two things which to him marked their conversion as genuine: they recognized the word which they had heard as God's word, not a human being's, and their reception of that word was tested by suffering (1 Thess. 2:13–14). Peter instructs us not to think trials a 'strange' ('foreign', Gk *xenos*) element in normal experience – our calling is to be made like our Saviour in his sufferings (1 Pet. 4:12–13; cf. 1 Pet. 2:20b–25). James goes even further, urging us to count trials 'pure joy' because they are part and parcel of the way forward to maturity (Jas 1:2–4); and Hebrews reminds us that educative discipline (Gk *paideia*) is inseparable from being a beloved child of the Father (Heb. 12:7; cf. Deut. 8:5). Peter also points out that while we indeed 'suffer grief' (Gk *lypeō*) as a result of 'all kinds [Gk *poikilos*] of trials', they all have the purpose that 'the proven genuineness of [our] faith . . . may result in praise, glory and honour when Jesus Christ is revealed'. He compares this process of testing to that of gold being refined in the crucible (1 Pet. 1:6–7). The mocking voice of Satan poured scorn on Job's faith, claiming that the Lord had made life all too easy for him, and scoffing that if he were to lose all that made his life pleasant, he would 'curse [God] to [his] face' (Job 1:10–11). Job's faith, however, was proved true, and he was confident that 'when he has tested me, I shall come forth as gold' (Job 23:10).

In the light of even this small selection of Scripture, we see that when the word of God arrives in our hearts and lives, testings and trials come too as God's appointed way for his children to grow spiritually and to come into the arena of Christlikeness. Even our poor understanding of such things can see that this must be so. Many Christians are given the opportunity in Sunday worship to affirm, 'I believe in God, the Father almighty.' This is all well and good, but we do not actually know that we truly believe in such a God until Monday faces us with experiences which suggest that he is far from almighty and pretty unfatherly! Testing has its place and purpose, and this applies not only to the outward trials of adversity and circumstantial difficulties, but also to the individual realities of besetting sins, temptation and the ceaseless warfare of the spiritual life.

Unless, therefore, we are prepared to rewrite the Bible, we must face the fact that Israel, having sheltered beneath the blood of the lamb, launched out into pilgrimage (Exod. 12:11) to face the wilderness (Deut. 8:15) in a divinely planned programme to test obedience, bring loyalty to light and prove the faithfulness of God (Deut. 8:1–4; cf. 1 Cor. 10:6–13).

d. False expectations: selective listening

Israel's complaint to Moses that he had only succeeded in making Pharaoh a worse overlord than he had been before is instructive (5:21). It accurately describes what had happened, of course, but it also describes what they should have expected to happen. According to 4:30, *Aaron told them everything the LORD had said to Moses*, and this would have included at least the words recorded in 3:19 and 4:21. What did they think a harder heart would do to them? The answer would seem to be that they did not think, because they did not hear. They heard only the good news that the Lord was on the move, and, indeed, Moses and Aaron were themselves infected with the same spirit, as is evident from their bumptious and triumphalist presentation of the case to Pharaoh (5:1). They had no expectation of trouble ahead, yet the word of God was quite explicit. They *believed* (4:31), but they did not listen when God's word warned that there is no such thing as an untested faith.[1] It could be said that the root of all disaster in the Christian life is the failure to hear and believe what the word of God says and to act accordingly.

e. Moses, too!

Moses, too, was surprised, almost traumatized, by his failure (5:22). He had really thought that now at last, forty years after his initial disaster (2:15), he was 'on the victory side'. Plainly, from his whole approach to Pharaoh, bouncing into the royal presence (5:1), he too had not listened with close attention to what the Lord had said and had not taken the predicted heart-hardening seriously. In his mind it was 'all over bar the shouting'! But that is not what the word of God said would be the case, and for Moses, failure to listen attentively led to failure to obey precisely in the following ways:

He took *the wrong delegation*. He had been commanded to take 'the elders of Israel' with him (3:18), but he took only Aaron. He adopted *the wrong approach*. There is nothing comparable in 3:18 to the *This is what the LORD, the God of Israel, says* of 5:1. He used *the wrong terminology*. 'Hebrews' is used in 3:18, and this was the recognized name for the people (cf. 1:16; 2:6), whereas Moses spoke of *Israel* (5:1). He was told to say that God 'met with' him (3:18), which Cassuto suggests (with evidence) was a recognized way, in non-Israelite circles, of describing a theophany (cf. Num. 23:3).[2] Moses had made no allowances for what might or might not have been acceptable to Pharaoh as the Lord had commanded him to do. He made *the wrong request*. Instead of the moderate request for three days' leave of absence which the Lord had put into his mouth as his opening gambit (3:18), Moses made an absolute demand for national emancipation.

As if this catalogue of mishandling God's word was not enough, Moses went on to add what the Lord had never said by threatening plagues and slaughter (5:3).[3] The Lord commanded a corporate approach, couched in

---

[1] Cf. Ramm: 'We must not be too optimistic about these people. Later on they would turn to murmuring . . . idolatry. Christian experience is also such a "mixed bag". We are all children of dust and never too many paces away from error' (p. 45). Ramm might have also called attention to Israel's false expectations at 5:21 as their first failure.

[2] Cassuto, p. 42, cf. pp. 65–66.

[3] Later, when the damage had been done, Moses said what he had originally been told (5:3), but this only served to compound his error. At first, he replaced the Lord's word with his own, then he added his own words to the Lord's (cf. Fretheim, p. 86).

understandable terminology, making a moderate and limited request in courteous terms. Moses adopted an authoritarian approach,[4] alienating Pharaoh with incomprehensible talk (5:2), and laying down an absolute demand.[5] When we sit loose to the word of God, in matters small or great, when we subtract what it does say (cf. Gen. 3:4) and contribute what it does not (cf. Gen. 3:3), we doom ourselves to reap failure and disappointment.[6]

f. Handling failure

Moses' first failure came about through his rushing on without any word from the Lord to commission, direct and control him (2:11–14); his second failure came about through possessing the word of the Lord but not obeying it (5:1–3).[7] The old 'can-do' Moses of 2:12 had by no means ceased to exist. It is not, however, that Moses had knocked the Lord off course. His peremptory approach provoked an enhanced harshness, and the king's hard heart became harder as the Lord had said it would. Thus, history was still on track, for even when we get it all wrong and offer the Lord only a partial, self-willed obedience, he still works his purpose out. But the consequences were tragic as Israel was nailed down by savage new labour laws,[8] and Moses was devastated. But, wonderfully, he knew enough to get back to square one, to bring his failure to the Lord (5:22).

---

[4] Mackay notes that there was 'an Egyptian idiom in which "Thus says" followed by the name of a god was often employed to introduce the commands of that god' (p. 103). If so, Moses' approach was all the more confrontational.

[5] Was Moses consciously deceiving Pharaoh in asking to go three days' journey (knowing full well he had no intention of returning)? In his panic he may well have painted himself into this corner. To depart from the word of God leaves us at the mercy of our own devices. But, in fact, Moses simply said nothing of the future beyond the three days.

[6] The spontaneous threat of 5:3 may well have been the result of Moses' reflecting on his own experience in 4:24–26. It is a deadly thing to fall out with the Lord.

[7] Moberly (p. 26 n. 27) notes the difference between 3:18 and 5:1–3 and asks if 'the reader is to suppose that adherence to the wording of 3:18 might have produced a slightly less hostile response?' Pharaoh's question (5:2) could have been perfectly genuine and not an arrogant repudiation (especially if 'Yahweh' was a secret name among the Hebrews). 5:1 is the first time *God of Israel* occurs. But by 5:10 Pharaoh's angry arrogance has taken over (notice how *This is what Pharaoh says* mimics and mocks *This is what the* LORD . . . *says* in verse 1). The issue has become the personal one of whose word will triumph (cf. Jer. 44:28b). So also in 5:11, Pharaoh's *Go* mocks the *Let my people go* of verse 1, as if to say, 'If it's going you want, I'll give it to you!' It is also worth noticing the reference to Pharaoh's *sword* in 5:21, which answers the reference to Yahweh's *sword* in 5:3. Poor old Moses – having professed fear of Yahweh's sword he had put a sword into Pharaoh's hand.

[8] In the Hebrew of 5:6–21 there are seven references to hard labour, emphasizing both the dire consequences of Moses' mishandling of the situation and the completeness of Hebrew servitude. Fretheim adds that the details of this section 'reflect accurately Egyptian slave labour organisation' (p. 83).

2. Moses returns to the Lord (5:22 – 7:7)

a. A bridge and a map

Verses 22–23 of chapter 5 have a double function to fulfil. On the one hand, they form the introduction to the second section of the overall passage, which we shall consider in a moment. On the other hand, they are the proper conclusion to the first movement, the movement of failure, in Moses' Egyptian adventure. Thus, they are a bridge between the two sections.

How typically human Moses was, even at his best! His 'best' is seen in his returning to the Lord with his failure. Although this is always the right thing to do in such circumstances, it is frequently the most difficult. None of us wants failure, and few find failure easy to admit. The easy course is for us to retire into a corner and tell ourselves what a misery life is, how unfair it all is after we have done our best, a let-down, nothing ever comes right – and so forth. Furthermore, since the most prominent ingredient in our failure is so often guilt over 'letting the Lord down', the easy course, again, is to shun his presence. Moses is our example in not taking this easy way but in getting himself promptly back to the Lord. This is where he had started (3:1–4), and it was the place for a restart, if there was ever going to be one. Indeed, the very exercise of returning to the Lord implied a willingness to try again, coupled with a longing to do better. So, here too, Moses is our example. He had grown in stature, for when he failed the first time he ran away (2:15), whereas this time he ran back – back to the Lord.

Moses was typically human also in what he said. The question *Why . . . ?* in verse 22 is almost instinctive to us when trouble comes and things do not turn out as expected;[9] and the insistent *you* in *Is this why you sent me?* (22) and *you have not rescued* (23) is as neat a passing of the buck as ever occurs in the Bible.

In this Moses was practically wrong, for the fault was his through his inexact obedience to the word of God, but he was instinctively right. For

---

[9] The question 'Why?' arises when our ideas of what the Lord should do are baffled by what he actually does. As in the case of Moses, closer attention to the word of God would often, if not always, provide a corrective. Moses' dismay arose from his belief that the Lord is both 'Sovereign' (5:22, *Lord*) and also 'Yahweh' (5:23, *your name*, i.e. 'LORD'). Moberly comments, 'If the name . . . is meant to indicate [God's] dynamic presence, it surely ought to have made all the difference in facing Pharaoh. Instead, just when things start to get difficult, YHWH makes no difference . . . appears to be absent.' No wonder Moses was confused, although he need not have been, for the name Yahweh ('I am who I am') implies 'It is for me to decide when and how I will be actively present.' We cannot dictate to sovereignty or predict the ways of eternal Wisdom. God's name speaks of his presence, but we often have to face what seems to be his absence.

if we cannot blame God, neither can we trust him. This is a very delicate matter and needs much fuller treatment than can be accommodated here. But consider how, in times of crisis, tragedy or trouble, others encourage us, or we encourage the distressed, to trust God to be with us and to see us through. But if he was not there when the tragedy happened, when the baby died, the child was killed, the engagement was broken or whatever, how can we be sure that he is here now and can be trusted with our trouble? We are tempted to think that the Lord has become like Baal, the god who is never there or available when you really need him (1 Kgs 18:27). We may prefer to think of the Lord 'permitting' sinful plans to reach tragic outcomes and allowing the wrongs and sufferings inevitable in a sinful world to remain unchecked. We may prefer to take the more rigorous but more biblical way of seeing eternal wisdom presiding in absolute rightness and justice over everything, including what sinners do in their culpability (Acts 2:23) and what eventuates in a world of sin. Our God is the 'Father [transcendent] of all, who is over all [present and sovereign] and through all and in all [working perfectly, wisely, justly, lovingly, powerfully]' (Eph. 4:6). God's absolute sovereignty never excuses or connives at our sin, but neither is he ever knocked off course by our sin but rather works his purpose out, as one year succeeds the next. So, Moses *returned to the* Lord (5:22), and the Lord said, *Now* (6:1).

There are three sections within this passage.[10]

A   Moses despondent: the Lord's purpose (5:22 – 6:12)
B   Moses and Aaron commissioned: their humanity (6:13–27)
C   Moses and Aaron commanded to speak: the Lord's word (6:28 – 7:7)

Each of the sections is marked off by an *inclusio* (i.e. they begin and end in matching ways),[11] and each conveys a basic truth. In the first, Moses' despondency made no difference. The Lord did not tell him to cheer up, brace up or get a grip. He did not invite or even here promise any change in Moses, but rather renewed the revelation of himself. It was Moses 'warts and all' who was caught up into the divine plan. In the second, we

---

[10]   This outline is couched in terms of Moses and his needs. If we think of 5:22 – 7:7 as a fresh start, then headings focused on the Lord are equally possible: 5:22 – 6:12 The Lord reaffirmed; 6:13–27 The Lord's agents; 6:28 – 7:7 The instrumentality of the Lord's word.

[11]   The *inclusios* are: A 5:22–23/6:10–12, B 6:13–26/27, C 6:28–30/7:6–7.

are faced with the ordinary and real humanity of Moses as seen in his family tree.[12] This is the point emphasized in 6:27: *They were the ones who spoke to Pharaoh king of Egypt about bringing the Israelites out of Egypt – this same Moses and Aaron.* You can almost hear the note of astonishment behind the words. In the one corner, ordinary human clay; in the other, superpower royalty. But this 'mere' humanity had been commissioned by the Lord (6:13, 26). Finally, in the third section, the still-despondent Moses, completely lacking in self-confidence (6:30)[13] and warned again of battles ahead (7:3–4), at last settled down to obey the word of the Lord: *Moses and Aaron did just as the LORD commanded them* (7:6). As the rest of Exodus shows, Moses had learned this lesson well. Apart from his bad-tempered and costly disobedience in Numbers 20:11–12, he did not diverge again from the divine word and was consequently the master of every situation. Walking in obedience, Moses the despondent failure became, increasingly and progressively, the authoritative and victorious agent of the Lord and the master of the pharaoh.

b. Renewed vision of the Lord

The hinge of the whole Exodus enterprise comes with the *Now* of 6:1. It is a 'turn your eyes upon Jesus' moment, for transformation comes through seeing the Lord as he is, past, present and future.[14]

i. The past: a great revelation (6:2–4)

God told Moses that *I appeared to Abraham, to Isaac and to Jacob as* [in the character of] *God* [*El*] [who is] *Almighty* [*Shaddai*] (3). The meaning of *Shaddai* is still unknown, although many suggestions have been made.

---

[12]   The occurrence of this genealogy in 6:14–27 is typical of the way the Old Testament uses such material. Reuben and Simeon are mentioned only in order to 'place' Levi in the succession of Israel's sons. The sons of Levi mentioned are the 'great' levitical families of subsequent history. Aaron precedes Moses because of primogeniture. The genealogy thus both introduces those who will subsequently figure in the story – hence Moses' sons are not mentioned, but Aaron's are (e.g. Lev. 10:1–7) – and reminds Moses of his place in the outworking of God's plan, the flow of salvation history (cf. Esth. 4:14b). He may be merely human, but what humanity! Note how, true to the genealogy, Aaron precedes Moses in 6:26 and, true to the Exodus history, Moses precedes Aaron in 6:27.

[13]   Moses speaks of himself here as being (lit.) 'uncircumcised of lips'. Circumcision signifies one who has been given the promises of God and, therefore, has been touched by the transforming grace of God. Moses was unaware of any such change in himself.

[14]   Each of the three sections includes a command to speak (6:6, 9; 6:13, 26, 27; 7:7); each admits Moses' self-despair (5:22; 6:12; 6:30); each affirms the Lord's purpose to deliver (6:6–8; 6:13, 26–27; 7:5); and the three in turn focus on the leading dramatis personae of the exodus: the revelation of Yahweh (6:2–8); the ancestry of Moses (6:14–26); Pharaoh and Egypt (7:3–5). There is also the 'I am' of divine revelation (6:2); the 'these are' of human frailty (6:26); and the 'I have made you' (7:1) of transforming enabling.

If, however, we bypass dictionary discussions and look at the contexts in Genesis in which this great title occurs, we find that a satisfactory meaning emerges. *El Shaddai* is revealed there as the God who is sufficient for personal inadequacies, as when the childless Abram became Abraham the 'father of many nations' (Gen. 17:1); the God who is sufficient for our helplessness against overwhelming odds, as when Jacob, sending his sons into the power of Joseph, the capricious ruler of Egypt, commended them to *El Shaddai* (Gen. 43:14); the God who is sufficient for the unknown future, as when Jacob left Canaan for Egypt on the strength of promises that God would go with him and bring him back (Gen. 48:3); and the God of miraculous transformation, as when Joseph, who suffered unjust imprisonment as a slave without remission or appeal, became in one bound second in command under Pharaoh (Gen. 49:25). In its actual use in Genesis, therefore, *El Shaddai* is predominantly the God who is sufficient – for his people's needs, for keeping his promises. When they are at their weakest, he is at his most potent.

ii. The present: the same God, the fuller revelation (6:3b–5)

The words *but by my name the* LORD *I did not make myself known to them* (3b) both reflects what we find in Genesis and implies that what 'the LORD'/ Yahweh means is now, at last, to be revealed – not as a new or different God but as the same God more fully known. In Genesis 17:1 Yahweh said to Abraham, 'I am *El Shaddai*', and this is typical of Genesis in that the God who is *called* Yahweh is *known* as *El Shaddai*, the God who is sufficient. Here, however, the situation is reversed and *El Shaddai* says, 'I am Yahweh' (2–3). The sufficient God is about to redefine his sufficiency, in new as well as old ways. The leading 'old way' is the reiteration of his covenant. In the covenant language of the Old Testament, the *established* of verse 4 is, rather, 'implemented', 'set in operation' (Heb. √*qûm*) *my covenant*. The reference is to Genesis 12:7, where the territorial promise of the covenant was first announced. This promise bridges the centuries and is the moving cause of the whole exodus work of God (5b; cf. 2:24). The present experience of the people may have been one of *groaning* and slavery (5) but, all appearance to the contrary, the promise had not been forgotten.

Acts 7:17 entitles the exodus period as the time 'for God to fulfil his promise to Abraham', and Joshua made the people look back and acknowledge that 'every promise has been fulfilled; not one has failed'

(Josh. 23:14). Our surest standing ground is always the promises of God, who never fails to honour his word.

iii. The future: deliverance, intimacy, inheritance (6:6–8)

These verses describe the Lord's work in terms of liberation and redemption. In connection with liberation (6a, *bring . . . out*, is the hiphil of √*yāṣā'*, 'to go out') the Lord makes a double promise: there will be liberation from both the experience of distress (*the yoke*) and the circumstances which provoked the distress (*being slaves*). When he turns to the distinct exercise of redemption (6b), the Lord links this with his intention to *take you as my own people* (7).

The verb 'to redeem' (√*gā'al*) is one of the loveliest in meaning and the most important in significance in the Old Testament. Its secular use concerns land which has passed, or seems likely to pass, into alien ownership and which must be 'redeemed' by purchase (Lev. 25:26; Ruth 4:3–4). In religious terms, if something is vowed to God which in the nature of the case cannot be given to him as such (e.g. a house), the one who makes the promise must 'redeem' the vow by paying the market value (Lev. 27:13–31). Within the community, the redeemer was the next of kin, who had the right to avenge a murdered relative (Num. 35:12–27; Deut. 19:6, 12). We can see from these examples that within the concept of redemption there are two separate ideas. On the one hand, there is the next-of-kin relationship between redeemer and redeemed,[15] and on the other, the idea of paying the equivalent price (e.g. Lev. 25:24, 52–55). The former explains how the verb can be used in the general sense of superintending care (Gen. 48:16, niv 'delivered'; esv 'redeemed'), for the verb expresses a personal and close relationship of concern. From Exodus 6:6 onwards, however, the price-paying emphasis is always present: the Lord knows and possesses his people and is ready to pay whatever price is needed in order to implement his next-of-kin right to redeem them and to take upon himself all their needs as if his own.

Who, then, is Yahweh, the Lord? In what ways do these verses supply what was held back in Genesis and extend what was taught in 3:13–15? They tell us that the Lord keeps his word (4), feels our woes (5), sets us free (6a), brings us close to himself (6b, 7) and will eventually lead us home (8).

---

[15] See Motyer, *Look to the Rock*, pp. 55–56, 199. Mackay thinks of 'redemption' as the action of the next of kin of the 'firstborn' of Exod. 4:22 (p. 121).

Faithfulness, empathy, deliverance, intimacy and inheritance are all embraced by the gracious *inclusio*, *I am the* LORD (2, 8).

Additional notes

6:2–3 These verses have been a battlefield of differing interpretations. E.g. see the contrasting views expressed in Motyer, *Name*; Moberly, *Old Testament*. See also W. J. Martin, *Stylistic Criteria and the Analysis of the Pentateuch* (Tyndale Press, 1955). The view taken here is that Exodus 6:3 means (and the evidence of Genesis supports) that Abraham and the other patriarchs knew 'Yahweh' only as one way of identifying *El Shaddai*, but as yet no distinctive revelation of God had been attached to it. Its *meaning* was not revealed until Moses (cf. 3:13–15; see also Cassuto). We may, therefore, treat 6:4–8 as the classical exposition of the revelation of God summed up in the divine name. See Motyer, *Name*, p. 29 for the use and significance of *El Shaddai*.

6:4 The Old Testament has a rich vocabulary related to the covenant that is not, alas, always sufficiently noted in translations. √*Kārat* ('to cut') is used of inaugurating a covenant (Gen. 15:18); √*nātan* ('to give, put, place, appoint') is used of the covenant as the continuing mode of relationship between the two parties (Gen. 17:2); √*qûm* ('to rise', in the hiphil 'to raise up') is used of implementing the covenant or bringing it into operation (Gen. 6:18; Exod. 6:4). Cf. also √*zākar*, 'to remember' (Exod. 2:24); √*šāmar*, 'to keep the covenant stipulations' (Exod. 19:5); √*pārar*, 'to break, annul' (Jer. 31:32). A covenant is made 'with' ('*ēt*, Josh. 24:25; '*im*, Exod. 24:8) someone, in the sense of bringing the two parties together in fellowship (cf. *bên*, 'between', Gen. 9:16); and 'for, to the benefit/advantage of' (Josh. 24:25).

Exodus 7:8 – 13:16

9. Viewpoint

Before we launch out into the darkish waters of 7:8 – 10:29, it will help us to stop for a moment to do what Moses did from Mount Pisgah (Deut. 34:1–3) and, as the hymn writer puts it, 'view the landscape o'er'![1]

1. The turning point

Moses had experienced a long, long probation before coming to what, we can see with hindsight, was the turning point described in 7:6. His history is written much more in terms of facts than of feelings; the experiences he passed through, rather than, on the whole, what he felt about it all. It is the story of two failures, in each of which Moses achieved nothing but rejection both by his own people and by Pharaoh (2:11–15; 5:1–21). Following his first failure, he settled down to forty years of shepherding another man's sheep in Midian (3:1). In so far as we can enter into Moses' mind during these years, 2:21 says he 'was willing/content to live with the man'. And in doing so, can we guess what he was saying to himself? Did he see his life with Jethro as an enforced interim, during which he continued to seethe with concern for the oppressed Hebrews and with rebellious animosity against their Egyptian masters? The words and the 'feeling' of 2:21 suggest rather acquiescence in failure, letting the dead past bury its dead, making the best of a not-too-bad job – he had, after all, a life, security, his own home, his wife and family. It was not, perhaps, what he had envisaged, but it was not at all bad. So, did he give his firstborn

---

[1] Isaac Watts, 'There Is a Land of Pure Delight'.

son a name that reflected his own state of mind, 'A resident alien – that's what I've become – in a foreign land!' (2:22)?

Moses' period of foreign residency was brought to an end by divine initiative when he found himself confronted by God (3:1 – 4:17). In the ensuing conversation we discover, however, how deeply the experience of failure had bitten into Moses' psyche. He had no sense of self-worth, awareness of ability, desire to change, or confidence in the face of envisaged challenges. He was a man whom it is so very easy for us to identify with: a failure who had settled for being a failure and accepted second best. The get-up-and-go which had made Moses a would-be liberator had evaporated under the sickening blow of rejection and the realization of the royal power ranged against him (2:14–15), and yet this was God's chosen man.

Argued into a corner by the Lord's persistence, Moses returned to Egypt and failed yet again, but this time, though he does not explain himself to us, he fled, not to Midian, but back to the Lord (5:22). And out of the experience of renewed revelation of the Lord and his promises (6:1–8), the still failing, self-doubting Moses (6:9) also had his commission renewed (6:10–13). Here we see him in all the reality of his human condition (6:14–26). Yet out of that second interview came a new, different man. His initial bouncy self-confidence was plainly not absent from that first triumphalist explosion into Pharaoh's presence (5:1), but after the second session with the Lord it was replaced by the magisterial authority, the quietness of confidence, of the man with the word of God (7:6).

2. The crucial transformation

By what inward processes of thought and decision Moses reached his crucial transformation we are not told. He entered the presence of the Lord with complaints about his failure (5:22–23); he emerged, as subsequent chapters will prove over and over again, as the man who had no words other than those God had taught him, no acts other than those God had commanded, and no position except that of a man sent from God. Moses and Aaron had previously erupted into Pharaoh's presence with words of their own devising and had only made the bad worse, but now the lesson had been learned. The point of change is plain to see, but it is so understated in the biblical account that were we not alert to what had gone before and to how the story proceeds, the crucial words 'Moses and

Aaron did just as the LORD commanded them' (7:6) would slip off the tongue unnoticed.[2]

Simply concentrating on the broad outline, 6:28 – 7:7 runs as follows:

A^1 Moses, transmitter of the Lord's word (6:28–29)

   B^1 The Lord, sovereign over Moses' speech (6:30 – 7:2)

   B^2 The Lord, sovereign over Pharaoh's heart (7:3–5)

A^2 Moses, obedient in deed and word (7:6–7)

3. God's word, resisted and irresistible

In the long section that begins in 7:8 and ends at 13:16 Moses is found acting only at the divine prompting and saying only what he had been instructed to say. It is, for reasons we will explore in the next chapter, a prolonged trial of strength, throughout which Pharaoh pits his word against the Lord's word until at the end he capitulates and Israel leaves Egypt. Like the rest of Exodus, it is a balanced and rounded work of literary artistry.

A^1 Prologue: looking forward (7:8–13)

   B^1 The nine mighty acts (7:14 – 10:29; see below)

   B^2 The tenth mighty act: Passover and exodus (11:1 – 12:42)

A^2 Epilogue: looking back (12:43 – 13:16)

   a^1 The law of the Passover: the covenant people (12:43–51)

      b^1 The uniqueness of the firstborn (13:1–2)

   a^2 The Feast of Unleavened Bread: the free people (13:3–10)

      b^2 The uniqueness of the firstborn (13:11–16)

This outline needs little explanation. The prologue (7:8–13) sets the scene very vividly, as Durham holds, instancing what is to follow in one single event.[3] The transformation of the rod into a reptile had essentially the same

---

[2] The reference to Moses' age in 7:7 is unexpected. Does it point to the unhurried purposes of the Lord and the calm sovereignty with which he matured the historical situation and the man he had chosen until they were both ready? Is it intended to match the genealogy of 6:14–27 with its demonstration of the real humanity of Moses, so that just as 6:12–13 is recapitulated in 6:28–30 and 7:1–2, 6:14–26 finds a counterpart in 7:7? At all events, we need to guard against thinking of Moses in terms of today's octogenarians. Moses lived to be 120 and, therefore, at eighty he was, in our terms, in his mid forties.

[3] Durham, p. 90. Currid is fuller, calling it 'a paradigm of the plague narrative' which foreshadows Yahweh's humiliation of Egypt and defines the true issue at stake as 'not primarily between Moses and Pharaoh, or between Moses and the Egyptian magicians, or between Israel and Egypt' but as 'a heavenly combat between the God of the Hebrews and the deities of Egypt' (p. 159).

significance as when Moses performed it privately as a 'sign' for Israel,[4] but two matters distinguish this new event. First, Pharaoh is envisaged as asking for a *miracle* (9), but this cannot be seen as the request of a man open to persuasion. We know that Pharaoh had already taken up a position of hostile intransigence, and the Lord made no secret of the fact that this opposition was going to increase (7:3). Since, therefore, Pharaoh was not concerned for Moses and Aaron to establish their credibility, it must be that he thought to expose them as charlatans, pretending to supernatural authority but actually driven by political or humanitarian motives. Consequently, the serpent sign was repeated with all its direct relevance to the power claims of the Egyptian throne and to Pharaoh's supposed personal divine status.[5] Second, a different word for snake is used here. In 4:3 the rod became a *nāḥāš*, whereas here both Aaron's rod and those of the Egyptian magicians became *tannîn*. Both these words are non-specific, so the reptile in question cannot be identified. In the usage of *tannîn*,[6] however, there is often an emphasis on size, fearsomeness or hostility. The LXX catches this possibility by using *drakōn* ('dragon')[7] here, whereas it has *ophis* in 4:3.[8] In this way the narrative emphasizes the trial of strength as being on the highest level and makes the domination of Yahweh over the powers of Egypt all the more spectacular and convincing.[9]

4. The nine mighty acts

A fuller consideration of the nine so-called 'plagues' and the question of Pharaoh's heart (7:13) will be the subject of the next chapter. Here, however, we can note the artistry with which the author of Exodus presents the material.

---

[4] See the notes on 4:1–5 above.

[5] Currid also notes that transformations were a feature of magic in ancient Egypt and refers to a wax crocodile becoming real. Thus, he points out, Aaron was taking on the magicians on their own ground (p. 161).

[6] Cf. Gen. 1:21 (NIV, 'great creatures of the sea'); Deut. 32:33 (NIV, 'serpents'); Job 7:12; Pss 74:13; 91:13[14]; 148:7; Isa. 27:1; 51:9; Jer. 51:34; Lam. 4:3 (NIV, 'jackals').

[7] In Homer it is used to mean 'of huge size, coiled like a snake' and 'appears to have been really the "python" or "boa"' (Liddell and Scott, *A Greek–English Lexicon*, 8th edn [OUP, 1901]).

[8] Durham (pp. 89, 91) offers 'a monstrous snake'; Currid (p. 160), a 'cobra', noting a link with the uraeus of the royal crown; and Fretheim (p. 113), 'a much more terrifying creature than any snake'.

[9] Durham (pp. 91, 92) sets aside all merely 'naturalistic' explanations of this passage, saying, 'the whole point . . . is its miraculous element'. The Egyptians possess 'arcane arts . . . Pharaoh and his best minds are by no means . . . inept or lacking in power. Quite the contrary, they are formidable, a force to be reckoned with.' Hence the scene is set by focusing on the 'awesome potential of the two opposing forces'.

E. J. Young points out that the nine acts fall into three sets of three:[10]

A	B	C
1. Blood (7:14–25)	4. Flies (8:20–32)	7. Hail (9:13–35)
2. Frogs (8:1–15)	5. Animal diseases (9:1–7)	8. Locusts (10:1–20)
3. Gnats (8:16–19)	6. Boils (9:8–12)	9. Darkness (10:21–29)

Young notes that the first two plagues in each set were announced to Pharaoh beforehand, presumably at the palace (the first all taking place at early-morning confrontations with Pharaoh and the second all initiated by the command 'Go to Pharaoh'), whereas the third in each set happened without warning. In the first three plagues (A), the magicians vie with Moses, replicating the divine act in the first two and acknowledging 'the finger of God' in the third. The fourth, fifth and sixth plagues (B) introduce a distinction between Israel and Egypt (8:23), and after that point, Egypt alone is smitten by the various disasters. Indeed, after 8:23 it is only in the sixth and eighth plagues that no attention is called to the protection of Israel. Finally, in the first series of three plagues we read of Aaron's use of the staff (7:19; 8:5; 8:16); in the second series there is no reference to the staff; and in the third series it is the staff of Moses (9:23; 10:13) or his hand (10:22) that is mentioned. There are also other identities of thought and wording in the three sets of the acts of God, but these will suffice to indicate a presentation made with literary artistry and skill on the part of the author or editor. We are intended to see the nine acts as quite the opposite of chance or any haphazard occurrence. They were designed and planned as a whole with the aim not only of edging Pharaoh to the point of releasing the people, but also presenting proof to Pharaoh and Israel that the Lord is God (7:17; 8:10, 22; 9:16; 10:2).[11]

---

[10] E. J. Young, *Introduction to the Old Testament* (Tyndale, 1953), pp. 70f. Cf. W. S. LaSor, D. A. Hubbard and F. W. Bush, *Old Testament Survey* (Eerdmans, 1982), pp. 137–140, who hold that the literary structure of the plague narrative points to 'a long history of oral and written transmission' before it reached its 'current form' (although they do not say why) but insist that this process 'does not necessarily prejudge its historical worth', which 'can be decided only by determining whether what is transmitted fits the background . . . of which it speaks'. As to this, 'the nine plagues fit rather precisely the natural phenomena of Egypt'. See further in the next chapter.

[11] The traditional literary-critical distribution of the text between the hypothetical J, E, D and P documents is noted by Durham (pp. 90–144), where it can be studied in all its arbitrariness. Durham extends much kindness towards this fragmentation but constantly notes that 'the composite at hand' is 'the only form of the narrative about which we can be completely sure'. Young's observations of intricate unity tell strongly against the validity of the literary critics' methodology.

5. The epilogue

In the outline given above, 12:43 – 13:16 is described as an 'epilogue' with the subtitle 'Looking back'. These descriptions were carefully chosen. The great Passover event, which we shall deal with in detail in the next few chapters, brought three matters of central importance into the life of Israel. First, there was the Passover itself, including the obligation to keep an annual memorial of it (12:14); second, the associated Feast of Unleavened Bread (12:17); and, third, the prominence which the Passover gave to first-born sons (12:12). The time would come, as the rest of the Pentateuch shows, when the double feast would be given its formal place in the developed religious system of Israel. Until that day, however, Israel needed to know how to set out on their pilgrim path as the Passover people, equipped with such basic information as would enable the annual celebration of their unique foundation rites. Exodus 12:43 – 13:16 is thus perfectly in place.

The interleaving of the Lord's requirements regarding firstborn sons (13:1–2, 11–16) is also a 'matter arising' from the Passover. Was this the Lord's first and, so to speak, best intention for the provision of priestly ministry in Israel? For example, do the firstborn appear as the 'young Israelite men' offering the covenant sacrifices of 24:5? Very likely so. Later the tragedy of the golden calf (chapter 32) would intervene to defer the Lord's desire to have a priestly people (19:6; cf. 1 Pet. 2:5, 9), and the firstborn were replaced by the priesthood of the family of Aaron within the tribe of Levi (Lev. 8; Exod. 32:26; Num. 8:18). More about all this later. First, however, we must deal in more detail with the nine plagues, the Lord's moral sovereignty and Pharaoh's heart.

Additional notes

7:11 Four words are used to describe the magicians and their works. First, they are *wise men* (ḥākām), a general word for being 'in the know' and 'possessing know-how'. Then they are *sorcerers* (mĕkaššĕpîm), from the noun 'sorcery', which gives rise to the verb 'to practise sorcery'. Their knowledge, therefore, was specifically of magical or occult arts. Third, they are described as *magicians* (ḥarṭummîm), lit. 'engravers' or 'writers' but used in the sense of 'educated', particularly in occult wisdom. The fourth word, *secret arts* or 'enchantments', is lit. 'secrecy', from √lûṭ, 'to wrap up, keep under wraps'.

Exodus 7:14 – 10:29

10. Why the plagues?

1. The heavens rule

There are many titles we could have used for our study of this section of Exodus. A most dramatic title would have been 'One hand, one heart', for it is here that we meet the hand of God stretched out in power (e.g. 9:15–16), and the heart of Pharaoh increasing in opposition (e.g. 9:34–35). This is a section that focuses sharply on the conflict between heaven and earth, issuing in the same lesson which, in later years, Nebuchadnezzar had to learn the hard way: that 'the Most High is sovereign over all kingdoms on earth' (Dan. 4:25, 32).

2. The new Moses

We could have called this section 'Moses, man of calm and control', for the book of Exodus could fruitfully be treated as a study of the developing character of Moses – a man (as we say) 'growing into the job'. Where now, we might ask, is the impulsiveness of 2:11–13, the hesitancy of 3:12 – 4:13 and the triumphalism of 5:1? Alternatively, where has all this unflurried calm (10:29), total confidence in God (9:5) and pervasive fearlessness before the king come from? Why, as we read these chapters, do we find ourselves sharing the conviction that, for all his power and position, Pharaoh cannot win? And it is not simply because we know in advance how the story will end; it is the sense of an assured outcome that pervades these stories from the start.

The answer to all these questions is – and how well we do to remember it – that Moses is now the man of the word of God, acting and speaking only as he has been told to do (7:6). 'The Holy Spirit', says Acts 5:32, is the one 'whom God has given to those who obey him.'

3. Why? Oh, why?

Instructive as such titles may be, they bypass the one thing which cries out to be answered – the question 'Why?' It is all very well, and a great lesson, to note that 'the heavens rule', but look at the way they rule. All that suffering, misery, disruption of life and, at the end, savage bereavement. It is all very well to learn with Moses the central lesson of obedience to the word of God, but look at what Moses actually did by the Lord's command.

The plagues run from the passing discomfort of water turned to blood to the revoltingly disruptive invasion of frogs, to the potentially disease-bearing gnats and flies, the commercially damaging animal sickness, the personally debilitating boils, the environmentally disastrous hail and locusts, and the terrifying darkness, and end at last with the heart-stopping sadness of the death of the sons. It is a terrifying tale of the woes which still mark and mar earthly life and which, then as now, prompt an intuitive, often rightly indignant and sometimes understandably hostile 'Why?' rising up from earth to heaven.

This questioning is exacerbated by the fact that from the start the Lord knew that it would have to come to the contest of the firstborn (4:22–23) and, therefore, that the earlier acts would prove ineffective. Why, then, did he not 'cut to the chase'? Why the prolonged agonies of nine ineffectual acts?

4. Obedience and disobedience

The immediate and basic answer is that in the eyes of the Lord disobedience is as greatly abhorred as obedience is prized. We can appreciate the latter by recalling that Moses' forty and more years of apprenticeship were designed to produce this one fruit: a man obedient to the word of God in action and speech. In respect of the Lord's abhorrence of disobedience, however, consider the garden of Eden, and the dire consequences for Adam and Eve of eating the forbidden fruit or, more exactly, the single act of disobedience to the single law of the garden. In that primeval perfection, the first man and woman enjoyed the garden as long as they lived within the sole restriction the Lord imposed on them. Their disobedience lost the garden for themselves and their human posterity and lost the manifold perfections of the garden for the whole of creation. Disobedience is as serious as that. Moses' obedience brought Israel out of Egypt, as we might say, against all the odds and in the face of the then world's superpower; his disobedience lost him the Promised Land. The terms in which this is expressed are telling: disobedience, as Numbers 20:12 and 27:14 reveal, rebels against the divine word, deserts the life of faith, scorns the holiness of the Lord and provokes his anger (Deut. 1:37).

If, as is indeed the case, the primary characteristic of the Lord's people is to obey what he has revealed, then, correspondingly, disobedience to the revealed word (in our case, the Bible) is the primary offence. On this point, by facing us with the horrific reality of the plagues, the book of Exodus speaks with unmistakable clarity to us as individuals and to the whole church. The great flood (Gen. 7), the destruction of Sodom (Gen. 19) and, in the New Testament, the striking down of Ananias and Sapphira (Acts 5) are all examples of the fact that the Lord sometimes gives a signal demonstration of how he feels and reacts. This is not because he intends on every occasion to act in the same way, but so that we may see into his mind, and fashion ourselves according to his serious concerns. The plagues reveal his love of obedience and his revulsion from disobedience.

5. 'In wrath remember mercy' (Hab. 3:2)

We, of course, live in a world of 'do-it-yourself' moral standards, in which, as Isaiah put it, darkness has replaced light and values are as subjective as matters of taste (Isa. 5:20). Absolutes are out, moral indignation or outrage is suspect, and what right, for heaven's sake, has anyone to say someone else is wrong? Paul spoke of sin's ability to spread like gangrene (2 Tim. 2:17) – in other words, increasing not only in area but in depth and in its capacity to replace the sound with the corrupt until the death-bearing corruption infests the whole. So it is with what started in Genesis 3:1–4. The subtlety of the serpent is seen in that he assaulted the woman at a point where our first parents had already tampered with the word of God. He was moving towards denying God's word (3:4), but he began at the point where Adam and Eve had added to God's word by importing a prohibition all their own – that of 'touching' the tree (3:3). As soon as we loosen our ties to the explicitness and sufficiency of what God has said – whether to deny or add – we are preparing ourselves to be seduced by what F. D. Kidner calls a 'flat contradiction . . . the serpent's word against God's', and, as he goes on to note – germane to our present discussion of Exodus – 'the first doctrine to be denied is judgment'.[1]

If, then, we make our way past peripherals (what a nasty experience to find water become blood!) to the heart of the matter, we have a problem with the plagues simply because we step back from the truth of the wrath of God against sin and the judgment of God upon sinners. We would prefer the bliss of a kingdom of God without moral absolutes, presided over by a God without wrath and entered through a Christ without a cross. But the price for this would be to discard not just this or that bit of the Bible (e.g. Exod. 7 – 10) but the whole God-given book, for in it God has revealed his absolutes and that he is a God of intense, fiery holiness. Jesus died bearing our sins in his body on the cross, for that is what sin merits, and saving us from the wrath to come, for that is where sin leads. If the plagues begin with the disasters sin brings, they lead inexorably to the death with which sin ends.

6. Warnings

God's first visitations were like warning shots across the bows of the Egyptian ship. Compared with the death of a son, water turned into blood is nothing. If Pharaoh had listened to the word of the Lord, no plague at all would have fallen on him and his people. If he had bowed before the visitation and sign of the water turned into blood (7:14–24),[2] he and the Egyptians would not have been bereaved of their firstborn (12:29). Thus, even the visitations of the wrath of God, however justly due, are held within the brackets of his inexplicable mercy. He did not visit Pharaoh and Egypt forthwith with the death their disobedience deserved but instituted a process of probation, at any point of which they could have stepped off

---

[1] F. D. Kidner, *Genesis*, TOTC (IVP, 1967), p. 68.

[2] Water turning into blood may have been, in one sense, the 'lightest' of the plagues, but in Egyptian terms it was loaded with significance. It was a direct challenge to the Nile. If Pharaoh was aware at all of the history of Moses (as we are), he would have observed the man who had been saved from the power of the Nile now claiming power over the Nile. The arena of the first trial of strength was well chosen. Note also how here (as in chapters 3–4) the God who speaks precedes the God who acts: the verbal revelation of 7:19 precedes the matching act of 7:20. Moses' staff was not, of course, a magic wand itself producing marvels, but an enactment of the word of the Lord – hence its smiting and the Lord's smiting coincide (7:20). The element of divine mercy or forbearance seen in the Lord's prolonged probation of Pharaoh is explicit in the unique warning of 9:19. It is the word of a God who longs to be merciful.

the ladder of discipline into the path of obedience and escaped the final penalty.[3]

7. Learning from the plagues: the God of moral probation

The plagues were designed to reveal the God who sent them and yet, surprisingly, they are recorded without any reference to the holiness of the Lord, even though that is the overriding impression which they leave with us.[4] They explicitly claim to teach four major lessons.

a. Knowledge of God as the Lord

Pharaoh had responded to Moses' initial, ill-judged approach by saying, 'Who is the LORD [Yahweh] . . . ? I do not know the LORD [Yahweh]' (5:2). Moses was sent back to tell Pharaoh that God was sending the disaster of the contamination of the Nile so that *you* [sing.] *will know that I am the LORD* [*Yahweh*] (7:17). The very first plague struck at the heart of Egypt's life as the whole country and its people were dependent on and sustained by the river they considered to be divine,[5] showing that there is a God greater even than the Nile, and it is his decision whether life on earth is sustainable or not.

b. Knowledge of the Lord as the only God

Pharaoh was told that the purpose of the plague of frogs was *so that you* [sing.] *may know there is no one like the LORD our God* (8:10), and that of the hail, *so you* [sing.] *may know that there is no one like me in all the earth* (9:14). Each of these references is important. The plague of frogs revealed the Lord's sovereignty of timing, for Pharaoh could not attribute the

---

[3] The Lord's probationary disciplines operate also within his family to bring our hearts into the way of obedience (Deut. 8:2), to reveal his faithfulness (Deut. 8:3a), to teach us spiritual priorities (Deut. 8:3b), to deal with us as his sons and daughters (Deut. 8:5) and, as such, to make us share his holiness (Heb. 12:7–10).

[4] Exodus is very much the book of the holiness of the Lord, with 3:5 and 19:10, 22–23 acting as the leading idea for its two halves. Everything that concerns the Lord is holy – his people, his place and dwelling, the instruments and celebrants of his worship – yet 15:11 is the only direct reference to the holiness of the Lord himself.

[5] Herodotus said, 'Egypt is land acquired by the Egyptians, given them by the river', but long before Herodotus 'the Nile was "the giver of life to the two lands"' (i.e. Upper and Lower Egypt). Currid quotes Khety's 'Hymn to the Inundation': 'Everything that has come into being is through [the Nile's] power . . . there is no district of living men without him' (Currid, pp. 164–165). Cf. the comments on the plague of frogs below. The same applies to the cattle sickness. Hathor was the cow-headed mother goddess, and the Apis bulls played a significant part in the royal cult. In all these cases the Lord is singling out the pretend deities for exposure.

removal of the frogs to happy chance or good luck as he was allowed to choose the time of relief. He chose *Tomorrow* (8:10), and, in answer to Moses' prayer, so it was, precisely. The plague of hail seems to have marked a point of no return in the Lord's dealings with Pharaoh, for he said *this time I will send the full force of my plagues against you and against your officials and your people* (9:14). Pharaoh had refused to respond to the initial 'sign' and the six subsequent plagues, in which there had been a mounting tide of evidence and pressure. In the first plague, the ability of the magicians to replicate the visitation led to Pharaoh's hard-hearted refusal (7:22).[6] The magicians were also able to replicate the second plague (8:7), but the removal of the frogs was according to an exact timing, proof of the presence and power of the Lord (8:10) and, by no means of least importance, proof of his response to Moses' prayer.[7] The magicians were unable to replicate the third plague and were forced to acknowledge *the finger of God* (8:18–19). When the fourth plague came, Goshen was set apart as a protected enclave (8:22–23), and once more the visitation ended in answer to prayer (8:30). Goshen was again exempted from the fifth plague, but this time Pharaoh sent investigators to convince himself of its immunity (9:7) and, of course, to load more evidence (and more guilt) on his own head. The sixth plague left even the magicians incapacitated (9:11). There is neat and telling use of two separate Hebrew verbs: the magicians *could not stand before Moses*, but the Lord could command Moses to *confront* [take your stand before] *Pharaoh* (9:11, 13). We see, therefore, that Pharaoh was faced with both a rising severity of divine action and a mounting body of evidence of the absolute power and incomparable nature of the Lord. His refusal on the occasion of the sixth plague (actually his seventh refusal in all) was decisive. Plagues now followed in

---

[6] The magicians could replicate but they could not remedy the situation. They could only make things worse, not better (cf. 8:7). In consequence of their ability, however, Pharaoh became obdurate (7:22b). Even so, Moses had no need to be anxious as it was all as the Lord had said it would be (7:22c). Since Egypt could not have survived seven days without water, the digging (7:24) must have been in some measure successful, and this would account also for the availability of water for the magicians to transform. The downhill path of the magicians is one of the lighter moments of the narrative: first they could replicate but not reverse; then they could neither replicate nor reverse (8:18); finally, they could not even stand (9:11)!

[7] In Egyptian religion frogs were seen as symbols of fecundity. The Lord took the picture of life and turned it into death and decay. It was the frog-headed goddess Hekhet who breathed life into bodies formed by her husband, the creator god Khnum. Note how the frogs were left to stink (8:14) so that the Egyptians could not deny that it was Yahweh who held the power of life and death. Previously, Israel had complained that they had become a bad smell to Pharaoh (5:21, ESV)! Here we see the first crack in the facade of Pharaoh's resistance as he recognizes that it is the Lord with whom he has to deal, not Egypt's gods or the magicians (8:8). 8:10 and 9:5 link the second and fifth plagues by this element of exact timing and show Yahweh as the Lord of time as well as event.

a crescendo of destruction and horror until at last the hardened heart was broken. Where, might we ask, did Paul learn the lesson that 'God cannot be mocked. A man reaps what he sows' (Gal. 6:7)? Had he been reading Exodus?

c. Knowledge of God as present in the land of Egypt

The immunity of Goshen in quarantine from the plague of flies – one of three distinguishing features of this plague, along with its severity (8:21, 24 [17, 20]) and the completeness of its removal (8:31[27]) – was *so that you* [sing.] *will know that I, the* LORD, *am in this land* (8:22[18]). In the case of such an all-encompassing visitation (8:24[20]), the exclusion of the flies from Goshen was a marvel of not insignificant proportions. It was a miraculous *sign* (8:23[19]) of divine presence and activity right at the heart of Egypt.

d. Knowledge of God as all-powerful

Both 9:14 and 16 introduce the idea of the Lord as God of all the earth. Verse 14 stresses the powers at his disposal (*the full force of my plagues*) and the extent of his sway – the king's heart and the resources at his disposal, his *officials* and his *people* alike. There is no power to be mobilized against God because all power is under him. Verse 16 shows that it is not just a matter of power in the immediate context (great as that was), for even history itself is an exercise of divine sovereign power – *I have raised you up for this very purpose, that I might show you my power and that my name might be proclaimed in all the earth* (9:16). Pharaoh was where he was, when he was, by divine appointment.[8] Plainly, this does not make him any less a responsible agent, as the stories make abundantly clear, but it does underline what the Bible insists to be the case, that all 'history' is 'his story'.

8. Learning from the plagues: the God of all power

As Durham rightly noted above, it would be untrue to the history recorded in Exodus if we were to exclude the supernatural. Exodus 3:20 is quite explicit when the Lord says that he will 'strike the Egyptians with all the wonders that I will perform among them'. 'Wonders' here is *niplāʾōt*. Its

---

[8] See Fretheim on 9:16 (p. 124): "'If I had not the intention of your knowing that there is none like me . . . I would have cut you off" . . . the Lord's larger purposes have preserved Pharaoh . . . and stayed the death penalty justly deserved.' And in the light of verse 16, we might add, Yahweh's purpose for the whole earth.

general use in the Bible is to point to people or events beyond the ordinary or incapable of naturalistic explanation, things that speak of an agency outside earthly or human scope. It is possible, as many commentators point out, for the Nile inundation to carry down red earth, giving the river a red appearance,[9] but the record says explicitly that the water became blood, and the simultaneous transformation of water to blood in jars and tanks (7:19)[10] shows that the Nile inundation cannot have been the cause. It is also possible to make a connection between the rotting heaps of frogs (8:14[10]) and the breeding of gnats and flies, and then to see these insects as disease-bearing, causing cattle disease and human skin eruptions. But there the linkage stops. Boils do not lead to hail, nor hail to darkness. And throughout it all, the exactness of timing, the relation of event to foregoing prayer, and the magnitude of the successive catastrophes point to a supernatural, organizing cause.[11]

The cause was the Lord's *hand*, the hand regularly being symbolic of personal intervention and action, or the Lord's *finger* (8:19[15]), the finger suggesting a more detailed involvement (e.g. Isa. 2:8). It is the Lord who puts a protective covering over his people (8:23), banishes the flies (8:31[27]), acts at appointed times (9:5), brings in the locusts (10:4), guides the wind (10:13) and changes its direction (10:19). It is he who delivers blow after blow[12] upon the disobedient. Regularly, the Old Testament indicates the presence of the Lord by the motif of disruption or violence in the elements and forces within the created order.[13] For this reason one of its most frequent titles of God is 'Lord of hosts',[14] pointing to the fact that he

---

[9] If we had been meant to understand that the waters came to look like blood, Exodus would have said something like 2 Kgs 3:22–23.

[10] The Hebrew simply says 'and in the woods/wooden things and in the stones/stone things'. The traditional understanding of this as referring to wooden buckets and stone jars is simplest. Some suggest a reference to wooden and stone idols or religious objects with the implied drama of the priests pouring water over them and finding it had turned to blood.

[11] LaSor attempts to trace out a naturalistic sequence in the plagues (*Old Testament Survey*, pp. 139–140). It has the advantage of showing that the exercise is not possible. By what natural sequence can 'boils/skin eruptions' lead to 'hail'? K. A. Kitchen also tries to show a natural sequence and notes that the hail fits in with climatic conditions at that time of year ('Plagues of Egypt', in *NBD*, pp. 932–934). But this is far from showing why hail should follow from boils.

[12] The plague narrative uses the synonymous verbs √nākâ (3:20; 7:17; 9:15) and √nāgap (8:2[7:27]) with its cognate noun, *maggēpâ* (9:14), emphasizing the relentlessness of the onslaught.

[13] E.g. Exod. 19:16–18; Josh. 10:11; Ps. 18:7–15[8–16]; Isa. 30:30; Rev. 16:21.

[14] The Hebrew syntax usually expresses a genitive relation between 'Lord' and 'hosts', with the 'hosts' as something that belongs to the Lord, but it could equally be an appositional genitive, with 'hosts' defining something about the Lord. In Ps. 80:4[5] 'LORD God' and 'hosts' actually stand in apposition (cf. Ps. 59:5[6]; 80:7[8]; 84:8[9]) and must mean 'the Lord who is hosts' rather than who simply 'possesses hosts'. The NIV usually prefers 'LORD Almighty', e.g. Isa. 1:9. See G. A. F. Knight, *A Biblical Approach to the Doctrine of the Trinity* (Oliver and Boyd, 1953), p. 21.

contains, within himself, and therefore has at his disposal, every potentiality and power. Yahweh is *Lord* indeed.

9. Learning from the plagues: the Lord and the heart

One of the most puzzling aspects in the story of the plagues, and at the same time one of the most interesting and important, is the seeming moral dilemma that the Lord hardened Pharaoh's heart (e.g. 4:21; cf. 11:10) and then, in consequence of his hard heart, visited the plagues on him.

It might be helpful for us to set the scene for examining this by considering something else entirely – the hail (9:13–35). A scientist's account of a hailstorm might run something like this: as moist air rises and freezes, ice globules form and then increase in size as more water vapour freezes around them. When they become too heavy to be sustained by upward air currents, they fall as a hailstorm. When the Bible says that *at this time tomorrow I will send the worst hailstorm that has ever fallen on Egypt* (9:18), it is neither offering us an alternative mechanism for hail, nor denying what weather experts now know. As is its customary way of cutting past second causes to the great First Cause, the Bible is taking for granted that the Lord will act in accordance with, and by means of, the mechanisms he, as Creator, has built into creation to achieve that particular end. If, therefore, Exodus 9:13 had started by telling us that as a matter of fact ice globules are even at this moment forming, because by tomorrow the Lord would send heavy hail, we would not worry over some supposed contradiction. The Lord of all creation uses, manages, directs and controls the way creation operates. The physical world is his world, and – to come to our present topic – so is the moral world.

a. Choices, habits and character

Humans are so created that the choices they make contribute to forming character, and character thus formed promotes the making of similar choices in the future. Sometimes it takes a very long series of choices to produce a fixed habit, sometimes one choice is enough, sometimes a prolonged series of choices still leaves the issue in question open. Choosing and habit-forming are things we all know about. What none of us knows is when the 'point of no return' will be reached. None of us can say, 'One more sound choice and this good habit is permanently mine'; nor can we say, 'I can risk one more choice and still retain freedom to give up this bad habit.' Sadly, we can pass the point where freedom to change has been lost and still retain the illusion that 'I can give it up any time I want!' Thus, the situation in which Pharaoh found himself was not peculiar to him but is intrinsic to the human condition. Only God foresees the decisive, freedom-destroying choice, and only he knows at once when the choice that kills freedom has been made. Indeed, the Bible goes further and claims that because he is God, it is he that fixes that point.

b. The vocabulary of Pharaoh's heart

Exodus tells us three things about Pharaoh's heart: that the Lord hardened it; that Pharaoh hardened his heart (8:15[11]); and that his heart became hard (7:13). In other words, it is possible to tell two stories about Pharaoh's heart, just as about the hail. One is the story of Pharaoh's moral choices, whereby his heart became increasingly 'set in its ways', committed more and more irretrievably to a course of genocide regarding Israel. The other is a mere statement that from the perspective of the Lord as moral ruler of his world, the point of no return had been reached and the hardness of Pharaoh's heart must now be judgmentally imposed on him as the justly due consequence of what his own choices had made him. All three components of our moral universe are brought together in 9:34 – 10:1: '[Pharaoh] made his heart unresponsive – he himself and his servant' [√kābēd] (9:34); 'Pharaoh's heart was strongly resistant' [√ḥāzaq] (9:35); and 'I, for my part, will make his heart unresponsive along with his servants' hearts' [√kābēd] (10:1).[15] With these words we are forcefully reminded that choices are the privilege and price of being human. Our privilege is that of being responsible beings, recognizing moral values, called to make responsible choices, and given the opportunity and obligation to live in the light of the foreseeable consequences of our actions. The price we pay is that every choice, for good or ill, goes to fashioning our characters, and whether in the long or short term – or both – makes us answerable to the Judge of all the earth.

10. Learning from the plagues: God's people in God's hand

Possibly the most obvious truth arising from the history of the plagues is of the immense, irresistible power of the Lord, its total command of every

---

[15] On all this, see Motyer, *Look to the Rock*, pp. 196–197.

possible resource and its total sway over the whole field of human life – place, person and event. All things, and everything, all peoples and every person lie 'uncovered and laid bare before the eyes of him to whom we must give account' (Heb. 4:13).

Indeed so! But, marvellously, the same power acts to shelter and protect us, to guard us, even from what we justly deserve.

As the story sweeps on its way, it is more and more a single combat between Pharaoh and Moses. Virtually the last word we hear from the slave people, whom the Lord and Moses would free, comes at 5:21, and it is a word of revulsion directed at Moses, despairing over the entire enterprise which had done nothing but make the bad worse. Can we say then that the people deserved the deliverance that they received? What we can say with certainty is that by the wonder of divine mercy, they were the Lord's people, the subjects of his saving activity, the people destined for deliverance and, in the meantime, in a world under his just and awesome judgment, a people set apart, the objects of his loving, protective care (8:22–23).

Additional notes

8:22 √*Pālâ* (in the hiphil) means 'to distinguish or make separate'. In 33:16 (in the niphal) it means 'to be distinct[ive]'. 8:23 uses *pĕdût*, 'to set a protection in place'. This is the only use of *pĕdût* with this meaning. It comes from √*pādâ*, 'to pay a ransom price', which lies close to the notion of 'covering (by payment)'. In contrast to the immunity of Goshen, 8:24 says the infestation was 'dense' (*kābēd*, lit. 'heavy') in the palace. *Kābēd* is one of the words used of Pharaoh's heart becoming unresponsive. Its use to describe the swarm is ironic, as if the Lord said, 'You choose "heavy" do you? Try this!'

9:12 This seventh refusal can hardly fail to be related to the use of seven as the number of completeness. Why was hail chosen as the *full force of my plagues* (9:14)? Was it an unusual event in the benign climate of Egypt? K. A. Kitchen says it 'fits the climatic phenomena of these areas', i.e. Upper Egypt and the Delta ('Plagues of Egypt', in *NBD*, pp. 932–934). This storm, however, was not only unprecedented (9:18, 24) but also unusual as (lit.) 'fire went this way and that in the middle of the hail' (9:23). The verb is the hithpael of √*hālāk* and is used of Abraham walking 'through the length and breadth of the land' in Gen. 13:17 (cf. Job 1:7). But 9:24 adds that the

111

fire was (lit.) 'taking hold on itself' (the hithpael of √*lāqaḥ*), an expression found again in Ezek. 1:4, and which possibly means 'self-perpetuating'. It was not lightning flashing but actual fire kindling and rekindling itself without need of fuel to feed on and spreading in all directions. The coincidence of two such mutually excluding elements as hail and fire must have been extraordinarily frightening and destructive. Hebrew uses opposites to picture totality, and the narrative demonstrates here that Yahweh is Lord of all power. The hail narrative is the longest of the plague histories and is presented in a shapely form:

A¹ Yahweh, Moses and Pharaoh (13–19)
   B¹ Comment: obeying/disobeying (20–21)
      C The plague (22–25)
   B² Comment: the immunity of Goshen (26)
A² Pharaoh and Moses (27–30)
   B³ Comment: destruction/non-destruction (31–32)
A³ Moses and Pharaoh (33–34)
   B⁴ Comment: Pharaoh's heart (35)

Pharaoh's heart: divine action in hardening Pharaoh's heart is expressed by three verbs. √*Kābēd* means 'to be heavy'. To 'make the heart heavy' (the hiphil of the verb, 10:1) is to make it impenetrable, unresponsive. √*Ḥāzaq* means 'to be strong' and carries the same meaning as our 'headstrong', self-willed, stubborn (4:21; 9:12; 10:20, 27; 11:10; 14:4, 8, 17). And √*qāšâ*, 'to be hard, rough', goes on to mean 'recalcitrant, dismissive of the feelings of others' (7:3). Pharaoh's own decision-making in setting himself against the Lord's word uses only √*kābēd* (8:15[11], 32[28]; 9:34). Cf. 7:22; 9:12, *he would not listen* (lit. 'he did not set his heart'), i.e. he would not pay attention. The resultant condition of the hardened heart uses √*ḥāzaq* (7:13, 22; 8:19[15]; 9:35) and √*kābēd* (7:14; 9:7).

9:16 *Power* is *kôaḥ*. Cf. Zech. 4:6, where *ḥayil* ('might/resources') and *kôaḥ* (the 'power/ability' that can use the resources) lie side by side.

10:1–20 The account of the plague of locusts is particularly telling. Once again, there is a religious 'edge' to the event in that the Egyptians worshipped Senehem, who supposedly protected Egypt from such pests. The Lord is master over every force, political or religious, earthly or supernatural, that might either oppose or challenge him. His purposes are not hindered by Pharaoh's opposition, Moses' inadequacies or Israel's unworthiness. So we see that even as huge and overmastering a thing as the locust plague is totally in his hand: he decrees its onset, sets its bounds and determines its duration. The narrative is presented with style:

A¹ The Lord, Pharaoh, Pharaoh's heart (1–2)

   B¹ Moses comes to Pharaoh: the plague threatened (3–6)

      C¹ Pharaoh negotiates, arrogantly, autocratically (7–11)

         D The locusts, exactly as threatened (note *all*; 12–15)

      C² Pharaoh pleads (16–17)

   B² Moses leaves Pharaoh: prays against the plague (18–19)

A² The Lord, Pharaoh, Pharaoh's heart (20)

In verses 1–2, note 'before him' (1; NIV *among them*) and *that you* [pl.] *may know* (2). The acts of God in judgment (on Egypt) and mercy (protecting Israel) establish a testimony to him. In verse 2 the NIV and ESV have *dealt harshly* and the NKJV has 'the mighty things I have done' to represent √*'ālal* in the hithpael. The base meaning is simply 'to act', and the context must decide what adverb qualifies the action. Cf. Num. 22:29 (possibly 'to make fun of', 'to treat dismissively or maliciously'); 1 Sam. 31:4 ('to treat unfeelingly' as with a plaything); Judg. 19:25. In Exod. 10:2 a possible meaning is 'acted at my own will and pleasure'. The darkness (10:21–29) strikes at Amon-Ra, the personification of the sun and chief deity of Egypt. Yahweh is Lord of the ordered processes of creation, to do with them as he will. On the breaking off of negotiations on both sides in verses 28–29, Durham (p. 144) remarks, 'The moment is like the scattering and confusion at Babel . . . the command to Abraham to sacrifice Isaac . . . the destruction of Jerusalem in 586 . . . the moment of the death of Jesus . . . Nothing more can be done . . . Yet the promises are the promises of *God*, so how *can* nothing more be done?'

Exodus 11:1 – 12:42

11. Why the Passover?

Four features, of varied importance, distinguish the tenth plague from its nine predecessors. First, as far as Israel's liberation is concerned, its success was announced beforehand (11:1). As we have seen, the nine preceding acts of God were probationary exercises. The Lord who knows all made no secret that they would not lead to Israel's deliverance (e.g. 3:19). Now, however, that period of moral probation was over and the die had been cast. The tenth act of God would succeed where the others had failed (cf. 12:30–33).

Second, this was to be a work of God without any mediation of Moses or Aaron. Previously, the rod of God had been lifted up (e.g. 7:19) or some other symbolic act performed (e.g. 9:8), but now the brothers were just as much spectators as anyone else. All ten of the disasters inflicted on the Egyptians were acts of God, but the final one was outstandingly so, for in its performance the Lord in person entered Egypt to exact a just judgment (11:4; 12:12). In this regard the sequence of plagues illustrates the awesome biblical truth that the final issue for recalcitrant humanity is to come face to face with God. Divine patience and forbearance wait while every avenue of moral probation is offered, tried and exhausted, but then comes the point which Jesus underlined in his parable, when he said, 'Last of all, he sent his son' (Matt. 21:37). The word of God cannot be refused endlessly. There always has to be an end, a meeting with the God whom our refusals have offended to the point of finality.

The third distinctive of the tenth plague lies alongside this – and indeed is at the heart of these central events of the exodus. Ever since the fourth plague, the people of Israel had been set apart from the Egyptians (8:22), but in each case it was the onset of the plague itself that made their distinct status evident. In the case of the plague on the livestock, Pharaoh had to send messengers to establish that Israelite cattle had been exempted (9:7). Now, however, before the onset of the tenth plague, Israel was commanded to put the public mark of blood on the houses where they were living (12:7, 13). Previously they had been segregated by the Lord without any cooperative or obedient act of their own,[1] but now, by command of the Lord, Israel must take a stand, self-declared as the people under the blood of the lamb.

The final distinctive mark of this tenth plague is the lengthy introduction given to it (11:1–10). Within the structure of the book of Exodus, these verses serve a double purpose. On the one hand, 11:9 and 10 form a 'match' respectively with 7:3–4 and 6, so that we can see 6:28 – 7:7 as a preface to the history of the nine acts and 11:1–10 as its conclusion. This also serves, of course, to set the coming tenth act decisively apart from the nine and, therefore, also to underline the Passover as the new beginning it claims to be (12:2). On the other hand, however, since the tenth act is substantially the subject of 11:1–10, the passage is also a preface to what is to follow, and the structure of 11:1 – 12:42 bears this out.

1. The impotent king and the sovereign Lord

If we think, then, of 11:1–10 as a preface, its main topics are the announcement of the final plague (11:1), the granting of favour to Israel when they made requests of the Egyptians (11:2–3), the coming of the Lord to Egypt (11:4), the nature of the coming plague and its timing (11:4–5),[2] the great cry of the Egyptians (11:6),[3] the command to leave Egypt (11:8) and a concluding comment that Pharaoh had not changed but was still resistant to the word of the Lord (11:9). These topics reappear in the epilogue of 12:29–42 – the coming of the Lord and the plague enacted as threatened at the time stated (12:29), the great cry (12:30), the terrified Egyptians

---

[1] See 8:22 – 'I will segregate' (NIV, 'deal differently with').

[2] Currid (vol. 1, p. 234) notes the timing of midnight in connection with 'The Hymn to the Aton', which mentions the Egyptians' dread of the night because it meant that the sun god had departed to the underworld, leaving Egypt unprotected. We should note as significant the extension of the plague from humans to beasts (11:5). Egyptian theology identified the gods with animals and portrayed them with animal heads. The death of the firstborn animals exposed the impotence of the gods.

[3] Cf. 12:30. The Hebrew is *ṣĕ'āqâ*, and when we recall that the exodus events began when the Lord heard Israel's *ṣĕ'āqâ* (3:7), we can see what a transformation has taken place.

commanding Israel to leave (12:31–34) and the Lord granting Israel favour when they asked for gifts (12:35–36). There is also a concluding comment recording Israel's departure from Egypt, so to speak, 'on cue' (12:37–42).

This structuring is deliberate, and the repetition involved is full of meaning. The first point is that the Lord does exactly as he says. He is a *sovereign* Lord, who announces his plans and fulfils them, makes his will known and performs it. He forgets nothing of what he forecasts, whether promise or threat: all happens according to his stated intentions (cf. Ps. 33:9). Second, those who will not bow to his word must bend to his judgment. God's foreknowledge told him that he would stretch out his mighty hand only to meet mighty resistance but, plainly, he was in no hurry to implement the final showdown he foresaw (3:19–20). As 2 Peter 3:9 says, 'The Lord . . . is patient with you, not wanting anyone to perish, but everyone to come to repentance' – Pharaoh included. But eventually the Lord's patience comes to an end, for he is a God of justice (Isa. 30:18) as well as mercy.

2. Passover faith

When Moses' negotiations with Pharaoh came to their abrupt end, nothing at all on earth had changed. Understandably, Moses' patience, for once, snapped, and he left the king's court in a flaming rage (lit. 'in heat of anger'; 11:8). To be sure, he had been given a new word from the Lord, but Pharaoh's resistance was unchanged (11:9), and the set of his heart was just as firmly opposed to the liberation of his slaves (11:10). It is against this background that we enter the sacred precincts of chapter 12 of Exodus. As far as outward appearances were concerned, the plagues had failed to achieve their purpose, and, more than that, Moses had failed and the Lord himself had failed. The slaves were still slaves, and freedom seemed as elusive and distant as ever. How could Israel have ever accepted that, nevertheless, this was a great new beginning (12:2) and that (of all unlikely – even absurd – things) their deliverance would hinge on what they were to do with a lamb and its blood?

What an act of faith it was, then, for Moses to command the Passover and for Israel to accept and obey his instructions (12:21). Yet, biblically, there was nothing special about what they did, for this is what 'faith' is – not a leap in the dark, but a leap into the light. There was darkness in abundance, all the misery engendered by slavery that had become even more deeply established, but in the darkness shone the *proved* beam of the word of the Lord – and that is the crucial point. Faith is action taken on evidence, driven by conviction. The evidence was the demonstrated trustworthiness of the Lord's word, verified in the course of the nine acts, and the resulting conviction was the holding fast to that trustworthiness and believing that the Lord was able to do what he said he would, that his promises would stand. The essence of faith is the trust that obeys, and this was the point to which Israel came in Exodus 12: knowing unmistakably how great was the power of the enemy, equally aware of their own weakness and helplessness, yet ready to pit all on bare obedience to the command and promise of God (cf. Rom. 4:18–22; Heb. 11:11–12; NIV, not NKJV or ESV).

3. The Passover narrative (12:1–28)

The account of the institution of the Passover begins with a directive and explanatory word from the Lord to Moses and Aaron (1–20). This is one of only two occasions when it is specified that the Lord spoke to Moses (lit.) 'in the land of Egypt' (1).[4] The emphasis is important for, as we shall see more particularly in verses 25–28, the Passover was intended specifically as a rite for Israel *in Egypt*. Once they had left Egypt, the Passover could not be repeated, only recalled and memorialized.

The Lord spoke to Moses about two matters: the Passover and its meaning (2–14; note how *This month* and *This . . . day* at the beginning and end form an *inclusio*), and the accompanying 'feast' of unleavened bread (15–20; this section has the references to unleavened bread as an *inclusio*). This can be broken down as follows:

The Passover (1–14)

    A^1 New beginning (2)
        B^1 The lamb (3–11)
            C The Lord the Judge (12)
        B^2 The blood of the lamb (13)
    A^2 Perpetual memorial (14)

---

[4] Cf. 6:28. If we are to find significance in this (as probably we should), the occasion was the renewal of Moses' commission. When Moses failed for the first time he fled to Midian (2:15). Here, following his second failure, the Lord hastened to him, keeping him in Egypt and renewing his revelation and vocation.

The seven-day feast (15–20)

   A¹ Seven days: no leaven (15)

      B¹ Two special days (16)

         C   Meaning (17)

      B² Two special days (18)

   A² Seven days: no leaven (19–20)

Leaving aside other details for the moment, the first important emphasis that we notice is on the Passover being a new beginning that must never be forgotten (2, 14). This is something that is not said about any of the plagues. The only other matter marked by the need for perpetual remembrance is the Lord's name (3:15), which gives some indication of how important the once-for-all, unique shedding of the blood of the Passover lamb is.[5] Sacrifice had, of course, a history stretching back a long way (Gen. 4:4) and had been accompanied by a complicated ritual and covenant significance for some time (Gen. 15:9–18), but never before had such a strong emphasis been laid on the shedding of blood. The Passover lamb truly constituted a new start.

4. The Feast of Unleavened Bread

The opinion of commentators that there was no original link between the feasts of Passover and Unleavened Bread has no foundation outside their own imaginations, and why they should want to support this fancy would not be easy to say.[6] It is markedly unperceptive to see no logic in the juxtaposition of the two feasts. The Passover has two distinct orientations. On the one hand, it is embedded in the events that took place on the particular night in Egypt when the Egyptian firstborn died under the judgment of God and those of Israel did not. We might call this the 'in Egypt' aspect of the Passover. On the other hand, Passover has an 'out of Egypt' aspect. Before the Passover, Israel could not leave Egypt; after the Passover they could not stay. This was not only because the Egyptians would not allow them to stay, but also, and fundamentally, because the Passover was a feast for pilgrims (12:11). The Israelites ate the Passover

---

[5] Compare the acknowledging of Jesus as the 'Lamb of God' at his baptism (John 1:29, 32–33) and the revelation of God as the Holy Trinity, Father, Son and Holy Spirit (Matt. 3:16–17).

[6] Cf. Durham (pp. 156–160) on Exod. 12:14–20.

meal as those committed to go walking with God. It is to this latter aspect of the Passover that the Old Testament constantly relates the Feast of Unleavened Bread.[7] The fact that the Feast of Unleavened Bread memorializes the circumstances of Israel's leaving Egypt (12:39) in no way conflicts with the fact that they were thus, as it were, inadvertently or perforce obeying a foregoing command of the Lord through Moses. Rather, just as the actual circumstances of their wilderness journey led to the memorializing of the Feast of Tabernacles (Lev. 23:39–43), so the readily foreseeable circumstances of their immediate post-Passover days were anticipated by the regulations of the Feast of Unleavened Bread and, thereafter, catered for its continued remembrance.

5. Leaven

It is not really until the New Testament that an explicit symbolism of leaven, or yeast, is enunciated in the Bible (1 Cor. 5:7–8), but once it is stated it makes sense. The first Passover constituted a new beginning of enormous proportions, and, inevitably, that emphasis continued. Paul, therefore, picking up on the New Testament insistence that the Lord Jesus is the Lamb of God, summons Christians to a decisive new beginning in Christ. The 'old yeast' of 'malice and wickedness' (*kakia* and *ponēria* – two broad words for any and every sort of 'wrong' in our lives) must go, to be replaced by the 'unleavened' reality of 'sincerity and truth'. The Old Testament, however, does not draw out this symbolism, and, indeed, it would not be appropriate to import it just like that into our understanding of Exodus 12, for it is not until the episode of the golden calf in chapter 32 that sin *in the life of Israel* comes to the fore as a fundamental issue. The Passover idea of 'leaven', then, is one of decisive newness: the old has passed away and all things have become new. So indeed it was.

6. Passover effectiveness

Having said all that, we are left with the question of why the Passover was necessary at all. The promise of liberation was linked with the tenth

---

[7] Cf. Exod. 13:3–10; 23:15; 34:18; Deut. 16:3. Other references simply to the existence and obligation of the feast are Lev. 23:6; Num. 28:17; Deut. 16:8.

plague, after which Pharaoh was to let the people go (11:1), so why not 'simply' have the plague and then the exodus?

In order to answer this question, we need to recall two things. First, according to the key passage of 6:2–8, the Lord had two purposes for Israel in Egypt, and liberation was only one of them. His promise was that 'I will bring you out from under the yoke of the Egyptians' and 'I will take you as my own people', and, allied to this, two verbs are used: 'free' and 'redeem' (6). The tenth plague achieved the first part of the promise, liberation and deliverance, but that still left the people's relationship to the Lord to be established by redemption. It was this that was to be the distinctive work of the Passover.

Second, we need to recall one of the distinctive circumstances surrounding the tenth plague which we noted at the start of this chapter – that it was accomplished without the mediation of either Moses or Aaron and was simply achieved by the coming of the Lord himself to Egypt (11:4) and by his direct, personal action in judgment (12:12). This intervention changed the whole situation, for when Yahweh entered Egypt as absolute Lord and Judge, Israel's problem was no longer how to escape Pharaoh but how to be safe before such a God.[8] Indeed, as the Passover history is recounted, this becomes the sole issue. The passage does not mention sin, on the one hand, nor the holiness of God, on the other. Even in the case of Pharaoh, while, of course, we cannot help seeing his plight against the background of a prolonged refusal to obey, this is not specifically raised. To allow sin a central place would be to distort a narrative in which the real issue is that unprotected, unsheltered humanity cannot stand in the presence of the Lord the Judge. Subsequent passages in Exodus will face the particular question of sin, and the Passover itself will be shown to have a special place in the system of sacrifices, with sin and atonement as their focal point, but in Exodus 12 all these matters are for the future. This is a single-issue chapter: 'How shall I, whose native sphere is dark, whose mind is dim, before the Ineffable appear, and on my naked spirit bear the Uncreated Beam?'[9] In Exodus 12, as in this hymn, the issue of sin cannot but lie plainly in the background. Had Pharaoh not refused and

---

[8] We can get the 'feel' of the situation in Egypt by thinking of the second coming of the Lord Jesus. Until that takes place, people have the option of considering all sorts of issues as their priorities – international problems, social issues, personal moral crises – but once he comes everything else will dissolve before the single issue of how they stand with him and what he purposes.

[9] From the hymn 'Eternal Light!' by T. Binney.

rebelled against the Lord's word, he would not at this point have been in the thick of divine judgment. Were we not fallen creatures, each of us with our personal record of sin, our native sphere would not be 'dark' nor our minds 'dim'. Nevertheless, for clarity of thought, we must defer this secondary question, however important, and focus on how, if at all, we may stand safely in the presence of God.

7. The blood

The hymn writer quoted above answered his own question by saying, 'There is a way for man to rise to that sublime abode: an offering and a sacrifice . . .' To put it in terms of Exodus 12 this is expressed by the blood of the lamb, for the Lord says, *when I see the blood, I will pass over you* (13). It is the blood which has the astonishing power to solve the problem of acceptance before God. Without the blood, all Egypt suffered a token but frightful judgment (30), but, having been marked by the blood, Israel was *passed over* (27). How can this be?

The explanation that emerges from the story has four aspects.[10]

a. The satisfied God

If the Lord's favour had been the ruling principle on Passover night there would have been no need at all for either the Passover ceremonies or for Israel having to hide away in their own houses with such strict orders not to emerge. The story of the six immediately preceding plagues proves that the Lord needed no markers or other aids to know where his people were and to exclude them from what was to take place. He knew the boundaries of their land (8:22), he could distinguish their cattle from the Egyptians' (9:4, 6), he could shelter them from the hailstorm (9:26) and give them light while Egypt was shrouded in palpable darkness (10:23). Such a God has no need of signposts. Therefore, the blood on the doors must have had some other significance, and this is borne out by the fact that it is not 'when I see you' that the Lord will pass over, but *when I see the blood* (12:13).

The God of judgment, who came to impose a penalty of death justly due, saw the blood and 'passed over' in peace. It may sound hazardous to speak of a 'change of mind' taking place in God, but the Bible allows us to see the

---

[10] Care needs to be taken when deducing truths from stories. Cf. V. Philips Long, *The Art of Biblical History* (Apollos, 1994); T. Longman, *Literary Approaches to Biblical Interpretation* (Apollos, 1987); S. Greidanus, *The Modern Preacher and the Ancient Text* (Eerdmans/IVP, 1988), chapters 4, 9.

Lord from a human perspective. It does this by using terms which suggest a likeness to human form (anthropomorphy) and human feelings (anthropopathy). In the present context there seems nothing for it but to say that the God who entered in wrath 'passed over' in peace. Something 'satisfied'[11] the God of judgment, so that he no longer found it necessary to exact the judicial penalty. The rest of the Bible teaches us to use other words besides 'satisfaction'. For example, there is 'reconciliation', the attitude of the judge towards the accused, turning from the alienation and offence caused to him and exercising acceptance with equanimity; and, above all, 'propitiation', the allaying and soothing away of wrath by whatever means the situation requires.

b. The people kept in safety

At three points in chapter 12 the safety of those within the blood-marked houses is brought to the fore. In verses 8–10 their sense of the safety is evident in that on Passover night they were feasting; in verse 13 this is undergirded with a divine promise, *I will pass over you . . . No destructive plague will touch you*; and in verses 22–23 there is a formal statement that behind the blood-marked doors they were guaranteed safety, for no destroyer could enter.[12] Objectively, they were made safe (or saved) by the blood of the lamb. The Lord saw the blood and passed over. Subjectively, they were made safe (or saved) by faith, the faith by which they believed and acted upon the word of God. They obeyed his commands to choose and kill the lamb, to smear its blood and to take refuge in the blood-marked houses, and they believed his promise that under that shed blood and within those houses they would be secure and immune.[13]

c. The lamb is a substitute for the Lord's firstborn

The time has come to ask the inevitable question of how the blood of the lamb could possibly have had such dramatic powers that it could turn the Lord away from judgment to satisfaction and provide security for those under its shelter in a night of judgment. The answer lies in bringing

---

[11] I.e. satisfied the Lord's just requirements and met the demands of his law.

[12] On the idea of 'the destroyer', cf. 2 Sam. 24:15–17; 2 Kgs 19:32–37. In Exod. 12:23 it is said that the Lord *will not permit* – like all else, the destroyer is under divine control and direction (cf. Job 1 – 2).

[13] The same objectivity and subjectivity is discernible in the salvation that comes through Christ. As Rom. 3:25 says, Christ was (objectively) 'set forth as a propitiation', i.e. a means of allaying, soothing and satisfying God's righteous wrath (NKJV), and that salvation comes to us (subjectively) 'to be received by faith'.

together two elements in the story. The first is present but easily over-looked. According to 12:30 *there was not a house without someone dead.* The judgment of God had swept through the houses of the Egyptians, from the royal family at the top to the single-parent family of the slave girl at the bottom (29). This is undeniably true and, indeed, is central to the narrative. What is not so obvious is that there was also 'someone dead' in the houses of the Israelites too, for the lamb had died and had been brought into the houses to provide the main part of the Passover feast (7).

d. Exactitude and perfection

The second element that we need to take into account is the way in which the lamb was chosen. The Exodus account uses four verses to elaborate this single matter (3–6) and thereby indicates that the making of a correct choice was a thing of primary importance. Precise instructions were given covering every stage of the proceedings to ensure that everything was done in accordance with the will and purpose of God.

First of all, it was established that the privileges conferred by the lamb belonged to *the whole community*[14] *of Israel* (3).[15] This was achieved by placing a great deal of emphasis on the matter of the sufficiency and death of the lamb for Israel. The lamb had to be chosen with extreme care so that it matched as exactly as was humanly possible those who would partake of it (3–4a). There was the general computation of *one for each household,* reflecting the principle of family inherent in the Lord's various covenant provisions,[16] but this was then refined further to take into account those families which would not manage to consume a whole lamb by them-selves and who were, therefore, permitted to make common cause with other households in a similar situation. In this way the identification between lamb and the number of participants was kept continually in the foreground.

---

[14] This is the first time Israel is called a 'community' or 'congregation' (Heb. *'ēdâ*). The word is used almost 150 times in the OT, by far the most often in Exodus and Numbers and almost always with reference to the corporate entity of Israel (but cf. Judg. 14:8; Ps. 68:30[31]). *'Ēdâ* does not necessarily refer to Israel gathered for worship but to the people's distinctness as a community.

[15] The issue of whether or not the Egyptians were made aware of this provision for safety is not raised in Exod. 12 and is, therefore, not a question we can answer.

[16] At the time of the great flood, the ark was said to be for 'you and your sons and your wife and your sons' wives with you' (Gen. 6:18). The wives and sons did not enter in their own right but only 'with you', because they were part of the family of the covenant man, Noah. Similarly, the covenant promise to Abram included the precious words (lit.) 'to be God to you and to your seed after you' (Gen. 17:7; cf. Exod. 20:6; Prov. 20:7; Acts 2:39).

It was not just numbers that were taken into account but needs also – *You are to determine the amount of lamb needed in accordance with what each person will eat* (4b). We can imagine the earnestness of discussion this would have involved, especially if two or more households had combined, with the almost anxious gathering of wives, the questions about levels of appetite and so on. It is a very human scene, but one full of crucial significance, for such care was taken to achieve as precise an equivalence as was humanly possible between the lamb, on the one hand, and the number and the needs of those who would eat it, on the other.

As far as the animal[17] itself was concerned, it had to be a year-old male and *without defect* (5). This insistence on perfection runs right through the sacrificial code. Malachi 1:6–14 explains that what is blemished is unacceptable to the Lord (13), unworthy of his greatness and brings a curse on the one offering it (14). By contrast, the perfection of the Lord Jesus Christ is predicted (Isa. 11:5; 53:7–9), described (1 Pet. 1:19; 2:21–22) and alluded to in the narrative of his trial (Luke 23:4, 14–15, 22, 41, 47). Only what is perfect is acceptable to God, as being commensurate with his dignity, but it seems very likely that behind the demand for 'perfection' lies the truth that while the imperfect can die for its own sins, only the sinless can bear the sins of another.

Even in matters of timing, there were precise instructions. The Passover lamb was to be chosen on the tenth day (3) but not killed until the fourteenth (6). This is an important point and indicates the care that was to be exercised in finding exactly the right beast. Hurried action or last-minute, panic preparation may have led to mistakes, and this was a matter into which no mistake must be allowed to intrude. Those responsible for organizing the sacrifice had to count the heads, assess the needs and, in a time frame that allowed for calm deliberation, examine the animal for flaws and set it apart. Only when all this had been done, and the appointed hour had come, were they to perform the sacrifice.[18]

The final element which bears on the equivalence between the lamb and those whom its blood would shelter is the regulation that anything

---

[17] We always think in terms of a 'lamb', but the Exodus account clearly says the animal could have been taken from either the sheep or the goats (5b). The Hebrew *śeh* (3, see NIV mg.) is non-specific and hence Durham (pp. 151, 153) has 'a flock-animal'.

[18] Cf. the death of Jesus (Acts 2:23; 3:18; Eph. 1:11; 3:11; 2 Tim. 1:9; 1 Pet. 1:20; Rev. 13:8).

left over from the Passover meal had to be burnt (8–10).[19] This means that the sole purpose and use of the lamb was to provide Passover cover and Passover nourishment for the people whose number and needs it matched, and once that had been achieved, it was not available for anything or anyone else. It was chosen precisely for the people and, having met their needs, had no other purpose or function so nothing of it was to remain once the meal was over.

e. Substitute

It has been necessary to approach this key idea of the lamb as substitute slowly, because this is the way the story does it, taking time in eight verses (3–10) to make it clear that the chosen lamb was an exact equivalent to the number and needs of its people and it was *as such* that the lamb died.

There seems, however, to be a flaw in the argument. For after all, in the houses of Egypt it was 'only' the firstborn son who died and, had any Israelite families neglected the Passover way of salvation, then, presumably, 'only' the eldest son in those houses would have died. If we are thinking in terms of substitution, then surely it would seem that the lamb was a replacement death for that of the firstborn alone? This is to forget, however, the point from which the whole enterprise of sending Moses into Egypt started. From the beginning it was revealed as a 'contest of the firstborn', for the Lord tells Pharaoh that 'Israel is my firstborn son' (4:22). Pharaoh's firstborn is a single individual; the Lord's firstborn is the corporate entity of Israel. The people were commanded to *take a lamb* (3) and to be sure that the chosen lamb matched the number and needs of the whole community. So, when the lamb died, it was as a substitute for the Lord's firstborn, the people whom he had chosen, and purposed to redeem.

---

[19] The lamb died by the knife and, in the end, was consumed by the fire. In the full sacrificial system that was to come these elements were symbolic – just as indeed Gen. 22:6–12 show that they were present in the Old Testament understanding of sacrifice from the earliest times. By the laying on of his hands, the person making the offering laid his sins on the head of the sacrificial beast so that when he killed it, it could be said to have laid down its life in payment for his sin (Lev. 1:4; 3:2; 4:4; 16:21–22). The fire on the altar spoke of the wrath of God against sin, and the burning of the beast, in whole or part, spoke of the satisfaction of that wrath. The knife and the fire, therefore, spoke respectively of a death to sin and the propitiation of wrath. The insistence that the lamb was to be roasted and not eaten raw (9) has the same significance: it had to be eaten after having passed through the fire. Sacrifice was practised from the earliest biblical times (Gen. 4:4) and, for all we know, the symbolism of knife and fire may always have been current and, therefore, recognized by the first participants in the Passover. Only the element of propitiation, however, is stressed by the narrative.

f. By the death of the lamb, salvation was actually accomplished

The blood that was smeared around the doors of the Israelite houses was a visible token that a life had been laid down in that place. Entering and remaining behind that door signified the personal appropriation by faith of all that the shed blood meant and had accomplished. We see this clearly in 12:11: Passover was a late-afternoon/early-evening meal, but it was to be eaten *in haste* by those dressed for the morning – a supper eaten by those taking a quick breakfast. In other words, the Passover was eaten by those already free to leave Egypt, already liberated and redeemed. Durham puts it well: 'Not in the relaxed dress of home, but in travelling attire; not at ease around a table, but with walking-stick in hand; not in calm . . . but in haste' (p. 154). In other words, they were not 'in slippers and dressing gown' as would befit supper, but booted, girded and ready as those equipped for the day ahead.

8. Free at last

And so it was.

The story of the Israelites' departure is told, with remarkable and moving restraint, in two parts: the tenth plague (29–30) and the frenzy which followed as the Egyptians understandably panicked and harried Israel out of the land (31–36); and the actual exodus itself (37–42). Typically of the book of Exodus, both sections are presented with balanced artistry:[20]

> **The tenth plague (29–36)**
> **A¹** People under judgment (29–30)
>   'The LORD struck' (29, *yhwh hikkâ*)
>   The Egyptians bereft (30)
>   **B** Reactions (31–34)
>   **b¹** Pharaoh (31–32)[21]

---

[20] Even if this book is not the place for an examination of the documentary approach to the Pentateuch, an occasional sidelong glance cannot be avoided. The structured approach to 12:29–36, 37–42 offered here is an indication that a different, and more fruitful, understanding is possible. Durham (pp. 166, 170) assigns verses 29–34 to J and verses 35–36 to E, but notes that 'the assignment to E is based on little more than the theory that E is *the* source for the "despoiling" tradition'. Noth and Coates, however, assign verses 35–36 to J. Durham assigns verses 37–39 'generally to J', but Davies says verse 37 was 'inserted by a D-redactor'. And, after all that, dare one ask, are we any better off?

[21] Pharaoh here calls the slaves *the Israelites* for the first time. To call them 'Hebrews' probably meant, in his mouth, a despised underclass. Has he at last in his panic recognized them as a distinct people? Can we

    b² Egyptian (33)

    b³ Israelite (34)²²

A² People under blessing (35–36)

    'The LORD gave' (*yhwh nātan*)

    The Egyptians despoiled (36)

The exodus (37–42)

A¹ Israel journeyed out (37)

    B¹ The camp followers (38)

A² Israel driven out (39)

    B² The Lord's hosts (40–41)²³

A³ Israel brought out (42)

Notes

The sense of tense panic in 12:29–36 contrasts markedly with the calmness of verses 38–42, where there is a cool sense of everything proceeding according to plan. Even verse 39, with its reference to being *driven out*, speaks volumes more of Egyptian terror than of Israelite agitation. Yet, obviously, there must have been some agitation, otherwise why would the Lord's command have included the idea of what might be called 'concerned urgency' (11)? To the Israelites themselves the whole exit from Egypt may have felt more 'chancy' and opportunistic than we often take into account. The people had had too much recent experience of Pharaoh's capacity as a mental quick-change artist. And, as later events were to show, he had not improved (14:5). Numbers 33:3–4 makes the interesting observation that Israel took the chance to get out of Egypt while the Egyptians were otherwise engaged with burying their dead. But it also says that they went (lit.) 'with a high hand, before the eyes of all the Egyptians'. We cannot

take *worship the LORD* as some sort of recognition of the God whose authority he had previously denied (5:2)? Is the request to *bless me* an acknowledgment that the gods of Egypt were impotent to restore the kingdom? All this would be very charitable, for nowhere does Pharaoh actually repent, and his later actions (14:5) are a surer indication of the cast of his mind at this point.

²² Commentators treat verse 34 (cf. 39) as a later attempt to explain how the Feast of Unleavened Bread came to be linked with Passover. According to Exodus, the link arose from the historical events themselves. Verse 34 is a demonstration of the Lord's providence by which he made it possible for the people to do (within the stressful circumstances of that time) what he wished them to do and to live as the Passover people. Thus, circumstances, in the hand of God, secured obedience to the command about yeast.

²³ Verses 40–41 give the exact figure of 430 years for the Israelites' stay in Egypt. Gen. 15:13 says 400 years and 15:16, four generations. To find a 'contradiction' here is a sure sign of being hard to please. The sojourn was sketched, prospectively, in broad terms as 400 years, but the clarity of retrospect made the exact figure 430.

excuse the 'high hand' of a touch of arrogance, triumphalism and self-confidence. It was that sort of occasion – even if wiser heads in the departing companies thought in their hearts that it was now or never.

But go they did, and the Lord did exactly as he said he would do (cf. 11:1–10), so that even those who thought in opportunistic terms were in fact walking in total security. The Israelites knew they were going out (37), some of the Egyptians thought they were driving them out (39), but the 'real' fact was that they were being 'brought out' by the divine hand (42). Even the seemingly most hazardous situation still finds those who have sheltered under the blood of the lamb safe in the Lord's care, and moving according to his predetermined plan.

Additional notes

11:1–10 Commentators sometimes find an awkward 'seam' between chapters 10 and 11. At 10:29 Moses breaks off negotiations with Pharaoh, but at 11:4 we find him still speaking, and he does not appear to leave Pharaoh's presence until 11:8b. For this reason, Durham (p. 149), for example, supposes a lost introduction to chapter 11. We need to remember, however, that we do not know the 'mechanisms' of revelation and inspiration. Isa. 38:4 shows that the word of God for a particular situation can come instantaneously, and this seems to be what happened here. Still in Pharaoh's presence (at 10:29), Moses became aware of the word of the Lord, perhaps a recollection of 3:19–22 and a prompting by the Lord to voice an oracle based on 3:21–22. Cf. Cassuto (p. 132), who says Moses 'recalled directives that were given him long ago'.

11:2 The error perpetrated by KJV in 11:2 of 'borrow' lives on. Durham (p. 148) refers to 'the theft of the Egyptians' valuables'! The verb √šā'al means 'to ask'. The situation was replicated in the subsequent regulation about providing for the freed slave in Deut. 15:13–15. Once more, this is what the Lord had said would happen (Gen. 15:14; Exod. 3:21–22).

11:4 The *I will go throughout Egypt* here should be compared with Gen. 41:45. In the Genesis account Joseph had just been given virtually pharaonic powers, and the way he took up and began to exercise this absolute authority over Egypt is expressed as 'Joseph went throughout [lit. 'out over'] the land of Egypt'. The same verb (√yāṣā') is used in 11:4, where the Lord says (lit.), 'About midnight, I am going to go out [√yāṣā'] into the middle of Egypt.' In other words, this was not just a coming into the land but a taking and exercising of dominant authority. Note the threefold exercise of the Lord's judgmental sovereignty over the land, life (human and animal) and gods. His dominance covers all things – territorial, animate and spiritual.

11:8 The same verbs (√šālaḥ and √gāraš) are used in 11:1 and 6:1, both in the piel mode, to mean respectively, 'to dismiss, send away [with authority]' and 'to drive out'. Things happened exactly as the Lord had said they would. See also the piel of √gāraš in 10:11 for the dramatic change in Pharaoh.

12:1–20 Some commentators (e.g. Hyatt [pp. 132–133] and Fretheim [p. 137]) see the Passover as a pre-Mosaic rite among nomadic shepherds, adapted by Moses to take on a new significance. Pretty much the only possible evidence for this is the brevity of Moses' command to (lit.) 'slaughter the Passover' (12:21), as if it was something the elders already knew all about. This is typical of the literalism with which the Bible is taken when it suits a particular theory, whereas the same commentators are elsewhere willing to sit loose to what is written – or to rewrite it. There is no reason to suppose that Moses did not at this point rehearse for the elders all that the Lord had said to him in verses 1–20, but in the record it is presented in summary form as 'slaughter the Passover'.

12:5 There seems to be no explanation why the Passover lamb had to be male. The same gender-insistence is found for the burnt offering (Lev. 1:3; 22:19) and the leader's sin offering (Lev. 4:23). By contrast, the peace or fellowship offering could be of either gender (Lev. 3:1, 6), and the sin offering of the 'ordinary' person had to be female (Lev. 4:28, 32; 5:6). Some suggest that in these matters the Lord was being deliberately considerate of economics, since the burnt offering was a twice-daily obligation and male animals were less valuable than female. A. Bonar (*Commentary on Leviticus* [London, 1874], p. 4) suggests that the fact that the Passover animal was male anticipated the maleness of the Lamb of God when, in the fullness of time, he came. This would fit with the maleness of the burnt offering, a symbol of perfect consecration and obedience, whereas the peace offering, focusing on the people's enjoyment of the benefits of peace with God, makes no gender specification.

Without defect means 'perfect' rather than 'without defect or blemish'. The verb (√tāmam) means 'finished up and gone' (Gen. 47:18; Deut. 2:16) and is used of the creation of a 'finished product' (Ps. 18:25[26]). The adjective (tāmîm) can be used to express both totality (Lev. 3:9) and perfection (e.g. Lev. 1:3) and is also used of the Lord's law as a 'finished product' (Ps. 19:7[8]) and the perfectly upright life (Ps. 15:2).

12:6 The *at twilight* of verse 6 is (lit.) 'between the two evenings' (*bên hāʿarbāyîm*). Cf. 16:12 where it refers to the time of the evening meal, and 30:8 where there is a reference to the time to light the lamps. This latter verse suggests the point when 'dusk' begins to become 'dark', i.e. when what we call afternoon becomes evening.

The NIV of 12:6 refers to *all the members of the community*, and this involves two words used of assembled Israel. The first is *ʿēdâ*, translated *community* in verse 3, and the second is *qāhāl*, 'assembly'. The verb √*qāhal* is found about 40 times, meaning 'to assemble' (e.g. in the intransitive [niphal], Exod. 32:1, and the transitive [hiphil], Num. 1:18). The noun can mean simply a 'gathering' or 'collection' (e.g. Gen. 28:3), but very often it is more specific and is used of an assembly of Israel as a whole for religious purposes. The experience at Horeb (Deut. 9:10) was 'the day of the assembly' (see J. P. Lewis, '*qahal*', in *TWOT*).

12:7 Considerable controversy has surrounded the meaning of the shedding of blood in the sacrifices. Many hold that the expression (lit.) 'the life of the flesh is in the blood' (Lev. 17:11) means that when blood was shed life was 'released' and thus made available either as a shield between Israel and the Lord (e.g. in the Passover) or as a gift to the Lord (as in sacrifices in general). See U. E. Simon, *Theology of Salvation* (SPCK, 1953), p. 212; T. C. Vriezen, *An Outline of Old Testament Theology* (Blackwell, 1960), p. 292. This is not only a most unnatural interpretation of the symbolism of shed blood, even in secular use (e.g. Gen. 9:5; 37:26; Ps. 30:9, NKJV), but also, as many others hold, contrary to a true understanding of Lev. 17:11 and incompatible with the 'price-paying' principle which underlies the sacrifices. See Motyer, *Look to the Rock*, pp. 51–53; L. Morris, *The Apostolic Preaching of the Cross* (Tyndale, 1965), pp. 24–26, 111–112 and *passim*; A. Stibbs, *The Meaning of the Word 'Blood' in Scripture* (Tyndale, 1947); J. R. W. Stott, *The Cross of Christ* (IVP, 1986), pp. 179–181 and the references to 'Blood' in the index.

12:11 *In haste.* This word (found elsewhere only in Deut. 16:3 and Isa. 52:12) is *ḥippāzôn* from √*ḥāpaz*, 'to be in trepidation' and 'to hurry', with a focus sometimes on the former, sometimes on the latter, and sometimes on both (cf. Deut. 20:3; 1 Sam. 23:26; 2 Sam. 4:4; 2 Kgs 7:15; Pss 31:22[23]; 104:7). Cf. *ḥopzî* (NKJV, 'haste', NIV, 'alarm') in Ps. 116:11. The noun catches perfectly the potential tenseness of the occasion. The requirement to eat the lamb *with bitter herbs* (8) is left unexplained. √*Marar* (qal, 'to be bitter', Isa. 24:9; piel, hiphil, 'to make bitter, show bitterness', Exod. 1:14; Exod. 23:21 uses the verb to express the bitter spirit that lies behind rebellion) yields the plural adjective *mĕrorîm*, 'bitter [things]', usually understood as 'bitter herbs' or some sharp relish. Cf. the general use in Lam. 3:15. The only other Passover reference is Num. 9:11, again with no explanation. Were the herbs intended to be a reminder of what the people had been rescued from? Cf. 1:14 where √*marar* is used to describe Egyptian cruelties. It could be possible that the word passed into common currency for what the Hebrews were suffering; in this case, the Passover usage would have been perfectly understandable at the time.

12:13 The Hebrew for 'Passover' is *pesaḥ*. In Exod. 12 √*pāsaḥ* is used in parallel with √*'ābar*, which means 'to cross over, pass through'. The Lord 'passed through' (√*'ābar*) Egypt and in doing so 'passed over' (√*pāsaḥ*) the blood-marked houses. The verb and its noun are used as technical terms for the Passover, but whatever meaning they had, if any, outside of this is not known. See both Durham and Currid on Exod. 12:11. There is some justification within the Old Testament for a meaning like 'to protect, cover' (Isa. 31:5), 'to limp' (qal, 1 Kgs 18:21; NIV 'waver'), 'to become lame' or 'be lamed' (niphal, 2 Sam. 4:4), 'to leap, hop', maybe even 'perform a ritual dance' (piel, 1 Kgs 18:26). The adjective *pissēaḥ* ('lame') occurs 30 times (e.g. 2 Sam. 9:13). There is no clear way of connecting this word group with the Passover, and it is best to think of a different verb with identical spelling. Outside the OT, Akkadian offers *passahu*, meaning 'to placate, propitiate' (see Davies, p. 112).

12:17–20 Even though the Old Testament does not elaborate a moral symbolism of 'leaven', there are indications that such an understanding existed. For example, leaven (which is produced by the process of decay and spreads pervasively through whatever it comes into contact with) was prohibited as a constituent of the sacrifices (Exod. 34:25a; Lev. 2:11). This was because the sacrifices were essentially about purity, and only that which was itself untouched by the infection of sin could bear the sin of another (cf. Mark 8:15). Twice, however, leaven is commanded in Leviticus. In 7:12–13 a thank offering may include 'bread made with yeast', i.e. 'leavened bread'. Similarly, at the Feast of Weeks (Pentecost) the wave offering is to be brought from 'wherever you live' (lit. 'your dwellings') and is to include 'loaves . . . baked with yeast' (Lev. 23:17). The significance in each case is the same. In the first, the offering is made in a spirit of thankfulness and confession of sin and of faith, and in the second it is done in a spirit of commitment. In each case, the people making the offerings come 'as themselves' – warts and all, so to speak – and, by the element of leaven, their offerings represent this fact. Cf. G. J. Wenham, *Leviticus*, NICOT (Eerdmans, 1979), pp. 78, 123. Wenham urges that *tôdâ*, customarily translated as 'thanksgiving', has the wider meaning of 'confession of sin and of faith'. In Matt. 13:33 Jesus isolates the single element of leaven's capacity to spread, and not its corrupting influence, as the basis of his parable.

12:37 It is not possible to identify Rameses and Sukkoth, and this is typical of the seemingly insoluble problem of plotting the route of the exodus in detail. On the numbers given here, 600,000 men of military age would suggest a total company of, say, 3,000,000. The word translated *thousand* ('*elep*) is inexact and could mean simply a 'group', either social or military. See 'Number' in *NBD* (pp. 830–835). Currid (vol. 1, p. 261) takes the numbers as they stand, recalling the growth of the people which so alarmed the Egyptians (1:6–7). See also J. W. Wenham, 'Large Numbers in the Old Testament', *TB* 18 (1967), pp. 19–53.

Exodus 12:14 – 13:16

12. Remember and respond

Remembering is very important in the Bible. Indeed, it is a striking thing that looking back and keeping the past in mind is probably stressed just as much in the biblical record as looking forward, rejoicing in hope and living in expectation.

1. Words

As far as vocabulary is concerned, the verb 'to remember' (√zākar) occurs well over two hundred times in the Old Testament. It is 'supported' by two derived nouns, zēker (found twenty-three times, e.g. Exod. 3:15) and zikkārôn (also found twenty-three times, e.g. Exod. 12:14). As a broad comment, zikkārôn ('memorial') is the more 'concrete' word when compared with zēker ('remembrance'). Zēker is something held in the mind, whereas zikkārôn is something that prompts the mind. The examples given above are typical.

2. Gripping the past, holding the truth

Peter's words in 2 Peter 1:12–15 also show the scriptural emphasis on remembering. At this point, Peter is facing the imminent end of his earthly life and ministry, but the thought of death fills him with only this one fear, that the truth he has taught might slip from the memories of those who heard it. He is confident that they already know, indeed are grounded in, established Christian truth (12), but as long as he has breath, he will keep reminding them of what they know and providing them with a 'reminder' – as we might say, an aide-memoire – that will be ready to hand when he is no longer available (13–14). The fervour with which Peter speaks of the duty of reminding is striking: it is a ceaseless concern (12a), something right in itself (13a), a fitting preoccupation as death draws near (13–14), worthy of commanding his 'every effort' and the legacy he would want to bequeath to the church, the true 'apostolic succession' and the deposit of apostolic truth (15). So, from our point of view as Christian believers, the foundational truth of our faith must also be committed to memory (12), and our prize, our earthly inheritance, is the readily available reminder of this truth in the written Word of God.

3. Ezra, Peter and Jesus

Peter's vision and desire is identical with that of the Old Testament sage and teacher Ezra. In 539 BC Cyrus, the founder of the Persian Empire, permitted the exiles from Judah to return to the homeland they had been forced to leave seventy years earlier. Only a pathetically small company was prepared to leave the security of Babylonia to face the uncertainties of a ruined Jerusalem and of a land few, if any, of them, had known, but a small community was established in Judah. Nearly a century later, Ezra was sent by King Artaxerxes with a royal commission 'to enquire about Judah and Jerusalem with regard to the Law of your God, which is in your hand' (Ezra 7:14). In preparation for this mission, we are told that Ezra 'devoted himself to the study and observance of the Law of the LORD' with the aim in mind of teaching 'its decrees and laws in Israel' (Ezra 7:10). In other words, he set himself to teach and establish divine truth *where it was already known*, not by innovation but by repetition, with the aim not of proclaiming a new truth but of securing for the already revealed truth of God a solid lodgement in the minds of his people.

At the highest peak of all, when speaking of his impending redemptive death on the cross, the Lord Jesus made a striking bid to capture and hold the memories of those whom he had redeemed, saying, 'Do this in remembrance of me' (Luke 22:19), 'Do this, whenever you drink it, in remembrance of me' (1 Cor. 11:23–26). The legacy he left was embedded in his last supper with his disciples, but controversy has rocked and still grips the visible church regarding the true understanding of what he meant. All the arguments have focused on the one question, that of the relationship between the bread and wine on the table and the body and blood of Christ once for all broken and outpoured on the cross. This is a very proper and necessary question but, sadly, it has obscured the majestic simplicity which lies much closer to the heart of the Lord's intention: that he commanded us to break and eat bread, to pour and drink wine, 'in remembrance' of him. That is what he told us to do, yet often we are so intent on holding on to what we believe to be the truth – and avoiding what we believe to be the error – in understanding 'This is my body' that 'remembering' Jesus ceases to be the central component of our worship at the table.[1]

4. Psalm 78

Psalm 78 is yet one more example of the importance of 'remembering' in the Bible, and it brings out the practical significance of a sound memory and the risks we run if we become forgetful.[2] This long psalm consists of a double review of the history of Israel from Moses to David (12–39, 43–72). Both reviews tell a long tale of sin and failure, and the second, in effect, ends with a question: will the new beginning in David prove any better? But Hebrew poets never indulged simply in narrative poetry, and the point here is not just to record the past but to learn what the author Asaph believed to be the one great lesson which explains the past and sets the course for the future. Why did 'the men of Ephraim' (9), well armed though they were, suffer defeat? It was because 'They forgot' (11). How is Israel's long record of defection from the Lord to be explained? 'They did not remember' (40–42). What lesson, then, must be passed on to coming generations? That 'they would put their trust in God and would not forget his deeds but would keep his commands' (5–8). Forgetfulness and defection, remembrance and victory, are pairs of inseparable biblical concepts.

5. So remember

The institution of the Passover in chapter 12 begins with a double announcement of a new calendar – *the first month, the first month of your year* (2). So important was the Passover for Israel that from that time onwards the year was reordered so that it began with the death of the

---

[1] See S. Motyer, *Remember Jesus* (Christian Focus, 1995).

[2] On the structure of Ps. 78, see J. A. Motyer, 'Psalms', in *NBC(21)*.

Passover lamb. This represents a much wider reorientation of life itself, for Israel's existence as a nation began all over again and in a fresh and wonderful way when the lamb died. Further, the commemoration of this event was to be much more than a simple aid to memory; it would come to dominate and control memory and make the new beginning unforgettable. Indeed, that this was the whole point of the exercise is made clear by the double command about the fourteenth day with which this section of the narrative ends, (lit.) 'this day shall be to you a remembrance [*zikkārôn*], you are to keep it as a feast . . . throughout your generations, as a statute of perpetuity you shall keep it as a feast' (14). For all time and in every generation, not only the new start of the year but the setting apart of the fourteenth day as a festival was designed to keep Passover, the deliverance from Egypt and the death and blood of the lamb as a living memory.

6. Bidden to the feast: the family and the foreigner

The annual Passover celebrations, then, were a constant summons to Israel to *look back* and were never meant to be anything other than a 'Getting out of Egypt' feast, a commemoration of their deliverance and redemption. This idea is elaborated as 12:25–27 points forward to the coming occupancy of the Promised Land (25) and the insistence that the new situation would not make the old obsolete, but rather the new was to be celebrated by remembering the old. Indeed, when the Israelites came into Canaan, they did not celebrate with a feast marking their entry but rather recalled how it was that they had come out of Egypt. This is strikingly put in Joshua 5:10–12, which tells how Israel commemorated their long-awaited arrival in the land (marked by the crossing of the Jordan [Josh. 4] and the cessation of the wilderness provision of manna [Josh. 5:12]) by remembering the manner of their deliverance (Josh. 5:10). Just as Jesus instituted a perpetual remembrance of his death[3] to be the constantly central thought in his people's minds, a centrality nothing can ever replace, so not even the huge novelty of actually, at long last, setting

---

[3] Paul is emphatic about the cross-orientation of the Lord's Supper (1 Cor. 11:26). Partaking of it is a proclamation of 'the Lord's death'. Indeed, so exclusively is this so, that Paul at once links Jesus' death, not with his resurrection, ascension and enthronement in heaven, but with his return, for the proclamation is 'until he comes'. Those who create liturgies are not always as careful as they should be about this. The Book of Common Prayer (1662) of the Church of England is exemplary, but more recent liturgies include, along with Christ's work on the cross, his activity in creation, incarnation, resurrection and ascension. This is a serious error and a needless confusion.

foot in the Promised Land could replace or diminish the significance of the Passover in the minds of the Israelites under Joshua.

These verses also elaborate on the theme of remembering by bringing us right inside the house of feasting, where we can see clearly that Passover was essentially a family festival and a vehicle for passing the story of the Israelites' deliverance down through the generations (26–27). The situation is envisaged where future generations will have to face the inevitable question 'Why?' from their children, and they are instructed to answer it in terms of the historic past by recounting that the Passover re-enacts what the Lord did long ago in redemption (when he *passed over the houses of the Israelites*) and judgment (when he *struck down the Egyptians*).

The instructions for keeping the Passover are then applied, with certain conditions, beyond the immediate families of Israel to non-Israelites living within the community (43–49). This falls into three sections:

a. Participants (12:43–45)

'Outsiders', whether they are foreigners pure and simple who happen to be around at Passover or those who have taken up residence or employment within the community, are to be excluded. Only those who have undergone circumcision may take part (44). A non-Israelite had a personal decision to make: whether to remain as a 'resident alien' pure and simple or personally to embrace Yahweh and his promises.[4]

b. Regulations (12:46)

In view of the concession in 12:4 that neighbours could 'go shares' in the chosen lamb, it is easy to envisage that some families might have seen no harm in 'slipping back home' with their meal, but this is forbidden as there is no safety/salvation except where the blood has been shed. The additional regulation, appearing here for the first time, stipulates that the lamb must die by the knife (cf. Num. 9:12; John 19:36). There is no obvious reason for this in the foregoing text; it must either be a preparation for the subsequent significance of the knife as the death due to sin or else this was a significance already known in existing sacrificial practice.[5]

---

[4] On circumcision, see Motyer, *Look to the Rock* (pp. 105–106), and 'Circumcision', in *NBD*, pp. 204–205.

[5] See above on 12:10. Currid notes various views about the safeguarded bones of the lamb, though he is too polite to call them fanciful.

c. Participants (12:47–49)

This is not a mere repetition of *a*., where the purpose was to state the conditions for the inclusion of the non-Israelite in the Passover ritual. Here the intention is to define more closely the status of foreigners who opted for circumcision and participation in the worshipping community. Thus, verse 47 can be understood as announcing the topic as *The whole community* ['*ēdâ*] *of Israel*. That this is a community with two components, not two degrees or levels of membership, is rather more explicit in the Hebrew than is clear from the NIV: 'Every male belonging to him must be circumcised, and he may then draw near, and he shall be as though native-born in the land.' In other words, the covenant is true to its Abrahamic foundation that in Abraham all nations shall come to the blessedness they need (Gen. 12:3; 22:18). The circumcised alien is able to come into full membership under the same principle as the native-born (49; cf. Eph. 3:6).

7. Passover and exodus

It is a true intuition that goes on from this teaching on the wider participation in the Passover[6] and the accompanying record of Israel's obedience (50) to report that on *that very day* the Lord brought his people out of Egypt (51). Passover was always to be the 'coming out' festival, and it was as such that it was annually remembered – not repeated, but remembered. Within the Old Testament scheme all the sacrifices were repetitive (rather like repeat prescriptions from a doctor; cf. Heb. 10:1–4), and even Passover could be remembered only by repeated sacrifices. In the case of Passover, however, these repeated sacrifices had a solely commemorative function (14). The Passover was a 'Getting out of Egypt' sacrifice and festival, and once it had achieved this, its great and sole purpose, it could only be remembered. In its first and fundamental sense, Passover could not be sacrificed outside Egypt.

---

[6] This particular Passover stipulation was required by the Egyptian context. There is no need to think of it as a later addition or a development arising from a later situation. The NIV of 12:38 notes that *many other people* accompanied the departing Israelites (cf. Lev. 24:10–11; Num. 11:4). The ESV, NKJV and RV have, more precisely, 'a mixed multitude'. Surely not all of these would have been a rabble of camp followers. There must have been genuine friends made over the years and others attracted by the distinctive life of the Hebrews in Egypt or convinced by Moses' activity in Egypt of the truth of Israel's God (cf. 9:20–21). The 1956 film *The Ten Commandments* sentimentally pictured Moses' royal adoptive mother slipping into the Passover house – to which the only reaction is 'Hmm!'; but the idea was prompted by a true intuition of a very likely scenario.

This wonderful truth comes to full flower in Jesus and the cross. In its once-for-all aspect Passover foreshadows his offering 'for all time' of the 'one sacrifice for sins' (Heb. 10:12). At Calvary, by 'the sacrifice of the body of Jesus Christ once for all', everything that God required to be done, and we sinners needed to have done on our behalf, was accomplished, and accomplished so finally, fully and effectively that the sins of those for whom he died are not even remembered in heaven (Heb. 10:10–18). No further sacrifice for sins is possible (Heb. 10:18). Such a work of salvation needs no repetition and requires no re-presentation. It cannot be amplified; it can only be remembered. Thus, we come back to the central, memorial aspect of the Lord's Supper. In many traditions it is customary always to use the words of 1 Corinthians 11:23–25 as a central scripture at the table. This is not just as a reminder of the first supper, but it also enables us, the contemporary participants, consciously to constitute ourselves all over again as the 'people of the upper room' and sit with Jesus at his feast. So it was that our brothers, sisters and parents of old, when they had come out from Egyptian slavery, annually reconstituted them-selves as the Passover people, to remember and to revel in the recollection, truth and experience of their great salvation.

8. Giving remembrance its proper importance

We noted above how the topics of 13:1–16, the firstborn (1–2, 11–16) and the unleavened bread (3–10), mesh together in the Passover narrative. As we shall now see, these two topics underline the command to remember and may be understood to highlight two aspects of true remembrance.

a. The Feast of Unleavened Bread

This teaches us that life must be planned in such a way as to create an 'oasis of remembrance', thus giving remembrance its proper importance.

The institution of the Feast of Unleavened Bread is recorded in 12:15–20, and its root in divine providential ordering is noted in 12:39 (cf. Deut. 16:3).[7] Beyond the fact that the feast constitutes an annual remembering of the exodus, it is given no further explanation, but what we are told is enough. Passover was of such outstanding importance that its annual remembrance had to be protected from becoming merely episodic, a day

---

[7] See also 23:15; 34:18; Lev. 23:6–8; Num. 28:17–25; Deut. 16:3–4; 1 Cor. 5:6–8.

that goes as quickly as it comes. In this way, we can, without being too imaginative, 'feel' the concentration of minds that must have accompanied the Passover celebrations. The special days of assembly, the special diet for all the days, the additional sacrifices – all of this prompting over and over again the question, 'Why are we doing this?' and receiving the answer, 'Because the Lord brought us out from Egyptian slavery.' And then the supplementary question, 'How was it he brought us out?' with its answer, 'By the blood of the lamb.' Thus remembrance was hammered home, not as a casual, annual raising of the hat to a past truth, but as a serious focusing of life's programme on a foundational event of miraculous proportions and its continuing and contemporary significance.[8] Should not the birth of Jesus, his death, resurrection and ascension command a like ordering of our lives, lest these great memorial occasions become to us no more than flashes in the pan?

We noted earlier that the symbolism of leaven is not elaborated upon in the Old Testament and, therefore, there is no sure biblical answer for us prior to 1 Corinthians 5 as to why unleavened bread was considered an appropriate dietary arrangement to assist Passover remembrance. Christians will rightly want to follow up the directive of the apostle in 1 Corinthians and see the death of Jesus on the cross, our Passover, as a call to holiness and purgation. But since this aspect is not mentioned in Exodus 12 – 13, we should also ask what these chapters themselves say to us about biblical ways of remembering.

There is no single, exclusively compelling answer. In the vocabulary associated with leaven there may be one small pointer worth following through. Of the three words used in connection with leaven and unleavened bread, *ḥāmēṣ* probably refers to a spicy or sharp taste, and *śĕ'ōr*[9] as likely as not contains some reference to the process of cooking. The third word, *maṣâ*, occurs in the plural (*maṣôt*) for 'unleavened bread' as a

---

[8] This element of seriousness is further enforced by the sanction that a breach of the ban on leaven would result in being 'cut off from Israel'. Cf. the penalties for the breach of the circumcision stipulation (Gen. 17:14), for failing to keep the Passover (Num. 9:13), for the misuse of blood (Lev. 17:10) and for idolatry (Lev. 20:3, 5–6). What this 'cutting off' actually entailed is left undefined: did it imply the death penalty or excommunication from the worshipping community and, therefore, the loss of the spiritual benefits of the blood of sacrifice? The broad sense of the verb (√*kārat*) suggests the termination of life, but see M. S. Seale, *The Desert Bible* (London, 1974), p. 167 on 'to be outlawed'.

[9] In Exodus *ḥāmēṣ* also occurs in 34:25. Cf. the metaphorical use of the verb √*ḥāmēṣ* in Ps. 73:21 of an 'exacerbated' heart; the related word *ḥōmeṣ*, 'vinegar', in Prov. 10:26; *ḥāmîṣ* used of 'tasty' or 'spiced' food in Isa. 30:24; and *ḥāmûṣ* used of a 'sharp' colour that would stand out in the distance in Isa. 63:1 (see Motyer, *Prophecy of Isaiah*). For *śĕ'ōr* see Exod. 12:15, 19; 13:7. The root meaning is unknown, but the related noun *maśrēt* (Exod. 12:34) means 'bowl, trough, mixing bowl'.

finished product (Exod. 12:15, 19–20, 34, 39; 13:3, 7; 23:18; Lev. 7:13; Deut. 16:3). The verb from which this noun derives (√māṣâ) means 'to drain out' (Isa. 66:11, NIV 'drink deeply'), but what could this possibly signify when applied to bread-making? Does it refer to a 'straining' or 'draining' process in the preparation, or are we to think of bread 'deprived' of a customary ingredient? This last possibility suits well the unusual circumstances of the exodus, where the bread was made with the least possible complication. But at this point interpretation again divides into two: does the eating of unleavened bread point to days of deprivation, living on a much less than luxurious diet, or to days in which, in the interests of the greater good, life had to be made as simple as possible? Either or both of these ideas could be introduced as ways of making our times of remembrance more important. We could voluntarily embark on a period of special discipline (such as some exercise in fasting), not as though it were meritorious in itself but in order to devote our minds to the great truths and spiritual realities of the season of remembrance (cf. 1 Cor. 7:5). On the other hand, in the interests of the same good objective, we could adopt a markedly simpler diet and lifestyle.

Such thoughts are, however, only speculation. The serious lesson of the seven-day Feast of Unleavened Bread is that remembering the great, central acts of God on which our faith rests demands a larger and more concentrated allocation of time and a more focused ordering of our schedules than is now usually the case.

b. The firstborn

This teaches us that those who are the particular recipients of the blessings of salvation must accept and fulfil the consecration of life to which that salvation calls them.

There is no special reference to Israel's firstborn sons in the Passover narrative, but, as we suggested earlier, the whole story is, in fact, written on the basis of 4:22–23 and the contrast between Pharaoh's individual firstborn and the whole people of Israel as the Lord's firstborn. We must never lose sight of this fundamental truth, bearing so directly as it does on the substitutionary significance of the lamb. Nevertheless, the logic of the situation is that if any Israelite household had refused to obey the Passover regulations with their provision of the substitutionary lamb, then judgment would have fallen there also in the death of the firstborn son of that household. The firstborn sons, therefore, hold a special place within the Lord's salvation of Israel. Numbers 8:17 puts it this way: 'Every firstborn male in Israel, whether human or animal, is mine. When I struck down all the firstborn in Egypt, I set them apart for myself.' 'Set apart' could be translated as 'sanctified' (see the older English versions). We are not told, however, in what ways this 'sanctification' (or 'consecration', ESV) worked out in the lives of the firstborn. Were they intended to be the priests of Israel, and are they the 'young Israelite men' we find functioning as priests in Exodus 24:5? This has the ring of truth, for even though the Lord's highest purpose was that Israel should be a 'kingdom of priests' (Exod. 19:6), the sacrificial code would, simply as a practical necessity, have involved some delegation of function. Following the incident of the golden calf and the separation to God of the tribe of Levi (see Exod. 32), however, the Lord specifically says that he took the Levites for their special service (lit.) 'in place of all the firstborn sons in Israel' (Num. 8:18).

c. Priesthood

The Old Testament understanding of priesthood is a huge subject in its own right, and to look at it in any detail would take us too far away from our study of Exodus. In the interests of brevity and simplicity, however, we can note the position of Moses as 'the people's representative before God' (18:19).[10] This sums up one whole aspect of priestliness: the Levites and priests enjoyed, in their respective positions, the privilege of access to God – it was, indeed, almost a definition of what they were 'for' (Num. 4:23). The other side of their function, as God's representatives to his people, was to teach them divine truth (Mal. 2:7).

This double understanding of priesthood stands true as we trace its meaning into the New Testament. There we find the same privilege of access to the divine presence and the same possession of divine truth with the calling to understand and share it. But we need to make this journey into the full revelation of the will of God with exactness. In the New Testament, the title 'priest' (in the singular) is used only of the Lord Jesus Christ (e.g. Heb. 7:24). By contrast, the title 'priest' (in the plural) belongs to the whole people of God (e.g. Rev. 1:6). The existence of a distinct order of priests, so prominent in the Old Testament, is totally absent from the New,

---

[10] Lit. 'You, for your part, must be for the people in front of God.' The quaintness of the KJV at this point, with its 'for the people to God-ward', is effective.

and has no place in the New Testament church.[11] But the characteristic priestly functions are retained in principle for the Lord's priestly people to fulfil, as all who come to Christ are created into a 'holy priesthood, offering spiritual sacrifices acceptable to God through Jesus Christ' (1 Pet. 2:5) and are a 'royal priesthood', called to 'declare the praises of him who called you out of darkness into his wonderful light' (1 Pet. 2:9). In other words, the privileges of access and knowledge remain, though the 'caste system' is gone.

Hebrews 10:22–23 expresses all this perfectly: under our great high priest, we are to 'draw near' to God (22) and (lit.) to 'hold fast the confession of hope without veering away' (23). This is the essence of priesthood in the New Testament: to practise the presence of God and to hold tight to the truth of God. Those who are redeemed by the blood of the Lamb are his priests and have this double obligation imposed upon them.

Additional notes

'To remember' In the present section of Exodus, see 12:14, 15–20, 25–27, 42, and the comments below on 12:43 – 13:16. See the article '*Zākar*' by A. Bowlin in *TWOT* (pp. 241–243). In the New Testament the verb *mnēmoneuō* occurs twenty-one times (e.g. Matt. 16:9; Mark 8:18; Acts 20:31; Eph. 2:11). There are three significant related nouns: *mneia* (occurs seven times, but is used only of remembering people and remembering in prayer, e.g. Rom. 1:9; 1 Thess. 3:6); *mnēmē* (found only in 2 Pet. 1:15); and *mnēmosynon* (occurs three times, Matt. 26:13; Mark 14:9; Acts 10:4). See also the strengthened verb *hypomimnēskō* (occurs seven times, e.g. Luke 22:61; John 14:26; Jude 5) and the noun *hypomnēsis* (2 Tim. 1:5; 2 Pet. 1:13; 3:1).

12:15–20 Devotees of the documentary analysis of the Pentateuch view this description of the Feast of Unleavened Bread as a typical intrusion/insertion of P material and urge that a seven-day festival does not fit the context of the Passover meal (see Durham). They do not stop to explain why it does not suit the Passover – and indeed there is no reason for the allocation of the account to P except that it deals with a festival. If the Feast of Unleavened Bread has the practical link with Passover suggested in this chapter (and why should it not?), there is no argument

---

[11] See J. A. Motyer, *Ordination for What?* (Fellowship of the Word and Spirit, 1985), p. 7.

against the whole complex of celebration being revealed to and through Moses there and then in Egypt. According to 12:3, 21, the lamb was selected (lit. 'drawn out', i.e. from the rest of the flock) on the tenth day, and there were still four more days before the Passover, leaving plenty of time for the thoughts and instructions in verses 21–28. Note the careful structure of these verses:

A¹ The elders summoned (21a)
   B¹ The ordinance of the Passover: immediate practice (21b–23)
      C Perpetuity (24)
   B² The ordinance of the Passover: future observation (25–27a)
A² [The elders] accept and obey (27b–28)

On the Egyptian context, note also 13:3 where the NIV *out of it* is lit. 'from here' (cf. ESV 'from this place'), which is an incidental pointer to the Egyptian locus. In 13:4 *Today* denotes the contemporary nature of the record.

12:43–45 The vocabulary of 'foreignness' here is interesting. 12:43 refers to the 'stranger' (*nēkār*), i.e. the alien as such. In verse 45 we meet the 'resident' (*tôšāb*, from √*yāšab*, 'to live, dwell'; the NIV gratuitously adds *temporary*) and the 'employee' (NIV, *hired worker*, *śākîr* from √*śākar*, 'to hire, take on as a wage earner'). In verse 48 another category of non-Israelite is introduced: the 'resident alien' (*gēr*). The root verb, √*gûr*, refers to temporary residence, but the derived noun *gēr* came to be used for people who had been granted political asylum and given resident alien status. Cf. its use of Moses in Midian and of Israel in Egypt (Exod. 18:3; Deut. 10:17–19). See the article on *gēr* in *TWOT*, pp. 155–156.

13:14–15 makes implicitly the same point that is explicit in Num. 8:18. Because of this special claim of God on them, all firstborn sons were at birth 'bought back' from this absolute claim of God in a special ceremony of 'redemption'. The totality of the divine claim is seen in that an un-redeemed donkey had to be killed (13:13), i.e. pass totally out of human possession and use, but no reason is given why the donkey should be singled out for special treatment (cf. 34:19–20; Num. 18:15). Death by breaking the animal's neck seems a pitilessly cruel mode of dispatch and, one would have thought, not all that easy to accomplish. The verb so translated (√*'ārap*, cf. 34:20; Deut. 21:4; Isa. 66:3; and Hos. 10:2, where it is used of 'breaking down' altars) simply means 'to neck', and probably refers to some known, non-sacrificial method of easy execution. The redemption of sons, if Num. 3:46–47 expresses standard practice, was by monetary payment. At any rate, here 'redeem' is stated as a concept that does not need further explanation. Currid rightly explains that 'God is permitting a substitutionary payment'. Throughout the Old Testament, √pādâ refers, as here, to the 'price paid' as the alternative to death.

Exodus 13:17 – 18:27

13. The next stage: the companionate God

Exodus 1 – 13 is the record of how the Lord *came to his people* in their distress; Exodus 13 – 18 is the record of how the Lord *went with* his people on their pilgrimage. We can take 3:7–8 as the key verses of the first part of Exodus, especially the phrase 'I have come down' (8); and in the same way 13:21–22 are key verses of the second part, especially the statement that *By day the LORD went ahead of them in a pillar of cloud . . . and by night in a pillar of fire* (21). In 18:8, speaking to Jethro at Sinai, Moses summarized events in the same way: *everything the LORD had done to Pharaoh . . . all the hardships they had met along the way and how the LORD had saved them.* The saving Lord had become the Lord their companion.

1. Continuous, coherent, selective

Exodus 13 – 18 is the record of the first two months of freedom for the erstwhile slaves (19:1). It takes up the narrative where 12:37 had left off: the pilgrims made Sukkoth their first stop, and from there they moved on to Etham, which is *on the edge of the desert* (13:20). Having crossed the Red Sea, further wilderness days awaited the people (15:22), and Exodus records halts at Marah (15:23) and Elim (15:27). As their second month began, they entered the Desert of Sin[1] (16:1) and went, via Rephidim, to Sinai (18:5; 19:1–2).

This all makes for a coherent story, but, as in all history writing, the author has been selective.[2] Exodus 13 – 18 covers two months, within

---

[1] 'Sin' is related to 'Sinai' (cf. 19:1–2).

[2] Commentators sometimes seem to assume that if authors are selective they are being tendentious, forgetting that any history writing, ancient or modern, has to be selective.

which six events are recorded: the Red Sea crossing (14:1 – 15:21), the waters of Marah (15:22–27), the manna (16), water from the rock (17:1–7), the defeat of the Amalekites (17:8–16) and the arrival of Jethro (18). How much more we would like to know! But the purpose of the Bible is not to satisfy our curiosity but to meet our needs, which it does here by underlining the delightful truth that the redeeming Lord himself became the caring, providing companion of those who had sheltered under the blood of the lamb.

2. The companionate God

In 13:17 – 18:27 this great truth is given an artistic shape typical of the book of Exodus but possibly foreign to our ideas of straightforward history writing. Yet we must not think for a moment that there has been any tampering with historical truth in order to make it fit into a preconceived literary idiom. We can illustrate what we find here by thinking of sculpture. A true artist sees the potential in a block of wood or stone and proceeds to shape it accordingly. The resultant crouching beast or integrated group of figures does no violence to the material; rather the newly expressed symmetry displays, indeed enhances, what has always been there. In the same way, the biblical historian, telling the story of the journey from Egypt to Sinai, sees and brings out the pattern, symmetry, unity and wholeness of the events so that in presentation as much as in wording the truth is driven home.

A^1 **Prologue:** The Lord and Israel: Lord of the pilgrim people (13:17–22)
  B^1 Victory over the past: deliverance accomplished (14:1 – 15:21)
    a. The victory (14:1–31)
    b. The song (15:1–21)
    C The companionate God: provident and sufficient (15:22 – 17:7)
  B^2 Victory for the future: the Lord's continuing war (17:8–16)
    a. The victory (17:8–13)
    b. The promise (17:14–16)
A^2 **Epilogue:** The Lord and the world: salvation for the Gentiles (18:1–27)

A carpenter's eye follows the grain in the wood, so as to be aware of its strengths and weaknesses; a historian's eye traces out the flow of events so as to be aware of how and in what order they happened, so he or she can then recount them in a way that displays their significance. So, as we look at Exodus 13 – 18, we can say two things: first, that this is the way things happened; and second, that out of all the events of those crowded two months, the historian perceived and recorded those that best exposed the significance and true meaning of what took place.

At the centre of it all lay the revelation of a God who in all his glory was with his people in their wilderness walk (15:25; 16:10; 17:6), patient with their failings (16:3–4; 17:2, 5–6), in full control of all the forces, capacities and inhabitants of the created world (16:4, 12–15; 17:11–13), exasperated by disobedience (16:28), yet patient and beneficent in the face of plain distrust (17:2–4) and capable of meeting every need that his pilgrims experienced. This is the centrepiece of the historical presentation of these chapters. The way things happened is also the truth they declare.

3. Totality expressed by contrast: the pilgrim path under threat

This is important enough a point to make us pause here a little longer. One of the most widespread idioms in Old Testament Hebrew is its use of contrast to express totality.[3] Right at the heart of our present section of Exodus lies the mortal danger that threatened the pilgrimage, and the totality of this threat is expressed in the contrasting forms of hunger and thirst (16:3; 17:3), with the repeated assurance that the Lord was present to meet every need.

Moving out, however, from this central subsection (C), we find it bracketed by the experience of opposition and conflict (B[1, 2]). We are not, of course, told at any point what the exodus pilgrims expected, save that 16:3 and 17:3 indicate that they did not anticipate hardship and Numbers 20:3–5 shows, at the very least, that what they immediately got rather took them by surprise. The promise of the land flowing with milk and honey

---

[3] E.g. Isaiah, wanting to say that the Lord is going to remove everything that upholds Jerusalem, uses the masculine and feminine forms of the same noun meaning 'a prop' (Isa. 3:1; NIV, 'supply and support'). We cannot rightly reflect this in English – though a phrase like 'bag and baggage' illustrates the idea – but together the contrasting masculine and feminine forms express totality, every conceivable sort of prop. Amos 1:2 uses the contrast between (low-lying) 'pastures' and 'the top of Carmel' to indicate the whole land.

pervades the Pentateuch,[4] and, if our ancestors were anything like us, they may have erred significantly at the point of expectation and, in particular, found themselves baffled to discover that the pilgrim path is a place of conflict. Indeed, the New Testament imagery of warfare indicates that it is still our condition now (1 Cor. 9:7; 2 Cor. 10:4; 1 Tim. 1:18; 2 Tim. 2:3). Paul in his letter to the Ephesians not only calls us to put on God's whole armour (Eph. 6:10–20) but also teaches a truth easily overlooked or forgotten, that 'in Christ' 'the heavenly realms' are not only the place of total blessing (Eph. 1:3) but also the place where we battle with 'rulers . . . authorities . . . the powers of this dark world and . . . the spiritual forces of evil' (Eph. 6:12). And this element of conflict can so contradict what we expected (and sometimes also what our elders and betters have taught us to expect) that we are floored, not just by the severity of the pilgrim fight but by the simple fact that life in Christ is like that at all.

What, then, do Exodus 14 and 17:8–16 teach us?

4. The past and the future

These two sections (B[1,2]) offer yet another example of totality by means of contrast. Chapters 16 and 17:1–7 focus on the circumstantial difficulties besetting the pilgrim way, whereas, by contrast, in chapters 14 and 17:8–16 the hostility came from people. This is the first contrast: the source of opposition. But there is also a contrast in orientation. In chapter 14, Pharaoh and his forces sought to undo the work of salvation by bringing the Lord's redeemed back from pilgrimage into slavery, but in 17:8–16 the Amalekites attacked in order to prevent the Lord's redeemed from continuing their pilgrimage on into the Promised Land. To each of these opponents the Lord spoke a resounding 'No', but in a different manner in each case.

a. The past (14:1–28)

With about twenty-five separate references to it, we can reasonably say that the crossing of the Red Sea remained vivid in Old Testament memory. The first reference (10:19) could of itself pass unnoticed, but in hindsight

---

[4] E.g. Exod. 3:8; 13:5; 33:3; Lev. 20:24; Num. 13:27; cf. Deut. 26:9, 15. Exod. 14:12 reveals that Moses was opposed by the people of Israel themselves during the period leading up to the exodus. It was grace that brought them out, and their continuing complaining illustrates that it was only grace that could bring them into the Promised Land.

the use of the Red Sea to put paid to the huge locust threat is significant. The sea starts to become the location for a demonstration of the Lord's sovereign rule over every force within the created order and the locus of his power exercised against his enemies for the good of his people. At the crucial moment, it was not locusts but Egyptians that the Red Sea devoured – and did so in a final, decisive manner (15:4; Deut. 11:4; cf. Exod. 14:13, 30–31). According to Isaiah, the Lord's name was enhanced by his victory (Isa. 63:12), and the prophet saw the event in large-scale, supernatural terms as proof of the Lord's sovereignty over the 'gods'. From earliest times, pagan religion was preoccupied with the conflicts between the various supernatural forces, and the creator god Marduk could not perform his intended work of orderly creation until he had 'cleared the decks' by disposing of the turbulent, destructive power of the monster of the deep, Rahab.[5] But the Lord's wonders are not a matter of credulity concerning a supposed event before the world came into being: he disposed of the waters that opposed him in the presence of witnesses (Josh. 2:10; 4:23; 24:6–7), and his domination over the sea remained as evidence of his wondrous works, sovereign rule (Pss 77:14–20 [15–21]; 78:11–13; 136:12–15; Hab. 3:15) and readiness to answer prayer (Neh. 9:9), notwithstanding the rebellion and doubt of his people (Ps. 106:7–12; cf. Exod. 14:10–12).

No sooner, then, was Israel out of Egypt than a threat arose from their past: Pharaoh promptly regretted his decision to dismiss his slaves and wanted them back (14:5). The contest was, therefore, a matter of ownership. Who had the right to claim ownership of Israel – the enslaving, genocidal king who had long been their master, or their divine Lord who had come to Egypt to claim, redeem and deliver them? The future of Israel hung on the answer to this question, but the question was put at a time when they were themselves in no position at all to settle it one way or the other. Yes, they were out of Egypt, but how helpless and hopeless their position was when contrasted with the overwhelming forces of the hostile superpower ranged against them (6–9). This, of course, is part of what Peter has in mind in 1 Peter 5:8. Christians participate in the exodus that was accomplished by Jesus (in Luke 9:31 'his departure' is lit. 'his exodus'), but the satanic ruler from whom they have been delivered will no more give up the struggle for repossession than did Pharaoh long ago. In this

---

5 See Motyer, *Prophecy of Isaiah*, pp. 408–410, and *Isaiah*, pp. 322–323.

way, Exodus 14 is a description of the past which speaks volumes to the present at the two points of spiritual warfare and temporal duty.

i. The battle is the Lord's

In this case, the spiritual battle is to be left entirely to the Lord. Moses spoke the permanently directive word, *Stand . . . see . . . The LORD will fight for you; you need only to be still* (13–14).[6] Just as their deliverance and redemption (6:6) was entirely the work of the Lord, so their continuance as his redeemed people was something for which he took entire responsibility. He would not allow those whom he had made his own to pass out of his ownership or to be repossessed by their erstwhile king. To this end, he planned and achieved the destruction of their enemy (4, 14, 13, 30) and also in the meantime himself undertook the protection of his people (19)[7] that would make their continued pilgrimage possible (21–22).

ii. To be a pilgrim

As to Israel's temporal duty within this enclave of divine activity, protection and security, it can be simply stated: *Why are you crying out to me? Tell the Israelites to move on* (15). Here was something not even to pray about. The danger could not have been more extreme, and yet it was not a matter for prayer. As the author of Revelation declares, 'Salvation belongs to our God' (Rev. 7:10). And this is the case in its initial achievement, in the continuance of the saved in the salvation that has been given to them, and in the security of the eternal kingdom. It is all of God, and he will never let his people go; no-one can snatch them out of his hand (John 10:27–30). The pilgrims did, however, have an earthly task and duty to

---

[6] Israel's role as a *spectator* at this point is strongly emphasized and they are exhorted to (lit.) 'Take your stand and watch' (cf. 1 Pet. 5:1). With regard to the sufferings of Jesus we are 'witnesses'; with regard to the fruit of those sufferings we are 'partakers'. Also, verse 14 here emphasizes human non-participation in what the Lord alone does. The subjects are emphasized in the Hebrew: 'As for the LORD, he . . . ; as for you, you.' The Lord was acting for his people to the extent that even when the action was in progress not even a war cry could be uttered – they just watched in silence what was being done on their behalf.

[7] On the *angel of God* see on 3:2 above. In the Hebrew the 'pillar of cloud' is preceded by the conjunction 'and', used here (as it so often is) idiomatically, to introduce an explanation. The NIV ignores its presence, but it should be represented in translation by 'that is to say'. See GK 154a, note 1 (p. 484). The Hebrew of verse 20 is terse: 'and it was cloud and darkness, and it lit up the night'. The NIV offers one interpretation: that the pillar overshadowed the Egyptians and gave light to Israel. It could, of course, have been the other way around: the darkness would have protected Israel and light by night would have terrified the Egyptians, since their sun god Ra should have been underground by this time. But the words probably simply mean that the pillar acted in the usual way, and that as long as day lasted it was an interposing cloud, whereas by night it was an interposing light, thus forbidding any military action until the great deliverance was done. Understood this way, the pillar speaks of the unchanging God whatever the circumstances.

fulfil – they had to continue with their pilgrimage, for Moses was told (lit.) to 'Speak to the sons of Israel that they continue on their journey.'

b. The future (17:8–16)

In this section (B²) the threat was as great as in 14:1–28 (B¹), but the motivation of the attackers and the method of the counter-attacks were different. If the Egyptians had been victorious they would have brought Israel back to their old past, as if they had never been redeemed; if the Amalekites had been victorious they would have stopped Israel from moving forward, as if they had received no promises for the future. With the Egyptians, the Lord's resounding 'No' took the form of his sole action, with any, even the least, contribution on Israel's part expressly forbidden. To safeguard his people's salvation, accomplished once and for all, was the Lord's business. In contrast, with the Amalekites Moses commanded the people to *go out to fight*, while he took up a position on the top of the mountain with the staff of God held up in his hands (17:9). This is parallel to 14:15–16, where Moses held the staff of God and Israel was given the practical duty of going on with their pilgrimage in the face of adverse circumstances (then it was the sea, here it is the Amalekites). The redeemed are always pilgrims. That is their part, even when it involves some demanding step of faith (14:15) or some costly enterprise of warfare (17:9).

5. The mountaintop

The fight may have taken place in the valley, but the victory was won on the mountain (10b–12). Joshua[8] did the fighting and conquered the enemy (10a, 13), but it was Moses who won the battle (11–12). This is not to say that the battle in the valley was not 'real' and costly. We see this truth in the New Testament too, for when our adversary roars, are we not called to 'resist him, standing firm in the faith' (1 Pet. 5:8–9)? And are we not exhorted to don God's armour to carry out our fight against the principalities and powers (Eph. 6:10–18)? There is no such thing in the Bible as easy progress, victory without cost, or access on earth to some supposed

---

[8] Joshua appears abruptly here, and Durham notes that some have, for this reason, proposed a 'Joshua-document' from which this and other references come. Durham himself sensibly says Joshua was too well known as Moses' assistant to need an introduction, and there is no reason to make references to Joshua secondary additions. On Joshua, see Exod. 24:13; 32:17; 33:11; Num. 11:28; 14:6; 27:18; 32:12; 34:17; Deut. 1:38; 3:21; 31:3.

higher life where striving sacrificially against foes inside and out is a thing of the past. Such will heaven be, but not earth.

In this battle, the only one in Exodus, the victory depended on the uplifted hands of Moses. The symbolism of this is not explained in context, but there is no reason to believe it to be any different from what we find in the rest of the Old Testament, where it is the customary gesture of prayer or praise (e.g. Neh. 8:6; Pss 28:2; 63:4; 134:2; 141:2). The sustained prayer of Moses was the secret ingredient securing the military victory of Joshua. This, too, is an abiding scriptural truth, as the hymn expresses it:

> Work as if on that alone
> Hung the issue of the day;
> Pray that help may be sent down:
> Watch and pray.[9]

This 'watch and pray' theme comes from the Gethsemane experience of the Lord and his disciples: he trembled in Gethsemane (Mark 14:33) and, though stepping into the arena of extreme trial and suffering, never trembled again. The disciples slept in Gethsemane and never stopped trembling thereafter. Or, in better words, the Lord in Gethsemane made the place of trembling the place of prayer; they were called to prayer but refused the call. Without prayer, nothing will bring victory. The essential battle is the battle for the secret place.

Moses himself expressed it this way (lit.): 'For [there is] a hand upon the throne of Yahweh' (16). The uplifted hand touches the throne – so movingly illustrated by the moment when Esther touched the golden sceptre of her husband, the king (Esth. 5:1–2). It was this 'touching of the throne' which brought the help the Israelites needed (11; cf. Heb. 4:14–16) and was met with the response that the Lord would never cease to be the enemy of those who sought to hinder his pilgrims' onward march (15; cf. 1 Sam. 15:1–9).

6. An enduring truth

The pilgrimage pattern encapsulated in this single incident is set in the imperishable concrete of a divine oath. The account of the victory over

---

[9] Charlotte Elliott's hymn 'Christian, Seek Not Yet Repose'.

the Amalekites (8–13) by itself constitutes a brilliant vignette from Israel's journey to Sinai, but verses 14–15 point to its validity as a changeless lesson, especially verse 14.[10] The Lord committed himself to the obliteration of the Amalekites, the power which would stop the pilgrimage of the redeemed, and in doing this showed that he would always be there as the rallying point of his warrior people to bring about his victory by giving them the victory in battle, a victory which would come to them through their sacrificial commitment to the conflict and the use of the precious weapon of prayer.

7. 'Singing songs of expectation, marching to the Promised Land'[11]

Songs have a large part to play in the Bible and a particular significance, well illustrated by the song of Moses and the sons of Israel in Exodus 15. The heart of the matter is stated in Psalm 98:1: 'Sing to the LORD a new song, for he has done marvellous things.' The Lord acted and his people sang, celebrating his deeds and recording their own enjoyment of the ensuing blessings. He was the agent, they the beneficiaries. They had had no part to play in, or contribution to make to, the acts they were celebrating and so their song expressed their joy at entering freely into the good of what the Lord had done for them.[12]

The overall presentation of the songs of Moses and Miriam is artistically ordered:

A[1] The situation prompting the song (14:29–31)

   B[1] The song of Moses and the sons of Israel (15:1–18)

A[2] The situation prompting the song (15:19)

   B[2] The song of Miriam and the women (15:20–21)

---

[10] Verse 14 (*Write . . . make sure that Joshua hears*; lit. 'put it in the ears of Joshua') brings together the two forms of transmission, written and oral, but priority is given to the written. *On a scroll* is (lit.) 'on the scroll', where the definite article is idiomatic, i.e. the [now unidentified] scroll kept for that purpose.

[11] From the hymn 'Through the Night of Doubt and Sorrow' (B. S. Ingemann).

[12] Cf. Isa. 24 – 27, which has the quality of a cantata in which the Lord acts and his people sing, and Isa. 54:1, where no song is recorded but the command to sing symbolizes entering freely and without contribution into the work of salvation described in 52:13 – 53:12. See Motyer, *Prophecy of Isaiah*; *Isaiah*. The motif of song never strays from this central significance, that God has acted and we observe and enjoy as eyewitnesses of his sufferings and partakers of the glory (1 Pet. 5:1). The song of Deborah and Barak (Judg. 5) belongs with Exod. 17:8–16 rather than with Exod. 15 in that the Lord had won his victory through the armed forces of his people, but it was still the acts of the Lord they celebrated.

The men of 15:1[13] and the women of 15:20[14] exemplify again the idiom of totality by means of contrast: the whole people were caught up in the excitement of what the Lord had done and they had experienced. They celebrated the wonder of the dry pathway (14:29; 15:19b) and the end of the Egyptian threat (14:30; 15:19a) – in fact, the Lord's single-handed victory (14:31; 15:20–21) – creating a basis for confident faith (14:31). The experience of the Red Sea stands in the same relationship to their Passover redemption as the resurrection of Jesus does to his cross. The cross is the finished work of salvation (John. 19:30; Heb. 10:12–14), the resurrection is that act of God which confirms the reality of the finished work and gives us the assurance that our sins have indeed been forgiven and our eternity made secure. So, the Israelites saw the Egyptians dead and knew for certain that they themselves were saved and that the past was past.

The song itself has a beautiful shapeliness:[15]

A¹ Victory past (1b–5)

Pharaoh defeated

What God has done

The Lord's name

  B¹ The Lord's hand (6–10)

  The Lord supreme on earth

  Human foes overcome

  The sea covering

  Israel secure from the past (8)

  B² The Lord's hand (11–13)

  The Lord supreme among the gods

  The earth swallowing

  The redeemed secure for the future (13)

---

[13] In 15:21 *to them* is masculine, referring to the *Israelites*, (lit.) 'the sons of Israel', in verse 1.

[14] There is no need to create a mystery over Miriam being called *Aaron's sister* without reference to Moses. From childhood Moses had been absent from the family home, living in the palace with his adoptive mother. Miriam and Aaron were siblings, known as such within the community. To call Miriam 'Aaron's sister' is an indication of contemporary authenticity.

[15] According to W. S. LaSor, D. A. Hubbard and F. W. Bush, *Old Testament Survey* (Eerdmans, 1982), p. 142, 'Remarkable parallels with Ugaritic literature in language and structure show that the poem is considerably older than the prose accounts that surround it . . . W. F. Albright and others have dated the poem as early as the thirteenth or twelfth centuries.' The date of the poem, of course, cannot as such tell us anything about the date of the surrounding prose.

A^2 Victory future (14–18)
   Nations cowed
   Possession accomplished
   What God will do
   The Lord's dwelling and sanctuary

8. Victory past (15:1b–5)

This section announces its theme by an *inclusio*, beginning with the enemy *hurled into the sea* and ending with *sank to the depths like a stone*. The Lord's high exaltation (1) is one of the duplications of wording in the Hebrew (*gā'ōh gā'â*) which are characteristic of the song (cf. the *right hand* in 6 and *like you* in 11). The idea of exaltation suggests how the Lord had 'risen to the occasion'. The overthrow of *horse and driver*, that is, both the instrument of war and the agent of war, expresses a total conquest, whereby nothing remains to threaten. The words of verse 2 obviously lived on in the national memory and it became proverbial that the Lord ever furnishes whatever strength his people need and brings them into a consequent joy, himself undertaking the role of saviour (cf. Ps. 118:14; Isa. 12:2). *The LORD* in this verse is the diminutive form, *Yah*, expressive of affection and devotion, as, for example, in Isaiah 12:1 and Psalm 118. *I will praise him* is (lit.) 'I will beautify/decorate him', that is to say, as soldiers are 'decorated' for valour in battle. Every battle honour will be heaped on the Lord alone. On *my father's God* see on 3:6, above. *Warrior* (3) is (lit.) 'man of war', one who can cast himself into that role 'as to the manner born'. By defining his name in the exodus events, Yahweh is the God who redeems his people *and* overthrows his foes (on *The LORD . . . his name*, cf. 3:13–15). The divine name always has this double definition. Currid notes that *officers* (4; Heb. *šālîš*) is the same as the Egyptian word *srs*, meaning 'to have command of a corps', which is an Egyptian expression embedded in the song. The *deep waters* of verse 5 is a quasi-mythological word, *tĕhôm*, usually thought to be related to Tiamat, the monstrous 'deity' which was thought in ancient times to indwell the raging sea. This was the opposing 'divine' force which, in ancient mythology, the creator god Marduk had to defeat before he could perform his work of creation. The Genesis account knows nothing of any such pre-creation combat: there is only one God. Like Isaiah 51:9–11, the song links this mythology with crossing the Red Sea: what Marduk supposedly did when there were no witnesses to his victory, the Lord did before the watching eyes of his people when he tamed the Red Sea to his redeeming purposes. There is no force, temporal (Pharaoh) or spiritual (*těhôm*), that can challenge him.

9. The Lord's hand (1) (15:6–10)

Within the two sections on 'The Lord's hand' (6–10, 11–13) there are sixteen occurrences in the Hebrew of the second person singular, whether as a verb or a pronoun, underlining the sole activity of the Lord in the great victory. The *hand* is the organ of personal intervention and action – God did it, and he alone. The enemy's vainglorious confidence in his own *hand* (9) was shown to be hollow. In verse 7, *stubble* is, as ever, used as a picture of the speed and irresistibility of divine hostile action.[16] The Hebrew changes in verse 9 to a markedly staccato style of speech, reflecting the military tendency to 'bark' orders. Verse 10 is equally abrupt in expression, as if to say that anything they can do, the Lord can do better. They needed six verbs; he needs only three!

10. The Lord's hand (2) (15:11–13)

This subsection is bracketed by the *inclusio* of 'holiness' – the holy God (11) and his holy dwelling (13). The singular of the word for *gods* is *'ēl*, which when used of the Lord refers to his transcendent spiritual exaltation, his utterly supreme deity. There is always a cosmic and spiritual dimension to the Lord's historical acts. As Fretheim says, 'The historical victory . . . participates in the cosmic victory.' What happens in history is real, but part of its reality is its place in the warfare in the heavens. Verse 11 affirms three things which combine to make the Lord incomparable. First, he is *majestic in holiness* (see above on 3:5). Holiness is the essential attribute of the God of the Bible. Indeed, it is more than an attribute, it is the very thing that constitutes his essential deity. His 'otherness' is his total, perfect, absolute, changeless – and dangerous – moral purity. Second, he is (lit.) 'rightly to be feared in praises', in all about him that excites praise. In the present context this refers to his deeds in redeeming his people and consigning his (and their) foes to destruction. Third, he is one who (lit.) 'does wonderfully/supernaturally'. The word

---

[16] See Motyer, *Prophecy of Isaiah* or *Isaiah* on Isa. 5:24; 40:24.

(*pele'*) is the nearest Hebrew gets to the idea of the supernal, supernatural or miraculous, that which can be explained only by appeal to some power beyond what is current among people, 'out of this world'.[17] Because of all this there is a consummate ease in the way the Lord deals with his opponents. All he needs to do is extend his hand (12), for the created order with all its potentialities and powers is at his disposal. It is he who blows his wind, and sea (10) and earth (12) – totality expressed by contrast – serve his will. The creation always sides with the Creator. And this same Lord, working in conformity with *unfailing love* and *strength*, looks after his people, redeeming them in the past, caring for them in the present, and guaranteeing the blessedness of their future (13). *Unfailing love* translates *ḥesed*, which is the love which finds expression not in the beating heart (*raḥămîm*), but in the decisive will. Being 'in love' may move a couple to their wedding service, but the love they express publicly then is the love of decision and unconditional commitment which says, 'I will.' Such is the Lord's love for his *redeemed* people with whom he has identified himself as next of kin, and whose burdens he has shouldered as his own (see on 6:6 above). His goal is to bring his redeemed home (13). His *dwelling* is called *holy* because that is where the Holy One himself dwells, and his redeemed will live with him. *Dwelling* translates *nāweh*, but a more emotive word like 'homestead' is needed. It is used of the place where a shepherd lives (Jer. 33:12) and where he keeps [pens] his sheep (2 Sam. 7:8).

11. Victory future (15:14–18)

The future perspective sketched in verse 13 now takes over. Nations barring the way to Israel's inheritance will be gripped by terror before the power of Israel's God – as indeed happened (Josh.1:5; 2:8–11; 5:1; 9:9; 10:1–2). The Lord will achieve for his people exactly what he promised – that they will share his dwelling place (17). And the poem which opened with the triumphant Lord (1) ends with his everlasting reign (18). In verses 14–15a the verbs are in the perfect tense and are either 'perfects of certainty' ('bound to hear . . . doomed to tremble' etc.) or past perfects (the news of the Lord's triumphs running ahead of them, as in Josh. 2:8–9). Fretheim notes that 'the word has gotten around . . . The reputation of Israel's God goes out ahead.' What was poetically envisaged was historically

---

[17] See Motyer, *Isaiah*, on Isa. 9:6.

borne out. The word of God as a weapon of our warfare is mighty to pull down strongholds (2 Cor. 10:4). The reference to the neighbouring territories is a list of potential or inevitable opponents: Edom and Moab on the invasion route; Canaan, the promised possession; and Philistia, a more remote power but a future threat. In whatever category opponents fall, they are immobilized while Israel takes its promised possession (16). The guarantee of this is (lit.) 'the greatness of your arm', where *arm* is the symbol of personal strength. The beneficiaries are *the people you bought* – a strictly accurate rendering of √*qānâ*, referring back to the redemption price of the blood of the lamb. And the destination is the *mountain . . . dwelling . . . sanctuary* (17). These words express a growing intensity. Mountains were the traditional homes of the gods, well attested, says Currid, in Ugaritic literature of the fourteenth century BC. The assumption is, therefore, that Yahweh, too, has his *mountain*. The word *inheritance* (*naḥălâ*) more properly simply means 'possession', and *place* translates *mākôn*, an 'establishment' (related to the verb 'established', √*kûn*), a fixed, secure place 'for you to inhabit'. This reality of divine indwelling is further emphasized by *sanctuary* (*miqdāš*), a 'holy place', a place where the Holy One lives in all his holy fullness.[18]

12. God of Israel and of the world: one God, one salvation (13:17–22; 18:1–27)

The long section 13:17 – 18:27, the journey from Egypt to Sinai, is bracketed by a delightful prologue (13:17–22) and an unexpected but telling epilogue (18:1–27). The prologue sketches in three aspects of the Lord's relationship to the Israel of the exodus but focuses on his caring companionship. The epilogue recounts how Jethro (called Reuel, cf. 2:18) came to Israel at Sinai and what legacy he left behind him, but puts first how he heard of the Lord's deeds for Israel (18:1) and himself became a believer (18:11).

a. The prologue: the Lord and Israel – divine, caring companionship (13:17–22)

    A¹ Divine care in the choice of route (17–18)

       B Divine faithfulness in promise-keeping (19–20)

    A² Divine companionship on the chosen route (21–22)

---

[18] In English usage, a 'sanctuary' is a place to which needy people run for safety. Throughout the Old Testament, the Lord's 'sanctuary' is, as above, the place where the holy God himself comes to dwell in holiness.

We will return to verses 17–18 in the next chapter when we review the stories in chapters 13–17 from the point of view of divine providence. It is sufficient to note here that the people were not redeemed and then left to their own best devices. The Lord who appointed them for salvation also appointed their onward path, not just as a general directive but on a day-to-day, moment-by-moment basis (21). They never moved without the directive of God's presence in the cloud or fire, and the pillar never left them by day or night. The verb √nāḥâ (17, *lead*; 21, *guide*) is used as an *inclusio* and makes guidance the leading theme of the verses. In particular, we note first that God led (17–18), and second, that in doing so he fulfilled his centuries-old promise to bring the people out of Egypt (19–20). The promise was made to Jacob (Gen. 48:4), but the dying Joseph grasped the promise in the directions he gave about his burial (Gen. 50:25–26; cf. Josh. 24:32). It was the patriarchal custom to be taken home for burial (e.g. Gen. 50:1–13), but Joseph countermanded this loving custom in favour of awaiting God's fulfilment of his promise. What a testimony to faith in God's faithfulness! And as they carried Joseph's coffin with them, what a constant reminder it was of the God who is so reliably faithful. Third, God led them in a way that was unmistakable: the visible cloud by day and fire by night. They learned the (still-important) lesson that it is not for us to seek guidance but to wait for it. The God of the great moving pillar is still the same, still conducting the pilgrimage of his people. Though he has removed the visible sign, he will never remove his presence or fail to make his way known to those who watch and wait (cf. 40:36–38).

b. The epilogue: the Lord and the world (18:1–27)

Exodus 18 consists of two balanced statements involving Moses and Jethro.

The first (1–12) is bracketed by *Jethro . . . brought* and *Jethro received* (2, 12; lit. 'took', √lāqaḥ) and has Moses speaking to Jethro as its centrepiece (8). The second (13–27) is bracketed by Moses sitting to judge (13) and accepting Jethro's advice (24) and has Jethro speaking to Moses as its centrepiece (17). The whole chapter is bracketed by the arrival and the departure of Jethro (1, 27).

i. Personal response: Gentile acceptance

The theme of the chapter is, however, much more important than its structure. In verses 1–12 Jethro hears the truth about the Lord, the God of

Israel, delights in what he hears, praises the Lord personally for his saving acts, affirms the truth of the one and only God, revealed in and confirmed by what he has done, and brings his own offerings. We would say that Jethro came to faith, that he was converted – and the response of the Israelite leadership shows that Jethro was officially affirmed in the faith he had professed (12b). He exemplified the words of Paul in the New Testament that 'the Gentiles are heirs together with Israel, members together of one body' (Eph. 3:6).

ii. Gentile oneness

The whole tone of verses 13–27 sounds administrative and legalistic, but to leave it at that level would be to miss the point. Deuteronomy 1:9–18 should be read as a parallel – and illuminating – account, not of the setting up of lower and higher courts and of a supreme court as such, but of making arrangements whereby the word of God (20, *his decrees and instructions*) was made available right down to the smallest group, the extended family (the *tens*, 21), so that daily life could be ordered according to what the Lord had revealed through Moses. The whole Sinai event (chapters 19–24) 'fleshed out' the word of God under which the Israelites were to live, but 18:13–22 brought them to the point where they learned that the supreme obligation of the Lord's redeemed is to order their lives by the Lord's revealed truth.

It was at this central point that Jethro, the newly converted and welcomed Gentile, actually played a deeply significant part within Israel. His was a full, practising membership – no second-class citizen or merely officially tolerated entrant, but a fellow member, who could, presumably, had he so chosen (cf. Num. 10:29–32), have lived on in full fellowship, among Israel.

Additional notes

13 – 18 Many of the place names mentioned in connection with the route of the exodus are of uncertain location – indeed many of the names may have been peculiar to the Israelites and have arisen from what happened here. *Rephidim* (17:1) sounds like √*rāpad*, 'to spread out' (cf. Song 3:10 [*rĕpîdâ*]; the niv has 'base', but it may be a reference to a cloth-of-gold canopy 'spread out'). This suggests that the Israelites' first impression of Rephidim was of a 'comfortable/roomy' place to camp. Currid quotes the letter of an Egyptian soldier who had been sent to pursue two escaped slaves which mentions 'the enclosure wall of Tjeku', Utm and Migdol (cf. 14:2). Possibly Tjeku is Sukkoth, and Utm is Etham. While this does not locate them, it suggests that the exodus followed a known route out of Egypt.

The Red Sea is frequently mentioned in connection with the exodus (cf. Exod. 15:4; Deut. 11:4; Josh. 2:10; Ps. 106:7; 136:13). In Hebrew it is 'the sea of Suph'. *Sûp* occurs in Exod. 2:3 in a reference to the reeds along the Nile, and so commentators often suggest the translation 'sea of reeds' in preference to Red Sea. Currid thinks that *sûp* could mean not 'reed' but 'end', and that this is a reference to the waters 'at the end [of the land]', i.e. the Red Sea or one of its northern extensions.

14:5 Exodus uses different expressions for Israel's departure from Egypt. The most easily misunderstood is that they *fled* (14:5). The verb (√*bāraḥ*) usually means 'to fly [for one's life]' (e.g. 1 Sam. 19:18; 27:4), but it can be used simply of speed (e.g. Job 9:25; cf. Song 8:14 and Exod. 36:33, where it is used of a bolt 'slipping easily' into its housing). Doubtless, when Israel left Egypt speed and secrecy did combine. They had had abundant experience of Pharaoh's fickleness and acted with prompt opportunism when at last he conceded all they wanted (12:31–33). But the verb does not necessarily mean 'in a disorderly fashion'. Jacob 'fled' from Laban (Gen. 31:19–22), yet his departure was more akin to an organized withdrawal. So it was for Israel in Egypt. 14:8 says they were *marching out boldly* (lit. 'with a high hand', an idiomatic expression which means 'confidently', even 'arrogantly'), certainly as people who knew what they were doing and were not prepared to be gainsaid. Again, it was not the flight of a rabble, and indeed 13:18 says they *went up out of Egypt armed for battle*. The verb here (√*ḥāmaš*) is of doubtful meaning and sometimes suggests a military formation (Josh. 1:14; 4:12), but it is unlikely that Israel had any sort of army at this stage, and Currid sensibly suggests 'well organised for their departure'.

17:8–16 Cf. Deut. 25:17–19; 1 Sam. 15:2–3. In 1 Sam. 15:2 the NIV's 'waylaid' is good (lit. 'placed [for] himself on the road'). The verb (√*śûm*) occurs in 1 Sam. 15:2; 1 Kgs 20:12; Ezek. 23:24 in connection with general mobilization of forces. See C. F. Burney, *Notes on the Hebrew Text of the Books of Kings* (Oxford, 1903).

17:13 This verse uses the unusual verb √*ḥālaš* for *overcame*. See the note on Job 14:10 in E. Dhorme, *A Commentary on the Book of Job* (Nelson, 1967).

The meaning is 'to weaken', and Currid tellingly suggests that its use here relates to Deut. 25:18 ('attacked from behind all the weakened') and can be expressed by 'Joshua . . . disabled those who preyed upon the . . . disabled'.

17:16 The words 'a hand upon the throne of Yahweh' are brief to the point of opaqueness. The suggested interpretation seems best suited to the context, but others have translated the phrase, as is undeniably allowable, 'for [there is] a hand against the throne', i.e. the Amalekites got what they asked for. In attacking Israel, they had raised their hand against Israel's Lord. *Throne* translates the otherwise unknown form *kēs*, the usual noun being *kissē'*. GK 23f notes that the final aleph (a 'silent' consonant, like the 'h' in 'honour' or the 'n' in 'hymn') is sometimes entirely dropped. Thus, the plural of *gebe'* ('cistern, pool', Isa. 30:14) is found as if from *gēb* in 2 Kgs 3:16. The function of the staff in Moses' hand (9) is more difficult to determine. It is not mentioned again in this incident. It could be linked with the altar of verse 15 which memorialized the truth that *The LORD is my Banner*. The word *banner* (*nēs*) can mean a 'pole, flagstaff' (Num. 21:8; Isa. 30:17), a flag (Ezek. 27:7) or both together (Zech. 9:16). The idea of a flagstaff as a rallying point (e.g. Isa. 11:10) may be the best interpretation here: the fighting troops would see the uplifted staff and realize that they were enlisted in Yahweh's cause (cf. 2 Sam. 10:12). The victory, consequently, was to be remembered, not for Joshua's leadership, nor his troops' valour, but for the Lord's gift of victory (15) coupled with his assurance of victories yet to come (14).

18:1–12 Verse 1 sets the scene for the chapter. Jethro came, not out of family duty, which he also fulfilled (2–5), but as a serious enquirer after the Lord, a Gentile coming to the light (cf. Isa. 60:3). This chapter is also the death knell for the once-popular 'Kenite Hypothesis' – that Moses learnt the truth about Yahweh from Jethro. Quite the reverse! Fretheim notices that Jethro is called 'priest of Midian' only once, but 'Moses' father-in-law' thirteen times. 'Jethro identifies himself with *Moses'* understanding rather than the other way round.' On another level of evidence, we note the deference of Moses to Jethro, son-in-law to father-in-law. This is a mark of eyewitness authenticity. A later writer would have insisted on Moses' superiority.

For Jethro's glad cry *Now I know* in verse 11, cf. 1 Kgs 17:24; 2 Kgs 5:15. In each case, something had happened that changed the situation. To speak of Jethro's conversion to Yahweh is certainly not going too far (see

Durham). The end of verse 11 should probably be taken as 'greater than all gods – indeed/even in the matter in which they behaved arrogantly against them', with the implication that the Lord took on the Egyptians where they thought themselves strongest, even unassailable. Verse 12 does not say that Jethro offered the sacrifices himself (as a priest) but that he *brought* (√*lāqaḥ*) sacrifices, a verb used (as in 12:3) of the selection of fit beasts. As D. Kidner says, the burnt offering 'depicts a general self-dedication' (*Sacrifice in the Old Testament* [Tyndale, 1952]). Durham is quite mistaken to say that Jethro 'is presented by the narrative as . . . the sacerdotal leader'. Presumably, *sacrifices* here means what we know as 'peace offerings', i.e. including provision for a fellowship meal with invited guests. This is equivalent to receiving Jethro into unqualified covenant membership.

18:5 According to this verse, Israel was already camped at Sinai when Jethro arrived, yet 19:1 is a very emphatic record of their arrival at the mountain. This link might suggest that chapter 18 is meant to be a preface to the Sinai pericope (see Cassuto), but there seems no obvious way to link the content of chapter 18 with that of chapters 19–24, whereas the balance with 13:17–22 (as above) and the many links with chapter 17 point to it rounding off the account of the journey to Sinai. The orientation of 18:1–12 is consistently backwards: Jethro hears of the past (1); Moses recounts the past (8); Jethro delights in what the Lord has done (9) and himself retells it (10). Chapters 17 and 18 both cover two days: on the first day God provided for his people (17:1–7) and Jethro (18:1–12), and on the second day for the weary Moses (17:8–16; 18:13–27). In chapter 17 the world, represented by the Amalekites, opposed the progress of the Lord's people; in chapter 18 the world, represented by Jethro, came into accepted membership of the Lord's people. There are also significant verbal links: in 17:8 the Amalekites *came and attacked*, in 18:5–7 Jethro *came . . . greeted* (lit. 'each enquired of the other about peace'); 17:9 and 18:25 are linked by the choosing of men; 17:12 and 18:13 by Moses sitting; 17:12 and 18:18 by Moses being weary; 17:9 and 18:14 by *I will stand* and *all these people stand*; 17:12 and 18:13–14 by evening time; and 17:9 and 18:13 by *tomorrow/the next day*.

18:20 Here *teach* (√*zāhar*) is 'to illuminate'. The task of Moses was not to innovate but to teach the people by throwing light on what the Lord had revealed. *Decrees* is *ḥuqqîm*, a word related to √*ḥāqaq*, meaning 'to engrave', i.e. the word of God is unchangeable, as though engraved in rock;

instructions is the plural of *tôrâ*, which means 'teaching' and, specifically, what God has taught; *show* is 'cause to know', i.e. not 'set an example' but 'share the truth'; *way* (*derek*) is regularly used of customary conduct or lifestyle, i.e. the application of truth to life; *how they are to behave* is 'work', what is now to be done. In all this Moses was in the mediating position of verse 19, bringing issues to God, bringing revelation back to the people, and the work was spiritual, not narrowly 'legal'. People came (lit.) 'to seek God' – to learn of God, his will and his truth (15).

18:21 is the fulfilment of Jethro's recommendation. *Select* (√*hāzâ*, 'to see a vision, to exercise spiritual perception') is not elsewhere used in this sense of to 'envision' the right candidates, i.e. to appoint with spiritual insight. The criteria were capability (*capable men*), spirituality (*fear God*), integrity (*trustworthy* is [lit.] 'men of truth', i.e. loyal to God's truth and themselves true, through and through) and incorruptibility (*hate dishonest gain*). In verse 22 *judges* has its typical OT meaning of 'setting things to rights' (e.g. Ps. 98:9). Verse 23 insists that Jethro was not sharing experience as such – 'I have found this to be best' – but helping Moses into the will of God. It was a practical man's observation, but the real need was for divine authorization. He was not telling Moses what to do (cf. Cassuto rather than Childs, who translates 'as God commands you to do' – highly improbable!).

Exodus 13:17 – 17:16

14. God's curious ways

Walking with God is no primrose path!

1. Visual aids

To say that the book of Exodus is full of visual aids in no way calls into question its historicity. Rather, it is just because it is history that it is spiritually reliable: here is history ordered in the hand of God for the instruction of his people. We will see this working out most strikingly when we come to study the giving of the Ten Commandments at Mount Sinai, but for now, what are we to make of the fact that redemption brought Israel out of Egypt straight into the wilderness? It is a point on which Exodus is pretty insistent.

The narrative of the journey out of Egypt is picked up at 13:17 with the information that the people took *the desert road* [lit. 'the way of the desert'] *towards the Red Sea* (13:18), and the rest of their journey continued as it had begun. They may have set out *marching . . . boldly*, but soon they complained that Moses had brought them *to the desert to die* (14:9–11). They did not, however, die but continued their bold march through the sea on dry land. Nevertheless, *from the Red Sea . . . they went into the Desert of Shur* to the place of bitter water (15:22), then on, despite the welcome oasis of Elim (15:27), to the place of no food, the Desert of Sin, where again they felt threatened by imminent death (16:1–3). Rephidim may have been so called because it seemed to offer room and rest, but it turned out to be waterless (17:1–3) – and its very roominess made the people vulnerable to attack (17:8). And what next?

A long encampment in the Desert of Sinai (19:1). And beyond that, forty years – quick to say, slow to pass – in 'the vast and dreadful [terrifying] wilderness, that thirsty and waterless land, with its venomous snakes and scorpions' (Deut. 8:15).

We have become so accustomed to reading all this that it is easy to forget to ask how such things could follow on from becoming redeemed by the blood of the lamb. They are the very sorts of experiences that make us ask today whether we are indeed the Lord's people, or whether we have got our guidance wrong, or how Satan has got in and spoilt the Lord's perfect plans. Such hardships breed swarms of 'why?' questions – Why me? Why us? Why her? Why them? Why now? Why so protracted? Why so savage? – and it is an easy second step to wonder, 'Where did I go wrong?' or 'How could I have slipped so far out of the will of God?'

2. Nothing strange

John Newton would have known better than to ask such questions. In his marvellous hymn 'Begone, Unbelief!' he included the lines

> The heirs of salvation,
> I know from his Word,
> Through much tribulation
> must follow their Lord.

And the whole Bible concurs. Newton probably got his words from Acts 14:22, 'We must go through many hardships to enter the kingdom of God', but the personal and national experiences recorded in the historical books of the Old Testament tell the same story. Likewise, over and over, the Psalms wrestle with life's sad troubles (e.g. Ps. 42), its manifest inequalities (e.g. Ps. 73) and its sometimes impenetrable darkness (e.g. Ps. 88). Isaiah alerts those who would follow the servant path (i.e. be like Jesus) that they may walk in darkness and have no light (Isa. 50:10). The Lord Jesus Christ himself taught that the incoming 'seed of the word' is always challenged, and that it is by 'persevering' that those who have truly accepted the gospel 'produce a crop' (Luke 8:15). And Paul, writing to the Thessalonians, recalls how they, having received his word as the Word of God, showed their true membership with 'God's churches in Judea' in that they suffered from their own people 'the same things those churches suffered from the Jews'

(1 Thess. 2:13–14). Similarly, James exhorts us to 'consider it pure joy . . . whenever you face trials of many kinds' because facing and outfacing trials leads to spiritual maturity (Jas 1:2–4), and such endurance brings 'the crown of life' to those who love God (Jas 1:12). And Peter tells his readers not to be 'surprised at the fiery ordeal . . . as though something strange were happening . . . But rejoice inasmuch as you participate in the sufferings of Christ' (1 Pet. 4:12–13). There is no such thing as an untried faith, and we could go on with more examples to prove the point, but in the end we are doing nothing but expand on the principle enunciated by Jesus that 'A servant is not greater than his master' (John 15:20).

We can return, therefore, with confidence to the visual aid of Israel in the wilderness with which we began.[1]

3. Why?

To the troublesome question 'Why?', there are two fairly common answers offered (or surmised) by Christians. The quick 'spiritual' answer is that our troubles are all down to the malevolence of Satan, who is ever watchful to find and exploit some loophole in our defences. The other answer is that, knowingly or unknowingly, we have strayed out of the will of God and somehow got our guidance wrong. In certain circumstances there can be an element of truth in both these explanations, but neither of them tells the whole story. Nor are they the explanation that we find in Exodus, where the Word of God has something intensely important and fundamentally comforting to say to us: the Israelites were in the wilderness because the Lord had led them there.

4. 'On they march, the pillar leading'[2]

The symbolism of fire and smoke is a familiar one in the Pentateuch. The (lit.) 'oven [with] smoke and flame of fire' which was the visible sign to Abram of the presence of the covenant-making God (Gen. 15:17) became for Moses the fire in the bush, indicative of the presence of the Holy One (Exod. 3:2–5). And as the Israelites embarked on their journey of faith, it

---

[1] This is incidentally where John Bunyan began his *Pilgrim's Progress* – 'As I walked through the wilderness of this world'.

[2] From the original of John Newton's hymn 'Glorious Things of Thee Are Spoken'.

became the fire in the cloud that accompanied them (13:21–22).[3] It was to be transposed into the mountain that flamed to high heaven (19:18; 24:17; Deut. 4:36) when the holy God came to declare his law, and, finally, it was given its standard expression in the cloud on the tabernacle (40:34–38). The Holy One was in the midst of his people as their constant companion and leader from the very start of the journey.

The fundamental truth that we need to take note of in all of this is that for the Israelites guidance was made easy and unmissable. Every move in whatever direction, every stop and start, every turn of the pathway was by the will of God. Whether they were in the comforts of Elim or in the dire straits of Rephidim, it was because the Lord had led them there.

5. God's curious ways

As an illustration of the sheer oddity of life under divine leadership, Exodus 13 – 17 can hardly be beaten. At 13:17 the Israelites came to a crossroads and took the unexpected turn. Instead of taking them by the main road to the Promised Land, which led through Philistine country, at this crucial point *God led the people around by the desert road* (13:18). Our inability to determine the location of Sinai makes no difference to the point. Putting it bluntly, where the people expected to turn north, they turned south and ended up in the wilderness! And this was not because they had got God's directions wrong, but because they had got them right. And then, almost immediately, they experienced what seemed like a retreat, and one with disastrous consequences (14:2). The command to *turn back* was accompanied by precise instructions[4] so that they were left in no doubt where to retreat to, but their obedience led them straight into a life-threatening trap (14:9). They could have been forgiven if the thought came to them that the Lord had gone back on his promises (6:6, 8), his work of deliverance (3:8) and the love and care that he professed to have for his people. Did they say, 'How can we believe in a God of love?'

---

[3] In 13:21 *went* is a Hebrew participle, expressing an unchanging state of affairs. *In* a pillar could equally be 'as'. In 3:5 the flame in the bush was unapproachable, but from 13:21 the pillar of fire was in the midst of Israel. The event which brought about this change was the Passover, by which the people were able to approach the Lord (6:7).

[4] The locations named in 14:2 are uncertain. Currid says that *Migdol* ('tower'), a Semitic term, was much used by Egyptians of the New Kingdom, and could refer to any one of a number of defensive points along Egypt's eastern border at that period. In 14:3 *wandering . . . in confusion* is an excellent translation of √*bûk*, used elsewhere only in Esth. 3:15; Joel 1:18.

It is not recorded that they did, but it would have been characteristically human and deeply understandable.

Next along the line came one of God's disappointments. After three days without finding a water supply, and with any water they had brought with them presumably now spent, they saw an oasis in the distance. They found water there, but it turned out to be undrinkable. The spot was fittingly called Marah, 'the place of bitterness'. We can sense their disappointment at the frustration of their expectations. This incident is specifically linked directly with the crossing of the Red Sea (15:22), so it was against the background of that great triumph – and maybe even in a spirit of triumphalism – that they ran headlong into the hard graft of a wilderness journey, with the onset of debilitating thirst and the grim reality of undrinkable water.

But there was more to come. The hunger of the wilderness of Sin (16:1–3) and the thirst of Rephidim (17:1–3) form yet another picture of totality by means of contrast and are recorded for that reason. The Lord's people, like Bunyan's Pilgrim, make their journey through the wilderness of this world, and in it they meet with every possible variety of life-endangering circumstances. The world around them had more valleys of darkness than it had green pastures. And then they had to face the Amalekites (17:8), which completed the idiom of totality-by-contrast by balancing circumstantial hardship with human enmity.

Yes, indeed, walking with God is no primrose path!

6. Why then?

Faced with life's problems, we frequently say that we have no answers. The Bible, however, is full of answers – the only difficulty is that they are not the sorts of answers we want. Like Job's 'friends', we think we need answers which would make the unexpected fit into a logical framework covering the whole of our life. This, we imagine, is the sort of 'explanation' that would help us because we would then be able to see a purpose working out, and the 'problem' that had taken us by surprise would then 'fit in' with what had gone before and prepare for what follows. (And this, of course, is the sort of answer and explanation that only God knows – and could understand.)

The Bible's answers to the question 'Why?' are of a different order. They are true explanations, but they invite us not to think in terms of human logic, but to identify ourselves with God's purposes for us and to trust the divine wisdom which has decreed this or that particular twist in our pathway. Let us see how this worked out for the Israelites in Exodus.

7. God's purposeful ways

More than anything else, what bothers us when trouble comes is our loss of a sense of purpose. We cannot see why these things are happening to us, and it is at this point that Exodus addresses us most forcefully. The God who created us and redeemed us never ceases to work out his purposes – for the whole cosmos, for the church and for every individual in Christ.[5] This was how it was for the exodus pilgrims and it remains true for us today that nothing ever touches us except by God's determination and in accordance with his will and in order to achieve his purpose. He is too great and he loves us too much to allow it to be otherwise.

First in the purposes of God as revealed in Exodus is *his determination to bring his redeemed into the Promised Land*. He knows that it is in our nature to shun discomfort and to retreat from danger. Therefore, having ventured our feet on the pilgrim path, he would guard us from those threats which would prove too much for us and entice us into backsliding. This is vividly expressed in 13:17 – *the road through the Philistine country* was the 'nearest' route to the Promised Land, but it contained the possibility that the Israelites would *face war*, and they were not yet ready for such a challenge. It would presently be their lot (17:8–13), but by that time they would be a 'tougher' people, disciplined by the wilderness experiences they had endured. At the outset of their pilgrimage, however, the road through Philistine territory[6] would certainly have been too much for them, a trial under which they would have forsaken the forward pathway of the redeemed. They would have put their hand to the plough, only to turn back (Luke 9:62).

There are two interwoven truths here, each important in its own right. The first is that perseverance is one of the signs of a real faith. We have already noted that there is no such thing as an untested faith, for it is under testing that its genuineness comes out (1 Pet. 1:6–7). In other words,

---

[5] For the cosmos see e.g. Eph. 1:9–10; for the church see e.g. Eph. 5:25–27; for the individual see e.g. 1 Cor. 1:7–9; Eph. 1:4; 1 John. 3:1–3.

[6] Durham says that Egyptian records attest to 'a well-fortified, military road from the Delta to Canaan', which, according to Currid, was 'guarded by a series of Egyptian forts'.

it is persistent faith that patiently pursues the pilgrim pathway even (and especially) against the odds that inherits the promises (Mark 13:13; Heb. 6:11–12).

Now, put alongside this is the deeper and infinitely reassuring truth expressed in 1 Corinthians 10:13 that all this inevitable discipline of life, designed for our perfecting (Jas 1:2–4) and aiming at the crown of life (Jas 1:12), is under the closest divine supervision. This means that at every point there is a harvest of growth to be reaped, and at no point need the enemy of souls gain an advantage by turning or forcing us backward.

In this way, because he would have them come safe to the Promised Land, the Lord chose for the Israelites the hardships and hazards of the wilderness of the Red Sea and protected them from the trial that would have put too great a strain on their pilgrim perseverance.

8. Bodies on the shore

Second in the purposeful ways of God is *his determination to achieve a total victory over his and his people's foes*. This truth is too obvious in Exodus 14 to need elaboration. In 14:2 the Israelites were directed by God to backtrack to a precisely specified place. If ever an act of God must have seemed unloving, this was it, for all too soon they found that they had apparently been led into a trap, which rapidly closed upon them (14:9). And it was their God who had put them there! They were helpless, caught in a vice, and when they looked back on that day, they probably said, as we frequently find ourselves saying, 'We didn't know which way to turn.' What can the Lord have been thinking about?

But where the Israelites saw only an unwanted disaster, the Lord had a purpose that would minister to his glory, give them assurance of faith and secure the future from the menaces of their past. For on *that day the Lord saved Israel from the hands of the Egyptians, and Israel saw the Egyptians lying dead on the shore* (14:30). At this demonstration of *the mighty hand of the Lord . . . the people feared the Lord and put their trust in him* (14:31) and in his promise that *the Egyptians you see today you will never see again* (14:13). So, there was a purpose after all. God was working his purpose out, bringing his people a benefit which they did not know they needed, and dealing with a danger which they thought was past, but he knew was not.

Let us learn the lesson: it is the will of God that gives purpose to life. There is always the 'bigger picture' of which he is aware and we are not.

There are dangers and menaces, unknown to us, from which he is guarding us, and, above all, there is his conflict with Satan, within which, in ways we cannot possibly know or understand, the joys, sorrows, battles and testings that come upon us are playing their part. Had Israel not been caught – baffled, terrified and helpless – at the Red Sea, there would have been no final defeat of the power that had enslaved them.

9. Trusting and obeying: living in the way of grace

It is now plain that the explanations the Bible gives for the way life turns out call for simple trust and confidence in the God who does all things well. They are not logical patterns quelling the question 'Why?' at a rational level, but invitations to trust, rest, stand still and see the glory of God (14:13, 19–20).

The next three narratives – Marah (15:22–26), the provision of manna (16:1–35) and Rephidim (17:1–7) – are linked by the idea of 'testing' or 'proving' (15:25; 16:4; 17:2, 7). The people 'tested' the Lord, and he 'tested' the people, which according to the Bible are two sides of the same thing. At the place named both Massah and Meribah,[7] Psalm 81:7[8] says, 'I tested you at the waters of Meribah',[8] whereas Psalm 95:9 says, 'your ancestors tested me; they tried me'.[9] 'Testing' God involves putting him on probation, withholding trust pending evidence. For the Israelites it meant doubting whether he who had proved sufficient in the past was still sufficient now that things had taken a different turn (17:2–3). There is also an element of challenge to God, demanding that he prove his worth all over again: if, against all probabilities, he gets us out of this mess, then we will consider believing, but in the meantime we will suspend both faith and obedience. For these reasons 'testing' – or in the older translations 'tempting' – God is deeply sinful.

---

[7] The two names reflect the two sides of the situation. Massah (from √nāsâ) has the general meaning of 'to test worth, claims or reputation' (e.g. 1 Kgs 10:1) or 'to put to the test' (e.g. Dan. 1:12, 14). Meribah (from √rîb) means 'to contend with' (Exod. 21:18), 'to take to court or test at law' (Isa. 3:13). The Lord's tests were met with 'grumbling' (√lûn) on the part of the people. This word is found only in Exod. 15 – 17 and Num. 14 – 17 (e.g. Exod. 15:24; Num. 14:2) and in the comparable context of Josh. 9:18. It is the grumbling of open rebellion against the Lord, his ways and his chosen leaders (cf. the cognate noun tĕlunôt in Exod. 16:7–9, 12; Num. 14:27; 17:5, 10 [20, 25]). Exod. 16:4 notes that the goodness of God is also a 'test'.

[8] The verb here is √bāḥan, which means broadly 'to test worth, reality or genuineness' (e.g. Pss 26:2; 95:9 [NIV 'tried']), but more specifically is used of assaying gold (e.g. Zech. 13:9).

[9] 'Tested' here is √nāsâ.

When God 'tests' us, however, it is a different matter. He does so by bringing us into situations which call for trust and the endurance and obedience that prove our trust is real, so that, by the exercise of faith in the face of new challenges, our trust in him can develop and mature until we come to see that everything that happens to us is under divine supervision and is brimful of divine purposes for good.[10]

When we come to chapters 19 and 20, we will discover in a more basic way the interlocking of faith and obedience, and we will see that obeying God's word is the foremost characteristic of his believing people, but in the present stories the truth itself is as plain as historical visual aids can make it.

God's third purpose as revealed in the Exodus account is that obedience is what he seeks. The structure of 15:22–27 makes this point clear.

> A[1] 'Found no water' (22)
>> B[1] 'And they came to Marah' (23–25a)
>>> C 'A decree and a law' (25b–26)
>> B[2] 'And they came to Elim' (27a)
> A[2] 'Camped by the waters' (27b)

This structured analysis does no more than follow the clues offered by the Hebrew wording. The A sections express, by contrast, the varying experiences the people encountered; the B sections speak of the sufficiency of the Lord's leadership and provision (if the circumstance presents an unexpected disappointment, he can remedy it, and his leadership will forthwith, in any case, bring them into rest and plenty);[11] the C section brings out the central truth the passage would impart, putting the whole lesson of the Israelites' experience into words. In other words, the Lord used this single experience as a paradigm for future generations, presenting Israel with a perpetual choice, to either 'complain' or to obey. First, the redeemed must live under the Lord's laws (25b). Second, this way of obedience is the way to enjoy the Lord's promises. The Lord used the

---

[10] Cf. Isa. 54:16–17; Jer. 29:11; Matt. 6:26–32; 10:29–31.

[11] Preaching from this passage, I once said that, instead of grumbling, 'all they had to do' was press on a few miles more and there was Elim, waiting for them. A thoughtful friend said afterwards: 'Have you ever been there?' 'No.' 'I thought not – in that heat, without water, it is impossible to go ten paces, never mind ten miles.' My comment was based on the truth that the first duty of the redeemed must always be to continue as pilgrims. True enough! My helpful friend's corrective underlines that it is the Lord's interventions of transforming grace (25a) that make pilgrimage possible.

occasion of the divine healing of the waters to point to a truth about himself as *the LORD, who heals you.* Obedience and blessing are conjoined twins.[12]

Chapter 16 takes the link between faith and obedience a stage further, showing that just as *obedience is the proper expression of faith*, so also *faith makes obedience possible.*

On the whole, it is in our natures to be provident, to lay up today what we will need tomorrow, and, equally on the whole, Scripture commends this (Prov. 6:6–8; 10:5; 20:4; 24:30–34). But in the case of the manna, the way in which it was sent to the people required them rather to rest on the assurance that God would provide and to gather each day only what was sufficient for that day (4, 18). To gather enough for the next day was neither allowed nor possible (19–20), and this arrangement was specifically a test of obedience (4). But into this scheme the Sabbath intruded, with its prohibition of work, and this meant that there could be no gathering of manna. Again, there was a command to obey (5), and the Lord who delights in an obedient people himself intervened to make obedience possible in this matter (23–24). The Lord safeguards what he has appointed.

10. The guardian providence of God the Creator

So, the narratives of chapters 13–18, taken as a visual aid of the pilgrim path of the redeemed, forewarn us that our faith will never remain untested, assure us that in the midst of troubles and trials that seem meaningless there are deep purposes of God at work, and call us to the obedience of faith. They also illustrate the comforting truth of a God of providential care, foreseeing our needs, planning ahead for our welfare, and awaiting us with his solutions and sufficiency. In a word, the trials of the pathway may take us by surprise, but never him. They may catch us unprepared, but never him. Left to ourselves, they would be more than we could bear, but we are never left to ourselves. By ourselves, we would not know which way to turn, but we are not by ourselves. God has planned the course we are to take and walks with us. We can say with David,

---

[12] Ancient Egypt was notoriously unhealthy, but it is worth noting that verse 26 speaks not of 'Egypt' but of 'the Egyptians'. The Lord not only brought his people out of Egypt, but made them distinct from the Egyptians. Obedience is the key to being his distinct people (1 John 2:3–4). The reference to *diseases* could, of course, be specifically to the 'plagues' visited on Egypt as evidences of divine displeasure. There is nothing to displease the Lord in an obedient people (Col. 1:9–10).

'As for God, his way is perfect . . . and [he] keeps my way secure [perfect]' (Ps. 18:30, 32 [31, 33]).

11. Anticipatory providences[13]

When the people came to Marah and the disappointment of the undrinkable water, the Lord showed Moses (lit.) 'a tree' (15:25). In other words, the remedy had been in preparation long before the need arose and was there, ready and waiting. It was 'an anticipatory providence'. The same can be said of the manna and the quails. Manna is apparently a natural phenomenon in the Sinai[14] and is remarkable here only for the quantity in which it was available. The quails, following their annual migratory path, and flying as usual by night, flopped exhausted to the ground at daylight, to be caught easily and so provide for the needs of the Lord's people.[15]

We can follow the same line of thinking through to the great rock on the hill, where an underground water supply, provided by the Creator in the very fabric of creation, was in place through millennia to minister to a need which the Lord knew would arise far in the future and for which he would have the remedy in hand (17:6).[16]

None of this is said in order to deny or evade the 'miraculous' in Scripture. Of course, the Creator can do what he pleases in his own world (Ps. 115:3), and it would indeed speak volumes of his love and power were we to think of him intervening 'there and then' at each of these points of need to make a special arrangement to sustain his pilgrims. And, had he done that, it would have violated neither his own nature nor the creatorial order. But it speaks of love, care and power at an even deeper level if we imagine the Creator God saying to himself as he made the world, 'My people will one day pass this way, mortally thirsty and disappointed by undrinkable water – I will plant a tree to await their arrival . . . My people

---

[13] It was once my good fortune to hear Alan Stibbs, then vice principal of Oak Hill College, preach on Exod. 15:22–26, and he used the words 'an anticipatory providence'. I owe to him my approach to the stories of Marah, the manna and quails, and the smitten rock.

[14] According to Cassuto, 'Certain kinds of aphids exude the superfluous sugar they absorb from the trees in the form of drops that dry and become whitish . . . globules.'

[15] According to Currid, 'a miracle in timing and extent' (p. 341).

[16] There is a contrast to be noted here. When the people complained under Pharaoh, he deprived them even more (5:7); when they grumbled at the Lord, he fed them (16:2, 4). Cf. 16:8, where *because he has heard* could (should?) be 'in spite of his hearing'. In 16:10, when they *looked towards the desert*, i.e. set themselves to go forward on the appointed way, they saw glory.

will one day pass this way threatened with death by starvation and at that point my aphids will work and my quails will fly. It will all be ready for them. And one day I will lead my people to Rephidim and they will be in desperate need of water, so in anticipation of that day I will provide an underground supply and mark it with a great rock so that it can't be missed.' The ordering of creation and the providence of the Creator await and meet the arising needs of the redeemed on their pilgrimage. Our needs have already been anticipated in his foreseeing, far-seeing grace, which is ever on our side.

12. Working to a larger pattern

We noted above that chronologically chapter 18 belongs after 19:1, but thematically it follows on from 13:17–22, and we saw also a little of its significance in context.

This chapter is one of the points where we suddenly become aware of the wider world in which our redeemed brothers and sisters, the church of the Old Testament, made their pilgrimage. From Genesis 12 onwards, the concentration on Abraham and his family is such that we could easily think of his descendants walking through an empty landscape and overlook how densely the land of Abraham's nomad days was populated and how Israel too lived and walked amid the wider world of large empires and small nations. This false picture is corrected when suddenly, in the person of Jethro, 'the world out there' walked right into the centre of Israel's camp. This prompts the question of whether the God of Israel had anything to say at this point to the rest of his creation?

Jethro arrived on a family errand.[17] He had obviously had some prior contact with Moses and knew where to find him and the Israelites in the Sinai region. We have no record that Moses had sent Zipporah and her sons to Midian (18:2), but then the Bible never tells us all the facts, and we must not misunderstand its silences. Moses' wife and children would have been safe in Midian, but now was the time to reunite the family.

Whatever else passed between the two men, or between Moses and his family, the narrative moves speedily to the point it wants to stress (18:8), the recounting by Moses at an early opportunity to his father-in-law of

---

[17] It was not, however, family duty which drew Jethro to come – that was simply the pretext; he was drawn by the hearing of the truth (18:1; cf. Josh. 2:10; 10:1–2).

the great, saving acts of the Lord and the fact that as a result of this Jethro came to faith in the Lord (18:10–11). He immediately expressed his unreserved commitment to the Lord by making a burnt offering (18:12)[18] and was welcomed into the fellowship of Israel. Thus, as we observed above, he is an example of the Gentiles as fellow members of God's people and fellow inheritors of his promises.

Two principles emerge from this: the salvation of Israel is the salvation of the world, and the experiences of the redeemed are a testimony to the world.[19] We do not know precisely what Moses said to Jethro, and we must not fall into the temptation of filling the gap with our own assumptions and thinking, 'Of course, Moses would have told him such-and-such.' What we do know is that Jethro was told all the Egyptian events (18:8a), the saving acts of the Lord by which he brought his people out. The way the Lord saved the Israelites became the message of salvation to Jethro and the saving truth he embraced for himself. There is no need of special ways of salvation for different people, nor of any adjustment of fundamentals to make them suit new circumstances. There is only what the Lord did in judgment and mercy, once and for all.

Moses also told Jethro about *all the hardships they had met along the way and how the Lord had saved them* (18:8b). In other words, the Lord's dealings with his people establish a convincing testimony to the world, and this is part of the purpose behind them. Had God not led them through the desert instead of by the way of the Philistines (13:18), and into the trap by the Red Sea (14:2, 9), and subjected them to disappointment at Marah (15:22–23), hunger in Sin (16:1–3), thirst in Rephidim (17:1) and assault by the Amalekites (17:8–13), they would have had nothing to say convincingly to the world.

The Lord works to a larger pattern than we can see at any given point. Paul was aware of this and, in the limitations and discomforts of his imprisonment, pronounced himself to have been put there 'for the defence of the gospel' (Phil. 1:16) and described himself as 'an ambassador in chains' (Eph. 6:20).[20] Purpose and providence rule.

---

[18] The burnt offering of Gen. 22:2, 8–9 is defined by the angel as evidence of 'not withholding' anything from the Lord (22:12). Cf. F. D. Kidner, *Sacrifice in the Old Testament* (Tyndale, 1952), where it is described as 'a general self-dedication which is worked out in careful and painstaking detail' (pp. 13–15).

[19] Chapters 17 and 18 reflect two aspects of the relationship between the church and the world. In 17:8–13 the world opposes and must be resisted (cf. Phil. 1:28); in 18:8 the world is won by the sharing of saving truth.

[20] The verb (*keimai*) could be translated 'to be on duty'. Douglas Vicary, in Wycliffe Hall Chapel, Oxford, August 1947, preaching on 'an ambassador in bonds', ended by saying, 'Whatever we find a "bind" calls us all over again to be ambassadors.' Cf. the testimony of 'Paul, the prisoner of Christ Jesus' in Eph. 3:1, 7–11.

Additional notes

15:22–27 The documentary theorists agree only in saying that verses 22–27 are a composite. There is a certain colour of possibility to this in that, at first sight, 25b–26 do seem intrusive. But Driver allots 22–25, 27 to E and 26 to R^{JE}, whereas Noth gives part of 22a and 27 to P, the rest of 22a and 23–25a to J, and understands 25b–26 as a D supplement. Apart from the fact that neither analysis helps us one whit in understanding the passage, such incompatible conclusions reveal subjectivity – and a determination to let the theory control the facts. Reflecting on similar allegations of a composite narrative in Exod. 14, Durham remarks that 'they begin to look not only subjective, but also somewhat arbitrary'.

15:25 The niv's *a piece of wood* is against the general use of *ʿēṣ*. As well as meaning 'a tree', the singular is used in a collective sense for the 'tree content' of a garden (Gen. 3:2) and in a generic sense for wood as compared with stone (Deut. 4:28). The plural (*ʿēṣîm*), as well as meaning 'trees', is used of wood as building material (Gen. 6:14), wood chopped for kindling (Gen. 22:3) and timber prepared for use (2 Kgs 22:6). Deut. 10 is a typical example: the singular in verse 1 is generic (the material from which the ark is to be made), but the plural in verse 3 refers to wood prepared and cut to size. The only place where I can find the singular used to mean a piece of wood in the sense of 'a stick' is Ezek. 37:16–22. Here in 15:25, therefore, the translation 'wood' does not correspond with Old Testament usage. 'Stick' or 'branch' could be justified, but 'tree' is the most accurate and is to be preferred.

15:25–26 *Ruling* and *instruction* are, respectively, *ḥōq* (the unchangeable regulation) and *mišpāṭ* (the authoritative directive). Verse 26 amplifies the point that the Israelites' privilege as the Lord's people is to hear his voice. They have the very word the Lord himself has spoken and, therefore, know what he wants. The eye is the organ of desire and aim, and so what is right *in his eyes* are the things he would have us aim at so as to please him. The ear is the organ of reception, and *pay attention* is (lit.) 'turn your ear to'. *Commands* (pl. of *miṣwâ*) are the Lord's words as designed to be obeyed. *Decrees* is the plural of *ḥōq*, as above.

16:1–34 This chapter falls into two parts (2–15 and 16–34), held together by the itinerary notes in verses 1 and 35–36 as an *inclusio*. The first part deals with the gift of the manna:

A^1 The threat of hunger misunderstood (2–3)

    B^1 The Lord to Moses: food provided, a test of obedience (4–5)

        C^1 Moses and Aaron to Israel: regular supply, the Lord's glory (6–7)

            D Moses' meditation: the same Lord hears complaints and gives (8)

        C^2 Moses and Aaron to Israel: the Lord's glory (9–10)

    B^2 The Lord to Moses: food provided, the Lord is God (11–12)

A^2 Hunger met: inexplicable, except as an act of God (13–15)

Following on from this, verses 16–34 set out the meaning of the manna in three sections:

A The way the manna is provided requires Israel to trust the Lord for tomorrow (16–22)

B Obedience is tested by the Sabbath, and the Lord makes obedience possible (23–31)

C The manna as a perpetual reminder of the Lord's work in the exodus (32–34)

The reference to the Sabbath before the commandment was given (20:8) requires some explanation. The commandment calls for 'remembrance', and this suggests that the Sabbath was already an ancient institution (Currid rightly says, 'a creation ordinance'). Verse 35 suggests that the narrative was written at a later date, and this would account for the reference to *the tablets of the covenant law* (34).

17:8 √*Rāpad* means 'to spread out' (cf. Job 17:13). Incidentally, the 'Desert of Sin' has nothing to do with the English word 'sin'. Sadly, Rephidim belied its name and, as Fretheim remarks, 'God's leading does not always move directly towards oases' (p. 188).

18:2 *Had sent away* is actually a noun, (lit.) 'her departing' (*šillûḥîm*). It appears in 1 Kgs 9:16 and Mic. 1:14 in the sense of 'parting gift'. The verb (√*šālaḥ*) is used of divorce (Deut. 24:1), but there is no need to think of this usage here. Zipporah was still Moses' *wife*. It is perfectly understandable that Moses sent his family to the safety of Midian when it became clear that events in Egypt were going to take time and might even turn ugly.

Exodus 19:1–2

15. Where we've reached and where we're going

The emphasis in 19:1–2 on the Israelites' arrival at Sinai indicates that we have reached a 'seam' in the book of Exodus. This is made plain by certain markers which we will note as we go along. We have noticed one already, namely that the encounter with Jethro also took place at Sinai (18:5) but is placed before the formal introduction of chapter 19. In other words, although the people had already reached Sinai (chapter 18), the Sinai events themselves and their aftermath require a fresh start. Sinai is thus marked out as special.

1. Surprise, surprise!

We know some of the things that happened between Egypt and Sinai, and we have been told some of the things – mainly grumbles – that the people said. Behind the grumbles lay the implied question, 'What are we doing here?' This was not what they had been promised! Indeed, from the traditional site of Mount Sinai in the deep south of the Sinai Peninsula, the Promised Land was still as far away as ever, and the people were not altogether wrong in moaning that their circumstances were in many ways worse than they had been in Egypt (16:3; cf. Num. 21:5).

Did even Moses know the whole answer to the dilemma? Did he remember that the Lord had said, 'This will be the sign to you [sing., i.e. Moses] that it is I who have sent you: when you have brought the people out of Egypt, you will worship God on this mountain' (3:12), and did the memory of it reassure him that the road they had taken was the right one even though it seemed to lead them further and further away from their goal? Did he wonder how it would all work out? Maybe he did. As for us, with the Bible in our hands and helped by hindsight, everything is explained, for what we have here is in fact the largest, most extended visual aid ever planned: the journey from the Passover in Egypt to the giving of the law at Sinai.

2. Sinai, a primary destination

Since no word of the Lord is without meaning, we must assume that he knew Moses would come to need some reassurance about his divine commissioning. Otherwise, the arrival at such a place as Sinai could well have become a low point in his confidence – the contrast between the promise of 'a good and spacious land, a land flowing with milk and honey' (3:8) and this wild, mountainous terrain could hardly have been greater or more depressing. Yet, according to the divine word in 3:12, Sinai was no accident brought about by misunderstanding or an adaptation of the Lord's plans to meet an unforeseen problem, nor was it a transient campsite like Elim or Rephidim. Sinai was in fact the primary destination of the journey from Egypt, the Lord's stated target. Now we can stand back and see the visual aid: the Lord's redeemed people had to be brought to the place where they could hear and receive his law. This can be broken down into three vital truths:

1. By the will of God, those whom he has redeemed must come under the direction of the word he speaks. The Israelites had been redeemed by the blood of the lamb, and now the Lord had brought them, as the primary destination of their pilgrimage, to the place where they could hear his voice and learn his law for their lives (cf. Deut. 4:34, 36–37, 40).[1]
2. The law of God is essentially his instructions on how to live a life pleasing to him, and it has this meaning not only in the Old Testament but throughout the Bible. God's law is not a 'ladder of merit' by which we try to climb, by grim obedience, into his 'good books'; it is a way of life revealed to those who are already by

---

[1] Mackay remarks that Moses was not given the law on his first visit to the mountain (Exod. 3). This would have implied that salvation is by works. Only when redemption has been accomplished can redemption be applied. The response of obedience flowed from gratitude for all the Lord had done for them.

redemption in his good books. He brings us to himself and then requires us to live so as to please him (19:4–5).

3. The grace of God precedes the law of God. His grace reaches out to save, and it is to those whom he has saved that he reveals his law. The first characteristic of the saved is that they possess, know and live by the word of their saving God. In the case of our ancestors in the faith, the Israel of old, that word came through Moses; in our case, inheritors of the new covenant in Jesus' blood (cf. Gal. 6:10, 16), it is the whole, completed Bible.

3. Sinai in Exodus

From 19:1 through to the end of the book of Exodus, Israel camped at the foot of Mount Sinai, a period covering the best part of a year (19:1–2; Num. 10:11–12). Exodus sets the story of the Sinai period in the framework of the seven ascents of the mountain by Moses into the presence of the Lord.

a. Preparation

The first three ascents are grouped together in chapter 19 and were preparatory in nature (3–8a, 8b–15, 16–25). During the first ascent (3–8a), the Lord called Israel to be obedient to his word: those whom the Lord has brought to himself (4) are obligated to hear and obey (5a), with promises of blessing to follow (5b–6). During the second ascent (8b–15), the Lord made arrangements whereby his people might receive his word. The obligation to obey is undergirded by the marvel of revelation (in this case through Moses, 9), and as only a holy people can meet with the Lord, there had to be a time of preparation while they awaited the trumpet of invitation (10, 14). With the third ascent (16–25), the people, Moses and the priests themselves were made aware of the awesome intensity and seriousness of the holiness of the Lord, and shown that this is a God not to be presumed upon or lightly encountered. Israel as an elect people were brought near to God and directed to obey revealed truth, and they had to be committed to personal holiness and sensitive to the presence of the holy God.

b. Direction

The Ten Commandments were spoken by the Lord, in his own voice to Israel (20:1; Deut. 4:12, 33, 36), but those who heard this found the experience terrifying beyond endurance (20:18–19) and appealed to Moses to become their mediator. Like the unleavened bread (12:15, 39), this is another example of what the Lord willed (19:9) being brought about by his providential ordering of events. As mediator, Moses ascended the mountain (20:21; cf. 24:3) to receive the Lord's detailed directions for the life of his people (20:22 – 23:33).

c. Worship

Moses was summoned for a fifth time to the top of the mountain (24:12),[2] and he stayed there this time for a period of forty days and nights. The purpose was for him to receive the 'tablets of stone' (24:12), but he also brought back with him plans for the location and manner of Israel's worship – the details of the tabernacle (25 – 27) and its priesthood (28 – 29). This linking of obedience (the Commandments) and worship (the tabernacle) is important: first, because it shows that the obedient life of the redeemed is not just conformity to a code but one aspect of living in worshipping fellowship and closeness to the holy God; and second, because when the Lord gave the law, he also gave the sacrifices for sin and all that made them possible. Obedience is the primary obligation; the sacrifices were instituted to deal with the inevitable failures and lapses in the life of obedience and to hold a committed though fallible people in the fellowship of the Holy One.

d. Intercession

Moses' sixth ascent (32:30) followed on the dire sin of the golden calf. His previous forty-day stay on the mountain had tested the people's patience, and they had failed (32:1). Even more seriously, Aaron had failed them, acquiescing in and promoting their lapse into religious falsehood (32:2–6). The Commandments were broken before they were even delivered, and Moses' action in shattering the stone tablets on the mountain (32:19) was but a dramatic portrayal of what had already become a reality. Later, such offences against the Decalogue were to merit the death penalty, and Moses felt this doom hanging over the whole people. Not for a moment did he countenance the suggestion that he would become the founder of a reconstituted nation (32:10), and he would rather have seen himself perish

---

[2] The ascent recorded in 24:9–11 is not to be reckoned in the list of Moses' ascents of the mountain. He went up, not in his distinctiveness as mediator, but as part of the symbolic delegation to eat a covenant meal with the Lord, the climax of the solemnization of the covenant of 24:1–8.

eternally than that the people should have to endure what their sin deserved (32:32). Moses was not looking for a cheap forgiveness, and the Lord listened to his costly prayer and, without violating his own standards of holiness (32:33), pointed Moses and the people forward to the Promised Land (33:1). As Paul was to say later, 'God's gifts and his call are irrevocable' (Rom. 11:29).

e. Restoration

Moses was commanded to ascend the mountain for the last time (34:1–5) and found that the Lord does not change. He rewrote the broken law without alteration (34:1), renewed the broken covenant (34:10), commanded the completion of the tabernacle (35:1) and resumed his leadership of his people's onward pilgrimage (40:34–38).

Additional notes

19:1–2 Childs says this makes 'a sharp break with the history which has led up to the arrival at Sinai. The goal of the journey from Egypt has been reached.' 19:1 has no introductory 'And it came to pass' (*wayĕhî*) linking it with what has gone before. By the words *on the very day* the date is underlined, giving it the force of a fresh beginning. This is further stressed by the way verse 2 recapitulates the last days of the journey. *That very day* is not explained but, by analogy with 12:41, we may be dealing with an idiom, meaning 'on the same day as they had left Egypt': they journeyed from the 14/15th day of the first month (12:6) to the same day of the third month. Driver quibbles that the original order was 'doubtless' that verse 2 preceded verse 1. This is pretty incomprehensible as Hebrew narrative often puts the substantial fact first and fills in the details after it. The Hebrew conjunction with which verse 2 opens is to be taken as an example of a *waw explicativum*, 'That is to say, . . .' Following upon this, the emphatic *Then Moses* (*ûmōšeh*) of verse 3 marks a new paragraph. *Desert* is, of course, not necessarily a barren sandy waste, and here Cole has 'grazing country, not settled'.

Exodus 19:3–25

16. To meet with God

We come now to look in more detail at Moses' seven ascents into the Lord's presence on Mount Sinai. The first three can be labelled 'introductory', not because they come first but because they offer a useful preview of the rest of the book. The first ascent (3–8a)[1] centres on the call to Israel to be obedient (5), and this is developed in the giving of the Ten Commandments (20:1–20) and the elaborated application of the Lord's law revealed during the fourth ascent (20:21 – 23:33). The second ascent (8b–15) calls the people to holiness (10) and to a careful respect for the Lord's holiness (12). This matches the instructions for the tabernacle and its regulations revealed to Moses during his fifth ascent (24:12 – 32:15) and accomplished in 35:20 – 40:33. Finally, the third ascent (16–25) makes Moses face a seriousness of divine holiness which not even he had previously contemplated (20–23) and is matched by the, again unexpected, barring of Moses from entering the completed tabernacle (40:34–35).

Exodus is indeed the book of the presence of the Lord among his people. We have seen this already in his coming to share their humiliation in Egypt (3:8) and in the gracious condescension of his walking with them, bearing with them and providing for them as they journeyed from Egypt to Sinai. Now, however, we begin to learn alongside the Israelites that Moses' initial exclusion from the presence of the holy Lord (3:5) is a

---

[1] The wording of 19:3 suggests that Moses began to ascend the mountain before he had heard the Lord calling him, and it should be understood this way. J. C. Rylaarsdam, in *The Interpreter's Bible*, vol. 1 (Abingdon, 1952), says, 'As Moses ascends the mountain, apparently before he has gone far, God calls', and Durham agrees. The implication is that at least by the time he reached Sinai Moses had recalled the Lord's promise (3:12) and knew the Lord would be there to meet him. He therefore ascended the mountain on his own initiative.

paradigm of the reality that sin excludes and holiness threatens. The fire in the bush (3:1–3) and the fire on the tabernacle (40:38) may seem manageable and 'domesticated', but they are both the same as the raging inferno of holy fire which descended on Sinai (19:16–18).

1. The obedience of the redeemed (19:3–8a)

The message and meaning of the first ascent are unmistakable once we see its structure:

> A[1] Moses' ascent, the Lord's call to Moses (3a)
>> B[1] Moses commissioned to speak to Israel (3b)[2]
>>> C[1] What the Lord has done (4)
>>> C[2] What the Lord requires (5a)
>>> C[3] What the Lord promises (5b–6a)
>> B[2] Moses commissioned to speak to Israel (6b)
> A[2] Moses' descent, Moses' call to the elders (7–8a)

The sequence of the three central C sections is extremely important for our understanding of the Old Testament and, indeed, of the whole Bible and of our place as the covenant people within it. The sequence is the saving acts of the Lord (C[1]), our response of obedience (C[2]) and the blessings which obedience brings (C[3]). Nothing must ever be allowed to upset this order. Notice, therefore, the past tenses of verse 4 and the contrasting future tenses of verses 5 and 6. The Lord's great act of deliverance and salvation has already been done (4), and this is why verse 5 can speak of the Lord's covenant[3] as an existing reality and something to be 'kept', that is, preserved and guarded. It was in pursuance of his covenant promises that the Lord came to his distressed people in Egypt (2:24) – not to make them his 'sons' but because Israel was already his 'firstborn son' (4:22). The redemption he achieved for them fulfilled the great covenant promise that 'I will take you as my own people, and I will be your

---

[2] The double designation Jacob/Israel looks back to Gen. 46:8 and Exod. 1:1. The people who went down to Egypt and encountered oppression there are the very people whom the Lord has delivered. Mackay suggests the doubling is deliberate, to increase the solemnity of this statement of the covenant. Kaiser thinks of 'Jacob' as a reminder of humble origins and 'Israel' as an indication of what the Lord made them.

[3] Hence it is referred to as *my covenant*, not 'our' or 'your'. Cassuto is quite mistaken in seeing verse 5 as implying 'a bilateral covenant', as though his people's obedience was part of negotiating a quid pro quo with the Lord. Childs (p. 366) is precisely inexact in speaking of 'the invitation to a covenant'.

God' (6:6–7). It was not, therefore, that they were ordered to obey in order that they might enter the covenant, but that, already being within the covenant, they were called to obey so that they might enjoy the benefits and privileges of God's people. What was true of the 'old' covenant is true of the 'new', and we enter on exactly the same basis of grace and continue in exactly the same obedience of faith.

2. Possessing our possessions

The telling phrase 'to possess one's possessions'[4] is used by Obadiah (verse 17) and expresses the idea of us entering into full enjoyment of what has long been and is rightfully ours. This is exactly what is meant here in verses 4–6: the Lord has acted, securing benefits for his people (4), and obedience to him (5a) brings the enjoyment of what he has achieved (5b–6a).

a. What the Lord has done (19:4)

The three instances of divine action in verse 4 are a deliberate summary of Exodus 6 – 19. The Israelites had seen it all; that is to say, they knew it at first hand. They were not, like Jethro (18:1), being told what had happened to someone else. They had been there when the Lord devastated Egypt: it had happened before their very eyes. They knew all about the caring, safeguarding wings of their divine 'eagle', and now they were in the very company of their victorious, sufficient Lord.[5] The use of the eagle as an image of guardian care and the journey's end in the Lord's company are easy to define. The people had experienced the watchful and supportive guardianship of one so infinitely stronger and more able than themselves, and now they found that they had been welcomed into his presence and accepted into intimacy with him, not by their own efforts or merits, but because *I . . . brought you to myself.*

---

[4] The Hebrew is *wĕyār̆šu . . . 'ēt-môrāšêhem* and is rightly translated in the kjv, rv and esv as 'possess their possessions'. In the niv it has been mistakenly altered to 'possess [their] inheritance'.

[5] According to McNeile, 'God is represented as having his dwelling place on the mountain', and Driver translates verse 4 as 'my abode in Sinai'. But if Sinai was God's abode, then why is he represented as 'coming down' on the mountain for this specific occasion (18)? The point is not arrival at the Lord's 'place' but the consummation of a relationship. Cf. G. H. Davies, who says, 'The Lord of Sinai descends upon the mountain. Sinai is not his dwelling place so much as his terrestrial manifestation point.' Cole remarks, 'Israel never thought of Yahweh as living on Sinai (as the Greeks thought that their gods lived . . . on Olympus) but only as appearing there.'

The initial divine act – *what I did to Egypt* – is a complex of ideas, not to be narrowly pinned down. First, Yahweh is Lord of all the earth. He is God over Egypt as much as over Israel. Second, his divinity is expressed in sovereign control and direction of earthly events. Egypt, a superpower of the day, was utterly without power against the will and visitations of the God of Israel. Third, in Egypt the Lord implemented his ancestral choice of Israel; he 'remembered his covenant' with their forefathers (2:24). So, along with sovereignty and victory, we can number election among the things the Lord 'did in Egypt'.

When we are discussing election we need to remember that we cannot and must not rationalize it, so as to reason, for example, that the God of Israel is such that he is always on the side of the poor, the oppressed and the disadvantaged. Election is always a secret, hidden in the divine nature. Deuteronomy 7:7–8 says,

> The Lord did not set his affection on you and choose you because you were more numerous than other peoples, for you were the fewest of all peoples. But it was because the Lord loved you and kept the oath he swore to your ancestors.

In other words, the Lord loved you because he loved you! Thus, the deciding factor in the choice was not one, like poverty, which might appeal to human logic, but the hidden reason of love. This means, of course, a reason that satisfied the wisdom, justice and every other attribute of God, but which remained hidden within the divine heart and mind.

These were all things which the Lord had already achieved. There was nothing conditional about them. They did not await, nor were they dependent in any way upon, some particular response on Israel's part. Indeed, considering the Israel of Exodus 4 – 17, one might even say the Lord would have been better advised to have chosen a different people! But, irrespective of anything about them, he acted in such a way that they were liberated by his victory, cared for and protected by his providence, and brought to himself.

b. What the Lord promises (19:5b–6a)

A broad correspondence can be traced between the Lord's acts described in verse 4 and what he went on to promise – as though he were saying, 'These things are what I have already done for you; now enjoy them.'

First, by what he did in Egypt, he demonstrated that *the whole earth is mine*, and it was there too that out of all nations, he chose Israel, making them his *treasured possession*. The word is *sĕgullâ*, and it means a 'personal treasure'.[6] We must understand it against the background of the absolutist monarchies of the ancient world, where the king was the theoretical owner of everything.[7] Within this total ownership, he might gather and put to one side things that he specially prized and considered to be his own in a unique way. It was this that was his *sĕgullâ*, his choice, personal treasure.

Second, there is the idea of the priestly people, *a kingdom of priests*. Durham insists that to see here the root of the idea of the priesthood of all believers 'goes too far'. Understandably, he does not say why, for there is no reason to object to this, the plainest meaning of the words. The elect covenant people are citizens of the kingdom of the divine King, but within that kingdom, ideally considered, each citizen is a priest, with the privilege of priestly access to the king's presence.[8] This understanding suits not only the words themselves, but also the way in which the biblical story of priesthood developed. The sin of the golden calf brought home to Israel their unfitness to be the Lord's 'kingdom of priests', and the privilege of priesthood became vested in the tribe of Levi and the family of Aaron. This lasted until, in the fullness of time, the Lord Jesus Christ restored the lost ideal, making us – all believers – 'a kingdom and priests to serve his God and Father' (Rev. 1:6), possessing and called to exercise the blessed privilege of priestly access into his holy presence (Heb. 10:19–21).[9]

---

[6] 1 Chr. 29:3 and Eccl. 2:8 illustrate perfectly the idea of treasure which the king looks upon as particularly his own. So Hyatt translates, 'a king's private treasure . . . a private accumulation'. Currid quotes these verses as showing that the word includes the sense of 'put aside for a particular use', but the verses do not seem to support this extension of meaning. Durham has 'the jewel in the crown'. For more references to Israel as the Lord's private treasure see Deut. 7:6; 14:2; 26:18; Ps. 135:4; cf. Mal. 3:17.

[7] G. H. Davies sensibly sees *the whole earth is mine* as 'this monotheistic affirmation . . . not too late in the days of the prophets . . . not too early for the days of Moses'. In context it also stresses the freedom of God in his choice of Israel.

[8] Many interpret the priesthood of Israel as referring to them as a mediating nation, bringing the knowledge of God to the world (e.g. Mackay, 'a servant nation . . . to mediate between the divine world and the ordinary world', and Durham, 'the extension throughout the world of the ministry of Yahweh's presence'). This is certainly not the main understanding of priesthood within the Old Testament. J. B. Payne (*TWOT*, p. 431) says that the role of the priest as 'a minister for sacred things, especially sacrifice' is a much more accurate picture. The priest had religious/ritual duties (Exod. 29) and state functions (e.g. as judge, Num. 27:2, and in the holy war, Deut. 20:2). Priests were obligated to holiness (Lev. 22; Jer. 23:11); they were teachers (Deut. 17:18; Neh. 8; Mal. 2:7) and medical doctors (Lev. 13:13), and were called upon to intercede (Ps. 99:6) and to enquire of the Lord (1 Sam. 30:7). All these functions were in the context of the relationship between Israel and the Lord. The substantial truth, therefore, of the 'priesthood of all believers' in both Old and New Testaments (cf. Heb. 10:19–22) is access into the holy presence.

[9] It is essential to remember that in the New Testament the word 'priest' is used in the singular only of Jesus and in the plural only of all believers. There is no such thing as an order or 'caste' of 'priests', and Christian ministers should not be called, or allow themselves to be called, 'priests'.

Thus it was that the Lord, who in Egypt had implemented his choice of Israel as his 'jewel in the crown' and who came to them as protector and provider during all the miles of their pilgrimage, now gave them the right to come to him, to be free in his presence, to be his priests.

Third, how well all this links in with the reality of a *holy nation*. The word used here is *gôy*, which throughout the Old Testament generally refers to the 'pagan' nations, unenlightened by divine revelation. Israel is, from this perspective, one *nation* among the many which make up earth's peoples, but it is also a *holy* nation, distinct from the rest, commissioned with sharing and displaying the divine nature and living in the likeness of God their Saviour (2 Pet. 1:2–4). This is the point at which their privileged status (*my treasured possession*) and free access (*kingdom of priests*) becomes the public testimony of the holiness whereby they show themselves to the world in all their distinctiveness (cf. Num. 15:40–41; Deut. 7:6; 14:2, 21; 26:19; 28:9), and whereby God is 'glorified in his holy people and . . . marvelled at among all those who have believed' (2 Thess. 1:10).

c. What the Lord requires (19:5a)

We come now to the *if* which forms the bridge between what the Lord has done (4) and what he promises (5b–6a), the only 'if' in the whole sequence. Unilateral divine decision and action had made the Israelites the Lord's elect, the objects of his providential care and the people of his intimate presence. Before them, by promise, he set the enjoyment of those very things that he had done: to know themselves as his treasure, to have access to his presence as his priests and to show forth his holy glory to the world. But this can be so only if they *obey . . . and keep.*

d. The people of God and the word of God

The significant *if* with which verse 5 opens relates not to covenant status but to covenant enjoyment. Status comes by the acts of God; enjoyment by the responsive commitment of obedience. Obedience is not our part in a two-sided bargain, but our grateful response to what the Lord has unilaterally decided and done.

There are two aspects to this response of obedience. First, covenant people are required to *obey me fully* (lit. 'listen attentively to my voice'). Our God is a speaking God who communicates his word to us; we are to be characterized by obedience to what he says. The hallmark of the genuineness of the people of God is that they possess, listen to and obey the word of God.

Second, covenant people are called to *keep my covenant*. As yet the Israelites did not know what this would involve, but they would soon learn that there were particular stipulations or requirements for living within the covenant. The main dimensions of covenant living were marked out by the voice of the Lord himself declaring his 'Ten Commandments' (20:1–17; cf. Deut. 4:12–13) and the detailed applications revealed through Moses (20:22 – 23:19). This all amounted to a distinctive personal, social and national life – the lifestyle of the covenant people.

3. Moses' second ascent: the coming God, the prepared people (19:8b–15)

The whole scene in Exodus 19 is startlingly unique – awe-inspiring to the nth degree, and yet fully believable. It is logical and natural that Moses should have hastened back to the people with the revelation of the covenant (4–6) and then, with equal alacrity, brought their prompt response back to the Lord (8). Equally realistic is the way Moses' report does not come until the end of verse 9: verse 8b is the author's title of the second ascent, but Moses' report has to take second place to what the Lord wanted to say to him (9a), and Moses must await an opportunity to interject the tidings he had gone up to share (9b).[10]

> A[1]   Moses ascends to report to the Lord (8b)
> > B[1]   The Lord will descend to speak to the people through Moses (9)
> > > C[1]   Preparation: the consecration of the people (10)
> > > > D   The Lord's promised visible descent on the third day (11)
> > > C[2]   Preparation: the separation of Mount Sinai (12–13a)
> > B[2]   The people[11] may ascend the mount when summoned (13b)[12]
> A[2]   Moses descends to prepare the people (14–15)

---

[10]   See Mackay: 'It was only after the Lord had clarified Moses' position that he was able to deliver his report.'

[11]   In verse 13b the pronoun *they* in *may they approach* is emphatic, i.e. it is 'they' as distinct from Moses, whose unique dignity is seen in his freedom to come and go into the Lord's presence.

[12]   See T. C. Mitchell, 'The Music of the Old Testament Reconsidered', *Palestine Exploration Quarterly*, 124 (1992), pp. 124ff.

The people's impulsive response in verse 8 was totally correct – even if uninformed (they did not yet know what the Lord would say) and unaware of their own inability to sustain a life of obedience. But what else do we want to do when we recollect the divine mercies but to pledge total loyalty, to allow gratitude to overflow in commitment and to vow that life will be different and pleasing to God our Saviour from now on (cf. Rom. 12:1–2; Col. 1:9–11)?

a. 'What shall I do? . . . You will be told' (Acts 22:10)

But how is an impulse to become a way of life? It is necessary that God should speak and make his will known. In this way, the topic of the second ascent follows straight from the first. The people had pledged obedience, and the Lord now proposed to honour their intention by speaking to them (9). By doing this he leads his people on to the lifestyle in which their impulse to please him will work out in their obedience to the word he speaks. The Lord transforms impulse into obedience by his spoken word.

At this point another question arises, but we will best understand what Exodus is saying if we turn aside briefly to the New Testament.

b. Jesus is Lord

The great New Testament confession that 'Jesus is Lord' (e.g. Acts 10:36; Rom. 10:9; 1 Cor. 12:3; 2 Cor. 4:5) finds vivid expression in Matthew's account of the resurrection. Like all the four Evangelists, he begins his account with the empty tomb (28:1–15), but he records this event in such a way as to turn our gaze forward to what was yet to happen in Galilee (28:7, 10). For it was in Galilee that the gathered church was favoured with a vision of the risen Jesus who proclaimed that 'All authority . . . has been given to me' (28:18) – in a word, Jesus is Lord. This claim gives us perspective but not direction. We see ourselves as in the hand and at the disposal of that supreme Lord, and we see the whole cosmos, visible and invisible, spiritual and terrestrial, as the sphere where his writ runs. We never face a place or circumstance where he is not already Lord. This is wonderful, but it tells us nothing of what we must do, where we must go, how we must live – unless, God forbid, we are to be left to follow the whims of our own intuitions! When we turn, however, to Luke's account of the resurrection, this crucial gap is filled. In Luke 24 the risen Jesus – still the Lord of the empty tomb (24:1–12) – is primarily the Lord of Holy Scripture. Only in Scripture is he to be known (24:27, 32) and only as revealed in Scripture is he to be preached (24:45–48). Lordship is thus linked with revelation. We can obey because God has spoken.

We can now return to Exodus, where at Sinai we have the revelation of a God who is Lord indeed, sovereign over the world, absolute in power and majesty, wonderful in saving mercy and in protecting, providing care, and who chose his people by free, unfettered choice and brought them to himself. No wonder they promptly pledged obedience to such a God (8). But lordship has no specific meaning without revelation, as we see in the Acts account where Paul asks, 'Lord, what do You want me to do?' and receives the reply, 'You will be told what you must do' (Acts 9:6, NKJV). Moses was thus an essential figure for the exercise of divine Lordship and for the obedience of the elect. He was to stand between the two parties to hear the word(s) the Lord spoke and then communicate that to the people. The life of obedience arises out of the word of God. In our case this is the Bible, but specifically here it is the word spoken through Moses, which in fact continues as divine revelation *always* (9; cf. 'to us' in Acts 7:38). The connection between the life of obedience and the word God speaks is inseparable, for the word of God transforms our best intentions into actual conduct. Holiness is obedience to revealed truth.

c. Holiness without which no-one will see God (19:10–15)[13]

By moving directly from the word which God speaks (9) to the holiness which God requires if we are to meet with him (10), Exodus reflects the way biblical thinking works. The word of God is designed to be life-changing, and, as the Bible teaches us, nothing is truly 'known' until it permeates from the mind to the heart and will: understood in thought, loved in heart and obeyed in will.[14]

We are told nothing of the spiritual exercises the people engaged in during their three days of preparation. The washing of clothes is to be understood in the sense of 'having clean clothes ready to wear on the third day'. Frequently in the Bible, clothes are used as symbols of the nature and intentions of the wearer. If we were to stop a wedding car and ask the girl in white, 'Why are you dressed like a bride?', she would reply, 'Because I am a bride, and I am on my way to get married.' Exactly! Clothes point to

---

[13] Cf. Heb. 12:14.

[14] J. B. Phillips' representation of 2 Tim. 3:16 is particularly helpful: 'All scripture . . . is useful for teaching the faith . . . correcting error . . . *re-setting the direction of a man's life* and training him in good living' (my italics).

the nature and intentions of the wearer. When the Lord puts on armour, it is because he is a warrior and purposes conquest.[15] By the third day the people were ready to present themselves as purified in heart and purposing holiness, and their fresh clothes symbolized this.

The intervening days did, however, impose a discipline which required the people to keep the idea of holiness in the forefront of their minds. Living as they were at the foot of the mountain, imagine the constant anxiety of parents lest their children thoughtlessly violated the bounds that had been set;[16] imagine how the shepherds must have watched the grazing of their beasts lest they lose valuable animals. Not only must the people have constantly been aware of God's holiness, but they also had to accept their own position as unworthy to approach him and acknowledge the peril with which holiness threatened the unworthy. They also had to accept the discipline of submissive waiting and not venture onto the mountain until the trumpet called. All this could be called 'holiness in the mind', the keeping of all that the holiness of God means constantly in mind and memory, day and night, and living thoughtfully in the light of that holiness.

The further prohibition of sexual intercourse extended their preparation to holiness of the heart and the emotions. Paul had the same thing in mind when he counselled married couples not to 'deprive each other except perhaps by mutual consent and for a time, so that you may devote yourselves to prayer' (1 Cor. 7:5). The Book of Common Prayer used to remind wedding couples that marriage was 'instituted of God in the time of man's innocency', a most beautiful and exact summary of scriptural teaching. Marriage is God's idea and is not of human origin. It was instituted before the fall into sin and is not in any way a concession for sinfulness or an accommodation of sinful desires. It arose, in fact, from the divine perception that 'it is not good for the man to be alone' (Gen. 2:18). Marriage, therefore, is a prescription for holiness, for the perfecting of human life, with the married couple as 'heirs together of the grace of life' (1 Pet. 3:7, kjv, rv; cf. esv). The prohibition of sexual relations did not arise, therefore, from any idea of the sinfulness of sex, but from the

---

[15] See Josh. 5:13–15; cf. the Lord putting on the garments of salvation in Isa. 59:16–17.

[16] From the prohibition of trespassing on the mountain, Calvin observes that true knowledge of God does not result from human inquisitiveness but only from God's decision, in his time and way, to reveal himself. The same would apply to serious research in which the unaided human mind ventures to weigh God in its balances.

awareness that in a true and happy marriage, intercourse involves a total absorption of each with the other and is the deepest emotional delight and commitment known on earth. The restriction was put in place at this important moment in time because the Lord wished to have his people's hearts wholly for himself. As Calvin says, 'They were to be reminded that all earthly cares were, as much as possible, to be renounced . . . that they might give their entire attention to the hearing of the law.'[17]

4. The God of surprises (19:16–25)

All of this was leading up to one thing: Moses was preparing the people for the coming of the Lord (11). The actual meeting was heralded by a trumpet call (16), inviting the people within the sacred enclosure of the mountain, and Moses led them out *to meet with God* (17).[18] He was surprised by the news that further safeguards were needed, safeguards which, in fact, he had thought were already in place. The scene must have been one of high drama as the people's approach was halted by a summons to Moses to make his third personal ascent of the mount (20). When he entered the presence of God, however, he was sent back down with messages for both people and priests that there were to be limits to how far they could go (21–22). Moses neither expected this, nor did he see the need for it, but, of course, he obeyed. The heart of the matter is that we are dealing with a holy God, and not even the best-intentioned, best-sustained and most sincere efforts at self-sanctification make us fit for his presence, or his presence anything less than a mortal danger to us.

The third day (19:16–19)

The record of Moses' third ascent of Sinai is prefaced by the awe-inspiring description of the Lord's descent.[19] The whole of creation reacted to the

---

[17] Calvin in his commentary on Exodus. Cf. Deut. 5:29; 8:2; 30:6. The Old Testament later recognizes that sexual intercourse renders the participants 'unclean' (Lev. 15:16–18). Such 'uncleanness' is technical rather than moral but, in any case, it arose not from marriage as such but because the male semen (like female menstrual discharge, Lev. 15:19–24, and childbirth, Lev. 12:2–5) involves contact with the very essence of sinful, fallen human life. This sexual abstention also distinguishes Old Testament religion from the rampant sexuality of the worship of Baal.

[18] When the Sinai event was 'written up', it was a correct instinct to say that Moses 'brought the people out to meet the God', the definite article signifying 'the one who is God indeed, the true God, God's very self'.

[19] As we would expect, verses 16–19 have a formal pattern:
   A¹ Cloud on Sinai: trembling in the camp (16)
      B¹ Moses leads the people to meet God (17)
   A² Smoke on Sinai: the mountain quaking (18)
      B² Moses speaks: God answers (19)

coming of the Creator in thunder and lightning, the trembling and quaking of the physical world and its people (16, 18). The reality of the divine presence showed itself in cloud (smoke) and fire, and there was the particular feature of the Sinai narrative: the trumpet (16, 19). Many of these phenomena subsequently became standard scriptural ways of expressing the Lord's presence and action.[20]

'Fire' and 'cloud' are both motifs of the presence of God, each representing different aspects. The symbol of fire goes right back to Genesis 3:24, where it puts into effect the will of the Lord God to exclude sinners from his garden and to make their unaided return impossible. In Genesis 15:17, the 'oven that smoked and flamed' symbolizes the presence of God the covenant-maker, signing and sealing his promises. Exodus 3:5 makes an explicit link between fire and holiness, again as that aspect of the divine nature which forbids human approach. This leads directly to the inferno of fire on Sinai, again representing the excluding and life-threatening holiness of God.[21] The values of Sinai are perpetuated in Israel by the undying fire on the altar (Lev. 6:9, 12) and are given occasional dramatic exemplification in acts of divine judgment (e.g. Lev. 10:2; Num. 11:1–3).

The 'pillar of cloud' is one of the notable features of Exodus. By it the Lord was his people's guide (13:21–22), and this continued when the cloud settled on the tabernacle, also proclaiming 'God is here' (e.g. 40:34–38; Num. 9:15–22). The protective angel dwelt in the accompanying cloud (14:19), and it was in the cloud that God's glory appeared (16:10). Psalm 99:7 recalls the cloud as the place of revelation (cf. Exod. 33:9). The whole Sinai experience itself was especially marked by clouds.[22] Moses went up into

---

[20] Ps. 18:6–15 is a notable example. We read the history of David and Saul in vain to find any actual occurrences of what is described here. David is retrospectively meditating on divine intervention in terms which, from Sinai onwards, became conventions of Hebrew thinking and poetry (see Hag. 2:6, 21; Rev. 8:5; 11:19). See J. A. Motyer, 'Haggai', in T. McComisky (ed.), *The Minor Prophets*, 3 vols. (Baker, 1998). Durham urges that the Sinai event was written up retrospectively in the standard theophanic motifs of later days, but it is more reasonable to think that these became standard theophanic motifs because they were evidenced in the historical reality of Sinai. Donald Wiseman, in an unpublished lecture at Tyndale House, Cambridge, said that if Moses did not keep a day-to-day record of events under his leadership, he is the only known leader of antiquity to fail to have done so. It is seriously unthinkable that no contemporary (i.e. Mosaic) record of Israel at Sinai was made and preserved.

[21] Fire pervades the events at Sinai (e.g. Exod. 24:17; Deut. 4:11–12, 15). Ps. 89:46[47] shows how the Sinai concept of fiery holiness as a threat to sinners remained in Israel. Ezekiel (1:27) makes fire central to his understanding of the revelation of God and sees the outpouring of the central fire of God as the agent in just judgment (Ezek. 10:2, 6; cf. Rev. 8:5).

[22] See 19:9, 16; 24:15, 18; 34:5. Cf. the revelation of God to Ezekiel (Ezek. 1:4) and also Matt. 17:5; 24:30; Acts 1:9; Rev. 1:7.

the cloud and darkness where God was (20:21; 24:18), and in the Holy of Holies the cloud that was large enough to envelop Sinai contracted itself to rest on the golden cover of the ark (Lev. 16:2). Like 'fire', 'cloud' symbolizes the presence of God, but in the sense of the Holy One so shrouding (not abandoning or diminishing) his glory that he could accommodate himself to live among his people, to grace them with a presence which, in its awful holiness, would spell their destruction.[23]

5. Go down, Moses

When the events in Exodus 19 reached their climax, to every human eye everything was in order. The days of preparation were over, the trumpet had sounded, and the Lord was doing what he had promised, conversing with Moses in the hearing of Israel, and in this way establishing authorized lines of communication and revelation. To the divine eye, however, all was not well, and Moses, notwithstanding his protests (23), was sent back to put further safeguards in place.

The people, happy about their state following the preparation days, could so easily have become forgetful of their status: in a word, their 'holiness' is not God's holiness. They needed the warning that the holiness of God is such that no human self-preparation can ever satisfy its demands. Humans can no more fit themselves to stand in the Lord's holy presence than Adam and Eve, in their day, could find the road back to the garden and evade the angel with the sword of flame. But this needs God's eye to see, and Israel might easily have thought that now at last boundary markers were a thing of the past, and even the mediation of Moses was no longer required, but that they could converse directly with the Lord themselves. Verse 21 opens the possibility of the double error of, first, a false self-understanding whereby they might have thought themselves fit and at liberty to ignore the bounds the Lord had set; and second, a wrong motive in entering the sphere of the divine simply to *see*, moved by a curiosity devoid of awe.

---

[23] Noth, observing that in general we have no indications to enable us to locate Sinai, finds a positive pointer in 'the fact that volcanic eruptions were to be seen on it'. The J source, he says, preserves a 'volcanic tradition'. If so, then we can only assume that J's customary powers of description deserted him! The fire came down upon Sinai, not up and out from it. G. H. Davies asks how Moses got people to 'stand and remain at the foot of a volcano in eruption' (cf. Cole). *Smoke from a furnace* (18) occurs in Gen. 19:28 (the only other place, notes Currid), where it is also the outcome of outpoured fire from heaven (Gen. 19:24).

By contrast, the priests, happy about their status, could easily have become forgetful of their state. Their status gave them the privilege to handle holy things and take on holy functions, and it would seem they had confused privilege with fitness and neglected the required preparation in holiness (22). But there is no such thing as holiness by office. Verse 21 deals with those whose consecration might make them presume, and verse 22 with those who presumed on their consecration. For each party alike, approaching God with such an attitude could only have been a case of 'forcing their way through' (21, 24), 'breaking and entering'.[24] As has often been said, 'an easy-going people believe in an easy-going God'.

The example of the people and priests warns us against the sorts of presumptions that still come so easily: an unthinking assumption of divine grace, forgetful of its wonder; a casual rushing into the divine presence, neglectful of the need of Jesus our mediator (1 Tim. 2:5) and of the precious blood of Christ by which alone we are sprinkled clean (Heb. 10:19–22); and an unwarranted laxity in our address to God. But we must learn equally from the patient and compliant obedience of Moses, acting out the word of God even against his own best judgment (23–25). In this he is like Ananias, who thought the Lord not best advised to have any truck with the arch-persecutor Saul, but went, nonetheless, and addressed the one whose coming he had dreaded as now his 'brother' (Acts 9:10–17).

Additional notes

19:4 Whether *nešer* means 'eagle' or 'griffin vulture', or whatever else, need not concern us. Such identifications are probably now beyond certainty. Whatever the bird, the picture is plain: nestlings must not be allowed to remain nestlings, and if their growth to maturity demands leaving the nest, then the parent bird itself will drive them out (Deut. 32:11). But, in doing so, the wings of the parent become a safety net under the first feeble attempts of the nestling to fly. On Deut. 32:11 see J. G. McConville, *Deuteronomy* (Apollos, 2002); J. A. Thompson, *Deuteronomy*, TOTC (1974); W. W. Wiersbe, *Be Equipped* (Chariot Victor, 1999).

---

[24] Two different verbs are used in these verses. The NIV's *force their way through* is √*hāras*, which means 'to break down, demolish', as in (here) the tearing down a fence. *Break out* is √*pāras*, which is used of a dam bursting (e.g. 2 Sam. 5:20). The Lord's holiness is like a huge force held in check, but constituting an overwhelming menace if released.

S. R. Driver, *Deuteronomy*, ICC (1895) quotes an account of an eagle actually doing these things.

19:9 Some commentators (e.g. Durham) see verse 9 as a later addition because of the seemingly repeated reference to Moses' reporting of the people's words and because it introduces a 'new' theme, the role of Moses as mediator. Such reasoning is needless. First, Hebrew narrative style often opens with a summary statement – here, verse 8b – followed by a more detailed account of what actually happened – here, verse 9 – introduced by *waw explicativum*, the conjunction (omitted in the NIV) used in the sense, 'that is to say'. Second, regarding the theme of Moses the mediator, the crucial question is not 'Are we surprised by it?' but 'Is it suitable in context?' Since the theme of the second ascent is that of the Lord coming to speak, it cannot be out of place for him to say how he intends to do so, i.e. through Moses' mediation. In verse 9 *to you* is second person singular masculine, i.e. it refers to Moses, with the purpose of validating him as the mediator of the covenant (another 'anticipatory providence'), the Lord having known in advance how the people would react to the sound of his voice (20:18–19). In *put their trust in you*, the *in you* is very emphatic, further emphasized by the particle *gam* (which the NIV also omits) – 'and, in particular, [so that] it will be in you that the people trust for ever'.

19:16–25 The way in which the documentary theory complicates the study of 19:16–25 without explaining or clarifying anything can be conveniently seen in Durham's summaries. Durham himself seems to believe that the section is a multilayered composite, though it is easier to *say* this than to 'disentangle' the bits and pieces. But, in fact, the most obvious feature of verses 16–25 is neither its accumulating 'layers', nor its composite nature, but its surprising content – the cancellation of the planned meeting. We should see this within the setting of the developing revelation of the holiness of God in Exodus. With unbelievable gentleness the holy God 'domesticated' his holiness for Moses in the simple act of asking him to remove his shoes (3:5). After this, holiness as such does not obtrude into the reality of the divine presence with Israel until, at Sinai, there begins the serious instruction about holiness (19:16–25), which the people begin to 'feel' but not acknowledge as such in 20:18, and which will reach its normative proportions following the sin of the golden calf (chapter 32).

19:19 With verse 19, cf. Deut 4:11–12. The NIV's *the voice of God answered him* is the correct understanding of (lit.) 'and God answered him by a voice [*bĕqôl*]'. The NASB's 'with thunder' is also possible; in verse 16 the NIV's 'thunder' is 'voices' (pl. *qolôt*). Durham allows the ambiguity; Driver understands 'thunder'; Cassuto and Childs suggest 'articulately', which conforms better with the Hebrew. There would have been little point in Moses being 'answered' by a thunderclap! The verse seems deliberately to set up a dialogue. Both subjects, Moses and God, are in the emphatic position, and the verbs *spoke* and *answered* are (lit.) 'kept speaking' and 'kept answering'. *God* is 'the God', underlining the wonder of it all: 'God himself'.

19:20–25 These verses have suffered considerable mangling at the hands of the proponents of the documentary theory and yet they offer plain evidence of careful artistic unity of presentation.

> A¹ Moses' ascent to the Lord (20)
> > B¹ The Lord's renewed warning to people and priests (21–22)
> > > C Moses' demurral (23)
> > B² The Lord's insistence regarding priests and people (24)
> A² Moses' descent to the people (25)

Verse 23, Moses' immediate reaction in questioning the Lord, is far from being an intrusion into the text but is the pivot around which the passage 'works'. Is it significant that whereas the Lord looks for a sanctified people, Moses speaks of a sanctified place? We may note also that here, as ever, it is the Lord who sees where the danger lies and shelters his people from it. Calvin notes the humble obedience of Moses, 'preferring the command of God to his own opinion', or, we might add, his official dignity. Regarding verse 25, Hyatt and others urge that it breaks off abruptly (translating 'and he said to them') and that 'originally' some sort of speech must have followed. But the translation *and told them* is good, idiomatic Hebrew (cf. 2 Sam. 16:11; 2 Kgs 4:24; Job 9:7; Ps. 106:24). The verb √'*āmar* is frequently used 'absolutely' in the sense 'said [it]'/'told'. Driver is quite mistaken to say this meaning is 'illegitimate'.

19:22 Commentators are divided over the reference to *priests*. Those who hold to a documentary approach (e.g. McNeile) allege an anachronism here. Hyatt thinks it is an addition to the text to deal with a question that arose later about whether priests were included in the prohibitions. He does not explain who would be so stupid as to ask such a question. Others seek possible explanations. Cassuto thinks of the likely priestly office of the firstborn and Davies of 'unofficial family ministers' without pointing out that in patriarchal times the head of the house acted as priest to his own family. But the idea of 'priest' (*kōhēn*) was widespread in the ancient world, and 19:6 indicates that it needed no explanation in Israel.

Exodus 20:1–21

17. The ten words

The substance of chapter 20 comes as no surprise. The Lord had announced beforehand that he would speak to Moses in such a way that the whole people would hear (19:9), and now he proceeded to do that very thing.

1. The Decalogue introduced (20:1–2)

The introduction to the Ten Commandments says nothing that Exodus has not already said, but repetitions in the Bible are every bit as needful as the parent's cry, 'How often have I to tell you . . . ?' Some truths go beyond 'bearing repetition' to 'requiring repetition' because of their fundamental importance. In the present case the repetitions are about the Lord's law for the Lord's people. First, the words originated in God (1). Second, the God who spoke the words is Yahweh *your God, who brought you out of Egypt* (2a). And third, the people to whom the words were addressed were those who had been brought (lit.) 'out of the house of slaves' (2b), that is, they had already been liberated.

a. The words originated in God himself

The fact that these words were spoken by God himself is an indication of the uniqueness of the occasion. Throughout the course of the Old Testament, the word of God, expressed in the words of God, comes in the form of the famous prophetic claim, 'Thus says the LORD', or, to bring out its inner flavour, 'This is what the Lord has said.' This means that had the Lord himself come forward in person as the speaker, he would have said exactly what he chose to say through his servants the prophets. Although they used the vocabulary, literary style and skill natural to each of them,

203

their words were God's words, and his words were theirs. At Sinai, however, the people heard not only the words of God but also his voice.

The Old Testament calls what he then said (lit.) 'the ten words' (e.g. Deut. 4:13), a description which stresses both the verbal nature of the revelation and also that each commandment is a self-contained 'word' in its own right. But, we may ask, why ten and why this particular set of ten? The second question is more important than the first. Deuteronomy 5:22 notes that these 'words' were spoken by the Lord and then goes on to observe that 'he added nothing more'. This suggests that we should search for a wholeness, completeness or totality in this particular set of ten instructions. More of this in a moment, but first we will address the question of why these particular commandments?

'I am'

Before the Lord announced his law, he pointed to himself with the words, *I am the* Lord *[Yahweh]*. Leviticus 19 helps us to understand the significance of this. There we find an odd and jumbled collection of the Lord's laws – religious, domestic, social, horticultural, ritual, agricultural and sexual. The fact that they are in no discernible order may be deliberate, for life itself is a jumble, one thing after another, and the Lord wanted his people to live in every situation, in all the flux and whirl of life, according to his revealed will. But the jumble of Leviticus 19 is held together by the recurring affirmation, 'I am the Lord' (sixteen times in all). In our English translations this sounds like a demand to submit to his authority: 'Do what I tell you because I am the Lord.' We would, of course, be untrue to the Old Testament if we overlooked this authoritarian note (e.g. Deut. 6:1), but 'the Lord' is the divine name, Yahweh, and the recurring affirmation is equivalent to the Lord saying, 'I want you to live this way because "I am who I am"' (cf. Exod. 3:13–14). For this reason, Leviticus 19 begins with a call to the Lord's people to be like him: 'Be holy because I, the Lord your God, am holy' – you must be what you must be because I am what I am. The law of God reflects the character of God. It is the likeness of God expressed in precepts, and obedience to the law of the Lord 'triggers' in us 'the image of God' (Gen. 1:26–28) which is our real nature.[1] In other words, we live the truly human life when we obey the Lord's law.

---

[1] See J. A. Motyer, 'The Image of God: Law and Liberty in Biblical Ethics', the London Bible College 1976 Laing Lecture. A. Phillips, *Ancient Israel's Criminal Law* (Oxford, 1970), p. 37, speaks of the law as 'the self-presentation of Yahweh'.

b. The God who spoke the words is the one who delivered his people from Egypt

In other words, he is Yahweh. He 'spelled out' the meaning of his name in words (Exod. 3:12 – 4:23) and confirmed what he said by his subsequent acts in the exodus, so that Yahweh would for ever be the God who redeemed his people and overthrew his enemies (3:15), the God of saving mercy and just judgment (e.g. 34:6–7). When he addressed his people at Sinai, the stress naturally fell on his work of redemption/salvation/liberation. It was he who had 'brought them out' from the land of Egypt and, therefore, could now speak to them of his requirements for their lives.

Grace and law

This brings into full focus the grand theological and spiritual significance of all that had happened up to this point. It was the God of salvation who imposed his law on his people; the grace that saves preceded the law that demands. The people were given the law not in order that they might become the redeemed; rather it was because they had already been redeemed that they were given the law. The law of God is the way of life he sets before those whom he has saved, and they engage in that way of life as a response of love and gratitude to God their Redeemer.[2] Grace and law belong together, for grace leads to law; saving love leads to and excites grateful love expressed in obedience.

c. The words were addressed to those who had already been brought into liberty

The law of the Lord was addressed to those brought out of bondage, and its aim was not to bring them into a new bondage, but rather to establish them in their new freedom. As those who had come out of (lit.) 'the house of slaves' (2b), they needed to be instructed in the behaviour and lifestyle of the free. Such is the law of the Lord – it is the true 'law of liberty' (Jas 1:25, ESV).

Back to the garden

This is the biblical understanding of God's law. It began in the garden of Eden, where Adam and Eve enjoyed the liberty, and liberality, of the

---

[2] The word 'law' is not our best friend. Hebrew *tôrâ* derives from √*yārâ*, which means 'to teach'. What we call the 'law' of the Lord is more akin to the teaching that careful parents would give to beloved children for their well-being (cf. Prov. 3:1–4; 6:20–23). The beneficent intentions of the law – life, entrance, possession – are expressed in Deut. 4:1 (cf. Acts 5:32).

garden (Gen. 2:9, 15–16) for just as long, and only as long, as they kept its law (Gen. 2:17). That law – the single prohibition regarding the tree of the knowledge of good and evil – far from being a restriction on their freedom, was the guarantor of freedom. It was a law of liberty.

So also the Decalogue (and, more generally, the law of Moses in its entirety or, supremely, the Bible as a whole) is the law of liberty, the gateway to human freedom. We readily say when we see the degrading conditions some people suffer that 'no-one ought to be obliged to live like that'. Behind that instinctive comment lies a sense of the unique value of humankind and some sense of what might constitute a 'truly human life'. But if we want to go beyond instinctive reactions, we need a true definition of what 'humankind' is. We have to be able to say what human nature *is* before we can say what human life *ought to be*. The Bible supplies the definition: 'God created mankind in his own image . . . male and female he created them' (Gen. 1:27). This is the intensely practical importance of saying that each precept of the law expresses some principle, some essential feature, of the divine nature. Each commandment represents some aspect of the likeness of God, and, therefore, obedience to God's law gives expression to what we really are, beings in God's likeness, and results in our true freedom. Once more, so to speak, the law preserves for us the delights of the garden.

When we approach the Ten Commandments, then, it should not be in a spirit of foreboding, as if we lived under a constant threat. Rather, we must learn to cry with the psalmist, 'Oh, how I love your law!' (Ps. 119:97).

Through the Psalms we look, as through a great window, right into the church of the Old Testament and find at its centre a delighted, exuberant love of the Lord's word of commandment. We need to recover this for ourselves, to remind ourselves of the grace and goodness of possessing the law of God. We have not been left to fumble around in mist or darkness, we have been given directions. As the Lord's redeemed, it should be our delight to give pleasure to God our Saviour (Col. 1:10), and he has told us how. To us, as to our brothers and sisters in the church of the old covenant, these commands are 'a lamp and the teaching [law] a light, and the reproofs of discipline are the way of life' (Prov. 6:23, ESV). If 'reproofs of discipline' sounds over-threatening, try 'admonitions of correction',[3] for

---

[3] In Prov. 6:23 these important words are *tōkēḥâ* and *mûsār*. The former derives from √*yākaḥ*, which gives the meaning 'reason together' in Isa. 1:18 [ESV] (cf. 'decide', Isa. 11:3; 'argue the case', Job 13:3). The latter means 'to warn, correct' (e.g. Ps. 2:10). Together they summarize what we now call 'counselling', gentle and helpful correction and direction.

what the word of God is doing here is exposing some wrong path on which we are about to set our feet and pointing and urging us in a different way – what J. B. Phillips calls 're-setting direction' (2 Tim. 3:16). By the mercy of his law, the Lord 'resets' us in the direction of light and life, or as Psalm 119:45 puts it most strikingly, 'I will walk about[4] in freedom, for [because!] I have sought out your precepts.' 'Precepts' is the 'narrowest' word in the vocabulary of Psalm 119, covering every minute detail of applying the law of God to daily life. The verse thus voices a striking truth: the psalmist found that the more closely he tied his life to the word of God, the more he enjoyed the largest liberty.[5] This is the way we are to think of the Ten Commandments – not as cramping restrictions on a fullness of life that we might otherwise have enjoyed, but as the very gateway to the fullness we seek.

2. The law is for life, for all life and for the balanced life

The Ten Commandments are the Bible's fundamental statement of 'the law of liberty'. The fact that they are in the main a series of prohibitions has led to the unthinking charge that they are negative in tone and purpose. This is to forget that a negative command is far more liberating than a positive one, for a positive command restricts life to that one course of action, whereas a negative command leaves life open to every course of action except one! Once more, the law of liberty in the garden of Eden is the perfect illustration. The single negative command 'You must not eat from the tree of . . .' left open the broad prospect that 'You are free to eat from any tree in the garden.'

Not only do the Ten Commandments function the same way in our lives, but they also show what a rounded, perfectly balanced life should look like. This is demonstrated by the way they are presented. We are told that there were two 'tables' or tablets of the law,[6] and traditionally the first (commandments 1 to 4) has been spoken of as 'our duty to God' and

---

[4] 'Walk about' is used in Gen. 13:17 of Abram's roaming at will, in unfettered freedom, in the Promised Land.

[5] The verb 'walk' is the hithpael of √hālak (cf. Gen. 13:17; Job 1:7). The noun 'precepts' is piqqûdîm and derives from √pāqad, meaning 'to enumerate', 'to survey in individual detail'.

[6] On the form of the Decalogue see J. A. Motyer, *Law and Life: The Meaning of Law in the Old Testament* (Lawyers' Christian Fellowship, 1978). For the 'two tablets' cf. Exod. 31:18; 32:15; 34:1; Deut. 4:13.

the second (commandments 5 to 10) as 'our duty to our neighbour'.[7] This conveniently – if roughly – takes note of the content of the Decalogue, but it is undoubtedly an incorrect understanding of the two tablets. Much study has been made of the Hittite people and especially of the covenants made between the great Hittite kings and their vassals from 1800 BC onwards.[8] According to Hittite usage, a covenant could come into force only when it had been given written form. Two identical copies were made, one of which was retained by the Hittite king and the other by his vassal. It is significant that Israel kept both of the tablets produced on Sinai together in the ark (Exod. 25:16; 40:20). This shows that Yahweh, the Great King who is the covenant-maker, was also the resident king among his people, and the covenant was his to guard and guarantee.[9]

The Lord, wanting his people to enjoy all the benefits of the covenant he had made with them, set his law before them. Our study of the Decalogue so far, pending consideration of the fifth commandment, offers a provisional pattern:

A^1 **God**

a^1 Thoughts (commandments 1–2)

b^1 Words (commandments 3)

c^1 Deeds (commandment 4)

A^2 **Society**

c^2 Deeds (commandments 6–8)

b^2 Words (commandment 9)

a^2 Thoughts (commandment 10)

---

[7] This wording derives from the Catechism in the Book of Common Prayer, engrained by memorization in many of the older generation.

[8] From the nineteenth to the thirteenth century the Hittite empire extended (with uneven influence) southwards from modern Turkey to Syria and Palestine, and eastwards (from time to time) as far as Babylon. See F. F. Bruce's excellent survey, 'Hittites' (*NBD*). Regarding covenants, see F.C. Fensham, 'Covenant Alliance' (*NBD*).

[9] See Phillips, *Ancient Israel's Criminal Law*, pp. 6, 10. Phillips uses the striking expression that the ark, in which the tablets were deposited, became a 'portable Sinai'. Regarding the date of the Decalogue, he concurs with many on an early, even Mosaic, date: 'If the covenant concept is understood in the light of the Hittite . . . treaties, which during the fourteenth and thirteenth centuries seem to have been the recognised international covenant form throughout the ancient near east, it follows that exodus and covenant become inseparable, for the latter must be dependent on the former. Further, since the covenant would only have been entered into while the exodus event was a living reality, it would therefore seem that the Decalogue can be attributed to Moses, to whom both chronologically and geographically the Hittite suzerainty treaty form could have been known' (p. 8). See also H. H. Rowley, *Men of God* (Nelson, 1963), pp. 1–36; G. E. Mendenhall, *Law and Covenant in Israel and the Ancient Near East* (Pittsburgh, 1955); D. J. McCarthy, *Old Testament Covenant* (John Knox, 1972); *Treaty and Covenant* (Pontifical Biblical Institute, 1963). According to Durham (p. 282), 'We can now be confident of an earlier rather than a later dating.'

The Decalogue begins and ends (a[1, 2]) with the interior aspect of our obedience – how we are required to think about God and about our relationships with other people. It is thus quite wrong to think of it as a list of rules to which we simply conform and that it awaited the teaching of Jesus to extend obedience to the heart (Matt. 5:21–30). To the contrary, in each of the great areas of obedience there is a call for purity of mind and heart.[10]

The first commandment takes account of the fact that we Christians, as God's Israel in the present day, live in a world where there are 'many "gods" and many "lords"' (1 Cor. 8:5) and requires of us undivided loyalty to the only God. The second commandment adds the requirement that this only God be thought of in spiritual, non-physical terms. It brings us to the place of worship and states that the use of visual representations of the Lord are personally offensive to him and provoke his judgmental wrath *to the third and fourth generation*.[11] As we shall presently note, the thrust of the second commandment is that the Lord is to be worshipped without the aid or interposition of visible representations. Behind that rule, so sternly expressed and enforced, however, lies a theology, a doctrine of God, that he is spiritual and self-revealing and, when we turn to worship him, we must fill our minds and our imaginations with what he has revealed and the word he has spoken (Deut. 4:12, 15–19, 25–28).[12]

---

[10] Cassuto's discussion of the Decalogue makes many sound points, not least his tough advocacy of attributing it, in its original form, to Moses. He discounts any explanation of the Commandments which makes them the product of 'borrowing' from contemporary cultures. Rather 'we are confronted here with a basically new conception and a spiritual revolution'. He notes, in particular, the transcendental view of God to whom all nature is subject and who cannot be depicted, and that the idea of the Sabbath is innovatory and unparalleled. Where parallels do suggest themselves, the Decalogue stands out in its 'unqualified absoluteness', its placing interpersonal requirements on a par with Godward requirements, and the definition of 'coveting' as a sin – 'the yearning itself constitutes a trespass'.

[11] Enns finds the visiting of wrath on succeeding generations a contradiction of Deut. 24:16, which forbids that children should be 'put to death for their parents'. But two different contexts and two different exercises are involved. Deuteronomy is dealing with human jurisprudence, where it would be plainly unjust and illegitimate to treat a child as if he or she had done the specific deed for which a parent has been brought before the courts (or would have been had not the parent's death or disappearance supervened). The commandment, however, deals with genetic inheritance, the price of being human, a fact all too evident as one generation succeeds another. But, first, this 'visitation' (NKJV, ESV) or 'punishment' (NIV) is in the hands of and at the discretion of God himself, and, second, does not constitute an unbreakable entail (Ezek. 18:4, 14–17). Exod. 20:5 lacks definite articles and says (lit.) 'visiting the iniquity of fathers upon sons', thus stressing the genetic and generational factor. See W. Zimmerli, *The Law and the Prophets* (Oxford, 1965), p. 58; W. C. Kaiser, *Toward Old Testament Ethics* (Zondervan, 1983), pp. 86–87 and indeed his whole excellent discussion of the Decalogue, pp. 81–95.

[12] According to Currid this sets out 'what type of God he is, and how he is to be worshipped'. Kaiser says this was 'not to stifle artistic talent (cf. the "ornate appointments" of the tabernacle) but to avoid improper substitution'. 'The first forbids the worship of any but the one and true God; the second forbids the worship of the true God in the wrong way' (Charles, p. 15).

If we are to worship God as he would have it, in spirit and truth (John 4:23–24), then his word must dwell within us in all wisdom, for this is the root of true and acceptable worship (Col. 3:16).

a. Guarding the tongue, ordering the programme

The third commandment deals, says Kaiser, with 'the profession of the mouth in true adoration'.[13] That is a sufficient statement of its meaning for the moment. It concerns our words and in particular the way we speak the Lord's name.[14] Alongside it, the Sabbath commandment focuses on the one day in seven that was to be a day of rest – that is to say, free of unnecessary work and of the gainful employment that rightly occupied the previous six days. But we have already seen (Exod. 16) that the Sabbath cast its blessed shadow before it in that if it was to be a day of holy rest, it required thoughtful preparation and pre-planning. Because of this, we can summarize by saying that the Sabbath commandment is concerned with how life as a whole is to be ordered under God. It may even be that in the increasing complication of modern life, if the Lord's Day is to be kept 'special', ever more and more organization of life – business, shopping, homework, whatever – becomes necessary so that this unique day dominates the pattern of the ordinary days. In any case, this is one aspect of the Sabbath law. It encapsulates our life with God, summed up by the word 'deeds' in the diagram above.

b. Life around

When we turn to the community aspect of God's law, the same three areas are covered. Commandments 6 to 8 concern our conduct towards other people, our 'deeds'; the ninth commandment requires truth in what we say about others, our 'words'; and, as we have seen, the tenth commandment 'internalizes' this aspect of the law, like the first commandment and our 'duty towards God'. It is not enough that we do the right and avoid the

---

[13] Cf. Enns: 'To use the name flippantly . . . to associate the name with falsehood . . . say what is untrue about God'; and Murphy: 'to violate his essence [by] blasphemy'.

[14] As a broad truth, the Old Testament prescribed capital punishment for breaches of the Decalogue: e.g. the first commandment (Exod. 22:20; Deut. 13:5); the third (Lev. 24:10–16); the fourth (Exod. 35:2; Num. 15:32–36); the fifth (Exod. 21:15; Deut. 21:18–21); the sixth (Exod. 21:12); the seventh (Lev. 20:10). See Kaiser, pp. 91–92, 297–298. Old Testament law prescribed capital punishment quite widely, but this is not to say that the penalty was always applied – in the case of the rebellious son (Deut. 21:18–21), parents were unlikely ever to invoke the law, though its existence may have had deterrent effect. To what extent the New Testament reaffirms capital punishment is a matter of dispute, as is the question of the death penalty today. But in any case, the Old Testament witnesses to the seriousness with which offences against the Decalogue were regarded, and, at the very least, this seriousness should be reflected in modern practice.

wrong in deed and word; we have to ask ourselves if our thoughts about others respect them and their inalienable rights.

In this way, we see that the Decalogue is a comprehensive survey of our life with God and our life with other people. Thoughts, words and deeds encompass the whole of life; there is nothing else. Everything is to be covered by, and expressed in, obedience to the law the Lord has spoken. It is what he is, and we are to be what it directs.

c. The fifth commandment

We can now offer another diagram of the Decalogue that takes into account the fifth commandment and in so doing highlights its central and unique place in the law of God. It can be stated like this: our first duty after our obedience to God (commandments 1–4) is within the family and, in the same way, this is our primary area of obligation before we consider our obligations to other people (commandments 6–10). The fifth commandment belongs neither in the first group nor in the second, but in its distinctiveness it recognizes our first and primary earthly obligation.

A^1 Our duty to God (commandments 1–4)
  a^1 Our hearts (commandment 1)
  a^2 Our deeds (commandments 2–4)
      B Our family obligations (commandment 5)
A^2 Our duty to our neighbour (commandments 6–10)
  a^2 Our deeds (commandments 6–9)
  a^1 Our hearts (commandment 10)

So then, if we are to think biblically about the Ten Commandments, we do not have two 'tables' or sections but three. God comes first, the family comes second,[15] and the community around us third. When we come out from God's presence, our primary obligations are towards our families, and our obligations to the world around us are secondary. The command to 'honour' is hugely demanding and also tantalizingly vague, but there is no better way to seek to spell it out than in the three categories of thoughts, words and deeds.

---

[15] Cf. J. Stier: the fifth commandment is 'the last precept of the first table . . . the middle term of transition to the second' (*The Words of the Lord Jesus*, vol. 1 [T&T Clark, 1885], p. 149).

The whole *sphere* of life is to be found in the Decalogue: God, the family and the world. There is nothing else. And the whole *course* of life is there too, because there is nothing else other than thoughts, words and deeds. The balanced nature of the presentation – thoughts, words, deeds . . . deeds, words, thoughts – is surely deliberate, depicting a complete, 'rounded' law, the law of God, designed by him to 'trigger' into action every aspect of our true human nature and our redeemed persons (Eph. 4:20–24).

3. The law written on the heart

At this point, we must turn forward in our Bibles to consider what the New Testament has to say on the subject. We must not fall unthinkingly into the mistaken and misleading 'slogan' that the Old Testament is the book of law and the New Testament is the book of grace. We have one Bible, and it is our task to trace the great biblical truths and principles right through both Old and New Testaments.

So then, when the author of the letter to the Hebrews wishes to state the essence of the new covenant and the supreme accomplishment of Christ and the cross, he picks up Jeremiah's prophecy that the Lord will write his law on the hearts of his redeemed (Jer. 31:31–34; Heb. 8:7–13; 10:10–18).

From a passage so full of teaching we can pick out only three points. First, there is the failure of the old covenant. Jeremiah uses the marriage covenant as his basic model. The Lord, the 'husband', fulfilled his role and obligations: 'I was a husband to them', but (lit.) 'they on their side broke' my covenant (Jer. 31:32). Second, there is an additional aspect in the new covenant. When the Lord's people cannot rise to his requirements, he does not lower his standards but rather he lifts up his people. In this case, the law remains the same, but now it is written on their hearts (Jer. 31:33). This is another way of expressing the truth of regeneration, God's gift of a new nature and in particular a new 'heart', a whole personality, fashioned to match the precepts of his law. The inner, true reality of the Christian believer is that our new nature has been fashioned for obedience. Third, there is the way in which this is all accomplished. Sin is dealt with so completely and finally that all memory of our sinfulness has been blotted out even from the mind of God (Jer. 31:34).

In other words, the values of Sinai are carried over into the lives of New Testament people, for whom the absolute requirement of obedience as a sign of covenant membership remains the same but is now met by the completed and regenerative work of salvation in Christ.[16]

4. God first

An obvious feature in the composition of God's law is that while there is plainly no forgetfulness of social duty – far from it: it occupies six commandments out of the ten – our duty to God undeniably comes first, over and above all our other duties. It is not the same as, or to be confused or merged with, any duty we owe to other people, to family or to the world around. We must keep apart what God has kept apart. If any should say that their religion is reaching out to the needs of others, the only clear-thinking reply is that that is not religion, it is humanitarianism or social conscience. It has lost touch with biblical priorities. The service, love and obedience we owe to God is a distinct thing and comes before everything else. However closely the 'first and greatest commandment' and 'the second' may be linked – here, throughout the Bible, and in the mind of Jesus – they are not the same thing. Love of God is a distinct thing and must always come first.[17] This priority has several different aspects.

a. Sole loyalty

The reference to *other gods* in the first commandment is not an affirmation of the existence of other deities besides Yahweh but an acknowledgment of their allure – and their menace. Similarly, Paul, the dedicated

---

[16] This paragraph deals only with the continuance of the principle of obedience to the word of God as one of the great, unifying themes of the Bible – one Lord, one way of salvation, one family of Abraham (the Israel of God), one rule of obedience. If we think in a 'two Testaments' fashion, we create needless difficulties. We must think of 'one Bible' with cumulative lines of revelation. Some of these lines 'run out' in their intended fulfilment and their earlier forms no longer apply: for example, the sacrifices are fulfilled and concluded in the cross, the promise of the land of Israel becomes (as intended) the 'kingdom not of this world' and the 'Jerusalem that is above'. Some were rules for their own time and were later set aside, as Jesus set aside the food laws. Some of these regulations remain today as 'open questions'; for example, the death penalty is something about which Bible-loving believers reach differing conclusions. The fact that the New Testament nowhere restates the fourth commandment seems to put it in a similar category. Then there are the regulations which are reiterated in the New Testament as both principles and precepts and therefore still continue in force today. The insistent cry that questions of homosexual practice cannot be settled by appeal to ancient levitical prohibitions overlooks the fact that along the line of cumulative revelation Rom. 1:26–28 finds such acts contrary to creation, 1 Cor. 6:9–11 finds them contrary to (and capable of being remedied by) salvation, and 1 Tim. 1:9–11 finds them contrary to 'the gospel concerning the glory of the blessed God'. There is an excellent basic discussion in D. E. Holwerda, *Jesus and Israel: One Covenant or Two?* (Apollos, 1995).

[17] Recently used intercessions in the Church of England (e.g. Rites A and B services of Holy Communion) included the prayer 'that we may serve Christ in one another'. Whatever truth there may be in this, it is a confusion of what Jesus spoke of as the two 'great commandments', wherein the second is 'like' the first (e.g. Matt. 22:36–40).

monotheist, knew that 'there is no God but one', but he also knew that he lived in a world where the existence and worship of other 'so-called gods' abounded and that this worship exercised a potent and, in many cases, an understandable fascination (1 Cor. 8:4–5). Like every other aspect of our faith, monotheism never goes untested, and so it was for the Israel of the Old Testament. When we think of the crudity, cruelty and infant sacrifices that went with worshipping, for example, Molek, we might say, 'How could they have fallen for *that*?' On the other hand, Baalism, whatever else there was about it, offered the promise of material prosperity and a religion in which sexual experiences were integral to worship, and the allure was understandable. While Baal does not exist, Baalism certainly does.

The phrase *before me* ('*al-pānāy*, 'upon/to/at my face') is used in two ways in the Bible, covering both time and space. Genesis 11:28 says (lit.), 'and Haran died upon the face ['*al-pĕnê*] of his father', and the NIV rightly understands this to mean 'while his father . . . was still alive'.[18] The other, and rather more obvious, usage is 'in my presence'. So the commandment says, as long as the living God lives and as long as the ever-present Lord is present, no other religious loyalty is permissible. And what a necessary word this was, for Israel would not always be an isolated people, living alone at Sinai. Once they were established in Canaan, surrounded by many other nations, how easy it would have been for them to have said that the passing of time had brought the need for fresh thinking and that new situations demanded new solutions. There would have been the temptation to adopt the customs and values of the peoples among whom they were to settle and to look for fresh 'insights' and to develop a religion compounded of what others had found 'helpful' or 'practical' and what they thought was more relevant to their new settled existence. This was not to be. While the living God lives and the ever-present Lord is present with his people, no matter what the time or where the place, there is to be only one God, one sole loyalty, the total capture of the heart.[19]

b. Worship must be governed by God's word

With Egypt fresh in their memories, the people of Israel were aware that 'other gods' were worshipped with the help of idols. The second

---

[18] The same usage occurs in e.g. Deut. 21:16. Other references that may be usefully consulted are Gen. 32:21[22]; Job 1:11; 16:14.

[19] See the inspired Mosaic comment in Deut. 6:1–5. Cf. Phillips, *Ancient Israel's Criminal Law*, p. 38.

commandment, however, does not refer to the worship of alternative gods – that had been dealt with in the first commandment – but to the worship of the true God in a false way, and it lays down an absolute prohibition of the use of visible representations as an adjunct to worship. God is not to be represented by any human contrivance (*image*), nor identified with any aspect of the visible created orders.[20] The commandment insists that such representations provoke the Lord to jealousy,[21] which must mean that in his eyes they cannot but involve alternative objects of worship, giving to others what is due only to him. The first commandment, though it does not mention love, is concerned with our loving loyalty to the Lord; the second commandment, with its reference to his jealousy, raises the topic of his love to us, for 'jealousy' is part of the essence of true love, and the Lord so loves us that he cannot bear it when our desires and loyalties go elsewhere.

Calvin offers some helpful summary statements. Of the commandment in general and the ease with which mild disobediences might be justified on seemingly allowable grounds (such as 'helpfulness') he says, 'Let this be our wisdom, to acquiesce in what God has chosen to decree in this matter.' And on the bearing of the commandment specifically on how we worship, he remarks that if people should think that 'zeal for religion . . . is sufficient' they have not realized that 'true religion ought to be conformed to God's will as to a universal rule',[22] which is no more than was first written in Deuteronomy 4:12. Sinai brought no vision to the eyes, only a voice to the ears. Everything in worship must be ordered according to the word of God – a truth Jesus reiterated in Matthew 15:6b–9.

c. Reverence for God as he has revealed himself

The third commandment arises from the self-declaration of God, *I am the Lord* [*Yahweh*], with which this whole great statement begins (2). The Lord's *name* is shorthand for all that he has revealed about himself, with,

---

[20] The reference to *heaven* and *earth* etc. makes the second commandment strictly monotheistic: wherever one looks there is only one God. The (lit.) 'waters under the earth' do not picture a 'three-decker universe' for, as Kaiser points out, 'this is the Hebrew idiom for the shoreline', i.e. the seas, not the underworld (cf. Deut. 4:18).

[21] *Bow down . . . worship* (lit. 'serve') suggests a sequence. Idolatry could start with simply seeing the idol as representing some invisible spiritual potency but then move on to serving the thing itself. Hence Yahweh's jealousy. This would be the case even if the idol represented Yahweh himself. The reverence of worship ('bow down') leads to the expression of worship in life ('serve'); devotion becomes dedication. The commandment goes on to call this 'hating' the Lord, whereas it identifies love with 'keeping my commandments'.

[22] J. Calvin, *Institutes of the Christian Religion* (SCM, 1961), 1.4.3.

of course, particular reference to the central revelations made through Moses and confirmed in the events of the exodus. 'I AM WHO [or WHAT] I AM' (Exod. 3:13–15) is like an ample container into which the great truths revealed by Moses and through the exodus have been packed: the Holy One, the God of the covenant, the Redeemer, Deliverer, Judge, the caring God of daily providence, the God of reconciliation who brings his people to himself. Any particular misuse of the divine name would deny or scorn any one of these great fundamentals. But since each is an aspect of what God *is*, any misuse of his name is a personal insult to him.

Misuse the name of the LORD (traditionally 'take the name in vain') is (lit.) 'lift up the name . . . to emptiness [*šāw*]'.[23] The most obvious meaning of 'lifting up the name' is that 'lift up' is an abbreviation of 'lift up upon one's lips'. The use of the noun 'God' or the name of Jesus or the title 'Christ' as an expletive would certainly fall within this condemnation and, on a more serious level, so would the giving of one's loyalty to, or taking one's oath by, a false god – though this (supported by Currid) would be an extension of the primary meaning.

The third commandment is one of four commandments (the second, third, fourth and fifth) with some added comment. There is no ground for the common assumption among specialists that these comments were later additions and that all of the Ten Commandments were originally composed of no more than the succinct words with which they open. Indeed, it is of no small interest to note that these are the commandments most lightly flouted today – and why should we not assume that, in the unchanging realities of human nature, they were just as easy to belittle and just as much in need of reinforcement when they were first promulgated? At any rate, the third commandment is given the support of a most striking sanction, all the more frightening in being left vague: *the* LORD *will not hold anyone guiltless*.[24] The implication is that the Lord's name is intensely precious to him. It is he who notes its misuse and who matches the punishment to the crime in each and every case.

---

[23] *Šāw'* is a broad word for that which 'lacks objective reality'. In Ezek. 13:6 it is used of the delusion, rather than the deception, of false prophets; in Job 7:3 of life without substance or significance; in Isa. 1:13 of religious rites empty of spiritual reality, offerings that offer nothing; and in Hos. 10:4 of false promises.

[24] The word is √*nāqâ*, which in the niphal means 'to be free, exempt', i.e. 'to be guiltless, innocent, unpunished' (e.g. Gen. 24:8; 1 Sam. 26:9; Prov. 6:29). In the piel (as here) it means 'to acquit, leave unpunished' (e.g. Exod. 34:7; 1 Kgs 2:9).

d. An imitative life

Our responsibility to live our lives in imitation of God is the heart of the fourth commandment, for did not the Creator perform his perfect work of creation – the work which he pronounced 'good' (Gen. 1:31) – by working six days and resting one day? What is then the perfect life pattern for humans in the image of God? Is it not to work for six days and rest for one? This has nothing to do with Christians attempting (as they are so often accused of doing) to impose their standards on others who do not share their convictions. Far from it. When a doctor prescribes a certain course of treatment, the sick person does not round on that doctor by asking what right he or she has to impose a doctor's convictions on someone who is not a doctor. In such a case the doctor would reply, 'Don't be so foolish! I'm not imposing my standards on you. I'm telling you what to do because you're human, because you're a person, and this is the way human beings "work".' In exactly the same way, the Creator prescribes his pattern of working and resting for us because we are made in his image and this is our proper functioning procedure. It is ours because it was his. Our calling is to live out his pattern, to make his example the way we order our lives, to reflect what we are – beings created in the image of God.

Exodus concentrates on the Sabbath as a day free from work, with obvious reference to the gainful employment of the previous six days, the wage-earning days which provided an economic basis for family life.[25] The loss of one day's financial gain cut deeply into the commercially ambitious, as Amos 8:4–6 shows. The businessman in the Amos passage happens to be unscrupulous, but many an honest shopkeeper, or self-employed farmer, must have faced the fact that losing a day's income out of obedience to the commandment was costly. In this way, faith and obedience join hands in the assumption that the Lord will look after those who put him first, and the fourth commandment is pre-eminently a call for the obedience of faith. Incidents like those recorded in Numbers 15:32–36 and Exodus 16:23 show, both negatively and positively, that the freedom to be enjoyed on the Sabbath imposed a duty of careful forethought.

---

[25] The brilliant discussion of Sabbath observance in Isa. 58 exposes the fallacy of drawing the conclusion from Exod. 20:9 that 'work' is to be defined in a merely logical way (cf. Matt. 12:2). See Motyer, *Prophecy of Isaiah* and *Isaiah*. Jer. 17:19–27 indicates how important the Lord viewed the Sabbath law, making it a test case of national loyalty. In Exod. 31:12–17 the Sabbath symbolizes the special covenant relationship between the Lord and his people (cf. Ezek. 20:12, 20). Exod. 23:12 emphasizes the importance of the Sabbath in healthy living using three verbs: it is a day of *cessation* from the occupations of the previous six days (√šābat), a day for *rest* (√nûaḥ) and an opportunity for *refreshment* and *renewal* (√nāpaš).

The cessation of work is not, however, an end in itself but, so to speak, 'clears a space'; as Childs puts it, there was to be 'the cessation of normal activity . . . in order to set aside the Sabbath for something special'.[26] What that 'something special' was is left vague by the commandment, but three principles are clear. The Sabbath was to be a day of holiness, that is, a different day, a day set apart from all other days (8), a day belonging in some special way to the Lord and therefore to be lived uniquely for him (10), and a day essential to our imitation of him (11). The vagueness is doubtless deliberate, leaving room for individual choice and personal preference, but the one thing that is common to all three principles is that it was to be a different day. And that surely remains true today: Sunday should be not a second Saturday every week (as the term 'Continental Sunday' is found to mean), nor an idle nothing (as 'Sunday observance' has so often turned out to be), but a day positively different because it is being lived specially for God.[27]

5. Essential relationships

There is, however, no such thing as a concern for God that ignores our relationships with people. Think of the way the Decalogue is structured: responsibilities towards God – thoughts, words, deeds; responsibilities towards people – deeds, words, thoughts. It belongs together as one rounded, indivisible whole which cannot be sundered. It is the law of God. And, if we were to follow this through the Bible, we would have to say that our attention to the outward and visible realities of the second section of the law reveals how seriously we take the spiritual realities of the first. As John puts it, 'whoever does not love their brother and sister, whom they have seen, cannot love God, whom they have not seen . . . anyone who loves God must also love their brother and sister' (1 John 4:20–21).

In this way, our 'vertical' relationship to God and our 'horizontal' relationship to those around us must be in harmony. The second 'great' commandment, said Jesus, is 'like' the first (Matt. 22:39), and therefore

---

[26] The NIV's choice of *by keeping it holy* is a possible but not the most obvious translation. *Lĕqaddĕšô* is taken by most in its primary sense of purpose, i.e. 'remember . . . so as to make holy' and presupposes a thoughtful view of the Sabbath, preparing beforehand and excluding any activity or exercise that fails to promote the stated purpose.

[27] The ceremonial law makes the Sabbath a day of special religious worship (Num. 28:9), and Isa. 58 stresses the aspect of particular social concern, but the idea of rest, so often ruled out by an almost frenetic Sunday programme, is pervasive (see Exod. 16:23; 23:11–12; 31:15; 34:21; 35:2).

obedience to the first must be reflected in obedience to the second. Relationships matter as deeply as that. But one set of relationships in particular takes precedence. The fifth commandment is deliberately linked with the fourth by its positive form, so that the passage from the first half of the law to the second is seamless. The fourth commandment deals with the *ordering* of life in imitation of God; the fifth deals with achieving *security* of life by the honouring[28] of parents. The life ordered according to God's priorities will receive his blessing (11); the honouring of parents is the key to social stability and security of tenure in the land.[29] When we step out of the arena of 'duty to God', we step into the arena of duty within the family, our foremost area of obligation in the world.

The fifth commandment is addressed to children, and this is significant. Covenant law has regard to the family born within the covenant and imposes its obligations on the children of covenant parents. It treats such children as members of the covenant people, having been 'brought out' by the blood of the lamb just as much as their parents. It makes its promises to them and imposes its obligations upon them. Just as children, from infancy, come within the circle of covenant blessing (Gen. 17:7; Acts 2:39), so from childhood they must be taught to follow covenant ways and obey covenant law. We note also the equality accorded to both parents, for an identical attitude is required towards the father as towards the mother.[30]

a. Sins and crimes

Pretty well every society, notes Cassuto, counts murder, adultery and theft as forbidden acts, and to this extent the Decalogue contains nothing new. It is unique, however, in making their prohibition into 'fundamental, abstract, eternal principles, which transcend any condition . . . circumstance . . . definition'. It is also typical, we might add, of the Old Testament to make no distinction between crimes (committed against people) and sins (committed against God). The origin of the social prohibitions here is

---

[28] √*Kābēd* (here in the piel with the sense of 'to honour') is used of what is important or substantial (Gen. 13:2; Ezek. 27:25), serious (Gen. 18:20; Isa. 24:20, NIV, 'heavy'), dignified and possessing status (2 Sam. 6:20; Job 14:21). The honouring of parents therefore gives them the importance, seriousness and dignity that are their right. Cole says, 'Those who build a society in which old age has an honoured place may with confidence expect to enjoy that place themselves one day.' Childs (p. 418) calls attention to the strong emphasis in biblical wisdom literature on reverence for parents (e.g. Prov. 1:8; 15:5; 19:26).

[29] Ezek. 22:7, 15 relates the loss of the land to the breaking of the fifth commandment. The promised result *so that you may live long in the land* is, of course, an inducement to keep the commandment, but it is also much more: it is a statement of how things work.

[30] Indeed in Lev. 19:3 the mother is mentioned first.

the will of God, reflecting the character of God and expressing the fundamental rule, 'You must be what you must be, because I am what I am.'[31]

We can see this principle plainly at work in commandments 5, 6, 7 and 9, where a biblical link is forged with the thought of the image of God. In Genesis 5:1 we are reminded that Adam was in the likeness of God, and verse 3 proceeds to tell us that he 'had [lit. 'begot'] a son in his own likeness, in his own image'. In other words, the image of God (note the coincidence of wording with Gen. 1:26) continues down the generations – defaced and diluted, undoubtedly, but continuing. Is it for this reason that Paul teaches that 'all fatherhood' derives from God the Father (Eph. 3:15; see ESV mg.)?[32] The conclusion to be drawn, therefore, in relation to this commandment is plain: children must look on their parents (and, by implication, parents on their children) as bearing the image of God and must treat them as such.

Genesis 9:6 makes the fact that humankind bears the divine image the reason why murder is both a crime and a sin, and it is, indeed, the ground of the rightness and justice of the death penalty. Genesis 5:1–2 finds the image of God reflected in the first man and woman united in marriage, who in their togetherness bear the name 'Mankind' (Heb. 'ādām), with all that that implies. It is for this reason that the offence of adultery disrupts and defiles the image of God. We ought also to recall that the Old Testament defines marriage as a covenant and even uses it as an illustration of the Lord's covenant with his people.[33] It is in this way that the seventh commandment, like all the others, reflects the divine nature, for at Sinai the Lord had pledged his covenanted word to his people. As Jeremiah insisted, he 'was a husband to them' (Jer. 31:32) – that is, he was undeviating in faithfulness and committed to keeping and doing what he had undertaken. Marital infidelity involves going back on one's pledged word and therefore is a departure from the image of God.

Finally, in illustration of the image of God as the foundation on which the Decalogue rests, James 3:8–9 observes that the remembrance of the

---

[31] Cf. Amos 1:3 – 2:4, where a long list of what today would be called 'crimes against humanity' are exposed as sins against the Lord, noted and reserved for punishment by him. So also Amos 4:1–12. See J. A. Motyer, 'Amos', in NBC(21). In Ps. 51:4, regarding the sin of adultery with murder, David can say to God, 'Against you, you only, have I sinned' (see J. A. Motyer, 'Psalms', in NBC[21]).

[32] See the excellent discussions in J. Stott, The Message of Ephesians (IVP, 2020), pp. 99–100; and F. Foulkes, Ephesians, TNTC (IVP, 1989), pp. 109–110.

[33] E.g. Mal. 2:14. Jer. 31:31–34 sees the failure of the Sinai covenant as marital breakdown (see J. A. Motyer, The Story of the Old Testament [Candle, 2001], pp. 129, 131). The same thinking lies behind the pervasive use of adultery and prostitution as figurative of religious apostasy (e.g. Ezek. 16; 23; Hos. 1:2; 2:2).

divine image in other people should control our words about them, as the ninth commandment requires. In his blunt, practical way, James asks how it could be possible for the one tongue to bless and curse the same thing – God himself and his image in other people.[34] In this way the two 'sides' of the law are bound together. We are drawn in devotion and honour, sole loyalty and imitative life, to God because of what he is and has revealed himself to be, because of the glories of his nature. But the glories of that nature are reflected, however imperfectly, with however many blemishes and stains, in those created in the image of God. There-fore, we are called to a great derivative concern for how we live among other people.

b. Property, truth and the heart

The Decalogue does not go in for a 'league table' of sins – as is evident by the way in which it puts an offence against property alongside offences against life, marriage and truth. Currid notes 'the lack of specifics' following the prohibition of theft; the command 'simply transcends any conditions or circumstances', whether it is a matter of carrying off goods or kidnapping people and whether the thing stolen is valuable or trivial. In a word, Scripture respects private property and demands integrity over the whole range of personal, economic and commercial relationships.[35]

In a similar way, the ninth commandment, (lit.) 'you shall not answer in the case of your fellow [as] a false witness', has both private and public aspects. The primary reference may be to an answer under oath at a formal court hearing. In this case the thrust of the commandment is to treas-ure the integrity of the judicial system. Once again, however, we notice that the command is non-specific. On which side of the case is one envisaged as bearing witness – for the prosecution or the defence? Does the witness hold the accused innocent or guilty? Would a truthful word have unwanted side effects and a small lie foreseeable benefits? No such considerations are relevant. Telling the truth in court is, of course, sacrosanct, but it would be hard to prove – or even imagine – that the more general notions of talebearing, innuendo and direct character assassination are not equally

---

[34] See A. Motyer, *The Message of James* (IVP, 2021), pp. 106–116.

[35] One cannot deal with any of the commandments without observing how much supportive elaboration and application the rest of the Torah (and of the OT) contains. Yet none of this material became an elabor-ation of the original terse command – as some commentators allege happened in the case of the second to fifth commandments.

prohibited. In imitation of the 'God, who does not lie' (Titus 1:2), his redeemed should be people of the truthful word.

The tenth commandment is where the Decalogue ends, but it is, in fact, the point at which every breach of the law begins – when by our 'own evil desire' we are 'dragged away . . . and enticed' (Jas 1:14). King David violated the sixth and seventh commandments (2 Sam. 12:9), but his sin began with the lust prohibited by the tenth (2 Sam. 11:2): possibly he could not have helped seeing Bathsheba, but he could have helped looking! King Ahab (more than ably assisted by his wife Jezebel) sinned comprehensively against the sixth, eighth and ninth commandments (1 Kgs 21:1–16), but the root of the evil was in his covetousness (1–4). 'Improper desire,' says Murphy,

> is the root of all evil. It can seldom be reached by human legislation, but it is open to the Searcher of hearts. The intent is that which, in the last resort, determines the moral character of the act. This last 'word' is, therefore, the interpreting clause of the whole Decalogue (Rom. 7:7).

We should note that, unlike the case of commandments 6 to 9, the verb *covet* is here provided with a wide selection of possible objects and, indeed, is itself repeated. The intention is not to limit the scope of the commandment to these precise objects, but by heaping one possible object of coveting on another to drive home the seriousness of the sin of covetousness itself. Its target is, specifically and comprehensively, the contemplative sin – as is made all too clear by the way in which Jesus drew out its meaning and significance in Matthew 5:21–30. It is true, as Cole points out, that Exodus 20:6 binds together feeling and action, but it is the function of the final commandment to make explicit the internalizing of the whole law and the dire reality of sin in the heart.

6. Interlude: proper and improper fear (20:18–21)

The immediate place of these verses[36] is as a response to the voice of God heard directly at Sinai, and it is in that light we must consider them, for we must learn from the Bible not only what is the truth but also how to respond to the truth.

---

[36] For their place in the overall scheme see Additional notes.

Verse 18 stresses the people's sustained and personal experience of what happened at Sinai. The first verb is a participle, which we might render 'were observing'. It was an awesome experience of sight and sound. *Lightning* is not the word used in 19:16 (*bārāq*) but *lappîd* ('flashings'), a word not used in the Bible since Genesis 15:17, where it occurs as a symbol of the presence of the Lord the covenant-maker. Surely its reappearance here is deliberate. The people saw lightning flashes, and they should have discerned the approach of God in his grace, bearing promises. Likewise, they saw the mountain covered with *smoke*, but they forgot the pillar of cloud which had meant all the way from Egypt that they were the Lord's pilgrims under his care. They saw with their own eyes, but really they failed to see.

In the same way, when they heard the *trumpet*, the sound struck fear into their hearts. It was not meant to do so, and it ought not to have done. For the trumpet was the voice of God inviting them to come to him (cf. 19:13), giving them his permission to approach. Their fear was a wrong fear, and instead of responding to the invitation they stayed at a distance (21).

They were not, of course, wholly in the wrong. They still wanted to hear God's words, and they were still ready to express their commitment to obey. They also sought Moses as their mediator, which was what the Lord had planned for them all along (19:9) – for it is ever his way to bring his choicest plans to pass in response to his people's felt need and in such a way that they are ever reminded of their unworthiness and of the way a God of grace caters for their weakness. At the same time, their hesitations and fears were wrong for they had already been listening to the voice of God and it had not killed them! But they were hearing without hearing. Had they really been listening, they would have known that this was the voice of their Redeemer God (2) – just as Moses found, when he approached the darkness where *God was* (21), that he was in the presence of Yahweh (22), the God of all grace.

The people's fear, however understandable in such an awe-inspiring setting, was wholly improper. The marks and notes of grace, covenant, promise, welcome, redemption and the sheltering wings of the God of Israel were plainly visible and audible.

Yet there is also a true fear of God, and Moses wanted them to experience it (20). The Lord had just now laid down his law, and he had come to *test* his people to see if they had that proper reverential fear for him, the true fear which would turn them from the sins his law condemns and hold them to obedience to his commandments.[37]

Additional notes

20:1–20 Commentators of the documentary school tend to wish to relocate the Ten Commandments on the grounds that in their present position they disrupt the narrative (e.g. McNeile, Hyatt). Durham disputes this, but in his turn, he says that the Book of the Covenant (20:22 – 23:33) disrupts the Sinai narrative, and he wonders why the 'Exodus compilers' put it where it is. Exodus, however, comes to us in a stylish and coherent arrangement, reflecting the order of events as they happened.

> A¹ Preface. Moses on the mountain: covenant preparation (chapter 19)
> > B¹ Laws. The Decalogue: basic principles (20:1–17)
> > > C¹ Interlude. The fear of the Lord felt (20:18–21)
> > B² Laws. Applicatory: a distinct lifestyle (20:22 – 23:19)
> > > C² Interlude. The fear of the Lord preceding (23:30–33)
> A² Epilogue. Moses on the mountain: covenant ratification (24:1–11)

20:4 *Image* (NIV) is *pesel*, from √*pāsal* ('to cut, carve'), and has behind it the idea of a craftsman developing some idea of the divine and then fashioning it out of his imagination. See Deut. 12:2–31 as comment on this commandment (cf. Isa. 44:9–20). G. H. Davies comments, 'The prohibition of images, like that of murder, does not mean that there were no images and no murder in later Israel.' In other words, disobedience remained an option, but 'archaeological remains have not yet yielded any certain images of Israel's God'. Commentators (e.g. Durham) often speak of Exodus 20:5–6 as a later expansion and explain it as arising from the difficulty found in keeping the commandment. There is neither ground nor evidence for this. The contemporary world was notoriously idolatrous. For this reason, the prohibition needed vigorous reinforcing – otherwise who could have grasped that the dangers involved in disobeying would span

---

[37] Childs says that 'The fear of God in the Old Testament refers specifically to obedience to God . . . It has nothing to do with the mystical sense of deity . . . Deuteronomy [4:10] provides the best commentary . . . "Gather the people to me, that I may let them hear my words, so that they may learn to fear me"' (p. 373). Cole writes of 'that true fear of God, which would lead to the avoidance of evil'.

the generations? Cf. W. C. Kaiser, *Toward Old Testament Ethics* (Zondervan, 1983), p. 86.

20:7 According to Murphy, 'To take his name in vain is to violate his essence.' Cf. Kaiser, 'Name', in *TWOT*. For examples of the idiomatic use of 'lift up' (√*nāśāʿ*) see e.g. 2 Kgs 9:25 (the NIV 'spoke this prophecy' is [lit.] 'lifted up upon him this burden/oracle'); 19:4 (the NIV 'pray for' is [lit.] 'lift up a prayer for'); Ps. 16:4; Isa. 14:4; 52:8. A general meaning 'to publicize, give voice to' can be established (see Exod. 23:1).

20:8 The command to *Remember* the Sabbath means that Sabbath law antedates Sinai. According to Gen. 2:1–3 it is a creation ordinance (see J. Murray, *Principles of Conduct* [Tyndale, 1957], pp. 30–35, 43), and in Exod. 16 it was the first regulation enforced as soon as the people gained their liberty. Indeed, it is assumed that all through the years of servitude (when the people were presumably not at liberty to order their lives as they pleased) the memory of the Sabbath remained. The great formal statement of Exod. 20:11 traces the Sabbath to its ground in creation, while Deut. 5:15, addressing those who through the exodus were again free to order their own lives, understandably relates the Sabbath to redemption. Exodus makes Sabbath law a perpetual obligation on humans as humans; Deuteronomy makes it particularly binding for those who sheltered beneath the blood of the lamb. Present knowledge suggests that the Sabbath was unique to Israel (see Currid, Cassuto). No other nation simply counted days in sevens without reference to lunar, solar or astral cycles. In Babylon the first, seventh, fifteenth and twenty-eighth days had special religious significance. In Israel the Sabbath is the seventh day, no matter when it falls (see Kaiser).

20:13 √*Rāṣaḥ* ('to murder') is used over forty times in the Old Testament, always of the death of a person and usually of a killing that in some way involves the legal process. It is used in Prov. 22:13 of a lion killing a person, but the commonest use is of murder either premeditated (e.g. Num. 35:30) or, mostly, unpremeditated (e.g. Deut. 4:42). It is never used of death in war. See J. Stamm, *The Ten Commandments in Recent Research* (SCM, 1967), p. 99; E. Nielsen, *The Ten Commandments in New Perspective* (SCM, 1968), p. 111.

20:14 √*Nāʾap* is used six times in apparent quotation of the commandment (e.g. Jer. 7:9); eight times without being specific whether married or unmarried people are involved (e.g. Prov. 30:20; Hos. 7:4); eighteen times of an offence within marriage (e.g. Lev. 20:10); and once with a possibly non-marital reference (Isa. 57:3). The other main word for sexual misconduct is √zānâ, which can also be used non-specifically for sexual misconduct in general, not necessarily for money. As a broad observation, however, √nā'ap is used in cases of a breach of the marriage covenant, and √zānâ is used to refer to instances of sex for money. Both words are used metaphorically of religious infidelity (e.g. Jer. 3:8–9; Exod. 34:15–16). Durham remarks that 'everywhere in the ancient near east adultery was a crime against persons; but in Israel it was first of all, and even more, a crime against Yahweh'. See Kaiser, *Ethics*, pp. 92–93.

20:15 Noth is quite mistaken in seeing an exclusive, or even primary, reference to kidnapping for purposes of enslavement. Napier perceptively notes that the fact that the commandment found its home in a predominantly poor community, in which (for example) the loss of a garment left a person defenceless against the cold (Exod. 22:26), pinpoints the seriousness of theft *as such*. He observes further that the biblical principle that 'the earth is the LORD's' (Ps. 24:1; cf. Lev. 25:23) makes any theft a violation of his ownership. On the use of √gānab see e.g. Gen. 31:30, 32; Josh. 7:11; 2 Sam. 21:12; Prov. 9:17. Its basic meaning is 'to carry off', and Durham finds its 'special connotation' in the idea of surreptitiousness. This may be unduly narrow in the light of most of the Old Testament examples.

20:16 Could anything be more absurd than the Interpreter's Bible's allegation that 'it is probable that in the early books of the Old Testament lying . . . was looked upon as something of an art form' – on the grounds that Laban was a specialist? I ask you! Since when was Laban a clue to Old Testament morality? In Exod. 20:16 (lit.) 'a witness of falsehood' uses the word *šeqer*. This is more specific than the broad noun *šāw'* ('worthlessness', 'emptiness'; cf. v. 7, [lit.] 'in vain'). *Šeqer* is 'the lie, falsehood, untruth'. The word translated *neighbour* (*rēa'*) has an ambience extending from close friend (e.g. 33:11; Prov. 17:17) to a fellow member of the same community (e.g. 2:13; Prov. 6:29), an acquaintance (11:2), someone next door or nearby (e.g. Deut. 23:24), or simply some other person or someone else (e.g. Deut. 4:42; Judg. 7:13). The commandment surely contains all these in its purview and requires us to act with integrity towards anyone who comes within our orbit.

20:17 Exodus uses √ḥāmad twice, whereas Deut. 5:21[18] uses √'āwâ on the second occasion. Durham rightly sees these verbs as too closely identifiable to allow a fine distinction. Each targets 'impermissible subjective longings'. √Ḥāmad is used for a grasping desire (Deut. 7:25), sinners delighting in sin (Prov. 1:22), idolaters desiring their illicit worship (Isa. 1:29) and sexual desire (Prov. 6:25). The change of verb in Deuteronomy is typical of the variations we find between the Exodus Decalogue and the one in Deuteronomy 5. All of them are explicable if we take seriously the situation Deuteronomy proposes for itself: that of Moses preaching the law to Israel on the verge of entering Canaan and naturally introducing variations and emphases suited to the new circumstances and natural to one who had become a superb orator.

Exodus 20:22 – 24:11

18. The Lord means his law and loves his people

Did Israel at Sinai know – or stop to consider – what they were committing themselves to? With all the enthusiasm at a new, great experience, they leapt to promise obedience (19:8); and not long after they reaffirmed their undertaking while their hearts were filled with dread (20:19).[1] While their joyous commitment in 19:8 has all the marks of reality, one might ask more questions about 20:19! Either they had not pondered the Decalogue, or they lacked a true self-knowledge, or they were so overcome by nervousness that they would 'promise anything'. But this was not the case, for in the long run their initial enthusiasm and their subsequent timidity came to fruition in the considered undertaking of 24:7, *We will do . . . we will obey.* Thus, they model for us the true position and correct response of the redeemed. The Lord's Israel is ever to be, now as well as then, first and foremost a people obeying the Lord's word.

1. The Lord's double move

The Lord, however, seemed not prepared to leave it at that. He did not want his people to 'walk blind', and therefore he said to Moses (lit.), 'Thus you are to say to the sons of Israel' and 'these are the judgments[2] you are to

---

[1] 'Listen' is √*šāmaʿ*, 'to hear', often used, as here, in the sense 'to give heed', to take in what is being said and submit to it in obedience.

[2] 'Judgments' (*laws, mišpaṭîm*) is abundantly used, as here, not in the sense of 'passing judgment' but in the sense of 'giving a judgment', making an authoritative decision (see J. A. Motyer on Isa. 42:2 in *Prophecy of Isaiah* and *Isaiah*). The Lord's 'judgments' are his infallible decisions and directions for life. Currid has 'a case decision dealing with specific social and economic contexts'.

set before them' (20:22; 21:1), spelling out in detail, as we would say, the commitment he requires. This is the significance of 20:22 – 23:19.[3] The Lord means his law: he means it to govern his people's actual life, and he means obedience to be the keynote of their conduct in every aspect and activity. Moses' words in Deuteronomy 5:1 sum the situation up in four verbs: 'Hear . . . learn . . . keep . . . do.'[4] But obedience is impossible without commands to obey, and broad principles like the Decalogue require thoughtful application to the actualities of daily life. Hence the need for the teaching contained in 20:22 – 23:19.

2. Always grace as well as law

This long section, however, leads into two passages of reassurance (23:20–33; 24:1–11). It is as if the Lord were saying to his people, 'Yes, you have made a demanding and even frightening commitment, but I want to make you equally aware of my reassuring provision.[5]

He offered two such reassurances: first, that the *angel* of the Lord would prepare their way ahead, bringing them into the place prepared for them, and that their obedience was the key to the angel's presence, superintendence and blessing (23:20–22); second, that there would always be provision within the sacrificial system of the covenant to cover and cater for their lapses from the life of obedience (cf. 1 John 1:7). This becomes apparent in the ceremony of covenant ratification (24:1–11), where the

---

[3] The title 'the Book of the Covenant' is commonly applied to 20:22 – 23:33 (see 24:7). While holding with many that these chapters are 'multilayered' (i.e. they have been expanded and extended over a lengthy period), Durham recognizes that their purpose is to clarify and apply the basic principles (the Decalogue) of living in covenant with the Lord. 'The first of such applications may well have been made by Moses.' He finds no ground for thinking of the terms of the Book of the Covenant as 'borrowed' from neighbours in Canaan and sees the collection as 'an integral part of the Sinai narrative . . . Yahweh's requirements for those who would be his special people' (pp. 315–318).

[4] Lit. 'Hear, Israel, the statutes and the judgments which I am speaking in your ears today, and learn them and keep them so as to do them.' In other words, listen to the word of God, grasp its meaning, guard it from addition, subtraction or neglect, and give it your obedience.

[5] See above, p. 224, for an overview of 19:1 – 24:11. This same sort of broad parallelism continues:
    A[1] Moses' fourth ascent: Moses on the mountain with God (20:21)
        B[1] The laws (20:22 – 24:11)
            a[1] The law of the altar (20:22–26)
                b Specific judgments (21:1 – 23:33)
            a[2] The covenant altar (24:1–11)
    A[2] Moses' fifth ascent: Moses on the mountain with God (24:12–18)
        B[2] The tabernacle (25:1 – 31:18)
            a[1] Provision for the tabernacle (25:1–9)
                b[1] Specific tabernacle details (25:10 – 30:38)
            a[2] Agents for tabernacle work (31:1–11)
                b[2] The inviolable Sabbath law (31:12–18)

people, as they again promised obedience, found that they were covered by the blood of the covenant (24:7–8).

3. Living with God (20:22–26)

Exodus 20:21 sets a scene which does not change until 24:3: that of Moses on the mountain in the Lord's presence in order to hear his voice. In the light of this, verses 22–26 belong with 21:1 – 23:33 in 'the Book of the Covenant' (24:7) and can be seen as a transition. The presence and voice of the Lord gave rise to an overmastering fear (20:18–19). The people's solution to this, to appoint a mediator, was a sensible one, and so they put Moses forward. The Lord, however, had another plan as well, the institution of an authorized altar, where he will *come to you and bless you* (24). When the trumpet called them to ascend the hill of the Lord, fear held them back (18; cf. 19:13), but

There is a way for man to rise to that sublime abode:
An offering and a sacrifice . . .[6]

The people backed off from the promised meeting with God, but the Lord was not to be deflected from his purpose to meet with them, and the altar, the place of sacrifice, was his appointed trysting place (as they will soon more perfectly learn).[7]

In this way Exodus 20:22–26 emerges naturally from the dramatic turn of events in 20:18–21, but it also has its proper place in what follows.

A¹ Prologue: the one God and the altar as the one place of worship (20:22–26)

 B¹ Ordering the household: the care of servants/slaves (21:1–11)

  C¹ Capital charges: social (21:12–27)

   D Responsibility for property and family (21:28 – 22:17)

    d¹ Animals (21:28–36)

    d² Ownership (22:1–15)

    d³ Family (22:16–17)

---

[6] From the hymn 'Eternal Light' by T. Binney.

[7] In the balance of the book of Exodus, 20:18–21 is elaborated in 21:1 – 23:19. The people pledged themselves to listen to God's voice through Moses, and the Lord graciously followed this through. 20:22–26 is elaborated in 25:1 – 29:46: the provision of the altar as the place of meeting is developed into the tabernacle, where the Lord lived among his people, where he spoke to them, and where the sacrifices were continually offered. His voice from heaven (20:22) and his voice in the tabernacle (29:42) form a grand *inclusio*.

C^2 Capital charges: religious (22:18–20)
B^2 Ordering relationships in the light of former servanthood
(22:21 – 23:9)
A^2 Epilogue: the one God and the religious ordering of life (23:10–19)

Notes

20:22–26 Here, as always in the Bible, the word of grace (the altar, God meeting his people) precedes the word of law (the 'judgments' of 21:1 – 23:19).

21:1–11 Verse 2 refers to *a Hebrew servant,* and Durham suggests someone who is 'less than a full citizen but more than a full slave'. What does 'full slave' mean? No such thing as slavery on, say, the Caribbean model was envisaged by the Old Testament. Hebrew has no vocabulary of slavery, only of servanthood, and it is to be noted that conditions were such that the first item of legislation catered for the servant who loved his master and did not want his 'freedom' (2–6). Indentured apprenticeship and the extended family provide better models. While Gen. 17:12 distinguishes the native (born in the home) and foreign (purchased for money) servant, each alike became a member of the extended family and covenant community through circumcision. Doubtless some heads of households were better masters than others, but nothing that we would call 'slavery' was intended, and compulsory, lifelong servanthood is prohibited here. We may well ask why the careful terms of servanthood are the first item of the Book of the Covenant, and there seems no answer other than that sensitivity towards those who might otherwise be lightly mistreated or ignored looms large in Mosaic legislation, rooted in the revelation of the Lord and Israel's own experience of divine care (Deut. 10:17–19). We must also take note of the chiastic arrangement so loved in Old Testament presentations and the way B^2 roots all relationships in the divine choice and care of slaves. In verse 6 the ear-piercing ceremony is possibly related to the ear as the organ of hearing, therefore of obedience. The pierced ear was on the master's part a claim to obedience; on the servant's part it was a commitment to obey. Verses 7–11 take account of the fact that the female servant was not protected by circumcision and, therefore, measures were enacted to secure her rights.

This section shows the care taken in codifying the laws. In verse 2 the topic in principle is introduced by 'when' (*kî*), and various codicils follow with *if* (*'im*) in verses 3–4 and a continuative codicil *But if* (*wĕ'im*) in verse 5. A related principle topic 'and when' (wĕkî) in verse 7 is qualified by various 'if' clauses in verses 8–11. The regulations in verses 12–17 have a common universalizing participle construction *anyone who* in verse 12 with continuative participles in verses 15–17. Qualifying codicils are introduced by wa'ăšer (13) and wĕkî (14). The distinction between the participial form and the codicils could point to the gradual accumulation of case law. The study of topics and codicils can be continued into verses 18–36, and in chapter 22. Exodus 23:1–9 is a chiasm on the topic of fair, honourable dealing in and out of court:

A¹   Social and legal integrity (1–2)
    B¹   No favouring of the poor at law (3)
        C   Compassion to triumph over hostility (4–5)
    B²   No disfavour to the poor at law (6)
A²   Social and legal integrity (7–9)

21:12–27 Verse 13 anticipates the provision of the 'cities of refuge', which must already have been known in principle to Moses (Num. 35:6, 13–18; Deut. 4:41–43; Josh. 20:1–9). Commentators report that in pagan societies the shrine or altar provided sanctuary, but 1 Kgs 1:50–53 and 2:28–35 show that this was not the case in Israel.

Verses 22–25 insist on *objective* and *exact* determination of penalties. The husband's whim would likely make some excessive claim for compensation; therefore the law insists on the intervention of the courts and goes on to assert the great *lex talionis*, whereby the punishment matches the offence committed in both kind and degree (cf. Lev. 24:20; Deut. 19:21). This is often misused (as if 'an eye for an eye' was an expression of ancient savagery), but it is actually a poetic and dramatic demand that the punishment should match the crime, no more *and* no less. When English law hanged a person for stealing a sheep, it was not because the principle of 'an eye for an eye' was being practised but because it had been forgotten. Nowadays, the great rule of equity is more often breached by mistaken leniency. The *lex talionis* is, of course, a law for the courts, not for private vengeance. The Lord Jesus reclaimed it from this false application (Matt. 5:38–42). Cf. J. A. Motyer, *Law and Life* (Lawyers' Christian Fellowship, 1978), pp. 12–13. The reference to the *lex talionis* in the present context shows that its terms were illustrative, not prescriptive. Durham rightly approves of calling it 'an important advance in the history of jurisprudence'.

21:28–36 Verse 30 provides secular examples of two words which play a big part in redemption theology. The niv's *payment* translates *kōper*, and *redeem . . . by the payment* is *pidyôn*. The former is from √*kāpar* (e.g. Lev. 17:11), the latter from √*pādâ* (e.g. Exod. 13:13–15). *Kōper* is the (here monetary) payment judged to 'cover' the offence, and *pidyôn* the actual payment which discharged the *kōper* (cf. Ps. 49:8–9[9–10]).

22:1–15 Verse 8 is (lit.) 'shall be brought near to the God [i.e. God himself]' and possibly refers to seeking a divine oracle which would settle the matter, but verse 11 makes an oath before the Lord decisive, and that may be the meaning in verse 8.

22:16–20 According to Durham, the prohibition on sex with animals in verse 19 is there 'not only because it was a sexual deviation (cf. Lev. 18:23; 20:16; Deut. 27:21), but even more because of its associations with animal cults and fertility worship'.

22:21 – 23:9 This section focuses the three basic motivations of Israelite law: to live in the light of saving grace (22:21; 23:9), to live in the light of what the Lord is (22:22–25) and to live in holiness (22:29–31). The general 'duties to God' (22:29–31) are preceded by eight verses of care for the disadvantaged and followed by nine verses of care for truth and right. Verses 21–24 apply the *lex talionis* on a national scale. A nation careless of its disadvantaged will not be allowed to survive. There are national consequences of provoking divine wrath. Loans to fellow believers may be secured loans (26) but must not be loans at interest for personal advantage (25). In verse 28 the niv's *blaspheme* and even the esv's 'revile' are too strong and specific. Something like 'belittle', 'make light of' or 'treat as of trifling importance' would be better. *Curse* (√*'ārar*) is always used of a deliberately malignant word, aimed at hurting.

Verses 29–31 can be seen as countering the spirit which says, 'God doesn't matter.' From the lesser dues (*offerings*) to the more serious ones (*firstborn*; cf. 13:2, 12–15), from the great call to holiness to the humdrum matter of food purity, everything matters. God is honoured by our *scrupulous* obedience.

Note the neat balance in 23:4–5 between *your enemy* (someone you are hostile to) and *someone who hates you* (someone hostile to you). There is also a balance between (lit.) 'in the absence of your enemy' (4) and in his or her presence (5).

23:10–19 Some commentators suggest that the three pilgrim feasts (14–17) were in all likelihood borrowed from the Canaanites after the conquest. This is a needless supposition. Moses was legislating with Canaan in view, not the wilderness. The people of the ancient world did not live in sealed compartments. Moses could well have envisaged what a settled way of life would mean, and through Moses 'the Lord graciously used the agricultural year with its natural rhythm to stimulate the people in the worship of his name' (R. L. Harris, *Numbers* [EBC, vol. 2], p. 952). On the *Festival of Unleavened Bread* (15), cf. 12:3–20; Lev. 23:5–6; Deut. 16:1–8; on *Harvest* (16), cf. 34:22; Lev. 23:16; Num. 28:26; and on *Ingathering* (16), cf. 34:22; Lev. 23:34; Num. 29:12; Deut. 16:13.

Verses 18–19 contain in the main cautionary directives, regulating practice at the feasts. Verse 18 relates primarily to Passover, verse 19a to Harvest. In verse 19b, if *young goat* (*gĕdî*) is the same as *gĕdî-ʿizzîm*, this might refer to the *śĕʿîr-ʿizzîm* specified only for Tabernacles (Num. 29:16; NIV, ESV 'male goat'). If, then, boiling a kid in its mother's milk was a Canaanite fertility rite (as is widely suggested; cf. Kaiser, Cassuto), it would be appropriate to announce this prohibition here as a specific guidance for the third pilgrim feast.

4. Devotion and duty

Everything in the Word of God is precious and carries its own meaning, but in the present section, the message of the whole is just as important as that of the individual parts, and brings clear, broad lessons.

a. All life is to be held within the setting of spiritual and religious devotion

If we follow the pattern set in the Book of the Covenant, what we call 'walking with God', biblical spirituality, is the context in which we must consciously seek to live every moment, every day. Prior place is given to the altar as the place of meeting with God (A¹), and the Book of the Covenant circles round to its *inclusio* (A²) in the demanding ordering of life in the seven-year cycle (23:10–11), the seven-day cycle (23:12) and the annual cycle (23:14–19). In this way, life is encompassed by spirituality: God comes first and last as he comes to meet with us (20:24) and we go to meet with him (23:17). What concentrated attention must be given to the altar and what careful thought to the diary.

Balancing this practical commitment to live our lives for and with God (A²), 20:22–26 lays the foundation on which that life rests. First there is the heavenly revelation spoken by the Lord himself, the sure divine word (20:22). Our response to this is a commitment to the knowledge of and devotion to the one and only true God (20:23; cf. 23:13). The religion that results from this centres on the altar, the place of the shed blood (20:24; cf. Heb. 13:10–13). The place of atonement has to be the focal point, the heart of religious reality. The balance of wording between verses 24 and 23 makes the prescription of the altar very emphatic – contrasting what the people must not make (*gods of silver or gods of gold*) with what they are to make: *an altar*. It is religion to which we have contributed nothing[8] but which is directed and determined by God himself and is free of sinful contagion (20:24–26). It is not a religion of humans feeling after God but of God coming to his people, with the emphasis not on what we might do for God but on what he would do for us in blessing (20:24). The altar is his, the offering ours; he does not need our offerings for his nourishment (cf. Ps. 50:9–13) – we need them for our sins.

b. The word of God entering and directing every aspect of life

The topics covered by the Book of the Covenant are diverse and extra-ordinarily comprehensive: the household (21:1–11), capital offences in society (21:12–17), injuries to persons and beasts (21:18–36), protection of property (22:1–6), finance and business (22:7–15), sexual malpractice (22:16–17), capital offences in religion (22:18–20), humane concern (22:21–27), living under God's authority in state, church and personal character (22:28–31), integrity and honourable dealing (23:1–9) and the timetable of work (22:10–13) and of religion (22:14–19). All this, of course, is intended to be illustrative and exemplary rather than exhaustive – but it is, never-theless, enormously demanding. God merits entrance into all life. All of life is his arena, and for all of life he has prescriptions and ideals. On the other side of the picture, the Lord's people have a duty to bring all life under the scrutiny of his word, and to live all life as his word directs. If 19:5 insists on obedience as the prime response of the redeemed, and 20:2–17 sketches the chief areas and foundational principles of obedience,

---

[8] Verse 24b guards religion from ritualism. The altar and its sacrifices are not techniques for securing advantage or twisting the Lord's arm; the Lord freely comes to bless. Verse 25 prohibits shaping or carving, thus keeping the altar free of the pollution of our sinful hands and from expressing what we might think suitable or helpful – or even beautiful. Even the substance of the altar is provided by God: the soil of his earth and the rocks of his creation. Verse 26 separates religion from human powers of fertility. Fertility cults – indeed pagan religions in general – often required officiants to be naked. The Bible is emphatic in refusing such a practice.

then 20:22 – 23:19 extends the parameters of obedience out to the very limits of personal, domestic, social and church living.

Lord Melbourne, Queen Victoria's first prime minister, is reported to have said that 'if religion is going to invade a person's private life, things have come to a pretty pass'. He was a well-intentioned and a good, even religious, man to the extent of attending church on Sunday, but he wanted his religion safely packed away in a box and kept there. The Book of the Covenant says that this is not an option. Like a dog, religion too is not just for Christmas, it is for life. True religion cannot be confined. The Lord demands entrance into every aspect of the life of his redeemed, and he looks to govern every aspect by his revealed truth.

c. A very distinctive people

We have already observed that many of the practices required by the laws of Israel were also part of contemporary pagan culture. Yet even so, in Israel it was different because the distinction between crime and sin had been erased. A different motivation applied. The Lord always had to be included in the equation.

Joseph voiced this exactly when he was faced with the temptation to commit adultery and refused, saying, 'How then could I do such a wicked thing *and sin against God?*' (Gen. 39:9; my italics). It was not the crime as such that deterred him, nor ultimately the sense of the honour due to his master, but his sense of himself as a man living in God's sight, owing a higher allegiance and subject to heavenly law and judgment. The recurring theological appeal in Exodus 22:21 – 23:9 makes the same point within the Book of the Covenant, as it prescribes the care of resident aliens by recalling Israel's own experience as aliens in Egypt (22:21–23; cf. 23:9) and the welfare of the poor by referring to divine grace (22:26–27). It stresses the importance of judicial integrity by a reminder that divine justice will not treat the guilty as though they were innocent (23:6–7).

5. Distinctive through obedience

We could well pause at any and every prescription of the Book of the Covenant to underline the truth that the Lord desires his people to be distinct. What he wants in us, however, is the distinctiveness which arises as a by-product of obeying his word. He wants us to live in the courts of earth according to the rules of the courts of heaven (20:22b). Christians of older generations will still recall today the reactive distinctiveness which passed for 'separation from the world' when they were young. If it was customary in the world around, it was forbidden to Christians – and for no other reason! Generations of Christians were deprived of the pleasures and benefits of the arts, for example, because they were considered the province of 'the world'. But this sort of isolationist difference is not what the Bible looks for. We are called, rather, to ransack Scripture to discover the distinctive features of a godly lifestyle and to follow through with a discipline of obedience to the word of God. This is what the Lord sought in his redeemed at Sinai, and it is still the calling of the Israel of God (Gal. 6:16).

6. Committed to obedience, met with blessing (23:20 – 24:11)

Two important passages both round off Moses' fourth ascent of Sinai (23:20–33; cf. 20:21 with 24:3a) and also complete the Lord's actions in bringing his people into his covenant (24:1–11). Just as 20:22–26 uttered a comforting word of grace before the itemizing of the terms of Israel's obedience (21:1 – 23:19), so these passages bring deep comforts of grace to those who have now heard what is expected of them.[9]

a. Unfailing divine presence

There are two great truths in 23:20–33: the accompanying *angel* (20–26),[10] and the forerunning *terror* (27–33). The terror is not explicitly said to be

---

[9] It is not only verses like Acts 5:32 and passages like Rom. 6:15–23 which continue the emphasis on the obedience of the redeemed, but the New Testament returns constantly to the ethical demands of the gospel and the distinctiveness of Christian living. When Jesus linked love, obedience and the gift of the Comforter (John 14:15–18; cf. 14:21), he could have been summarizing the movement from the grace of Exod. 20:22–26 to the commandments of 21:1 – 23:19 and on to the accompanying presence of 23:20–33. We need to ask, however, to what extent the laws of the old covenant continue to apply to believers in the new covenant. Matt. 5:17–20 is the key passage, insisting that the Bible is not two Testaments but one book, united around the person and work of the Lord Jesus Christ. Jesus said that nothing of the written law would be 'demolished' (*katalyō*), not even the smallest letter (*iota*) or the least stroke of a pen (*keraia*); all would come to its full flowering (*pleroō*), everything would 'happen' (*ginomai*). We are, therefore, not at liberty to dismiss anything as 'Old Testament' without asking what its fullness of meaning, significance and application in Christ is. See J. A. Motyer, *The Story of the Old Testament* (Candle, 2001), pp. 8–13. Our task is not to harmonize two disparate documents (the 'Old' and 'New' Testaments) but to trace out lines of cumulative revelation which reach their fullness in Christ. As a broad position, even things which the Bible makes temporary as prescriptions for living remain on as principles of godly life, but everything must be judged in the light of the whole Scripture, i.e. in the light of Christ.

[10] On the angel of the Lord, see above. Note how in 23:20–26 the angel and the Lord alternate – his presence, my name; his voice, I speak; etc. According to Cassuto, 'In the final analysis, the angel . . . is simply God's action.' Mackay, surely correctly, sees the angel as 'a temporary, pre-incarnate, appearance of the second person of the Trinity'.

the angel, but identification is reasonable, since the angel will bring them into the Promised Land and drive out their foes (23), and this is what the terror does too (27–28). Also the angel and the terror are both in fact the Lord himself: when the angel speaks, it is the Lord who speaks (22), and when the terror drives out the inhabitants of Canaan, it is the Lord who is driving them out (28–29). Thus, the Lord who calls his people to costly and demanding obedience himself accompanies them in appropriate ways and goes before them to secure their victories and promised possessions.

A^1 The accompanying angel (20–26)

    a^1 The function of the angel (20)

        b^1 The perils of irreverence (21)

        b^2 The blessings of obedience (22)

    a^2 The function of the angel (23)

    B^1 The monotheistic people (24–26)

        a **No alternative allegiance or tolerance (24)**

        b **Sole loyalty and consequent blessing (25–26)**

A^2 The forerunning terror (27–33)

    a **Foregoing panic (27)**

    b **Foregoing victory (28–31)**

        b^1 Gradual possession (29)

        b^2 Assured possession (30)

        b^3 Complete possession (31)

    B^2 The monotheistic people (32–33)

        a **No alliances (32)**

        b **No cohabitation (33)**

Notes

23:21 The NIV's *Pay attention to him* (NKJV, 'Beware of him') is *hiššāmer mippānayw*. There is no other case of *mippĕnê* following the niphal of √*šāmar*. It must be emphatic: 'watch yourselves carefully in respect of him/because of his presence'. The angel's presence calls for sensitivity (21), his voice for obedience (22). In verse 21, *he will not forgive* needs careful thought, for if the Lord's name is in the angel (i.e. he possesses the full, revealed divine nature) then he is (as Yahweh is) a forgiving God, yet grace must never be presumed upon. When mercy comes it should always be welcomed as a surprise, never taken as a foregone conclusion (cf. 34:6–7).

23:24–26 Following verse 23 (what the Lord promises), these verses are not 'the other side of the bargain' (our reciprocal promises) but a unilateral, unconditional imposition of the terms of our responsive obedience. In verse 24 all the verbs are second person singular, indicating that the collective action of the community requires the deliberate obedience of the individual.

23:27 *Terror* is *'êmâ*, a very strong word, 'terrifying fear' (e.g. Gen. 15:12; Job 39:20; 41:14).

23:28–31 *Hornet* (28) is an uncertain translation of *ṣir'â*. It is found elsewhere in the Bible only in two other places (Deut. 7:20; Josh. 24:12), with the same sense in both places. Durham (without comment) suggests 'panic-terror' and Kaiser (with no elaboration or evidence offered, but cf. 'bees' [or 'flies'] in Isa. 7:18), 'discouragement' or perhaps the use of 'hornet' as a symbol of Egypt. Certainly the bee appears in pharaonic heraldry (Cole). Davis calls attention to the 'numinous panic' accompanying the 'holy war' of Joshua 10:10.

23:29 The Lord blends the fulfilment of his promises with his concern for all creation (29) and with his people's capacity to enjoy (30), but he will always do what he has pledged (31a), while his people will enjoy what he promises through active obedience (31b).

23:32 Note how *with them or with their gods* embraces social as well as religious distinctiveness. *With* is *lĕ*, which in covenant terminology means a covenant 'in favour of', 'bestowing benefits on'.

The benefit of an analysis like this is that when we follow it through, item by item, we are forced to pay attention to the Bible's details and in this way to dwell on its truth and differing emphases.[11] What we have in 23:20–33 is a classical statement of the fundamental covenant situation: absolute divine promises (20, 31), obedience as the entrance to enjoyment of what is promised (22–23), obedience as an absolute requirement (24–26), what is unconditionally promised is conditionally enjoyed (27), and the sovereign freedom of the Lord in deciding how his promises will be fulfilled (28–30), though ultimate fulfilment is guaranteed (31).

---

[11] Durham (p. 335) perceptively notes that it is 'hardly a coincidence that virtually the first (20:23) and last (23:32–33) words of the present sequence are Yahweh's insistence on the absolute loyalty of his own people'.

b. The sheltering covenant[12]

Exodus 24:1–11 seems logically and thematically in place. Durham's comment that verses 1–2 are less in sequence with what goes before than are the verses which follow (3–8) is surely unnecessary. It is hardly likely that the Lord would allow Moses to leave his presence without some direction about what was to happen next. At any rate, 24:1–11 as we have received it makes a fine epilogue to the prologue in chapter 19 and can be set out in this way:

A¹ Moses, Aaron, Nadab, Abihu and seventy elders to approach (1–2)
  B¹ Declaration and response: obedience pledged (3)
    C Formalization of the covenant (4–6)
      c¹ The written words (4a)
      c² The permanent relationship between Yahweh and Israel
          symbolized in the altar and pillars (4b)
      c³ The basis of the covenant: blood sacrifice (5–6)
  B² Reading and response: obedience pledged (7–8)
A² Moses, Aaron, Nadab, Abihu and seventy elders approach (9–11)

As distinct from the joyous but uninformed response of 19:7–8, the full Exodus/Sinai/Mosaic revelation of the Lord is here spelled out (4, 7) – its ground rules (20:2–17) and its typical applications (20:22 – 23:19). On the one hand, the sacrifices formalized the covenant from the Lord's side (5), and on the other hand, the people's considered response was their personal embracing of all that the Lord had done and said (7).

There are some things here that we do not know or cannot be wholly sure about. For example, there is no record of the Lord describing or commanding this covenant ritual, so where did it come from? Moses would, of course, have known from Abram's experience that the Lord's covenant is inaugurated by sacrifice (Gen. 15). It is also likely that, just as in Genesis 15:9, the Lord specified the beasts required but Abram apparently needed no instruction what to do with them, so here, the basic form of covenant inauguration was known to Moses. Again, we do not know

---

[12] Supporters of the documentary theory offer their usual confused picture of chapter 24. It is said to be 'mostly E' but with J components. Beer finds P in verses 15b–18b, and Hyatt finds R^D in verses 4a and 7. Durham (pp. 340–342) thinks that all this is speculative and that it obscures the function the chapter has in the narrative, which is as 'an obvious conclusion to the events set in motion' in chapter 19. He thinks it 'uneasy' in form but dramatically appropriate. On the place of 24:1–11 in the whole sequence, see above, p. 224.

who the *young Israelite men* of 24:5 were, but the most likely surmise is that they were the firstborn sons, set apart at this stage to act as Israel's priests (cf. 13:2). Likewise, we do not know precisely what the Book of the Covenant contained, but no doubt we are intended to assume – and it is reasonable to do so – that it was a written record of the Lord's direct statement of the Ten Commandments and the Lord's directives through Moses recorded in 20:22 – 23:19.[13]

7. An unmistakable symbol

There can, however, be no mistake about the meaning of the altar and pillars of verse 4. The Lord had taken it in hand to bring his people to himself (6:6–7) and had done so (19:4). This basic relationship was now, as we would say, 'set in concrete', and a stone altar was built to represent the Lord surrounded by the twelve tribes of his people who had been brought out of Egypt, protected from his judgmental wrath by the blood of the lamb, and who were now immovably established around him. The blood of the lamb, the blood of propitiation, was the just 'settlement' of the wrath of God. The sacrificial basis of the inauguration of the covenant was now completed by the other two great categories of sacrifice: the burnt offering, symbolizing the holding back of nothing from God (cf. Gen. 22:2, 12), and the fellowship or peace offering, symbolizing communion with God.

The first function of the blood is Godward, as Moses sprinkled half of it on the altar (6). It must be so. The primary need is that God should be satisfied, for it is his justly due wrath that constitutes our danger, and, in mercy, he has appointed that by substitutionary death – encapsulated in and symbolized by the shed blood – those endangered by his wrath are accepted into his presence and fellowship. Next, however, the people must affirm the reality symbolized by their burnt offering and ask themselves if they are really committed to God's way, holding nothing back, as the total consumption of the burnt offering on the altar depicts. So, the law

---

[13] In the introduction to his commentary on Jeremiah, J. L. Mackay reports that it was the custom in the Ancient Near East 'to secure the message from the deity in the most accurate way possible', and says we can assume that the same 'would apply for ancient Israelite prophetical texts . . . [which were] written down after they had been delivered' (*Jeremiah*, Mentor Commentary [Christian Focus, 2004]). This is surely correct. People conscious that their words were in full reality the very words of God would inevitably have been intent on their immediate preservation – and certainly not to consign them to a centuries-long game of Chinese whispers!

of God was read to them, and they gave their assent – *We will do everything the Lord has said: we will obey* (7). Henceforth they will be wholly people of the revealed word. But – and how significant this is – no sooner had they made this enormous commitment than the shed blood was sprinkled over them like a huge covering of mercy (8). They were committed to obedience – that was their prime concern – but God knows that the best intentions fall constantly short and provided the blood of sacrifice to be at the ready to cater for each and every lapse from his revealed way.[14]

---

[14] In 19:21 there was a warning not 'to see the Lord' (√*rā'â*), but now the assembled elders *saw the God of Israel* (10, √*rā'â*). God had veritably come to them and stood before them for examination (they saw *his feet*), in the full reality of his purity (*bright blue* is *ṭāhôr*, 'clean' or 'pure'). He accepted their gaze, and they went unharmed and experienced the sight in all their humanness (11; *God did not raise his hand against* them and they *ate and drank*), enjoying the fruition of the covenant in a communal meal (cf. Gen. 31:54; Isa. 25:6–9). This was not an 'out of the body' experience but, just as God came to them in his divine reality, so he welcomed them in their human reality. This, in a word, is the effectiveness of the shed blood of sacrifice. Following *and saw*, the reference to *his feet* suggests a reverential bowing down before him.

Exodus 24:12 – 27:19

19. The Lord's tent

In the wonderful variety of the Word of God, we come now to one of God's picture galleries.

The Bible teaches us in many ways. In the book of Exodus we have learned divine truth from the record of historical events and from the revelation of the Lord's laws. With the account of the tabernacle, however, we come to visual aids of spiritual realities.[1] Indeed, the tabernacle could make a strong bid to be the greatest of all biblical visual aids. We can think this way because the Bible insists that both the idea of having a tabernacle at all and also the detailed design according to which it was constructed came from the Lord himself.[2] On this ground alone it would be allowable to say that there cannot be a single detail of the tabernacle devoid of meaning – even though it is not necessarily possible, or maybe indeed safe, to stray beyond those main lessons which illuminate truths plainly taught in other passages of Scripture. William Tyndale was surely right to say, with his homely bluntness, that a truth derived solely from a 'type' and unaffirmed by plain teaching is as much use as 'a tale of Robin Hood'!

---

[1] It is easy for the study of typology (finding pictures of truth in institutions such as the tabernacle or foreshadowings of Jesus in people and events from the past) to get a bad name through fanciful applications and snatching verses, even bits of verses or individual words, out of context. But this is not to say that there is not a proper typology. The epistle to the Hebrews is itself sufficient to justify finding truth typologically expressed in the tabernacle (e.g. Heb. 9). See G. R. Osborne, 'Type, Typology' (with bibliography), in W. A. Elwell (ed.), *Evangelical Dictionary of Theology* (Baker, 2001); H. H. Rowley, 'The Interpretation of the Song of Songs', in *The Servant of the Lord* (Lutterworth, 1954), pp. 187ff.; J. A. Motyer's Introduction to H. Taylor, *Union and Communion* (Christian Focus, 1996). Cf. D. W. Gooding, *How to Teach the Tabernacle*; *The Account of the Tabernacle*. Older writers still well worth consulting include White, *Christ in the Tabernacle*; Dennett, *Typical Teachings of Exodus*; Rainsford, *The Tabernacle in the Wilderness*.

[2] See Exod. 25:8–9, 40; 26:30; 27:8; 36:1; Num. 8:4; cf. Acts 7:44; Heb. 8:5.

1. God alongside, really present, ever near

From the start, the Lord revealed the secret of his purpose: the Israelites were to *make a sanctuary for me, and I will dwell among them* (25:8). Cassuto comments that for as long as Israel camped at Sinai 'they were conscious of God's nearness; but once they set out on their journey, it seemed to them as though the link had been broken, unless there were in their midst a tangible symbol of God's presence'. The tabernacle was 'a perpetual extension of the bond that was forged at Sinai'.

The vocabulary of the tabernacle is important, and there are two key words used in 25:8. First, the verb 'to dwell' (√*šākan*), giving rise to the noun *miškān*, a 'dwelling', widely used throughout Exodus 25 – 40; and second, the noun *miqdāš*, 'a sanctuary' or 'place of holiness'. In addition to these words, *'ōhel*, the ordinary word for a 'tent', makes its appearance in 26:7 and occurs frequently thereafter. 'Tabernacle' has become the conventional name for the Lord's tent, intended presumably to express a sense of dignity and uniqueness, but we must not lose sight of the fact that it is the common word for 'tent' used to refer to the homes in which the Israelites themselves lived. It was, in fact, as Gooding says, 'the tent God used when God went camping'. Considering simply the words, *'ōhel* ('tent') points to the nature of the structure, a mobile home, *miškān* to its purpose as 'somewhere to live', and *miqdāš* ('holy place') to the divine character of the occupant.

Each word contributes to the significance of what happened. The Israelites were living in tents at the time (16:16), and for the Lord to command the pitching of his tent (*'ōhel*), therefore, symbolized his coming alongside, his identification with them and with their circumstances.[3] To call the Lord's tent his *miškān* indicates permanency, as though it were his 'address', the place where he was to be found living. Just as the glory *settled* (√*šākan*) on Sinai (24:16), that is, it was constantly there throughout Israel's stay at the mountain, so it was the Lord's intent to 'settle' among his people in the tent that would be pitched at the centre of their camp.

Even though *miqdāš* ('sanctuary') is found only once in the chapters dealing with the tabernacle, its importance is immense. In common

---

[3] Num. 2 outlines the camping and marching pattern of Israel in its wilderness days, with 'the tent of meeting . . . in the middle of the camps' (17). If the Judah tribes camped in an eastward line, the Reuben tribes southward, Ephraim westward and the Dan tribes northward, then the Lord's tent was pitched at the centre point of a huge cross, symbolizing the Lord in the midst of his people, sharing their lot and alongside them in their situation. So, for Cassuto (p. 320), the tabernacle section is not 'a disquisition on the antiquities of Israelite worship' but an instruction on 'the fundamental idea of the presence of God in the camp'.

English usage a sanctuary is a place to run to for safety. This is not what the word means in the Old Testament. Rooted in the verb *qādēš* ('to be holy'), the noun means 'a place where holiness is', and it specifies the tabernacle as the place where the Lord in his holiness, in the full reality of the glory of his holy nature, would come to settle among his people.

When we speak, popularly, of our church buildings as 'the Lord's house', we mean a place where we go to be with him; in the Bible, the tabernacle – and, later, the temple or 'house'[4] – is where the Lord comes to be with us.

All this is summed up in Exodus 29:42b–46. The tent of meeting is where the Lord keeps his appointments with Israel (42b, 43), where he speaks with them (42b). It will be a sanctified place because his glory is in it (43–44), and there the Lord will dwell (√*šākan*) (lit.) 'in the middle of the sons of Israel' (45) in fulfilment of the covenant promise to be their God (Gen. 17:7; Exod. 6:7). More than all this, however, the tabernacle sums up the whole divine purpose in redemption: he brought Israel out of Egypt 'so that I might dwell [√*šākan*] among them' (29:46). The consummation of the work of redemption is the Lord's dwelling among his people – a truth brought to its intended fulfilment in Christ. In 1 Corinthians 3:10–17 Paul teaches that Christians, gathered and built on the sole foundation of Jesus Christ, are in their collectivity 'God's temple' and that 'God's Spirit lives' in them (16). And in Ephesians 2:11–22 he says that the universal company who in Christ have peace with one another and with God are being built on the foundation of apostles and prophets to become 'a dwelling in which God lives by his Spirit' (22).[5]

2. Law and grace (again)

Having seen the central truth which this great section on the tabernacle teaches, we can now turn to the message of the structure of the account of Moses' fifth ascent of Sinai.

---

[4] Solomon's great question in 1 Kgs 8:27, 'But will God really dwell on earth?', is intended to elicit the marvelling answer, 'Yes indeed!'

[5] This is a perfect illustration of the concept of fulfilment, which applies equally to the consummation of the Old Testament sacrifices in the cross, the Jerusalem promises in the Jerusalem which is from above (Gal. 4:26; Heb. 12:22; Rev. 21:10–27), and the territorial promises in the kingdom not of this world (John 18:36). As the grain in a piece of timber 'runs out' into its own characteristic end grain, the New Testament is the intended fullness of expression of what the Old Testament anticipates. It is not an adaptation, certainly not an alteration, but the same proper growth to maturity that makes a sapling develop into a tree or brings the meagre first-year flowering of a perennial to its full floral display in the third or fourth year (cf. Motyer, *The Story of the Old Testament*, p. 10, 2b).

$\mathbf{A^1}$ The promise of the tablets of the law (24:12–18)

   $\mathbf{B^1}$ Materials for the tabernacle, according to the divine pattern (25:1–9)

      $\mathbf{C^1}$ Tabernacle specifications (25:10 – 27:21)

         Ark (25:10–22)

         Table (25:23–30)

         Lampstand (25:31–40)

         The dwelling (*miškān*) (26:1–37)

         The courtyard (27:1–19)

      $\mathbf{C^2}$ Tabernacle officiants (27:20 – 30:10)

         $\mathbf{c^1}$ Priestly duty: tending the lampstand (27:20–21)

            $\mathbf{d^1}$ Priestly robes (28:1–43)

            $\mathbf{d^2}$ Priestly consecration and work (29:1–46)

         $\mathbf{c^2}$ Priestly duty: tending the golden altar (30:1–10)

      $\mathbf{C^3}$ Tabernacle functioning (30:11–38)

   $\mathbf{B^2}$ Workmen for the tabernacle, according to the divine pattern (31:1–17)

$\mathbf{A^2}$ The gift of the tablets of the law (31:18)

Notes

24:12–18 This fifth ascent is reported in seven separate 'words': 25:1; 30:11, 17, 22, 34; 31:1, 12. Certainly from the second word onwards it is easy to imagine Moses' questions provoking divine answers.

25:1–9 The Lord proposed to live among his people, but his indwelling awaited their responsive giving which would provide the materials for the tent. The repetition of the blessings of Sinai (19:17–18) depends on willing hearts (2), costly giving (3–7) and meticulous obedience (9). This same situation, centuries later, gave rise to Haggai's message: the people's neglect of the house of the Lord spoke of an uncaring attitude whether the Lord was among them or not: his presence still 'awaited' their obedience. See J. A. Motyer, 'Haggai', in T. McComiskey, *The Minor Prophets*, vol. 3 (Baker, 1998). All the materials specified for the tabernacle could easily have been in Israel's possession as a consequence of both what they asked from the Egyptians (12:35) and the 'large droves of livestock' (12:38) they owned.

Sanctuary (8) applies to the whole complex about to be described, not just to the part subsequently described as the *Most Holy Place*.

25:10–22 The construction of the ark, the table and the lampstand (10–40) preceded the construction of the tent to house them. Cassuto

(p. 328) says, 'The Tabernacle serves . . . them. They do not serve the Tabernacle.'

In 25:17 *an atonement cover* is *kappōret*. The noun is of the same formation as *pārōket* (NIV 'curtain', e.g. 26:31), from √*pārak*, 'to shut or close', hence it conveys the idea of the 'shutting' rather than the 'thing' that does it, i.e. the curtain. Therefore, *kappōret* is 'the atoning/making atonement', the active expression of what happens. It comes from √*kāpar*, which in the simple active (qal) means 'to cover over' (e.g. Gen. 6:14, NIV 'coat'). The intensive (piel) *kipper* derives from the technical, religious use of the noun *kōper* as the price paid to 'cover' an offence and means 'to pay such a price, to atone'. Durham (p. 359) calls it 'a primary Old Testament term for propitiation'. The solid golden lid of the ark was both its *cover* and also the place where the atoning blood was sprinkled (Lev. 16:14). The ark contained the law of the Lord; the *kappōret* was a precise 'covering', and when identified with the atoning blood – the price paid in respect of sin – there was an exact covering/payment/atonement. Cf. the use of √*kāpar* in Lev. 17:11, and see J. A. Motyer, *Look to the Rock*, pp. 51–53.

For other occurrences of *cherubim* see Gen. 3:24; Exod. 25:22; Num. 7:89; 1 Sam. 4:4; Ps. 99:1; Ezek. 9:3.

The 'testimony' (21 ESV, *ʿēdût*) is that which testifies to God and his requirements and is used of the law as the Lord's 'testimony' to himself. It comes from √*ʿûd*, meaning 'to attest, bear witness to/against'. The ark, its cover and the testimony are a single unity. The throne of the Lord rests on the foundation of the exact matching and mutuality of law and atonement. This is where God meets his people and speaks.

25:23–30 Durham (p. 362) says the table was 'a special symbol of Yahweh present with his people . . . his giving nearness. Any idea of food being provided for Yahweh is as removed from this provision as from the offering of sacrifices . . . No such thought in Israel.' The bread was for the priests. The Lord is the nourisher of his priestly people. 'He is here, and here as one who gives sustenance.'

25:31–40 Brightness, fire and gold symbolize the presence of the Lord (see 27:20–21; 30:7–8; 40:4; Lev. 24:3; Num. 8:4; 1 Sam. 3:3). The first duty of the priests was the care of the lampstand. Gooding (*How to Teach the Tabernacle*, p. 32) says it was 'made to look as if it were a living tree . . . [with] buds, blossoms and almonds . . . the three stages of life', the tree of life. Moberly (p. 11) sees the lampstand as a stylized representation of the burning bush. On *almond flowers* cf. Jer. 1:11. Durham calls it 'the life-promising . . . tree'.

26:1–37 On 26:15 Cassuto (p. 354) says acacia wood was plentiful in the wilderness of Sinai. Commentators differ whether *frames* (NIV, ESV) or 'boards' (NKJV) is the correct translation of *qĕrašîm*. Gooding (*Account*, p. 15) favours 'a kind of skeleton framework'. This would allow the beauty of the embroidered curtains to be seen through the gold framing.

Verses 32–33 are one place where we become aware that, though every detail of the tabernacle was revealed to Moses, not every detail is recorded for us. How was the curtain hung on the four pillars? Where were the hooks, and to what were the clasps attached? Perhaps we should think of V-shaped sockets at the top of each pillar, holding a crossbar from which the curtains hung – indeed it is hard to see how it could have been achieved without some such arrangement. But we are not told. The width between the pillars meant that the ark had to be *in situ* before the pillars were set up (see 40:20–21). Or maybe the curtain was suspended from the line of hooks/clasps which fastened the roof-curtains together? The same problem applies to the door screen (36). In 36:37–38 the doorposts were fitted with gold 'bands' (NIV; ESV 'fillets'), which were, perhaps, braces or tie rods between the pillars and between the end pillars and the corner braces of the tabernacle. Without some such bracing, the weight of the covers would have pulled the side walls inwards. Gooding (*Account*, p. 15, on 27:10) says, 'It is not clear whether the Hebrew denotes an ornamental band round the pillar . . . or whether it means a connecting rod . . . between the pillars.'

27:1–19 The specifications of the altar given here (1–8) make all reconstructions hypothetical. Its *horns* (2) are never explained throughout the Old Testament (see 29:12; Lev. 4:18; 1 Kgs 2:28–34). In verse 3 *meat forks* is a speculative translation of *mizlĕgôtaw* (cf. the related *mazlēg* in 1 Sam. 2:13).

The positioning and use of the *grating* ('lattice', 'network') in verses 4–5 are very obscure. Was the grating inside, to permit ash to fall through, or was it some sort of openwork step from which the priests officiated? Gooding (p. 18) says, 'It seems practically certain that it was not a fire-grate.'

The attempts to reconstruct the courtyard have to be conjectural. We are not told what timber was used, how the draperies were suspended, or where the tent and the altar were placed within the area. *Pegs* are mentioned (19) but not their use, and 35:18 refers to 'ropes'.

27:20 – 30:10 The directional movement of the account reverses at this point. Hitherto it has been from within outwards. The supreme sign of the Lord's presence is the ark (cf. 25:22 with its firm 'There'). The account then moves from the Most Holy Place to the Holy Place, with the table and lampstand, and then out into the courtyard, the bronze altar and the enclosing draperies. Now, however, the movement changes and becomes from outside inwards. It is no longer God coming out but the people going in to God and accessing his presence – the priesthood and their essential works (see Dennett, pp. 279–280). The point reached at 27:19 is that God has come among his people, and the question now is how he is to be approached.

27:20–21 Notwithstanding the 'movement' observed above, it is at first sight surprising to find the care of the lampstand and the golden altar (30:1–10) here. The connection forged between the two activities (30:7) emphasizes that they form a designed *inclusio* to the descriptions of priesthood (28:1 – 29:46). In other words, they are not just chance insertions or later additions (cf. Durham, p. 400) but are purposely placed to make a point: priesthood brought many duties, covering many areas of religion and life, but what was priesthood really about? Respectively, the *inclusio* passages answer. The priest was to enter and stand in the full light of God's presence (27:20–21) and to effectuate access into the Holiest, bringing the people to God and maintaining an intercessory relationship with the Lord (30:1–10; cf. 30:36 where the 'incoming' incense finds the Lord waiting to 'meet with you'). The tending of both the light and the incense is specifically priestly, belonging to Aaron and his sons (21; 30:7–10). The priestly privilege is access; its responsibility is mediation (cf. Heb. 7:24–25; 9:24; 10:19–22).

28:1–43 The priests and their robes:

A^1 The priestly family. The significance and importance of the robes
    (1–4)
    B   The robes (5–38):
       The ephod (6–14)
       The breastpiece (15–30)
       The robe of the ephod (31–35)
       The plate of pure gold (36–38)
A^2 The significance and importance of the robes. The priestly family
    (39–43)

Verse 1 emphasizes Moses' key part: (lit.) 'And as for you/you for your part must bring near to you' (cf. Lev. 8:2). Moses' agency is stressed because priesthood was by divine appointment, not popular election. In Exodus the garments (rightly) come before the persons in chapter 29. The garments represent the priesthood in its ideal reality (e.g. holiness, 36) which Aaron and his sons could never personally embody (cf. Heb. 5:1–3; 7:26–28; 9:7).

On the ephod as a priestly garment, see 1 Sam. 2:18; 22:18; 2 Sam. 6:14. 'The' ephod is mentioned in 1 Sam. 21:9, and is used in divination in 1 Sam. 23:9–11; 30:7–8; cf. Neh. 7:65. In verse 6 does *gold* mean 'cloth of gold'? The ephod seems to have been something like the back and front of a waistcoat held together by the jewelled clasps (12), or perhaps it was more like a kaftan? 'Gold' (as always) speaks of the presence, dignity and purity of the Lord. As to the stones on the breastpiece (17–20), their identity is a matter of surmise. Cassuto (p. 375) recalls that they are the precious stones found in Eden (Ezek. 28:13) when 'man [was] free from all sin'. Verse 30 is a beautiful picture of the high priest having his people on his heart – as well as bearing the burden of them on his shoulders (12). (On 'Urim' and 'Thummim' see *NBD*.) What, however, does it mean by (lit.) 'Aaron shall bear the judgment [*mišpāṭ*]'? The phrase *nāśā' mišpāṭ* does not occur elsewhere. The NIV offers one possible meaning, but it could also mean that the high-priestly garments displayed what the Lord thought of his people – his 'decision' about them, that they are his jewels, his precious ones (cf. Mal. 3:17). The *robe of the ephod* (31) was worn under the ephod and sounds like a poncho or surplice. In verse 32 *collar* and NKJV's 'coat of mail' are both uncertain renderings of *taḥrā'*. The ESV excusably cops out with 'garment'. *Plate* (36) renders *ṣîṣ*, from the verb 'to blossom/sparkle', and may be suggesting a 'polished' or 'sparkling' piece of gold. The *plate* declares what the high priest is in the mind and purpose of God (Heb. 4:14; 7:26–28). In verse 38 this holiness is linked with bearing iniquity, in accordance with the scriptural principle that only the sinless can bear the sins of another. Here the 'holiness' of the high priest makes good every deficiency of the people, who inevitably fall short even in their best endeavours to offer acceptable sacrifice to God. Everything less than sufficient in Israel's devotion is laid at the priest's door and made his responsibility. Verse 42 registers the customary biblical opposition to the sexual orientation of pagan rites, which often demanded that the officiant be naked. The emphasis on perpetuity (43) shows the intensity of the rejection of a sexual component in Yahweh's worship. The worship of Yahweh must be distinct, because he is distinct; the divine nature dictates the divine worship.

29:1–46 This also is a coherent and balanced presentation:

A¹ The priestly consecration offerings (1–3)

   B¹ Their cleansing: symbolic washing (4)

      C¹ Aaron and his sons taking possession of their priesthood (5–9)

         D The full cycle of offerings for Aaron and his sons (10–25)

            Sin offering (10–14)

            Burnt offering (15–18)

            Peace offering (19–25)

      C² Aaron and his sons enjoying their priestly possessions: holy food, holy garments (26–34)

   B² The seven days of consecration (35–37)

A² The regular (daily) priestly offerings (38–46)

Notice how the first act is the washing (4). Aaron has to be the prefiguring of the absolute purity of the perfect priest, without spot (cf. Heb. 9:14). Likewise, Aaron's vesting (5–6) precedes his anointing (7): he is anointed not so that he may become a priest but so that he may function in the character the garments typify. So far there has been no blood sacrifice involved: he is anointed without blood because he is the 'type' of the sinless Jesus. The *other ram* (19) is also called the *ordination* ram (26, 27, 31); the NKJV has, much more correctly, 'consecration'. Hebrew expresses the idea of consecration as 'filling the hands'; cf. verse 9, (lit.) 'you shall fill the hands of'. When we say, for example, of a mother with a brood of young children that 'she has her hands full', we mean 'more than enough to occupy all her time'. This is the biblical thought behind 'consecration'. 'Ordination' is the authorization to hold an office, and this is a minor thought, if it is there at all, in the present passage. Consecration, personal absorption in the Lord and his work, is the leading idea. The touching of the ear, hand and toe with the blood of the burnt offering (20) signifies respectively to hear alone, act alone and walk alone for the Lord. This was the blood of the *other ram* and was a fellowship or peace offering. The meaning, therefore, is that the hearing ear, active hand and directed 'walk' mark and totally preoccupy those who are at peace with God. The intense seven-day focus on sin offerings points up the tension between the holiness the priests represented and the sinfulness of their actual human state – and the need, therefore, to be super-conscious of the required cleansing (cf. Lev. 8:33–35; Ezek. 3:15). To *make atonement* (36) is ʿal-kippurîm, from √kāpar. In verses 38–46, matching verses 1–3, the offerings *for* the priesthood, we have the daily offerings *by* the priesthood. Daily worship, morning and evening, was a burnt offering (39, 42), i.e. the primary concern of the Lord for his people – and of his people for the Lord – was dedicated living that held nothing back in consecration. Dennett (p. 310) rightly notes that the burnt offering is 'an emblem of the sacrifice of Christ . . . his devotedness unto death . . . his obedience to the uttermost . . . the "sweet savour" [is] the acceptability of his death to God'.

The offerings to be made are specified (38–41) and their significance is spelled out (42–46): the place of sacrifice is where the Lord meets and speaks with his people (42); he will indwell his tent and be available for his people (43); he will guarantee the effectiveness of his appointed means of approach, altar and priesthood (44); and he will indwell his people and thus fulfil the purpose of their redemption (45–46). In verse 42 the NIV's *regularly* should be 'continually' (cf. Lev. 6:8–13). In principle the burnt offering was constantly burning, day and night.

30:1–10 The priesthood had to guarantee the outshining light and the incoming prayer. Durham (p. 400; cf. Cassuto, p. 389) says 'there is little reason why the use of incense and altars cannot be as early in Israel's worship as the Old Testament suggests'. The Lord comes to meet his people (29:42) and makes himself available to prayer. Mackintosh (p. 311): 'In the brazen altar we have Christ in the value of His sacrifice . . . in the golden altar we have Christ in the value of his intercession . . . there must be a brazen altar and a priest before there can be a golden altar and incense.' The Old Testament does not explicitly explain the symbolism of incense; but see Ps. 141:2; Luke 1:9–10; Rev. 8:3–4. The idea of a sweet scent usually signifies what delights and is acceptable to the Lord (Gen. 8:20–21; Lev. 1:9). The burning of incense is the third of the specified priestly actions – along with tending the lamps and offering the daily burnt offering.

30:11–38 This little section is widely thought to consist of odds and ends of later, random insertions. In the light of all we have seen of the careful structuring in the book of Exodus, this is unlikely. Of the four items included here – ransom money (11–16), the basin for washing

(17–21), anointing oil (22–33) and incense (34–38) – the last three concern the needs of the priests in their office and work, and there is no problem in seeing why they are here in the tabernacle account. The washbasin provided for incidental defilements contracted in the priests' actions (hands) and their 'walk' through life (feet), just as the shed blood of 29:10–21 secured once-for-all cleansing (cf. John 13:10). Thus the removal of all that is unsuitable by washing is matched, in the anointing oil, by the symbolic enduement with every divine gift and grace for the work (29:7); and the incense made provision for one of their leading duties. Oil for the light is dealt with in 27:20. All this, however, leaves one further question: for whom is the tabernacle and its ministry designed? The priests are appointed, anointed and equipped. To whom do they minister? To entitle verses 11–16 *Atonement money*, as does the NIV, creates an understandable but wrong focus. The verses are not really about the money but about the people who chose to give it. In verse 13 (cf. 38:26) we read of (lit.) 'every one crossing over to those who were numbered'. Picture, then, a queue of people waiting to be enrolled in the census. One by one each registered his name and became an enrolled member. Ramm (p. 172) says it was 'the way in which the covenant was made personal . . . each Israelite . . . willing to be counted'. Thus the general pledge of 24:7 became an individual commitment. This, then, was a religious census as the one recorded in Num. 1 (cf. verse 3) was military. The half shekel, says C. A. Coates, 'speaks of the redemption rights of Christ' over each whom he has redeemed – 'that we should own and answer to the rights [he] acquired through redemption . . . he is entitled to the recognition of those rights'. The need of a 'covering payment' arises from the unexplained hazard in taking a census at all (12; cf. 2 Sam. 24:3).

31:1–17 *The Spirit of God* (3) brings 'skill', 'ability' and 'knowledge'. According to Durham (p. 410), this is 'the ideal combination of theoretical knowledge, problem-solving practicality, and planning capacity'. In turn, the words are *hokmâ*, mostly translated *wisdom*, the ability to grasp truth and to know what to do about it; *těbûnâ*, 'discernment' (NIV *understanding*), the ability to see to the heart of a matter and solve inherent problems; and *da'at*, 'knowledge and know-how'. There is, however, no room left 'for creative variations on the plans Yahweh has given' (Durham on 6, 11). Verses 12–18 are a beautifully succinct repetition of the significance and law of the Sabbath. It is a *sign* (13, 17): that is, keeping the Sabbath is evidence of the Lord's creation of a distinct, separated people (13, *makes you holy*), and their distinctness (17) shows itself in copying him. The Sabbath obligation is enforced by the sanction of excommunication (14) and is to be held in perpetuity (16). The hallmark of the Sabbath is rest (15). Sabbath enforcement reiterated here is meant to alert the workers that circumstances do not alter cases: their work may be exceedingly holy, but the Sabbath is holier still. This reminder is addressed to all – for at this point who knows who will be enrolled according to the terms of 31:6. Exceptional duties do not permit exceptions to the keeping of the Sabbath.

3. Obedience is the priority of those who would enjoy grace

While the above outline of Exodus 24 – 31 has the stylish arrangement that is customary in Exodus, its most notable feature is that while it begins and ends with the gift of the law ($A^{1, 2}$), there is nothing about the law at all in the long intervening chapters. There are, of course, detailed directions – for example, for the priests – but the law as inscribed on the tablets is absent. Yet the gift of the law is both the declared purpose of Moses' fifth ascent of Sinai (24:12) and its outcome (31:18). This has a most important lesson to teach. In a word, we will not understand the tabernacle correctly unless we see it in the context of the law; and we will not understand the law correctly unless we see the tabernacle at its centre.

In 24:7 (cf. 19:8; 20:19) the people made a common commitment to obey the word of the Lord, and in the census of 30:11–16 each individual male implicitly made the same commitment. Obedience should not be considered as our part of an equally balanced bargain with the Lord, a quid pro quo, but, nevertheless, throughout the Bible obedience figures hugely in covenant thinking. It does not bring us into the Lord's covenant, but it constitutes our response to his redeeming grace and brings us the enjoyments of our covenant membership. The Lord brought his redeemed not by the direct route to Canaan but via Sinai in order that they might hear his word and receive his law. Hence, the spoken word (20:1) became the written word (24:12) and was placed in the ark in the midst of those who were called upon to hear and obey (25:16). When we see the pattern of events in this light, the whole tabernacle system becomes an elaboration of the single symbolic act of the sprinkling of the blood (24:7–8): those who were called to obey had at the centre of their life an established availability of grace to cater for their lapses from obedience.

4. Grace is at hand for those committed to obedience

The Old Testament, and indeed the whole Bible, is opposed to ritualism – the supposed effectiveness with God of some ceremonial performance or act. The essence of Canaanite religion was sympathetic or imitative magic, the performance of certain rituals which would prompt the god to do something similar in return. But magic has no place in biblical religion, even though biblical religion – New Testament as well as Old – can just as easily be corrupted into ritualism as any other.[6] Clearly, one of the main thrusts of the tabernacle regulations is that everything must be done in precisely the correct way. The Lord had detailed plans for his worship, and no variations were to be tolerated. This sounds like an open invitation to ritualism. For this reason, the context of the tabernacle revelation was the giving of the law. That was the priority in the mind of God and was to be his people's primary concern. When they made their communal (24:7) and individual (30:13–14) responses, they must surely have entertained inward doubts about their ability to fulfil what they had undertaken. Whether this was so or not, only a little time was to pass before they discovered the huge gap between promise and performance. Into this gap stepped the Lord with his gracious provision of the tabernacle, which, with its rounded system of sacrifices and its constantly burning fire consuming the burnt offering, spoke day and night of an atonement, forgiveness and cleansing available to cater for every lapse from the life of obedience that the people had bound themselves to (cf. 1 John 1:7).

5. Tabernacle metals: gold, silver, bronze

We have noted already that there is a two-way 'movement' in the description of the tabernacle in Exodus. On the one hand, the Lord comes to live among his people, his indwelling presence symbolized by the ark and its contents, with everything else as an enclosure for the ark. On the other hand, there is also an inward movement, evidenced by the fact that both sections of the tabernacle – the Most Holy Place (sometimes referred to as the Holy of Holies) and the Holy Place – have entrances, as does the courtyard that enclosed the whole (26:31, 36; 27:16). The people would

---

[6] Amos protested against the ritualism of his day in his 'plumb-line' oracle (Amos 7:7–8, NKJV, ESV; the NIV wrongly introduces the word 'true'). See J. A. Motyer, *The Message of Amos* (IVP, 1974); 'Amos', in *NBC*.

soon discover that although the Lord was the central resident of their camp and, as the sequence of entrances implies, there was a way into his presence (cf. Heb. 9:8), he was not, so to speak, 'at home' to callers (40:35). In this way a dilemma was created: the provision of entrances, and yet the implicit erection of a sign that said, 'No Admission'.

The Holy of Holies (26:1–31) must have been a most beautiful place. The overwhelming impression would have been of pure gold – the ark itself and on three sides the supporting gold-plated frames forming a 15-foot cube, with the white linen curtains, decorated with blue, purple and scarlet cherubim,[7] showing through the frames. Then, the Holy of Holies was separated off from the east end of the tabernacle with another beautiful white linen curtain decorated with blue, purple and scarlet (26:31). The symbolic significance of gold is not plainly stated in this passage.[8] Found at the beginning of creation in Eden (Gen. 2:11–12), its scarcity and beauty mean that it has always been a sign of royal dignity (e.g. Gen. 41:42; Pss 21:3; 72:15). In the book of Job, refined gold is used to typify purity and perfection (Job 23:10). Solomon made gold the distinctive adornment of his temple (1 Kgs 6:20–21), and there it served the same function as in the tabernacle. Psalm 29:9 says, 'And in his temple all cry [or 'everything cries'] "Glory!"', and we cannot go beyond that: gold is the glory of the divine nature, the glory of God actually and fully present in the beauty of his holiness.

If, however, we look carefully, we notice one element of silver in the inmost place of golden holiness: the bases into which the supporting frames and pillars were set were made of silver (26:19, 21, 25, 32). Silver was also used for the pillars supporting the curtains and the door screen of the tabernacle courtyard (27:10, 17). There is a link here with the silver atonement money referred to in 30:11–16 and further described in 38:25–27. The silver used within the holy enclosure serves as a reminder to us when we enter the Lord's presence that we do so as the Lord's redeemed for whom payment has been made and redemption accomplished (cf. Heb. 9:11–12).

---

[7] Ezekiel saw 'living creatures', which he identified as the cherubim (Ezek. 1:5–10; 9:3; 10:1). They were great winged beings with four faces representing all created excellence – a lion (the greatest of wild beasts), an ox (the greatest of domestic beasts), an eagle (the greatest of birds) and a human being (the greatest of all creatures). The cherubim, therefore, represent all creation in its perfection in the presence of God the Creator (cf. Rev. 4:6–8).

[8] The lovely hymn 'O Worship the Lord in the Beauty of Holiness' by John S. B. Monsell speaks of the 'gold of obedience and incense of lowliness'. This is helpfully emotive poetic licence but without biblical sanction.

Not all the pillars within the tabernacle complex had silver bases. The curtain for the entrance to the tent was supported by five pillars with bronze sockets holding them in place (36:38), and the pillars surrounding the courtyard, including the four pillars supporting the 30-foot-long entrance screen, had sockets of bronze (27:16–17). Once more, there is no mistaking the symbolism intended by this, for the great altar in the courtyard, situated along the line of approach between the gate and the tent, was overlaid with bronze, and all its ancillary parts, utensils and carrying poles were likewise bronze (27:1–8). This altar was the place of regular sacrifice (Lev. 1:5; 3:1–5; 4:7), daily burnt offerings (Exod. 29:38–42) and undying fire (Lev. 6:9). Fire itself, as we have seen, is a symbol of the holiness of God in its pure and awesome hostility to sin. Sinners have standing before God only on the basis of, and by means of, those appointed substitutionary sacrifices by which the demands of divine holiness are met and satisfied. Bronze, therefore, speaks of holiness, wrath, satisfaction and acceptance.[9]

6. Special curtains

Three special curtains or screens were included in the construction of the tabernacle: an internal screen separating the Most Holy Place from the Holy Place and hung on four pillars, topped with gold and with bases of silver (26:31–32); an external screen, which provided, so to speak, a 'door' into the Lord's tent and had five pillars with gold top-fittings and bronze sockets (26:36–37); and the entrance to the tabernacle court, extending for 30 feet, supported by four pillars with silver tops and bronze sockets (27:16–17). Should we look for any significance in the differing number of pillars? No hint is given about this, but the broadly spread pillars of the entrance to the courtyard (there could have been 7 feet between them), the narrower gaps in the entrance (with spaces of between 4 and just over 2 feet, depending on how the pillars were set), and the even narrower gaps between the pillars of the Most Holy Place, would visibly say 'Come in' and then 'Keep out'. Maybe this was what was intended, and it would have been in keeping with the 'thus far and no further' regulations of the tabernacle as a whole.

---

[9] See Motyer on Isa. 6:5–6 in *Prophecy of Isaiah* and *Isaiah*.

All these special screens or curtains were of the same design – blue, purple and scarlet on fine white linen – and the writer to the Hebrews teaches us to see them as a representation of the Lord Jesus Christ. The writers of an earlier generation did not hesitate to make a more detailed application, and surely they were right to do so. They saw the blue as symbolizing Christ's heavenly origin, the purple his royalty, the scarlet the blood of his sacrifice and the white linen his spotless purity and moral majesty. Beyond question, however, is that the sameness of the screens must mean that there is only one way from outside into the very heart of the divine presence, and the letter to the Hebrews insists that this one way is the Lord Jesus Christ. In the rending of his flesh, the curtain of the temple was 'torn in two from top to bottom' (Mark 15:37–38) and the way into the Most Holy Place was opened for us (Heb. 9:7–8, 11–12; 10:19–22).

Additional notes

25:8 For √*šākan* see 24:16; 29:45, 46; 40:35 (pp. 244–245 above). The NIV translates *settled* in the first and last references and to *dwell* in the rest. *Miškān* is translated 'tabernacle' in all its fifty-seven occurrences (e.g. 25:9; 26:1, 6, 7; 40:2, 5, 6, 9). The NIV conflates two occurrences into one in 26:27 and 36:32. The noun transliterated *šĕkînâ*, meaning the indwelling presence of God, is post-biblical, but, as R. A. Stewart remarks, 'the concept saturates both Testaments' ('Shekinah', in *NBD*). *'Ōhel* (discounting the examples in 33:7–11) is used forty-eight times of the tabernacle. The NIV translates it as 'tabernacle' on its first appearance (26:7) but thereafter as 'tent' (e.g. 26:9; 40:2, 6, 7, 12). In 40:19 *'ōhel* is the fabric stretched over the *miškān*; and in 40:29 the *miškān* ('tabernacle') and the *'ōhel* ('tent') are the same thing. *Miqdāš* occurs in 25:8 for the only time throughout the chapters on the tabernacle. It has already appeared in 15:17 and is, of course, abundantly used later (e.g. Lev. 12:4).

Exodus 27:20 – 30:10

20. The way into the Holiest

1. Mediation

It is hard to read the ending of Exodus without getting the feeling that Moses was taken aback when he was unable to enter the completed tabernacle. He had overseen the whole operation, making sure that, down to the last detail, it was what the Lord wanted (39:42–43). Yet when the glory of the Lord filled the tent, 'Moses could not enter' (40:34–35). The Lord was present indeed in his tent, but his tent was not open to callers.

That, however, was not the end of the matter. We need to remember that the division between Exodus and Leviticus is a traditional separation of an originally continuous text. We should actually move without interruption from the reality of exclusion at the end of Exodus to the reality of drawing near in Leviticus 1:1–2. Out from the tabernacle, from which the people were excluded, came the voice of the Lord, saying (lit.), 'When anyone of you brings near a bringing near to the Lord . . . you shall bring near your bringing near.' The verb is √qārab ('to bring near'), and the noun is qorbān (NIV, 'offering'). While sin excludes, the prescribed offerings are able to 'bring near'. Holiness bars the way, but mercy opens it.

This is the significance of God's appointed priesthood, Aaron and his descendants in their unique and essential role as mediators. We will see presently that there was another dimension to Israel's religion besides its formal, public expression in the tabernacle – a personal, informal, private spirituality. But, as is true throughout the Bible, everything ultimately rested on the work of the priest – Aaron in the Old Testament, Jesus in the New – and on the divine provision of sacrifice (cf. Lev. 17:11).[1] Just as

---

[1] See Motyer, *Look to the Rock*, pp. 52–53, 106, 173.

Israel could stand secure in the Lord's presence only through the shedding of blood (24:4–6), sin offering, burnt offering and peace offering, so the continuing system of these threefold offerings was given for this purpose; that sinners might live in the presence of the Holy One and he dwell with them (see e.g. Lev. 1 – 7).

This is what the tabernacle and its priesthood was all about.

2. Pictures of the true

The typological symbolism of the tabernacle is a deep mine of truth, but only a summary of some main points is possible here.[2]

a. Do we want him?

The section on the tabernacle begins and ends with the responsibility of the redeemed people (25:1–9; 31:1–11). Israel had to provide the materials for the tabernacle, and the construction work had to be done by skilful craftsmen (31:6; lit. 'and in the heart of everyone wise of heart I have put wisdom, and they will do everything I have commanded you'). In other words, the Lord, for his part, was willing and ready to dwell in the midst of his people, but it was for them to decide if they wanted him to do so. If they did want him, then they had to fulfil the conditions he laid down. We can put it this way: they had a 'means of grace' at their disposal, and it was up to them to use it. It is the same for us; we can either engage in or neglect those things which make 1 Corinthians 3:16 a reality corporately and 1 Corinthians 6:19 a reality individually. We too have means of grace at our disposal: public and corporate means such as Christian fellowship, the ministry of God's Word and the Lord's Table, and private means such as time apart with God for prayer and Bible reading. We can, however, choose to live at a distance, neglecting those things which would bring God near to us and us near to him. The tabernacle is a depiction of a reality as well as an ideal. In it we can see represented the indwelling God, the God near at hand, and the avenues of approach, which can be either cultivated or neglected. Has the chief failing of the Lord's people through the ages always been that we do not live up to our privileges?

---

[2] The older books (e.g. those by Dennett and White) are well worth reading, even if at times they may seem to us over the top. See also the moderate position of Gooding in his all-too-brief booklet *How to Teach the Tabernacle*.

b. The triumph of grace

It is commonplace to note that the description of the tabernacle and its arrangements starts on the inside and works outwards (25:10). This means that everything about the tabernacle was determined by the meaning and purpose of the ark at its centre. The tent, the courtyard, the surrounding curtains and the priesthood with its ritual duties were nothing more than subsidiaries to it. It determined them, not they it.

The ark represented the Lord in his unapproachable holiness. It was the sole piece of furniture in the innermost shrine, with not even a stand to support it. As a box, it contained the stone tablets of the law, which stated in ten precepts both what the Lord is like in his holiness and what he requires his people to be. As such, the ark exposed the sins and short-comings of those the Lord had redeemed by contrasting what he in his moral distinctiveness is like with what they in their moral weakness are like. It was a physical reminder of why God lives in isolation and why his people cannot enter his presence.

No image, as in pagan shrines, occupied the central place in the taber-nacle; just a wooden box containing the law of holiness. There was, however, more to it than just that. In the details of the construction of the ark (all of which are full of meaning; see Heb. 9:3–5) it is explicitly required that a golden lid be made to match the dimensions of the box so as to be its exact covering (25:17). Without this lid, the ark was not a box, and without the box, the golden cover was not a lid. Each needed the other for completeness. But why was this lid prescribed for the ark?

The solid gold of the 'atonement cover' (Heb. *kappōret*)[3] – or, in the emotive rendering William Tyndale devised, 'the mercy seat' – did not long retain its pristine purity. It soon bore the stains of the shed blood of sacrifice (Lev. 16:13–14). This is why it was called *kappōret*, as it was not so much a 'cover' as a 'covering', more 'atoning' than 'atonement'. The blood, which symbolized a substitutionary life laid down, both allayed the wrath of the holy God over his broken law and, at the same time, sym-bolically (in the person of the high priest) admitted to his presence those

---

[3] The carved cherubim were integral to the whole. Understanding them as the four-faced heavenly beings of Ezek. 1, they can be seen to represent all created excellence, and their inward and downward gaze symbolizes the truth that the shed blood of atonement is central to the divine worldview and the subject of heaven's adoring wonder. The same symbolism is wonderfully caught in John's record of the angels seated at the head and foot of where the body of Jesus had lain (John 20:12). There indeed is the concept of the atonement cover in all its intended completeness.

who, though they had broken his law, were now covered by the blood of sacrifice (cf. Heb. 10:12–18, 19–22).

It was not, therefore, the sacred box of the ark as such that was central to the tabernacle, nor even the law which it housed, but the triumph of mercy over wrath, of forgiveness over offence, of admission over exclusion, and of the unmerited working of grace over well-deserved judgment.

3. The priestly people and their priests

Even though the tabernacle was the focal point of the actual dwelling of the Lord at the heart of his people's life, they did not enjoy direct, unmediated access to him. From the time of leaving Egypt, Israel had been served by 'priests'. The word itself is not applied within Israel in Exodus until 19:6, where it refers to the Lord's plan that Israel itself should be a 'kingdom of priests'. But the same chapter notes the existence of 'priests' within Israel, indicating that the title had already been given to those who officiated for the people in special ways (19:22–24; cf. 24:5). With the institution of the tabernacle, however, priestly functions were concentrated in one family, that of Aaron and his sons.[4] One way or another, therefore, whether the redeemed people could live up to 19:5–6 or not, they needed a priest – indeed, they needed priesthood in its perfection.

4. Garments before persons (28:1–43)

In the Bible, clothing is often used as a symbol to express outwardly what the wearer is, or ought to be, inwardly, in character and also in intention. Thus, in Joshua 5:13–14 the 'drawn sword' reflects the reality of the Lord as warrior; in Isaiah 59:17 the garments of salvation and vengeance reveal the God who is fit and able to accomplish these things and who intends to do so. As part of the instructions for the construction of the

---

[4] We can trace a cumulative revelation of the ways of God with his people from Genesis to Exodus. Throughout Genesis there was direct fellowship with the Lord. The patriarchs walked with him, and he spoke to them (Gen. 5:24; 15:1; 17:1; 18:1–33). We are not told what conditions obtained in Egypt during the Israelites' sojourn there, but the fact that Aaron was called 'the Levite' (Exod. 4:14) may suggest that even then the tribe of Levi was accorded some special status. In any case, at the appropriate point, Exodus notes the introduction of 'priests', and in this way a formalization of relationships. As we shall see, the incident of the golden calf (Exod. 32 – 33) takes matters another step forward to their normative Old Testament pattern. No particular conclusion should be drawn from the move from firstborn sons in general to Aaron and his sons. Wilderness conditions sometimes allowed for arrangements which were later formalized and given proper expression (see Deut. 12:8).

tabernacle, the people are told to *make sacred garments for . . . Aaron . . . for his consecration* [lit. 'to sanctify him'], *so that he may serve me as priest* (28:2–3). The garments were to express not what Aaron was in himself but what he represented, what he was meant to be, what his office ideally required him to be, even though the human reality may have been so tragically different. It is for this reason that the garments come first, before the solemn inauguration of the persons in chapter 29, and it is this note of sanctification, the holy separation unto God, expressed by the garments that forms the *inclusio* of the account (28:1–4, 40–43). The garments are figures of the true. By his robes, the ideal priest is revealed.

a. The high priest as the heavenly man

Space forbids attempting more than to cut a swathe through the rich and detailed symbolism of the Exodus accounts of the tabernacle and priesthood. In the description of the priestly garments it is clear that colours were an important factor: gold, blue, purple, scarlet and white feature throughout, in the ephod (28:6) and its belt (8), the breastpiece (15) and its cord (28), and the robe (31) and its cord (37). Even the robe's hem was decorated with blue, purple and scarlet pomegranates and hung with gold bells (33–34). There was also a lavish use of *pure gold* for chains, rings, settings and, on the turban, a medallion engraved with the words HOLY TO THE LORD (11, 13–14, 22–27, 36). The fact that the same colours, fabrics and gold were used for the garments as for the tabernacle itself shows how the high priest was regarded as the appropriate and prepared person to perform the duties that were to take place within the tent. He was, in this sense, 'made for' his work, as was, in a far greater sense, the Lord Jesus. He is our great high priest, suited to our needs, 'holy, blameless, pure, set apart . . . exalted' (Heb. 7:26), perfect for his priestly work on our behalf, the man from heaven.

If, as seems to have been the case, the *robe of the ephod* (31–35; 29:5) was a poncho-like garment, worn under the ephod,[5] then, as the first garment to be put on (after the linen underpants), it represented what the priest is, first and foremost. As soon as the Old Testament priest donned the first of his robes, he symbolized the 'heavenly man'.

---

[5] As 2 Sam. 6:14, 20 shows, an ephod was by itself a somewhat skimpy garment and should not have been worn without the 'robe' of the undergarment.

b. The high priest and the wisdom of God

It was a practical necessity to describe the ephod before the breastpiece (6–14, 15–30), but the list in verse 4 gives the breastpiece priority. The ephod was 'for' the breastpiece, not vice versa. As a pouch, the breastpiece contained the Urim and Thummim (30). There is no explanation of what these were, so presumably their significance must have been known at the time.[6] We are told, however, that because of the Urim and Thummim, Aaron (lit.), 'when he goes in before the Lord, will bear the judgment of the sons of Israel upon his heart before the Lord continually' (cf. ESV). The expression 'bear judgment' (*nāśāʾ mišpāṭ*) is not found elsewhere. One possible meaning is that chosen by the NIV, *bear the means of making decisions*. There are, however, other and wider possible meanings. The Hebrew *mišpāṭ* can be as narrow as the 'decision' which settles a single issue (e.g. Num. 27:21; Judg. 4:5) or as wide and non-specific as a biblical term for the revelation of divine truth. For example, in Deuteronomy 5:1 *mišpāṭ* is used for 'laws' (NIV; ESV, 'rules'; NKJV, 'judgments'), and in Isaiah 42:1 it means 'binding truth' ('justice'; NIV, ESV, NKJV). What is meant here in Exodus may well be that the high priest, ideally considered, was an organ of revelation, an earthly source of the wisdom and direction of God (cf. 1 Cor. 1:30).

c. The high priest, representative and responsible

The *names of the sons of Israel* occur twice in association with the ephod and breastpiece. The pouch of the Urim displayed their names on its twelve engraved stones (17–21), and in addition it was attached to the ephod by golden *braided chains* fastened to golden shoulder settings with two onyx stones engraved with the names (9–14). The Exodus account does not dwell on the value, colour or lustre of the stones but on the responsibility of the high priest as he brought his people before the Lord on his shoulders and heart (12, 30). He was known before the Lord not by his own name but by their names. It was with their names that he entered the Most Holy Place. He carried them as one making himself responsible for securing their entrance into the Lord's presence (cf. Heb. 9:24; 10:19–20). They could enter only because they rested on him (Heb. 10:21–22). He, on his part, bore all their burden and brought them with him because they were on his heart (cf. Gal. 2:20; Eph. 5:2; Rev. 1:5).

---

6 See J. A. Motyer, 'Urim and Thummim', in *NBD*.

d. The high priest, the holy one

Strikingly, the high priest was given no words to say as he entered the Holy Place (cf. Lev. 16). There were no priestly mantras, no incantations or liturgical formulae. Aaron entered in the character of the word on the plate attached to his turban which silently proclaimed that he was (lit.) 'Holiness to Yahweh' (36–38).[7] However these words are translated, it always comes back to the fundamental affirmation that here is a holiness that the Lord requires and accepts, and it was in this character that Aaron entered and was accepted.[8] He represented an ideal he could never himself attain, and for this reason he and his sons had to begin their installation as priests by making a sin offering (29:10–14; cf. Heb. 5:1–3). The mercy of God operated on the assumption of the ideal, and he passed over the sins that would have vitiated the work of the Old Testament priesthood (cf. Rom. 3:25). The glories of the Lord Jesus Christ and the sufficiency of his sacrifice are retrospective (catering for Aaron) as well as prospective (catering for us) and eternal (catering for Aaron and us). In Jesus, the ideal and the actual coincide. He steps, in his own person, perfection and unquestioned right, into the very presence of God, there to appear on our behalf (Heb. 9:11–12, 24). In Christ, at long last, the Holy One himself comes as priest into the holy place.

Every shortfall, imperfection and wrong of the people was taken under the wing of the perfect holiness displayed by Aaron (38). When our brothers and sisters of old brought their sin and other offerings, they did so according to God's perfect will, but their sinfulness contaminated the very sacrifices they offered. But just as Aaron was accepted under the holiness of the medallion he wore, so the people were accepted because their names were part of his dress. In other words, both his true reality and all their inadequacies were brought under the same wondrous covering,[9] and they were 'accepted in the Beloved', just as we are (Eph. 1:6, NKJV).[10]

---

[7] 'Holiness belongs to Yahweh', 'Holiness for Yahweh', even 'Yahweh's Holiness'. Some, noting correctly that the root idea of holiness (√qādaš) is separation, urge 'Separate unto Yahweh', but since this prompts the question, 'In what sense separate?' and the reply 'Separate in [ethical] holiness [as Yahweh is]', the net result is the same.

[8] Note the gentle stress in verses 37–38 on the medallion being to the forefront.

[9] The wording *he will bear the guilt* in verse 38 (√nāśā' 'āwôn, 'bear the iniquity') occurs again in Lev. 16:22 in the provision of the scapegoat. It represents a complex of ideas to do with accepting someone else's burden as one's own, taking responsibility for it and carrying it away. In Scripture, only the sinless can bear the sins of another.

[10] *So that they will be acceptable* is 'to secure their favourable acceptance' (the noun rāṣôn, from √rāṣâ, 'to accept with favour'). The high priest wore *their names*, not his own; he came *as them* into the Lord's presence under the medallion of holiness that he wore.

e. The high priest, separate from sinners

We come now to the subject of the priests' underwear! *Tunics* and *sashes* are brought together here in verse 40 and in Leviticus 8:7 but are mentioned separately in verse 4. Other references to tunics indicate that they were fairly substantial garments, and indeed the word can refer to outerwear. In the case of the high priest and his sons, the tunic was made of white linen woven with a pattern, and in this way the purity and beauty intrinsic to priesthood were continued even into what was hidden from view. In addition, the priests wore *linen undergarments . . . from the waist to the thigh* (42). The word is *miknĕsê* (from √*kānas*, to 'gather together'), expressing here the idea of a 'close-fitting' garment, registering, says Cassuto, opposition to the practice of performing religious rites naked. The emphasis on the perpetuity of this ordinance (42–43) and on its necessity at all times of ministry points to the strength of the Bible's opposition to the inclusion, even the suggestion, of any component of human sexuality in Yahweh's worship. This contrasts sharply with Canaanite ideology and practice, which made human sexual potency central to its rites, the idea being that Baal could be prompted to get on with the task of making land, animals and people fertile by his worshippers doing something similar in the hope that he would see and 'catch on'. These rites involved the use of men and women, as officiants of the Baal shrine, devoted to, and available for, the sexual acts inherent in the cult. To the Canaanite mind this was 'holiness', living a life 'separated' to the god Baal, but the Old Testament will have none of it. With its customary sturdiness in 'calling a spade a spade', the acts, the people involved in them and the profits accruing from them were all alike 'abominations' to the Lord (e.g. Deut. 23:17–18 ESV).[11] So it was that the high priest possessed inwardly, in that which was hidden from the eye, the beauty and the purity of holiness. He was to be 'pure, set apart from sinners' (Heb. 7:26–27), an ideal realized in Jesus and in no other, the only priest who 'does not need to offer sacrifices . . . for his own sins', for he has none. In Campbell Morgan's memorable words (speaking of the ascension of the Lord Jesus Christ),

---

[11] In Deut. 23:17–18 the female involved is referred to as *qĕdēšâ* and the male as *qādēš* – 'holy' women and men, i.e. in the sense that they were devoted to or set apart for the worship of their god. The money made by them is called (lit.) 'the hire-charge of a prostitute' and the 'purchase price of a dog'. It is what is called not mincing one's words!

He was the first Man to enter into the perfect light of heaven in the right of his own holiness. Heaven had never before received such a Man . . . On that Ascension Day there came into heaven a Man Who asked no mercy. Pure, spotless, victorious, He came into the light of heaven, and caused no shadow there.[12]

5. The making of the priesthood (29:1–46)

There is so much detail to pause over – indeed, to marvel at – in these chapters that we can easily lose sight of the bigger picture. It is important to remind ourselves that this section of Exodus has two central chapters, 28 and 29. Chapter 28, as we have seen, is a portrayal of the ideal high priest, a foreshadowing or 'type' of Christ. But it also contains references to Aaron's sons (1, 40) and, therefore, in a way, to us too as the numerous family – the 'many sons and daughters' – whom the Father has brought to himself through the author of our salvation, the 'merciful and faithful high priest' who made atonement for our sins (Heb. 2:10–18). Jesus alone is the full expression of the ideal priestly beauty of holiness, and we, as his disciples, are called to fill our eyes with him, and live in his likeness. It would be good to retrace our steps through chapter 28 so as to say not only 'This is what Jesus is' but also 'This is what we are to be', we who, because we belong to him, belong to the priesthood of all believers and are called to be like him.

Chapter 29 follows on in logical sequence. Aaron and his sons were introduced into their priesthood, and alongside them we can learn how to step into our priestly status and work as those who, through Jesus, are 'a kingdom and priests to serve his God and Father' (Rev. 1:5–6). To this we will turn directly, but not before reminding ourselves that the two central chapters are bracketed by linked priestly duties: the lampstand (27:20–21) and the altar of incense (30:1–10). We must simply let the symbolism speak to us of the outshining light and the uprising incense. On the one hand, we – each and every believer, as his priestly people – have the priestly duty of bringing to the church and to the world 'the light of the knowledge of God's glory displayed in the face of Christ' (2 Cor. 4:4–6), and, on the other hand, of making sure that 'the voice of prayer is never silent' in priestly intercession. In all of this, Jesus, of course, is the

---

[12] G. C. Morgan, *The Acts of the Apostles* (Pickering & Inglis, 1924), p. 55.

perfect light (John 1:9; 8:12) and the perfect intercessor (Heb. 7:25), and he sets us an example of our priestly priorities.

In chapter 29, certainly, we continue to see Jesus portrayed. For example, he actually achieved the perfect consecration to God depicted in verse 20, and also he is the perfect reality foreshadowed in the sin offering, the burnt offering and the wave offering of verses 10–26. But the main subject of the chapter is how ordinary sinful people – in this case, Aaron and his sons – can enter upon their priesthood. They, as Hebrews 7:27 sees them, 'need to offer sacrifices day after day'. It was as sinners that they ministered to sinners, and it was as sinners that they entered their priestly office. In chapter 29, therefore, there are many, many ways in which we can see ourselves pictured rather than Christ.

The shape of the chapter tells its story:

A¹ The consecration offerings: the hallowing of priesthood (1–3)
Their purpose: 'to set them apart to act as priests to me'
The offerings *for* the priesthood
  B¹ The washing of Aaron and his sons (4)
    C¹ Aaron and his sons vested: entering upon their priestly possession (5–9)
      D The full cycle of offerings for Aaron and his sons (10–25)
the bull, the sin offering (10–14)
the ram, the burnt offering (15–18)
the ram, the wave/peace/consecration offering (19–25)
    C² Holy food, holy dress: Aaron and his sons enjoying their priestly possession (26–34)
  B² The seven days of consecration for Aaron and his sons (35–37)
A² The perpetual offerings: the function of priesthood (38–46)
The purpose: divine indwelling, meeting and revelation (42–46)
The offerings *by* the priesthood

Notes

29:1–3 Leviticus 8 'enacts' Exodus 29 in matching detail. For the three offerings (Exod. 29:1, 10–25), cf. Leviticus 8:2, 18, 22. The *wave offering* of verse 24 is called a 'consecration' offering, *'êl millu'îm* (cf. 26, 27). *'Êl* is the appropriate (construct) form of *'ayil*, 'ram'. BDB and KB, noting that *millu'îm* is used of 'setting' jewels (e.g. 25:7), treat *millu'îm* as 'installation'. It is, however, related to √*mālē'*, 'to be full', and should rather be linked with the Hebrew idiom for 'consecration', 'to fill the hands' (cf. 29:9, where to 'ordain Aaron' is [lit.] 'fill the hand of'). Consecration is total preoccupation and engagement with something, to have one's hands full. Note how the *'êl millu'îm*, 'the ram of fillings', is at once put into Aaron's hand (24), and henceforth he is a man 'with his hands full'!

29:4 It might be thought that the full cycle of offerings (10–25) would have been sufficient to make Aaron and his sons acceptable as priests. Why, then, the need for this washing? The order of events is self-explanatory. The offerings were not for Aaron and his sons as persons but as priests; therefore, they must be robed (5–6) before the offerings were made, so that it was as the Lord's priests that they stood to receive the benefits of the sacrifices. But garments of beauty and glory cannot be put on the unclean, and, therefore, a ceremony of cleansing (4) must precede the robing. The symbolism of water for cleansing is a regular feature of tabernacle worship (cf. 30:17–21). Here, however, it is a cleansing of the whole body (not just the hands and feet; cf. John 13:10) so that Aaron may become a type of him who was personally without spot. Verse 9 observes that once Aaron and his descendants have been dressed, *the priesthood is theirs.*

29:10–25 The order of the offerings here is sin offering (14), burnt offering (18) and wave offering (24), more generally called a peace or fellowship offering (cf. verse 28). In Leviticus 1 – 5 the order is burnt offering (1:3), fellowship offering (3:1) and sin offering (4:2), while in Leviticus 6 – 7 the order is burnt offering (6:9), sin offering (6:25) and fellowship offering (7:11). None of this is haphazard; it is all meaningful. Leviticus 1 – 5 gives the order of divine desire: the Lord wishes a completely dedicated people (cf. Gen. 22:12, the offering which holds nothing back), living in peaceful fellowship with one another and with him (cf. Deut. 12:17–18), and with the provision of the sin offering to cater for their lapses from obedience (in Lev. 4:2, to sin 'unintentionally' is to do so against the intended, committed course and purpose of their lives). Leviticus 6 – 7 is the order of priestly ministry: the burnt offering was the priest's daily preoccupation (cf. Exod. 29:38–42), the sin offering would be the point at which the people mostly approached God through him, and the fellowship offering was their consequent joy in God as forgiven sinners. The order in Exodus 29 is the order of individual need of being forgiven, wholly dedicating oneself in gratitude to the Lord, and rejoicing in fellowship with him and one another.

29:26–34 Cultic legislation does not help us to distinguish the significance between the wave offering (26; *tĕnûpâ*) and the *thigh that was presented* (27; *tĕrumâ*, [lit.] 'heave offering'). From their titles we would presume that the former was presented to the Lord with a side-to-side movement and the latter with an up-and-down movement. (See Wenham, *Leviticus*, p. 126; Coates, p. 305: 'Does the wave-offering suggest divine appreciation of what is offered . . . while the heave-offering indicates rather the energy in the affections of the offerer?')

29:42–46 This section merits detailed examination:

A¹ The Lord meets his people when and where sacrifice is offered (42)
 B¹ The tabernacle indwelt (43)
  C The sanctification of the means of approach (44)
 B² The people indwelt: the covenant fulfilled (45)
A² The Lord indwells his people on the grounds of redemption (46)

The actual place of offering was the altar (42; cf. 36–38), but by specifying the 'door' (NIV, *entrance*), i.e. where the altar is (30:18), attention is called to the effectiveness of the offerings in implementing 'meeting' – bringing us to the Lord and him to us. The NIV's *regularly* represents *tāmîd*, 'continual/perpetual' (cf. Lev. 6:8–13). The fire of the burnt offering was never allowed to go out, day or night. It could well have taken the whole day or night for the morning or evening offering to be consumed. According to Dennett (p. 312), 'The moment the sinner is led to take his stand upon the "sweet savour" of the sacrifice, God can meet with him in grace.' The inclusion of Aaron's sons (44) calls attention to the priesthood as a perpetual institution, matching the perpetuity of sacrifice. This verse is central to the passage, holding together the blessings of hearing the word of God (42) and enjoying the presence of God (46).

6. Creating priests

There were four elements that contributed to making Aaron and his sons priests of the Lord: washing (4), robing (5–6, 9), anointing (7) and the threefold cycle of divinely appointed sacrifices (10–25). Of these, only one can be applied in any direct sense to our great high priest, the Lord Jesus. His anointing is foreshadowed in Psalm 45:7 (cf. Heb. 1:9), where the king's impeccable righteousness is proof of his divine anointing. Also, of course, his title as the 'Christ' (from *chriō*, 'to anoint', e.g. Acts 4:27) proclaims his anointed status – as does its Old Testament equivalent, Messiah (√*māšaḥ*, 'to anoint', 7).[13]

All four elements do apply, however, to Christian believers as priests under the priesthood of Jesus. We have been 'washed' from our sins by his blood (1 Cor. 6:11; Heb. 10:22),[14] clothed in his righteousness alone,[15] and we too have our anointing,[16] with, as always, its double significance of being set apart and endowed for whatever particular duty is in mind (2 Cor. 1:21; 1 John 2:27). And, above all, we come within the scope of the all-sufficient saving work of Christ, the shedding of his blood in his substitutionary death on the cross. Hebrews 10:10–18 is a central New Testament text on this wonderful theme, and we ought to note how it moves immediately and logically from the sufficiency and finality of the cross to our entrance, through the high priest, into priestly realms and duties (Heb. 10:19–23).

7. Responding to the given

The creation of the priests was followed by their response, both active and passive, to the new status conferred on them. They accepted the obligation to live the consecrated life (19–22), they fed on the food of the sacrifices (31–33), and they engaged in days of special withdrawal into privacy and 'retreat' (35). All of this has clear resonances for the life of priestly reality which is ours as believers in Jesus. For we are called to feed upon the food of Christ's broken body and shed blood (John 6:35, 51–58), both in the quality and persistence of our personal, spiritual communion with him (John 6:62–63) and in the communal eating and drinking at his table (1 Cor. 11:23–26). We deeply and desperately need to practise the presence of God, to engage in, or to recover, if necessary, the all-too-often-neglected 'quiet time', that early-morning meeting with God – not necessarily

---

[13] Cf. Isa. 61:1 with Luke 4:18; Acts 4:27; 10:38. The baptism of Jesus is specifically excluded from any association with cleansing. As the conversation with John the Baptist in Matt. 3:13–17 reveals, Jesus came to John as the sinless one who needed no washing. Rather, his baptism was the first public act of his identification with sinners which culminated at Calvary (cf. Isa. 53:12).

[14] Rev. 1:5–6 makes a direct link between this washing in the blood of Christ and our priesthood.

[15] The wonderful doctrine of 'imputed righteousness' runs through the Bible; e.g. Gen. 15:6; Isa. 54:17; Rom. 4:3–6; 1 Cor. 1:30; 2 Cor. 5:21; Phil. 3:9. For the imagery of 'putting on the Lord Jesus Christ', see Rom. 13:14; Gal. 3:26–27.

[16] See J. A. Motyer, 'Anoint, Anointing', in *NBD*.

frantically early, but 'first thing' – so that we start the day with him as Jesus did (Isa. 50:4; Mark 1:35).

The ceremony of putting some blood on the ears, thumbs and toes of the priests (20) seems at first sight an alien practice, but it is worth pondering. The blood in question was that of the *other ram* (19), here called the *wave offering* (24) but in principle a peace or fellowship offering. The sequence is that sin had been covered and cleansed (the *sin offering*, 10–14), unqualified commitment to the life of obedience had been made (the *burnt offering*, 15–18), and now with the wave offering Aaron and his sons entered upon a joyful life of fellowship with the Lord (cf. Deut. 12:7).

But such a life has to be on his terms, consonant with his holiness and directed into his ways: hence, the hand (life's actions), the foot (life's directions) and, first and foremost, the ear (life's listening, the hearing of divine truth) must be brought 'under the blood'.

8. The heart of the priestly life

After the priests' consecration and response, their life was, for the most part, a daily grind of performing the repeated sacrifices (38–42; cf. Heb. 10:11). The year had its high spots – for example, Passover and the Day of Atonement – but for the most part the Aaronic priest was like a doctor writing out repeat prescriptions. Each day must have been very much like any other, and the rituals the priests were asked to perform can hardly have retained their early freshness or excitement. Yet it was the life to which God had called them; it was the life characteristic of their priestly privilege; the framework of their walk with God was to be one of patient continuance in well-doing.[17]

So, year after year, the ministry of Aaron and his successors, his sons and their successors went on, and, if ever they wearied with the 'daily round and common task', please God the central reality of their priesthood came to their rescue and never failed to thrill their hearts and hold them steadily on course. The purpose of their ministry – even in its mundane routine – was to realize the presence of the living God among his people (46) and to hear and share the word which he would speak (42; cf. Mal. 2:5–7). The priestly life was indeed concerned with patience and perseverance in daily duties and activities, but at its heart was the calling to live in

---

[17] Cf. Acts 13:43; 14:22; Rom. 2:7; 5:3–4; Col. 1:11, 23; 1 Tim. 4:16; Heb. 6:12; 10:36; 12:1; Jas 5:7–11.

the presence of God, to be occupied with the things that made his presence real, and to wait upon him to hear his word.

Additional notes

27:20 – 30:10 The structure of this part of Exodus is as instructive as ever.

- A^1 Priestly duty: the Lord's outshining light (27:20–21)
  - B^1 Priestly robes: figures of the true (28:1–43)
  - B^2 Priestly consecration: provision for the times (29:1–37)
  - B^3 Priestly offerings: the continual burnt offering (29:38–46)
- A^2 Priestly duty: the rising incense (30:1–10)

Note how the light and the incense are linked (30:7–8). This whole priestly pericope is enclosed by a beautiful picture of the priest as mediator, responsible for the Lord's light reaching out to his people and their solemn and acceptable worship reaching up to him. Seen in this way, this section fits smoothly into its context. The furnishings so far described (chapters 25–27) represent the Lord's coming to his people and his presence among them, and this can be seen as summed up in the light. The remaining furnishings (chapter 30) are concerned with the approach to the divine and the fitness to come near, and these can be seen as amplifying the picture provided by the incense.

28:1–43 The structure of chapter 28 is equally instructive.

- A^1 The priestly family: the significance of the robes (1–4)
  - B^1 The ephod (5–14)
  - B^2 The breastpiece (15–30)
  - B^3 The robe of the ephod (31–35)
  - B^4 The golden medallion of holiness (36–38)
- A^2 The priestly family: the significance of the robes (39–43)

This bears out the reason given above for why the description of the robes precedes that of the institution of Aaron and his sons.

28:4 KB traces *ephod* (*'ēpôd*) to √*'āpad* ('to fit neatly or closely'). The ephod itself is sometimes thought of as a kind of apron or pinafore, or (so to speak) the back and front of a long waistcoat, held in place by a belt (8) and joined by shoulder pieces (9–12). Some less ornate or utilitarian ephod was the distinguishing garment of a priest (1 Sam. 22:18) or levitical servant (1 Sam. 2:18). David, presumably in his royal role as the Melchizedek priest, wore an ephod on the occasion of the arrival of the ark in Jerusalem (2 Sam. 6:14).

28:9–14 Durham (p. 387) is right in saying that 'the varieties [of precious stones] can only be surmised … we cannot translate … with any accuracy', but the resultant beauty, richness and preciousness is undeniable. In both cases – the shoulder stones (12) and the stones in the breastpiece (21) – Aaron brings his people before the Lord. That is to say, this is how the Lord's people appear before him, how he sees them – his 'precious and honoured' ones (Isa. 43:4), his 'treasured possession' (Mal. 3:17), (lit.) 'the riches of the glory of his inheritance in the saints' (Eph. 1:18). This is the other, and richer, meaning of the words that Aaron (lit.) 'bears the judgment of the children of Israel' (30) – he is a visual display of the Lord's 'judgment', his opinion regarding his people, the visible beauty and value of the stones and the hidden reality of Urim and Thummim (*'ûrîm*, 'lights', and *tummîm*, 'perfections', are both plurals of amplitude, meaning 'every sort of … ').

28:15 The word represented by *breastpiece* is *ḥōšen*. It is of obscure derivation and used only of this item of the robes. Any translation is, therefore, guesswork. KB suggests that √*ḥāšan*, unused in the Old Testament, means 'to be beautiful', and no doubt the finished article, a square pouch made from a folded rectangle of 'tabernacle weave', was beautiful (15–16).

28:36 Usually represented as a 'plate' of gold, *ṣîṣ* means a 'blossom, flower'. It derives from √*nāṣaṣ*, 'to shine, sparkle' (cf. Ps. 132:18, ESV). In 39:30 the 'flower' (NIV, 'plate') is defined as 'the sacred diadem', (lit.) 'diadem of holiness'. It was neither a crown nor an encircling tiara, for it needed cords to secure it to the headdress. Probably we should think not of a rectangular 'plate' but of a highly polished golden medallion, floral in shape.

28:39 *Sash* is *'abnēṭ*. √*Bānaṭ* is not found in the Old Testament, but KB suggests 'to wrap up'. The sash held the tunic firmly to the body as a close-fitting undergarment.

For *kĕtōnet* see e.g. Gen. 3:21 ('garments'); 37:3 ('robe'); 2 Sam. 13:18 ('robe').

28:4 uses the adjective *tašbēṣ* and 28:39 the verb √*šābaṣ*, which means 'to weave with a pattern in the weave', maybe a plaited pattern. We are not told what the pattern was, but it went beyond plain linen to be an ornamented garment of beauty in its own right.

Exodus 30:11 – 31:18

21. Practicalities

This section may look at first sight like a collection of odds and ends – maybe things the author simply forgot to include at their logical place earlier on in the narrative. But there are indications that this is not so.

First, we note that the account of Moses' fifth ascent of Sinai, which began with the promise of the gift of the tablets of the law (24:12–18), ends here with the fulfilment of that promise (31:18). In addition, the section concerning the materials for the construction of the tabernacle and the law governing their use (25:1–9) is balanced here by the identification of the artisans to whom the work was committed and the law governing their working pattern (31:1–18).

Additionally, there is the way that the items now described in this section 'flow' from the passage dealing with the incense. The constantly burning incense was a symbol of access and leads into this examination of the who (30:11–16), the how (30:17–38) and the where (31:1–11) of Israel's approach to the Lord – that is, the people who may approach,[1] the priesthood, fitted and equipped for its work, and the place and utensils of worship.

The three topics of this section, then, are the Lord's people (30:11–16), his priests (30:17–38) and his work (31:1–17).

---

[1] Dennett (p. 325) points us in the right direction when he observes that before the priest engages in his work 'there must be a redeemed people on whose behalf' he acts. The section on the people (30:11–16) is literally enfolded in priestly access to the Lord (30:1–10, 17–21).

1. Personal commitment (30:11–16)[2]

The Old Testament does not seem to explain anywhere why taking a census was such a dangerous matter, but the fact was apparently well known, so that even a hard-headed 'man of the world' like Joab counselled David against doing such a thing (2 Sam. 24:3). Was it that numbers engendered human pride and so offended the Lord? We do not know, but the seriousness of the possibility of provoking divine displeasure was recognized even here where the Lord himself had commanded the numbering to be done (12).[3] Typical of the divine mercy, however, the danger foreseen was met by a provision of a ransom price (12, 15–16).

It is not for us to ask how the payment of money could effect a ransom (12a), avert divine wrath (12b) and make atonement (15–16), any more than we are allowed to ask in Exodus 3:5 how the removal of sandals could make it possible for Moses to stand in the Lord's holy presence. It is always for the Lord to say what he is prepared to accept as satisfactory, and here, in respect of the census, it was the silver half shekel of the redemption money.[4] The glorious truth is that the same God whom the census offends is the God who reveals the protective covering against his own wrath.

Responsibility

Each individual was made responsible for paying his own ransom. It was not paid out of tabernacle funds on behalf of Israel, but out of the pocket of each Israelite as a personal decision. It is in this same spirit of individual commitment that those enrolled are spoken of as 'crossing over' (13–14), an expression found only in these two places. We do not know how exactly the census was taken, but the picture that seems to emerge here is of the census-takers sitting in a certain place and those who wished to be

---

[2] The tabernacle was set up on the first day of the first month (40:2), so we may presume that this census, which was a religious census, preceded it. The census in Num. 1:2 was commanded on the first day of the second month, and was a military census. But since the two happened so closely together and took into account the same males (Exod. 30:14; Num. 1:3), it is not surprising that the result was the same.

[3] Ramm (p. 172) suggests that exact knowledge of the number of his people was the Lord's prerogative and that it was dangerous for humans to trespass on this.

[4] The NIV translates different forms of the same word variously: *ransom* (12), *to atone* (15) and *atonement* (16). The verb is √*kāpar*, and the nouns are *kōper* (12) and *kippurîm* (16). The taking of a census exposed participants to a *plague* (Heb. *negep*, 'a striking, blow'), but the *ransom* or 'atonement price' covered them. The linked thoughts are clear: on the one hand, divine displeasure or wrath issuing in a 'blow' and, on the other, the price which covered.

enrolled queuing behind them and passing by, making their payment and having their names registered and counted before going on to join those who had preceded them. It must have been in some way like this that they could be said to have 'crossed over'.

We are not told if any of the people decided not to be counted; we are told only that the census was individual and voluntary. The Lord would have each and every one of his covenant people memorialized before him in the silver of the tabernacle (16),[5] but each one must individually undertake the responsibility, make the decision and pay the price. This was in essence a spiritual, not a social or national, matter. It was not decided solely by Israelite birth. The issue was to escape the wrath of God, and the question was not 'Are you an Israelite?' but 'Are you redeemed?' So, the individual decision to be made was whether or not one wanted to see one's name added to the roll, under the covering of the redemption money. The Israelite nation as such was something one was born into (and this carried immense privileges with it), but being an actual participant in the spiritual blessings focused in Israel – enjoying the tabernacle and the nearness of the Lord it afforded and coming under the spiritual cover of its sacrifices – all this was a matter of individual conviction, choice and commitment.[6] Those who 'crossed over' did so by personally participating, through the giving of the half shekel, in the Lord's provision of redemption.

2. Holiness constantly refreshed (30:17–21)

The extent to which the revealed will of God dominated everything about the tabernacle is enormous. It was a matter of the giving of not just the 'blueprint' (e.g. 26:30), but also the practical details of ministry – for example, the exact payment of the redemption money (30:14–15), the ordinance of priestly washing (30:20–21) and the composition and use of the anointing oil and the incense (30:23–25, 34–38). There was nothing

---

[5] According to Dennett, 'The silver on which the tabernacle rested [Exod. 26:19–25] testified, on behalf of the children of Israel, that atonement had been made for their souls. They were all represented in the atonement and had their memorial ever before the Lord.' A *memorial* (*zikkārôn*) is 'an object or act which brings something else to mind or which represents something else' (*TWOT* 1.242) (e.g. Exod. 12:14; 17:14; 28:12, 29).

[6] The title 'Jew' and what we know today as 'Judaism' are, of course, later than the Old Testament, but using the terminology of his own day, Paul expresses these same truths in Rom. 2:28–29 (cf. Rom. 3:1–2). Ramm (p. 173) observes that in the census, the covenant 'was made personal' with each Israelite 'willing to be counted . . . owning up to the covenant. The call of revelation is a call to decision.'

casual or whimsical about Israel's worship. When the element of 'doing what one finds helpful' came in at a later period, it was the subject of condemnation (Amos 4:4–5). The Lord insisted on being in charge of his worship, and the consequences of departure from the rule of his will were dire (30:21, 33, 38). Any sort of casual assumption that whatever we do sincerely is as valid in heaven as it may be enjoyable on earth finds no endorsement in the Bible (cf. Mark 7:7–9). There was a price to pay for offering 'unauthorised fire' to the Lord (Lev. 10:1–5; Num. 3:4).

The institution of the bronze basin for ceremonial washing enforced a single divine rule of worship. Isaiah expressed it succinctly: 'Be clean, you who bear the vessels of the Lord' (Isa. 52:11, nkjv). The Lord Jesus brought all his sinless perfection to his tasks as our high priest, but for us Christian believers, our priestly liberty to draw near through the veil under the protection of his blood is allied to the necessity to wash with pure water and to have our hearts 'sprinkled' to cleanse us from a guilty conscience (Heb. 10:19–22). So, the basin was not for the Lord's benefit, but for his people's.

In their daily duties the priests of old did not have to repeat the cycle of sacrifices specified for their consecration in 29:10–25: that had been done once and for all. The washing of the whole body (29:4) was never repeated either: that too represented a once-for-all fitness to don the robes of their holy office.[7] But on a daily basis the water in the basin provided for the cleansing of any defilement contracted by the priests. The situation is exactly as in John 13:10 – there is the bath, and there is the wash-hand basin! And our mothers were right when they called us to the family table, not with 'Have you had your bath?', but with 'Have you washed your hands?'

So, what does the basin of the tabernacle mean for us today? First, we must take account of the dire consequences for the priests if they dared to perform holy duties or enter holy places without washing. They were warned that to enter God's presence in an unfit state brought the threat of death (20–21). Unhallowed worship brought a real threat to life (Lev. 10:1–2). Paul, in his careful, caring way, warns the Corinthian church that it is possible to come to the Lord's Supper in a way that brings judgment on them and 'that is why many among you are weak and ill, and a number

---

7 Dennett (p. 333) makes this washing a 'figure' of being born again, 'and this cannot be repeated'. But, says Mackintosh (p. 314), those once washed needed to be 'preserved in fitness'.

of you have fallen asleep' (1 Cor. 11:29–30). The fact that the Lord in his mercy withholds the infliction of the penalty that pertained in ancient times (e.g. 1 Sam. 6:19–20; 2 Sam. 6:6–7) is no indication of a dilution of his holiness or that the offence is any less serious or our sinfulness any less offensive. The Lord invites and allows us to come freely; we have no permission to come carelessly or casually.

The basin was set in the tabernacle, accessible and available for God's people of old, and the same mercy opens fountains of cleansing for us. Confession of sin brings cleansing from sin (1 John 1:8–9), and the blood of Jesus, though shed once and for all on the cross, is the constantly available agency of cleansing for those who would walk in the light of God's presence (1 John 1:7). The New Testament also speaks of 'the washing with water through the word' (Eph. 5:26) and says that we 'have purified [ourselves] by obeying the truth' (1 Pet. 1:22) and are 'clean because of the word I have spoken to you' (John 15:3). Even though the New Testament commands self-examination only as preparation for the Lord's Table (1 Cor. 11:28), dare we enter that holy presence at any time without thoughtful confession and without taking up the Word of God to allow its sanctifying truth to shower upon us (Ps. 119:9), permeate our beings and to bring us all over again into obedience and sanctification (John 17:17)?[8]

3. The essential touch of God (30:22–33)

We have looked at two of the elements used for sanctification in the tabernacle: blood and water. The simplest, as well as the most basic, distinction between them is to link the blood with propitiation and the water with cleansing. The wrath of God had been revealed against sin, whether in the human agent or in that which human hands had infected, and the shed blood of substitutionary sacrifice propitiated that wrath and laid it to rest, bringing the sinner into line with the demands of the holy, now-reconciled God. The washing with water dealt with the continuing defilement which would make sinners and what they had defiled unfit to have any engagement in holy things. Therefore, the blood of sacrifice speaks to us of the cross of Christ in its once-for-all dealing with sin, and

---

[8] Coates (p. 260) warns, 'We might well fear the allowance of any soil on hand and foot . . . Whatever might move in one's spirit that is not in accord with divine holiness necessitates washing.'

the water speaks to us of that same blood in its everlasting, continuing efficacy for cleansing.

The third element of sanctification, the anointing oil, differs from the other two in that it possesses the positive efficacy of marking, fitting and enabling for the service of God.[9] In the case of Aaron and his sons, the sequence was washing, robing and anointing – that is, the removal of defilement, the identification of Aaron with ideal priesthood, and the Lord's acknowledgment and enabling of him as such for his priestly work (29:4–7).

It was not just the priests, however, that were to be anointed, but also all the articles of worship (26–28). In what sense did anointing them make them holy? Did it 'magically' transform them so that after anointing they were somehow different in substance from their ordinary counterparts? This question is still of importance today, for in some church circles officials are called in to 'consecrate' buildings, furnishings, land and some of the other material adjuncts to worship and service. It can hardly be the case that the anointing of old or the consecration of today 'magically' effects some mysterious change for the better within the thing concerned, for the Bible nowhere deals in anything approaching magic. No, the objects connected with the tabernacle worship were anointed as a sign of the Lord's recognition, acknowledgment and approval of them as items to be used exclusively in his service. The anointing oil was not to be used as a consecrating or sanctifying agent for anything that was merely a human 'good idea', but only for what had been made at his command and according to his revealed pattern. It was his public 'Yes' to the institution of the tabernacle, and once that 'Yes' had been pronounced, all the ministries of the tabernacle could be undertaken with the assurance that this was acceptable to him and effective for his worshippers. In our case, we need to be very careful that the buildings we use and the articles of worship they contain conform to the nature, standards and truths of New Testament worship.

---

[9] Christians have their anointing, as did the priests of old. It is referred to in general terms in 2 Cor. 1:19–22, where God's anointing of us (22, *chriō*) is linked with his fundamental, initial saving work in and for the individual. It is associated, on the one hand, with the gift of the promises of God in Christ, and, on the other hand, with the Holy Spirit as 'seal' (*sphragizō*) and 'deposit' (*arrabōn*; cf. Eph. 1:14). The verb *chriō* is used of the Lord Jesus as the anointed one (Acts 4:27; 10:38; Heb. 1:9) and also of believers (1 John 2:27; cf. references to the 'pouring out' of the Holy Spirit in Acts 2:33; 10:45, and especially Titus 3:4–7). Hence, Rainsford (p. 128) speaks of the anointing oil as 'the Old Testament emblem and promise of the Divine and infinite fulness of the third Person of the Blessed Trinity'.

4. A fragrance unto God (30:34–38)

Like the anointing oil, the incense was to be made according to a specified 'recipe' (34–35). There were certain essentials that had to be included in specified amounts, and nothing was to be introduced other than what had been prescribed.[10] In verse 37, where the NIV (also the ESV) has *to the LORD*, the NKJV has 'for the LORD'. Both renderings are allowable. Only when the incense is compounded with the prescribed ingredients and in their exact proportions is it acceptable to the Lord; only as such is it a sweetness for the Lord's delight. As we noted above, the Bible does not explain the use of incense, but there is sufficient information to draw out a double significance: the incense has a sweetness which is delightful to the Lord, and its rising fragrant cloud represents the ascending prayers of the Lord's people or, maybe more accurately, their access by prayer into his presence. Through the work of the priests, the people were to be ever acceptable and delightful to their God, and where they themselves could not go, their prayers could. The incense is described as *most holy to you* and *holy to the LORD* (36–37). This expresses how precious our acceptance before the Lord and our prayerful access into his presence ought to be to us, and also how precious we are to him and how he, for his part, finds delight and satisfaction when we come before him.[11]

5. The Lord's work done in the Lord's way (31:1–17)

a. The Spirit of God

Bezalel and Oholiab may not have had the ceremonial anointing with oil of the priesthood, but they had the reality which it symbolized, the filling of the Holy Spirit (3). It is not only for what we might class as 'spiritual' work that the Holy Spirit comes to equip us. He was there when the craftsmen's drawings were made (4), when the wood was carved (5) and when the carpentry was done (8). He was the inspiration of the weaver and the smith, the needleworker, the tailor and the chemist (9–11). Wherever a willing heart commits itself to hear the call of God and to do the will of

---

[10] In July 1984 I listened with great benefit to the late, and greatly loved, John Caiger (then Pastor of Gunnersbury Baptist Church) at Crosthwaite Church, Keswick. He said that if our lives are to be fragrant for God, we must, first, embody essential biblical truths; second, exclude what is extraneous to the Bible; and third, hold truth in biblical balance and proportion. It is a blessing to recall this lovely man of God.

[11] For other uses of the idea of a 'sweet odour', see 2 Cor. 2:14–16; Eph. 5:2; Phil. 4:18.

God, the filling of the Spirit of God may reverently be assumed. Helping and administration are as much his concern as healing and speaking in tongues (1 Cor. 12:28).

b. The will of God

It is not enough for the willing-hearted to follow the whims and fancies of their hearts – doing the Lord's work means doing the Lord's will. A fundamental principle of service is enunciated in verse 11: the craftsmen are to do their work *just as I commanded you*. The 'pattern shown you on the mountain' (25:40)[12] must govern every detail. And this is a truth carried through intact into the New Testament. Throughout the Bible, the will of God is not only that sovereign exercise of divine grace and power whereby he does what he wills in heaven and earth and in our individual lives, but it is also that perfect plan and pattern he has for each of us, in matters great and small alike.[13] Knowing the will of God for everyday things (as well as for the big life-changing decisions) is a huge topic, but the example of Israel in the wilderness lays down a great fundamental principle. Israel did not 'seek' guidance, they waited for it, because the directive will of God was expressed to them by the movement of the cloud (40:36–38). For them, guidance was a matter of waiting and watching. So also for Jesus: as foreseen in Isaiah 50:4–5, the will of God was made known to him in the daily discipline and privilege of meeting with the Lord and waiting upon him 'morning by morning' for his word.

c. The commandments of God

It is important to note that immediately after the verses which speak of the divine appointment of Bezalel and Oholiab and, later, immediately before the commencement of work on the tabernacle, the law of the Sabbath was enunciated (12–17; 35:1–3). This emphasis on the Sabbath was surely meant to alert the workers on the tabernacle to the fact that the uniqueness and holiness of their task did not allow them to sit loose to the law of God. The commandment was not addressed specifically to Bezalel and Oholiab but to all Israel (13), for no-one knew at this point who was to be included in the workforce. No-one was permitted to say either

---

[12] Cf. 25:9; 26:30; 27:8; Num. 8:4. Commenting on Exod. 31:6, 11, Durham notes that 'no room is left for creative variations on the plans Yahweh has given'.

[13] Pss 115:3; 135:6; Rom. 1:10; 12:2; 1 Cor. 4:19; Eph. 1:4–11; 2:10; 5:17; 6:6; Col. 1:9; 4:12; 1 Pet. 2:15.

that the abnormal circumstances of Israel's wilderness life or the exceptional nature of the work in hand allowed adjustments to be made. As ever, God's work must be done in God's way.[14]

Exodus 35:1–3 is an unelaborated restatement of the Sabbath law – its divine origin (1), its terms and seriousness (2) and its applicability to the details of everyday life (3). As always, the Sabbath required a thoughtful approach to life's schedules, so that in this case all necessary food preparation had to be done on the preceding days. In summary, these verses say that there was to be no relaxation of the very stringent requirements of the Lord's law. The following verses (31:12–17), however, while emphasizing the same inviolability of the law, dig deeper into the meaning of the Sabbath as such:

A[1] The Sabbath: a sign that the Lord has set his people apart as holy (13)
   B[1] The Sabbath: an obligation enforced by penalties (14)
      C The Sabbath law: its rule and its seriousness (15)
   B[2] The Sabbath: an obligation in perpetuity (16)
A[2] The Sabbath: a sign that the Lord's people must imitate the Lord (17)

While we must take note of the fact that the New Testament never quotes the fourth commandment, and Colossians 2:16 rules out any legalistic approach to the question of Sabbath observance, nevertheless we must be careful to take account of the rather wonderful – and deeply theological – understanding of the Lord's Day given here in Exodus. The Sabbath is to be a sign to the world of our holy separation as the Lord's holy people (13), and that separation itself is a sign of our determination to fashion our lifestyle in imitation of the Lord (17). It is not meant to be an exercise in restriction but in devotion, for in this situation as in others, 'imitation is the sincerest form of flattery'.

Additional notes

30:13 Coates (pp. 257–259) carefully observes that 'ten . . . is the number of responsibility' (cf. Dennett, p. 327). The gerah, as the twentieth of a shekel, is mentioned in Lev. 27:25; Num. 3:47; 18:16; Ezek. 45:12.

---

[14] So Cassuto (p. 403): 'Although I have commanded you to perform the work of the Tabernacle, do not forget that I have forbidden you to do any work on the Sabbath.'

30:18 No measurements are given for the bronze basin, but according to 38:8, it was made from the 'mirrors of the women who served at the entrance'. The translation 'mirrors' here depends on ancient renderings of the Hebrew. *Mar'â* has the general meaning of 'sight' or 'vision' (e.g. Num. 12:6; Ezek. 1:1). Those (e.g. Cole) who query whether the basin is mentioned here in its proper place usually want to move it back to follow the bronze altar in 27:1–8, but it is linked with priestly *needs*, not with priestly *ministry*. It is, however, bronze, in keeping with the altar. The altar establishes the symbolism of bronze as the outworking of divine fiery judgment in substitutionary death. 'Nothing can be allowed in the service ... of the holy priesthood that is inconsistent with the death of Christ' (Coates, p. 259).

30:22–33 The balance of the passage brings out its main emphases and central affirmations regarding the oil for anointing:

A¹ Its revealed composition (23–24)
  B¹ Its holiness and use (25)
    C¹ Anointing and sanctifying the articles of worship (26–29)
    C² Anointing and sanctifying the personnel of worship (30)
  B² Its holiness, exclusive use and composition (31–32)
A² Its inviolable composition (33)

30:34–35 On the reference to salt, cf. Lev. 2:13 and Num. 18:19. Salt is evidence of a covenant relationship, and in 2 Kgs 2:20–21 Elisha threw salt into a spring as evidence that the curse had been removed and the covenant restored. The KJV has 'tempered together', a usage of √*mālaḥ* that is unsupported elsewhere. Cassuto, however, offers 'ground small', but the grinding to a powder is mentioned in verse 36.

30:34–38 Bonar (*Leviticus*, p. 295) and Rainsford (p. 136) both make the point that while the efficacy of oil was inherent, that of the incense needed fire to draw it out, to show, says Bonar, 'that acceptance is effected by justice itself', for on the Day of Atonement at least this needed fire was taken from the bronze altar. Wenham says the incense of Lev. 16:11–13 served to 'create a screen which would prevent the High Priest from gazing upon the Holy Presence' (*Leviticus*, p. 231). It should be noticed, however, that this 'screen' was required when Aaron brought the sin offering for himself, but it is not mentioned when he entered the second time with the offering for the people's sin (Lev. 16:15–16). This would have been because on the second occasion he entered in the character of the perfect priest, his own sin offering having been made. This suggests that the cloud of incense was rather to hide Aaron's imperfections. By contrast, Jesus 'entered heaven itself, now to appear [*emphanisthēnai*, 'to be seen in his true colours'] for us in God's presence' (Heb. 9:24).

Exodus 32:1 – 34:35

22. A dreadful step back, a huge step forward

Sin has not figured much in the Exodus story so far. Even in chapter 12 there is no reference to any sinfulness of Israel in connection with the blood of the Passover lamb. The exclusive effectiveness of the blood on that memorable night was to allay the wrath of the Lord, so that he could pass over Israel's houses in peace. What references there are to sin are few and far between. Pharaoh refers to his sinfulness three times (9:27; 10:16–17), and we can make of that what we wish. Then, Moses alludes to the value of a proper fear of the Lord in restraining the people from sin (20:20), and the reason for driving out the existing inhabitants of Canaan was because 'they will cause you to sin' (23:33). In the last two cases,[1] 'sin' seems as if it were something that might yet happen, but need not. In the same way, the narratives touching on Moses' relationship with the Lord and on the Lord's providential care of his people have more in common with the stories of Genesis – a carefree relationship within the broadest of parameters (e.g. Gen. 17:1; cf. Rom. 4:15b; 7:8b).

All this is in marked contrast to Exodus 32 – 34 where, on a simple word count, there are eleven references to sin[2] as compared with ten in the book up to this point. But the reality of the situation runs even deeper. Israel was now directly charged with having *committed a great sin* with

---

[1] In all the foregoing references Hebrew uses words of the √ḥāṭā' group, with its basic sense of 'missing the target, coming short'. Two other words for sin are pešaʿ ('wilful rebellion'; 20:5, 'sin'; 22:9[8], NIV 'illegal possession', ESV 'breach of trust'; NKJV 'trespass'; 23:21, 'rebellion') and 'āwôn (usually translated 'iniquity', the hidden bias towards sin within the human heart; 28:38, 43, 'guilt').

[2] The √ḥāṭā' group, 32:21, 30 (twice), 31, 32, 34; 34:7, 9; 'āwôn, 34:7, 9; pešaʿ, 34:7.

only a *perhaps* that atonement could be made (32:30). It was a sin of such dimensions that it imperilled the status of Moses himself in the Lord's *book* (32:32) and, apparently, called into question the continuing presence of the Lord among his people (33:3). Furthermore, it is in these chapters that Israel experienced a conviction of sin for the first time, consciously accepted for themselves the position of the guilty, and mourned for what they had done (33:4–6).

1. The golden calf (32:1–35)

The nature and meaning of the holiness of the Lord is as plain in 3:1–5 as it will ever become in the rest of the Bible, but divine mercy made entrance into the Lord's holy presence so easy for Moses that we might well question whether anything fundamental about holiness and sin entered his mind. In the same way, the Sinai experience brought the Lord's holiness home to the people so that, momentarily, they experienced the fear of sinners before the Holy One (20:18; cf. Heb. 12:18–21) but, there again, the issue was sidestepped by the putting forward of Moses as their intermediary, as if nothing more would be needed (20:19). Likewise, while they had truly committed themselves to obey the Lord's law (19:8; 20:19; 24:3), it was not until the incident of the golden calf that they faced the full seriousness of the call to obedience, the Lord's stark refusal to compromise regarding his law, and the dire consequences of breaking it.

Their actual sin was simple and compound at one and the same time. The 'simple' fact is that they requested and worshipped a 'god' they had made themselves (1, 5–6, 8). The part Aaron played in this was, of course, criminally feeble.[3] First, he acquiesced in the doubt cast on Moses (1), failing even to remind the pressure group that Moses had commanded them to wait for his return (24:14). Should he not at the very least have urged, 'Moses said "wait" and that's what we are going to do! Just wait! You'll see – Moses will be back'? Because of this, the character of Moses was denigrated, and, in the light of Moses' record to date, unjustifiably so. Second, Moses had not committed the leadership to Aaron alone, but to Aaron and Hur (24:14) – not to mention Nadab, Abihu and the 'college' of seventy elders (24:9). Aaron could, if he had wished, have played for time and insisted that these others must be consulted.

---

[3] Bentley (p. 313) attempts a defence of Aaron.

2. The strength of fellowship

There was, however, a more serious fault here. Very few, if any, people in positions of leadership are capable of 'going it alone'. The strength that there is in fellowship is recognized by both folk wisdom ('Two heads are better than one') and the Bible (Eccl. 4:8–12). Even a powerful leader like Elijah collapsed under the strain of his solitary position (1 Kgs 19:1–3), when he could have gathered to him the strength of a hundred prophets of the Lord (1 Kgs 18:13), not to mention the newly invigorated people who had accepted his leadership (1 Kgs 18:39). If the mighty Elijah could not succeed alone, how much less the effete Aaron![4]

So, the gold was collected, melted down and fashioned into a calf (3–4). Much of this gold must have been the 'spoil' of Egypt, acquired when the Lord himself acted to give the people favour in the sight of the Egyptians (12:36). Now, however, the riches brought by the Lord's work of redemption were squandered – and, indeed, never enjoyed again (20).

Not only, however, did the people show this disrespect to the work of their redemption, they also broke the first three commandments. As to the first commandment, their intention was that Aaron should make for them some alternative to the God of Moses.[5] The broadest understanding of the second commandment forbade the making of any image, but, as we saw above, what it specifically forbade was the worship of Yahweh under the form of some model derived from the created order. This was the grossest element of their sin. Aaron, looking at the golden calf, said, 'Tomorrow there will be a festival *to the* LORD' (5; my italics), and it was this affront that loomed largest in the Lord's mind when he first alerted Moses to what Israel had done (8). In this way, the Lord's name was taken and applied to the unreality of a 'god' fashioned by human hands, out of

---

[4] But was Moses wholly guiltless? Was his leadership so 'dominant' that it left no room for others such as Aaron, Hur and the elders to grow into leadership roles? Did his personality so loom over everything that had happened that – at this late stage – the people could speak of *this fellow Moses who brought us up out of Egypt*? Did Moses allow himself to become too 'centre stage', so that the exodus was seen in solely political terms, as a matter of human policy and success? What a leadership fault this would have been. Phil. 1:1 addresses church leaders as 'together with' (*syn*) the saints, i.e. the ideal of companionate leadership, with leaders alongside, in and with the fellowship.

[5] The most frequently used Hebrew word for 'God', *'ĕlōhîm*, is plural. When it is used of the Lord, the word may be understood as a plural of majesty or of fullness, i.e. the 'Great God' or 'that God in whom every divine attribute coexists'. The plural noun is used here (1; cf. 23) with a plural verb, possibly indicating that the people asked for 'gods'. The one God seemed to have disappeared along with Moses (cf. Durham, p. 419). Monotheism is an exercise in putting all one's eggs in one basket. With polytheism there is always 'someone to turn to' – as they would have learned in Egypt. The Apis bulls of Egypt represented a complex of gods – Ptah of Memphis, Hapi, the god of the flooding Nile, and Osiris (when the Apis bull died it became the god Osiris).

earthly material, according to a created shape[6] and in defiance of the third commandment.

Their sin was compound indeed. Their use of the gold contradicted the redeeming work of the Lord, as represented by the tabernacle; the making of the image contradicted his word; and calling it by his name contradicted his revealed nature. The people had exchanged the invisible God who had led them by his spoken word for a visible 'thing' which could not speak.[7]

In summary, the Israelites fell into sin and broke the Lord's law. They then began to feel something of the horror of his alienation and of the heavy reality of his wrath (cf. Eph. 2:12; Heb. 10:31).

3. How the history was written

The story of the golden calf is simplicity itself – Moses' prolonged absence, the onset of doubt and impatience, the pathetic Aaron, the idolatrous, pagan festival invoking the sacred name of Yahweh, Moses' angry return and its aftermath. But, as always with Exodus, the narrative is given an instructive balance of presentation. This is one of the ways in which history becomes prophecy, the bearer of the truth of God.

A¹   Moses doubted (32:1–6)

   B¹   Covenant under threat: Moses' intercession (32:7–14)

      C¹   The broken tablets (32:15–19)

         D¹   False security: longing for the visible (32:20–24)

            E¹   Practical devotion (32:25–29)

               F¹   The angel leading: sin faced (32:30–35)

               F²   The angel expelling: sin acknowledged (33:1–6)

            E²   Spiritual devotion (33:7–11)

---

[6] We are not told why a bull calf was chosen. It is possible that the calf ('ēgel, 'a young bull') was suggested by the Apis bulls of Egypt, part of a cult reaching back nearly to 3000 BC and representing the incarnation of deity in this symbol of potency and royalty (see 'Apis' in Bunson, *Encyclopedia of Ancient Egypt*). On the stupidity of it, see Ps. 106:19–21; Isa. 44:6–20. Even if there was a grain of truth in the claim that as the molten gold solidified it took a form suggestive of a calf (24), the actual production of the finished article was Aaron's work. It was he who took the lump of gold and went to work with some sort of marking tool, to produce the desired result. Durham (p. 431) suggests that the burning of the idol (20) points to there being a wooden base with gold leaf or plating. *Tool* in verse 4 is *ḥereṭ*. In Isa. 8:1 the word is used of a pen or some sort of stylus, and therefore it must have been an instrument capable of engraving the metal to make the likeness clear.

[7] Cf. Ps. 115:4–8; Rom. 1:22–25. According to Mackintosh (p. 328), 'The human heart loves something that can be seen . . . which meets and gratifies the senses. It is only faith that can "endure as seeing him who is invisible"' (cf. Heb. 11:24–28).

        D^2 True security: not the visible but the audible (33:12–23)
        C^2 The replacement tablets (34:1–4a)
     B^2 Covenant renewal: Moses' devotion (34:4b–28)
     A^2 Moses validated (34:29–35)

Notes

32:1–6 In verse 1, *so long* (NIV; ESV, 'delayed') represents *bôšēš*. The same form (the piel of √*bôš*) – with a context seemingly requiring the same meaning – occurs in Judg. 5:28 and means 'to be ashamed, disappointed of what one had hoped'. A translation like 'had disappointed them in respect of coming down' is possible. Cf. Cassuto, p. 411. (The intensive forms of stative verbs carry the corresponding transitive meaning.) G. F. Moore, *A Critical and Exegetical Commentary on Judges*, International Critical Commentary series (Edinburgh, 1908), p. 170, offers to 'disappoint the expectation of his coming'.

With verse 6, compare and contrast 24:11. The latter is the uplifting enjoyment of covenant fellowship with God and his people, the former the orgiastic frenzy produced by false worship and issuing in human degradation. It is surely significant that their worship included no sin offering.

32:7–14 In verse 11, *sought the favour of* is (lit.) 'softened/weakened the face of' (cf. 1 Sam. 13:12; 1 Kgs 13:6; Jer. 26:19). √*Ḥālâ* is 'to be sick, weak'. In the piel (*ḥillâ*, as here, with *pānîm*, 'face') means 'to weaken, soften'.

For the most part √*zākar*, 'to remember' (13), takes a direct object, but sometimes (as here) an indirect object attached by *lĕ*. In the present case this is a 'dative of advantage' – 'remember, for Abraham's good/in Abraham's favour' (cf. Ps. 132:1, 'in David's favour/for David's sake').

32:15–19 Four truths are discernible about the tablets: Moses was the intermediary (they were *in his hands*); they were important for Israel (a 'testimony' [ESV], i.e. a declaration of the divine character); they were complete and sacrosanct (*inscribed on both sides*, i.e. leaving no room for addition); they were authoritative (being, in general, *the work of God*, and, in detail and wording, *the writing of God*). Cf. 31:18, where 'stone' indicates their permanency, and 'the finger of God', his direct personal expression of his word and will, binding and authoritative.

The appearance of Joshua here seems sudden and unexpected to us, but it needs no special explanation. Just as in general the Bible tells us only what we need to know, so in narratives it usually tells us only what we need to know when we need to know it. Joshua had accompanied Moses when he left Aaron, Hur and the elders (24:13). We learn now that Joshua only went so far and then waited – showing more patience than did Israel and Aaron! Moses returned to him and they began their descent together.

The basic meaning of verse 18 is as in the NIV, but its details are more difficult. The noun *qôl* ('voice, sound') comes three times, and the intensive (piel) infinitive *'annōt*, three times. There are four verbs in the Bible spelled *'ānâ*. The most frequently used means 'to answer', but this never occurs in the piel, nor does *'ānâ* here mean 'to be occupied with'. *'Ānâ*, 'to be humiliated, downcast, downtrodden', offers a piel, meaning 'to humiliate'. The fourth verb means 'to sing' – though Jer. 25:30 shows that the 'singing' can be of a vociferous, vigorous nature, verging on a shout (*'ānâ* is paralleled with √*ša'ag*, the pouncing roar of a lion). So, 'It is not the sound of the singing of military prowess, nor the sound of the sing-song pleading of the crushed – the sound of pervasive singing is what I am hearing!' The piel (intensive) of *'ānâ*, 'to sing', certainly occurs in Isa. 27:2.

The documentary theorists profess to find problems in the various references to Moses and his anger (see Durham, p. 430), but the story seems coherent: in verses 7–14 Moses does not probe behind the Lord's anger. He reacts to the problem – of covenant revision – as presented to him and successfully pleads against it; in verses 15–19 he sees for himself the full reality of Israel's sin and explodes; in verses 20–29 he takes his own remedial action; and in verses 30–35 he faces the deepest problem, that of what the Lord will do in the face of the people's sin, which still remains. Moses responds with his truly amazing prayer (31–32).

32:20–24 The sequence of burning, grinding and scattering is found in the destruction of the god Mot, in Ugaritic mythology (see Durham, p. 431). This suggests that it could be a formulaic description for total destruction – as we might use 'root and branch' of things that have neither. The verbs may also point to the material out of which the calf was made: wood which could be burned, gold which could be ground to a powder, and both being able to be scattered on the water. Cole recalls verses like Deuteronomy 12:2–3, where Israel is instructed to be as ruthless with internal idolatry as with the religious artefacts of the heathen.

Making the Israelites drink the cocktail of their sin (20) should be understood in the light of the ceremony formalized in Num. 5:11–31. The instances are not completely parallel, but in each case the drinking stands for bringing home to the accused the judgment of God upon what has been done. (See Cole on Num. 5:27, p. 219: 'As Israel had been unfaithful to her heavenly "husband", so the curse will fall upon her.')

32:25–29 In verse 25 *running wild . . . out of control* represents two forms of the verb √*pāra*'. The thought is rather 'let loose', 'free from restraint'. Aaron had lifted the old restrictions, former guidelines had been cancelled, and nothing mattered any more. Num. 5:18 illustrates the verb. The word translated *laughing-stock* (*šimṣâ*) is very uncertain. Possibly, 'to [their] belittlement among their opponents'. The form *šemeṣ* occurs in Job 4:12, 16, where commentators suggest 'a little, a little something, a fragment' or (from the context) 'a whisper, sound'.

Considering the total population of Israel, the (comparatively) small number who fell (verse 28) suggests that by no means all the people were directly involved in the worship of the calf.

Verse 29 *You have been set apart* (ESV, 'ordained for . . . service') is (lit.) 'They have filled your hands today for Yahweh.' 'They' is the Hebrew idiom known as 'third person indefinite' and is really equivalent to a passive verb: 'Your hands have been filled' (just as, today, 'they say' can mean 'it is being said'). 'Having one's hands full' is the imagery of consecration, as we have already seen. *For you were against your own sons and brothers* is rather 'indeed each even at the cost of his son and his brothers' (cf. ESV) and is an allusion to the costliness of consecration (cf. Deut. 33:9; Luke 14:26).

32:30–35 Moses' *perhaps* (30) is understandable and correct. Brashness and cockiness are never suitable, even before the Mercy Seat. Note also the wonderfully broken sentence in verse 32 (see ESV, NKJV) where the initial (lit.) 'If you will forgive their sin . . .' is just left hanging in the air. Mackintosh (p. 334) rightly notes, 'How different is this from what we see in Christ! Having done all, He went back to heaven, not with a "peradventure" but to lay upon the throne the imperishable memorials of an atonement already accomplished' (cf. Heb. 9:12).

On the Lord's *book* (33), cf. Pss 56:8; 69:28; 139:16; Dan. 12:1; Mal. 3:16; Luke 10:20; Phil. 4:3; Heb. 12:23; Rev. 5:1–14; 13:8; 17:8; 21:27.

33:1–6 The quaintness of the documentary theory can be examined in these verses (see Durham, p. 435). Beer accords verses 1, 3, 4 to J[2], verse 2 to JE, and verses 5–11 to E[2] and E. Noth suggests deuteronomic origin for the whole; Hyatt, a D redaction of J and E. Durham comments that 'the variety of these opinions' suggests that certainty is impossible.

33:7–11

A¹ Seeking the Lord: the tent was for everyone (7)

    B¹ The watching people: standing to watch (8)

    Moses' customary use of the tent

        C Reality of fellowship with the Lord (9)

    B² The watching people: bowing in worship (10)

    the Lord's customary advent

A² Meeting the Lord: the special privilege of Moses (11)

    the ordinary privilege of Joshua

33:12–23 We ought to take chapters 32–34 simply as a statement of what happened and the sequence in which it happened. Thus 33:1 'resumes' 32:34 – the Lord's unchanged purpose for Moses and Israel. The tent (7–11) gives Moses the opportunity of further exploration of the Lord's will, and verses 12–23 offer an example of what transpired when, in this setting, the Lord spoke to Moses (11) (see Mackay, p. 554; Currid, p. 301).

Moses' words to the Lord in verse 12 begin with 'See' (*rĕʾēh*), omitted in the NIV. It forms an *inclusio* with *see . . . not be seen* (both √*rāʾâ*) in verse 23. In verses 12–23 √*rāʾâ* occurs seven times, 'face' (*pānîm*) occurs seven times, and, either as verb or noun, √*ḥānan* ('grace') occurs seven times. The longing for something visible, sinfully exemplified in the golden calf, is not overlooked, even though (as ever in biblical religion) the audible – the hearing of the word of God – takes precedence.

In 33:1 the Lord renewed Moses' commission to lead and reiterated the destination; in verse 2 he specified the foregoing angel. But Moses was confused because the promise of the angel had been linked with the negation of *I will not go* (3). Hence, here in verse 12 he asks for clarity and is given the assurance that the angel is Yahweh himself present with his people.

In verse 13 *rĕʾēh* is not *Remember* (as the NIV) but 'And see', with the force of 'And look here!' The people in question are not Moses' people (as in verse 1), nor merely an ethnic entity ('this people', 12) but *your people*. Moses moves the question from one of 'grace' to one of reliability: will the Lord prove faithful to what he has undertaken to do?

My Presence in verse 14 is (lit.) 'my Face' (as in 20, 23). Just as we recognize people by their faces, 'face' stands for the essential reality of personal presence (cf. Ps. 139:7–8[8–9], where 'presence' is [lit.] 'face' and is parallel to 'Spirit' as the mode of the divine omnipresence). That the Lord spoke with Moses *face to face* (11; cf. Num. 12:7–8) and yet *you cannot see my face . . . and live* (20) only shows how the attempt to describe the indescribable strains language to its limit. God is spirit and can, at will, take on a 'form' suited to his invisible glory and in this 'form' allow himself to be seen (Num. 12:7–8). The angel is one such form (e.g. Gen. 16:7–13). See Motyer, *Look to the Rock*, pp. 63–79; 'Old Testament Theology', in *NBC*, p. 29.

34:4b–28 This section is an account of Moses' seventh and last ascent of Sinai. Its theme is the renewed covenant:

A¹ Moses and Yahweh. The tablets prepared (4b–5)
   B¹ The name of the covenant-maker (6–9)
   B² The restated covenant: its stipulations (10–26)
      a¹ The covenant affirmed (10a)
         b¹ The Lord's acts, Israel's response: in principle (10b–11a)
         b² The Lord's acts, Israel's response: in particular (11b–24)
            Exclusivity (12–13)
            Worship and obligation (18–24)
         b³ Summary: worship, obedience, exclusivity (25–26)
      a² The covenant inscribed (27)
A² Moses and Yahweh. The tablets written (28)

It is common (see Durham, pp. 458ff.) to understand this as a parallel/doublet account of the Sinai covenant, with the commandments forming a 'ritual Decalogue'. Wellhausen dates it earlier than chapter 20; Pfeiffer, far later; to Rudolph it is an earlier form of 20:2–17; Langlamet sees 34:11–16 as 'intermediate between J and D'. These theories, says Durham, 'remain altogether too subjective'. He thinks 34:1–18 has been 'woven into' its present position to suggest 'the renewal of the covenant relationship'. But why 'woven into'? Where is the difficulty in saying the verses are where they are because that is the way things happened? For this is not a 'second covenant' in any sense: it is inaugurated on the basis of the 'ten words', inscribed on two tablets. The stress on *reiteration* in verses 1–4 must be given full weight. Verses 10–27 are the same sort of comment on the 'ten words' as is the Book of the Covenant in relation to 20:1–17. Yet, while the Book of the Covenant focuses inwardly upon Israelite society, the amplifications and applications here take into account the golden calf and the temptations that lay ahead in the land of Canaan. Thus the Lord insists that he alone is God – note how the idea of the jealous God (14) is underlined by the added words *whose name is Jealous* and, in the light of the envisaged entry into Canaan, by his insistence on exclusivity (12–17), the distinctive hallowing of Israel's life by the annual and weekly festivals (18–25), and by scrupulosity over details (26).

On *break its neck* (20), cf. the comments on 13:13 above.

Note the same insistence on Sabbath-keeping in verse 21 as, in principle, in 31:15. There, not even the extreme sacredness of the work on the tabernacle allowed variance of the Sabbath rest; here, not even the crucial demands of getting the harvest home are allowed to supervene. The emphasis in the Hebrew is well reflected in the NIV's *even* . . .

34:29–35

A¹   Moses leaving Yahweh's presence: the beaming face (29)
    B¹   The visibly beaming face: the awe in recognition of spiritual status (30)
        C   Moses, the accredited mediator of Yahweh's words (31–32)
          The Sinai revelation (31–32)
          Continuing revelation (33–34)
    B²   The visibly beaming face: veiled because of Moses' humility and sensitivity (35a)
A²   Moses entering Yahweh's presence: the unveiled face (35b)

Was radiant (29, 30, 35) is √qāran, from which is derived qeren, a 'horn'. It is probable that the original root is unused, but a verb qāran has been developed from the noun (a denominative verb), meaning, 'to send out horns' (cf. Ps. 69:31[32], where the NIV translates the niphal participle, 'with . . . horns'). Durham (p. 467) notes that were it simply a matter of 'shining', the hiphil of √'ôr would have sufficed, but quotes Moberly (without approval), that since they chose a horned god (the bull calf), Yahweh accredited a horned Moses. The implication is that Moses' face did more than 'glow', as with some internal brightness – it sent out visible rays of light (cf. Hab. 3:4, where Yahweh's splendour is described in terms of 'rays [flashing] from his hand', qarnayim miyyādô lô, [lit.] 'he had "horns" from his hand'). That Moses *was not aware* (29) indicates that this outshining light was not the product of a subjective experience but was an imposed transformation arising from divine fellowship, (lit.) 'because he spoke with him'. It was a two-way interchange: the Lord spoke with Moses, and Moses spoke with the Lord.

On verses 28–35, see Cassuto (p. 447): Moses 'attained to an exceedingly lofty spiritual height and drew very near to the Lord'. His prolonged fasting indicates 'that he was uplifted above the everyday plane of life and tangibly approached the divine sphere. In the light of this we can understand that . . . Moses' face shone.'

We will use the outline of the golden calf narrative above to explore its meaning a little more fully, but as we do so we must constantly keep in mind the very crucial part it plays in the development of the book of Exodus, and in the rest of Old Testament and biblical religion – a matter to which we shall return at the end of this chapter. It is the point at which Israel began to see sin as the Lord sees it, to understand themselves as sinners before the holy God, and therefore to grasp in its true setting the marvel of the divine indwelling (chapters 35–40) and the place and function of the sacrifices as the appointed means whereby sinners could approach the Holy One and he could take up residence in their midst (Leviticus). With the incident of the golden calf, sin, atonement, 'the wrath of a sin-hating God'[8] and the necessity and power of substitutionary sacrifice all became and remained the fundamental concerns of biblical religion and the centrepiece divine revelation.

a. Moses and the faithfulness of God (A[1, 2])

The narrative begins with doubt being cast on Moses by the impatient people (32:1–6)[9] and ends with the same people standing in awe of Moses as the man bearing the marks of divine validation (34:29–35).[10] The example of the people in this incident is a sharp warning against allowing impatience to take over. Impatience is a form of unbelief, a lack of trust, and like all other manifestations of the wrath of human beings it cannot produce the righteousness that God requires (Jas 1:20, ESV). Moses, however, was totally unaware of events below him in the camp until the Lord alerted him. He could not, therefore, have taken any action in self-justification (not that he would have done, or that any believer should). It

---

[8] From the hymn 'A Debtor to Mercy Alone' by A. M. Toplady.

[9] 32:1–6 is bracketed by the references to Moses 'coming down' (1) and the people 'getting up' (6). 34:29–35 opens with Moses leaving Yahweh's presence (29) and ends with him entering the presence (35b).

[10] Note the verbal *inclusio* formed by 'coming down' in 32:1 and 34:29.

can safely be left to the Lord to look after his cause, his servants and their good repute – in his own way and time. In this case, with what drama the Lord made it known that Moses was indeed his man as his face 'beamed' with the light of the Lord's presence. In 32:1 *this fellow Moses* says it all, but the man fresh from God's presence utterly dominated his erstwhile denigrators, striking awe into them and communicating with unquestioned authority what the Lord had spoken to him. Yet just as Moses did not know he was being criticized and rejected, neither did he know that his face shone with spiritual light and commanding authority. It was the Lord's doing, his mark upon his man.

Unheralded and unsought, this transformation happened to Moses, but it did not happen without him. We read in 34:28 that he accepted the discipline of seeking and cultivating the presence of the Lord, speaking to him, listening to him, receiving and recording his word, and consequently it happened to him just as the old hymn[11] promises to us:

Whene'er we leave the silence of that happy meeting place
We will bear the shining image of the Master in our face.

In the Gospels we read of the occasion when Jesus went to the mountaintop to pray and, as he continued in prayer, he was transfigured (Luke 9:28–29; cf. Isa. 50:4–9). The Lord's transformation of Moses did not happen independently of Moses' perseverance in fellowship with God. He 'looked to him' with fasting and self-denial for forty days, and as a result of this he became 'radiant' (Ps. 34:4–5).

b. The characteristics of effective prayer (B[1, 2])

The main uniting theme of these two passages is that of covenant endangerment (32:7–14)[12] and, against all the human odds, covenant renewal (34:4b–28). What we will see to be the central truth of this whole narrative (F[1, 2]) is in fact brought out again and again in the course of telling the story: the Lord is changelessly faithful to his purposes, irresistibly set upon what he has, of himself, determined to do. It was not for any goodness in them that he chose Israel in Egypt, and here their lack

---

[11] 'In the Secret of His Presence' by E. L. Goreh.

[12] The *inclusios* here are *your people* (7) and *his people* (14) and the two references to Moses, the Lord and the tablets (34:4b–5 and 28).

of goodness did not make him change his mind. From beginning to end he loves us simply because he loves us (Deut. 7:7–9), and the love which brought us out will bring us in (Deut. 4:37–38).

This is always the case and cannot be said too often: God loves because he loves and is faithful because he is faithful. Our whole salvation is of God, beginning, middle and end. Nevertheless, into this wondrous and blessed truth of an unchanging God of salvation, the story of the golden calf raises the question of whether the Lord would have remained faithful were it not for the fact that Moses prayed. After all, did he not say *leave me alone so that . . . I may destroy them* (32:10), and did he not relent in answer to Moses' intercession (32:11–14)? It certainly seems so, and, since Scripture is the Word of God in the words of God, accurately reflecting the mind of God and infallibly revealing the ways of God, this impression must lie there in order that we may learn a mighty lesson.

We are aware that the Lord knows the end from the beginning and that he has not only planned both the beginning and the end but also plotted the course in between. Now, while it is true that he does not change, there is at the heart of his changelessness a 'mystery', a 'revealed secret', that the sovereign, unchangeable God accomplishes his purposes through the prayers of his people. For example, the birth of the forerunner of the Messiah was predicted by Malachi four hundred years before it took place and set for a date predetermined in the divine calendar (Mal. 3:1; 4:5–6; cf. Mark 1:15; Gal. 4:4; 1 Tim. 2:6). Yet when the time came, Gabriel said to Zechariah concerning the birth of John the Baptist, 'Your prayer has been heard' (Luke 1:13). In this way, the fixed purpose was fulfilled because an old and childless couple prayed for a baby. Prayer is one of the 'laws of God' by which he runs his world.

The Lord's prompt response signals the effectiveness of Moses' prayer. This prayer can provide an object lesson for us on the marks of true and effective prayer.

1. True prayer does not seek – rather refuses – glory for self. We do not know how severe a test it was for Moses when the Lord offered to make him the founder of a fresh start, but Moses brushed the temptation aside.

2. True prayer matches the known will of God. The Lord said, *your people, whom you brought up out of Egypt* (32:7), but Moses replied, *your people, whom you brought out of Egypt* (11) and based his prayer on that known reality. If God has made his mind known on any given matter, no amount of prayer will change it. It is pointless to say, 'We've prayed so

much about it, it must be right.' Where God has made his will known, true prayer will take that as settling the issue, and pray accordingly. We must learn to pray, 'Help us to do your will', rather than, 'Please be so good as to hear us when we ask you to think again.'

3. True prayer pleads on the basis of what the Lord has done. In verse 11, Moses mentions two things – the Lord's choice and work of redemption and deliverance (*your people, whom you brought out of Egypt*), and the power at his disposal (*with great power and a mighty hand*). In the Bible the Lord's 'hand' is a representation of his personal intervention, the application of his power to a particular point, his 'touch' of power. Whether we are praying about other Christians, those who are not yet Christians, or circumstances, these truths apply. As we pray we should think of other believers in the context of the Lord's loving, personal choice, those still outside salvation in the light of the almighty power of God to save, and every worldly circumstance as being wholly subordinate to the Lord to deal with as and when he chooses. He is the God of exodus almightiness.

4. True prayer is concerned for the Lord's good name. Moses refused glory for himself but could not bear that the Lord's name should be derided or misrepresented or that his power should seem inadequate (12).

5. True prayer rests on what the Lord has promised in the confidence that, as the Baptism Service in the Book of Common Prayer so beautifully puts it, 'what he has promised he will most surely keep and perform'. Moses based his confidence in God on the promises made to Abraham concerning his descendants. Joshua too knew that the Lord could be trusted to keep his word, and in his farewell speech exhorted the leaders of Israel with these notable words, 'You know with all your heart and soul that not one of all the good promises the LORD your God gave you has failed. Every promise has been fulfilled; not one has failed' (Josh. 23:14).

c. Unchanging God, unchanging word (C$^{1, 2}$)

The two accounts of the broken and replacement tablets have identical emphases.[13] The words were the Lord's words (32:16; 34:1); they were the same words each time (34:1); and they were engraved on stone – always a

---

[13] 32:15–19 is marked off by the opening reference to the tablets in the hands of Moses and the closing reference to them flung from his hands. 34:1–4a is bracketed by the command to chisel out the tablets and Moses doing so.

motif of what is permanent and indelible (32:16; 34:1, 4a). In the first passage Moses descended with the tablets (32:15), and in the second he ascended to receive them (34:1–3). Each passage is integral to its context. The conversation of 32:17–18 shows that Joshua was not with Moses on the mountaintop (cf. 24:13), and 34:2–3 is a renewal of the rules governing the Sinai event with the separation of the mountain and Moses as the Lord's sole invitee.

Between these two events, however, it would seem that there had been basic changes – and yet nothing had changed! The people who had pledged obedience had proved their inability to obey and that they lacked patience and perseverance to wait for the word of God (32:1). This was no minor matter, for it was a case of the people of the revealed word proving themselves unwilling to be ruled by the revealed word. In particular, with open eyes and willing hearts, they had set about violating those particular stipulations which required, and would prove, their sole loyalty to Yahweh. They were not only rebels but traitors. So, what did the Lord do when his law was broken, his character denigrated and his people shown to be unable, unfit and unwilling? The answer is that he reiterated what he is in his holiness (34:3) and repeated his word unchanged (34:1, 4a). He adjusted neither his holy character nor his holy law to suit the sinfulness and weakness of his people.

Jeremiah 31:31–34 offers the Bible's comment on all this, stating that the weakness of the 'old' covenant was on the human side, and the Lord was totally faithful to his covenantal undertakings ('they broke my covenant, though I was a husband to them', 32). This expression not only highlights the covenantal privilege of an intimate relationship with the Lord but, more particularly, states that within that intimacy no charge could be laid at his door as 'husband' within the covenant 'marriage'. In the envisaged new covenant, the law of the Lord ('my law', 33) remains unchanged. It is not that the standard is reduced to whatever level the people can manage but, rather, they are lifted up to match its demands by the inward reality of a 'mind' and 'heart' brought into conformity with the law now written there. All this is to come about by a final dealing with sin (34, 'For I will forgive'; my italics; cf. Heb. 8:7–13; 10:10–18).

While Jeremiah looks forward to the new covenant, Exodus remains within the old, but the principle is the same. The broken law was reiterated. It can never be diminished, adjusted or banished. But the God who called his people to obey made provision for their failure to meet his demands.

The law remained, but so did the tabernacle, the priesthood and the sacrifices, and so, of course, does the once-and-for-all sacrifice for sins with its abiding efficacy to cleanse those who would walk in the light of God's truth (Exod. 12:13; Heb. 10:12; 1 John 1:7).

d. The longing for spiritual certainty and the secret of it (D[1,2])

The next two passages to be considered are 32:20–24, the destruction of the golden calf, the 'god' the people (or some of them) needed to *go before* them (23), and 33:12–23, where Moses feared for the future unless the Lord went with him (33:15).[14] The great thematic link between the passages is the desire – maybe better, the need – for some visible focus of the supernatural.

With the 'disappearance' of Moses, the people felt that they had lost their visible link with Yahweh. They suddenly seemed adrift, lacking any 'markers' in an alien world. Aaron recognized this as the heart of their problem, but went his own compromising and pathetic way to meet it by gesticulating at the calf with the words, 'This is your god . . . who brought you up out of Egypt' (32:4).[15] Of course, he was wrong to do it – and his bewilderingly ludicrous excuses (32:22–24) show that he knew it – but nevertheless, frightfully wrong though he was, he gave the Israelites a point of reference, a sense of belonging somewhere, having a past and a future in an otherwise rudderless existence. Even if nothing else, they now had something to dance around.

i. No idols

The second commandment expressly forbade the making of idols and the worshipping of Yahweh under some form derived from creation (20:4). The reference there to Yahweh as 'jealous' – that is, passionate to have his people's devotion all and exclusively for himself – underlines one peril of idolatry. It is inevitably a weaning away of love from the Lord to the visible object. Anything – and for any reason whatever – that usurps his exclusive lordship and centrality is a provocation to him and an offence in us. Exodus

---

[14] For the *inclusios* of these passages, cf. 32:20 (*in the fire*) with 32:24 (*into the fire*). 33:12–23 is marked off into two sections: verses 12–17 by references to *name* and *grace*, and verses 18–23 by the plea *show me* (lit. 'let me see', √rā'â, 18) and the promise *you will see* (√rā'â, 23).

[15] In 32:4 should we read 'gods' (NIV, ESV, RV) or 'god' (NKJV, NASB)? The plural noun *'ĕlōhîm* can be used with singular intention even with a plural verb (as here, and e.g. Gen. 20:13; 35:7) or with a plural qualifying adjective (e.g. Jer. 10:10). It is pretty inconceivable that Aaron (daft though he was) would have spoken of 'gods', so that in this context 'This is your God' is preferable.

34:13–14 returns to this theme of the jealous God when it looks forward to the people's entry into Canaan and their meeting there the seduction to worship Canaanite gods in Canaanite ways, or to worship Yahweh under Canaanite forms. Plainly, that sort of grossness would provoke the Lord to jealousy, but no less an offence, says 32:5–10, is the association of the divine name with a physical, human-made representation.

Deuteronomy 4 returns to the same theme, as Moses made his people recall the wonder of what happened at Mount Sinai. There they 'saw no form' (15), and the setting aside of this fundamental fact and the making of an 'idol' was to 'corrupt' themselves (16). We see this corruption at work in the worship of the calf. Just as worshipping the Lord and obeying his word lead to wholesome purity of life and of society, so turning to alternative ways and objects of worship corrupts life and society. The holy Lord is the fount of holiness. Every other fount is corrupt and brings corruption. Hence we read that the people *sat down to eat and drink and got up to indulge in revelry* (32:6) and that, on his return, Moses saw that Aaron *had let them get out of control* (32:25). Egyptian religion was not founded on orgiastic rites as was Canaanite religion, but the choice of a bull calf, a prime symbol of sexual potency, leaves little to the imagination as to what direction its worship would go.

ii. The 'visibility' of the Lord (33:12–23)

Without Moses the people lacked certainty for the future and desired the leadership of a visible god. In principle, Moses himself was no different. He too was unprepared to venture alone into the future (12), he too desired some certainty that the Lord was still prepared to go with him and Israel (13–15), and – ideally, as he then understood it – he too wanted something he could see (18). As it turned out, his desire to be certain of the Lord and his presence was blameless, but to see the face of God was an impossibility (20). Yet the Lord, in marvellous graciousness, set about meeting Moses' needs, and he did so with a promise (14), a glimpse of the glory (20–23) and a word to rest on (34:5–9) and live by (34:10–27).

The promise of the Lord's presence in 33:12–17 forms the first half of this deeply important section of Exodus. In verse 12 Moses sought confirmation of his place in the Lord's plans: how would he be enabled to fulfil his commission, and how did he stand personally in the Lord's esteem? The answer comes in verse 17: the Lord had heard Moses' plea and, yes, Moses did have his place in the Lord's esteem. If we entertain any surprise at this display of uncertainty on Moses' part, we need to remember the shock given to the Israelites' system – including, apparently, Moses' – by the episode of the golden calf. It brought to the fore, *for the first time*, the issues of sin, death and judgment. If we discern them underlying the earlier Exodus narratives, it is because we have the benefit of hindsight. But now they have become the main issues and, seen clearly in Moses, there is a proper trembling before God, a big question mark over the future and a need for fresh assurance about whether such a God could indeed continue to march with such a people (see especially 32:7–14, 19–21, 28, 30–32). And to be frank, Moses might well have been confused, for the Lord's recent words to him could scarcely have made sense. What good was it to be promised angelic presence (32:34; 33:2) if it meant that the Lord himself was to be henceforth absent (33:3)? Can we wonder that Moses needed assurance?

The assurance he needed came in the sweetest, gentlest word of promise, given in the central verses of the passage (33:14–15). 'Who is going with me?' Moses asked. 'I am,' the Lord replied. Relief must have flooded into Moses' battered spirit and he burst out, *If your Presence does not go with us, do not send us up* ['cause us to go up'] *from here.* We can feel the spiritual heartbeat of a real man of God, who deemed it better to remain permanently in a desert place than to get into a land flowing with milk and honey and find the Lord was not there with him.

As we try to understand the message of Exodus, we need to remember that the Lord's presence with his people was, throughout, secured by the angel. It was the angel of the Lord who appeared to Moses in the bush (3:2), it was the angel who went ahead of the people in the pillar of cloud and fire (14:19a) and who moved protectively to cover their rear (14:19b–20), and it was the angel who, before ever they sinned in the affair of the golden calf, was to be the companion of their way and the guarantor of their victory (23:20, 23). Yet, throughout all that happened, both the narrative and the experience of the main participants make it clear that the accompanying angel was the Lord himself (cf. 13:21–22 with 14:19).

In other words, the incident of the golden calf had changed nothing, but it had brought a true understanding of the Israelites' position and plight as sinners before the Lord and an explanation of why he came alongside them in the person of the angel. First, the story up to the point of the golden calf explains how it was that the Lord could say both *my angel will go before you* (32:34) and *my Presence will go with you* (33:14).

The Lord and the angel are one. But, second, the incident of the golden calf and the revelation of the seriousness of sin as alienating the holy God and inviting death as its result (32:10) revealed why the Lord could say both *I will send an angel* (33:2) and *I will not go with you* (33:3) and *If I were to go with you . . . I might destroy you* (33:5). The angel is not a diminution of the divine presence, but an adjustment whereby the holy God can, in all his holiness, come among and accompany sinners and bring them into an inheritance from which their sinfulness would have excluded them. The angel is the whole divine nature in an outreaching of grace.

The terms of the Lord's actually taking up residence in the tabernacle among his people were not simply 'God in the midst of Israel' but 'the holy God living among sinners' (cf. 1 Cor. 3:16–17; 6:19–20).

In 33:18–23 the structure reveals all:

A¹ Moses' prayer: 'Show me' (18)
    B¹ Promised divine self-revelation: goodness and name (19)
        C The unbearable reality (20)
    B² Promised divine self-revelation: glory and care (21–22)
A² The Lord's reply: 'You will see' (23)

Notes

33:19 The expression *all my goodness* is not used in any other self-revelation of God. *Goodness* is *ṭûb*, used of the beneficence of Yahweh in blessing and saving (e.g. Neh. 9:25; Ps. 25:7; Isa. 63:7), the attractiveness of Yahweh's house (Ps. 65:4) and rich abundance (Gen. 45:18). Here it conveys the idea of a display of all that is lovely, beneficial and generous in the character of the Lord.

Note the sequence here: the *goodness* is encapsulated in the *name*, the main ingredients of which are *mercy* ('grace', √ḥānan) and *compassion* (raḥam). The wording *I will have mercy on whom I will have mercy* underlines that it is wholly the Lord's decision on whom he bestows his undeserved favour ('grace'), the heartbeat of his love ('compassion'), the knowledge of his name and the vision of his goodness. Cassuto (p. 436) says, 'It is impossible for you to know when, or if, I shall act thus. I shall be gracious . . . if it pleases me, when it pleases me, and for the reasons that please me' – and, we might add, 'to whom it pleases me'. Not even Moses has a 'right'. It is all of grace, and sovereign grace at that.

33:20 Note the equivalence of *my face* to *me*. The Lord's *face* is his very person and personality. Cf. Ps. 139:7, where 'Spirit' and 'face' (NIV, 'presence') are used in parallel.

It was part of Moses' uniqueness that he was able to stand 'face to face' with the Lord. Numbers 12:8 indicates that the vision granted to Moses here in Exodus was by no means a 'one-off', no matter how special it was. Moses enjoyed person-to-person conversation (lit. 'mouth to mouth I will speak to him') with the Lord and was able to see his 'form' (lit. 'the distinctive representation of the Lord he will observe').[16] On every such occasion Moses saw the Lord truly but, Exodus insists, he never saw him fully. The same grace which sovereignly granted the vision also guarded and graded the revelation to what Moses could bear. If we speak about the Lord 'accommodating' himself, we must be careful not to permit any thought of the Lord 'diminishing' himself.

All this is precisely what Israel and Moses learned in consequence of the golden calf: that the Lord had always made himself present among them in the person of his angel, and that he would continue to do so (32:34; 33:2). The angel is his 'real' and 'true' presence, but it is particularly his presence 'adjusted' to dwell among sinners, so that he can accompany them, lead them and bring them into what he has promised. In other words, the angel of the Lord is a 'preview' of our Lord Jesus Christ, the second person of the Trinity. When we believe in him, we believe in the Father; when we see him, we see the Father; and when we hear him, we hear the Father's words (John 12:44–45, 49–50). He came from the Father to make the Father plain (John 1:18), and the answer to the plea to see the Father is to look at Jesus (John 14:8–9). God himself shines in our hearts to give the light of the knowledge of his glory in the face of Jesus Christ (2 Cor. 4:6).

Our situation is exactly that of the people in Deuteronomy 4:12 (and, indeed, of Moses) but yet it is so incomparably fuller, higher and more glorious. They had 'no form . . . only a voice', but we have the fourfold manifestation of God in Christ which we call the Gospels. The time will come when 'his servants will serve him. They will see his face' (Rev. 22:3–4), but in the meantime every possible delineation of God in Christ

---

[16] The key word here is *tĕmûnâ* (e.g. Deut. 4:12; Ps. 17:15), which is related to *mîn*, 'kind, species, distinctive sort' (e.g. Gen. 1:12). It is the visible representation of what is distinctive or unique.

is there for us in the rich technicolour of the inspired page. Even Moses felt he could not proceed without the special reassurance of his eyes (33:18), and the understanding Lord met his needs with promise (19), caveat (20), protection (21–22) and satisfaction (23). The major revelation was not, however, what Moses saw but what he heard (34:5–27): the word of God in disclosure (5–8) and direction (8–26). Moses was commanded not to draw a picture of what he saw but to write a record of what he heard (27). The people of God are to find all their assurance and confidence in the Word of God, and it is in his Word that we too can look, with unveiled faces, upon the face of Jesus and, with reassured feet, go forward.

e. Dimensions of devotion (E[1, 2])[17]

Moses' call for a deliberate taking of the Lord's side creates what is in fact the customary earthly state of the visible church: a combination of those who have participated in the rites and ceremonies, shared the general experiences, and, in a formal sense, identified themselves with the church, and those who have made their personal commitment, come out with conviction and commitment to be the Lord's, and identified themselves as separated and distinct people.[18]

i. The devotion of practical commitment: the people within the people (32:25–29)

The rigour and vigour of the response demanded of the Levites (32:27–28) dismays and shocks us, but if we need to remember that our ways are not their ways, we must also recall that their day was not our day (cf. 1 Kgs 18:40). We should not ask if they were right to do what they did, but rather what would be the equivalent of their committed response today? It is wrong to ask, 'Should we do as they did?' It is right to ask, 'Do we feel as they felt?' Are we as horrified as they were when we face spiritual disloyalty and abandonment of divine truth? Is our commitment as firm, realistic, adequate and morally charged as theirs was?

---

[17] E[1] (32:25–29) is bracketed by the contrasting references to the people, now without moral restraint (25), and the Levites, who 'filled their hands' in devotion to the Lord. E[2] (33:7–11) begins and ends (7, 11) with seeking and meeting the Lord: the tent was for everyone (7) but was also special to Moses and Joshua (11).

[18] Cf. Isa. 8:11–18; Rom. 2:28–29. Moses cried, *mî layhwh*, 'Who is Yahweh's?' (i.e. who 'belongs to' or is 'for' Yahweh in personal, committed distinctiveness). He did not ask what they may have been, or whether or not they had participated in the worship of the calf, but he simply asked if they would now 'get up out of their seats' and take a public stand.

We must go on asking the right questions. Does it appal us that some god other than the Lord should be worshipped, or that he should be worshipped in defiance of his Word and to the denigration of his character? Are we as convinced as the Levites were that there are fixed standards, moral absolutes and revealed rules for the people of God? Do we see and feel sin to be hateful, disastrous and deserving of death, a thing to be eradicated from within ourselves and from the community of the Lord's people?

No, the Levites do not set us an example of an action to follow, but they do challenge our complacency and our lack of pure indignation and moral outrage. Their example does not call us to 'strap a sword' to our sides, but it does call us to stand up, to stand out, to stand for and to stand against. We are called to belong to the Lord and to be on his side and, therefore, to wage spiritual warfare against sin in ourselves, in the fellowship to which we belong and in the whole professing church. We are still the people of God's armour, taking 'the sword of the Spirit, which is the word of God' (Eph. 6:17).

ii. A different devotion of practical commitment: the people within the people (33:7–11)

If Moses summoned the Levites to declare themselves to be on the Lord's side and by their action to set an example of being the 'people within the people', he also made it possible for those who had committed themselves to the Lord to enjoy regular, individual fellowship with him by pitching a *tent of meeting* (7). In parallel with the action of purging the disloyal, there was a 'gathering in' so that those who desired to enjoy the divine fellowship could identify themselves and do so.

The way in which the pitching of this tent is described makes it clear that it was not a temporary substitute for the tabernacle. The verbs that are used throughout the passage are in a form that expresses habitual action ('Moses used to take . . . used to pitch . . . used to call . . . everyone used to go out . . . all the people used to rise and take their stand', etc.), and this indicates that the pitching of this tent went on and on, even after the tabernacle had been instituted. This underlines for us the truth that alongside the established forms of religion open to all who associate themselves with the church and conform to its ceremonies, there is also a private, personal religion of individual conviction and devotion. As 33:7 expresses it, the tent of meeting was a provision for personal spirituality (*anyone enquiring of the* LORD),[19] a place apart (*outside the camp*) and a reality of divine fellowship (a *tent of meeting*). Israel's relationship with the Lord had been grossly sullied by the abomination of the golden calf, but there was a double avenue of restoration: the way of contrition and repentance, a real sorrowing for sin (6), and, with repentance, a personal 'seeking' after God (7). In this Moses set the example of regularity (8, lit. 'it used to be') and Joshua, the example of persistence and consistency (11, lit. 'used not to stir from'). Moses stands for the spirit that returns from the secret place to serve the Lord and his people; Joshua represents the fact that 'in spirit the servant does not leave his sweet retreat' but 'is always in spirit "outside the camp"'.[20] And in all of this, the Lord gave proof positive that he honoured the desire of his children to be with him, for he came in person to the meeting (10).

f. The undefeated, undefeatable, unchanging God (F[1,2])

We come finally to the two matching passages which lie at the heart of this section. Their common topic is the presence of the Lord's angel as both the leader of the onward journey to the Promised Land (32:34) and also the conqueror of its existing inhabitants (33:2). He is the one who accomplishes the whole work of inheritance; he both leads in and drives out. Surrounding this central idea, the section opens with Moses' awareness of Israel's sin (32:30) and ends with Israel's own awareness of their sin (33:6). A further link is the balance between 32:31–33, where sin merits the sinner's banishment, and 33:3–5, where sin merits the Lord's alienation.

The two passages, then, taken together, bring us to the crucial turning point in Israel's walk with God, where sin comes to the fore as the fundamental issue. As Paul will later write, 'Sin was in the world before the law was given, but sin is not charged against anyone's account where there is no law' (Rom. 5:13), and in Acts 17:30 he says, 'In the past God overlooked such ignorance.' 'Ignorance' is an accurate description, for again according to Paul, it is 'through the law' that 'we become conscious of our sin' (Rom. 3:20). Throughout Romans he continues this theme of the difference made by the giving of the law. For example, 'where there is no law there is no

---

[19] Lit. 'seeking' the Lord. This is a regular OT idiom. Here √bāqaš is used, in other places, √dāraš (e.g. Ps. 34:4[5]), without any variation of significance. The idea is never that of searching around for something that has been lost and one is not too sure where it may be, but always of a determined approach to the place where the desired object ('the LORD') is known to be and sure to be found.

[20] Coates, p. 286.

transgression' (Rom. 4:15); 'I would not have known what sin was had it not been for the law' (Rom. 7:7); and 'when the commandment came, sin sprang to life and I died' (Rom. 7:9). The apostle might well have reached this conclusion by reading Exodus. Chapter 32 is living proof of Paul's personal contention that 'when the commandment came, sin sprang to life and I died'. Up to this point, Israel had grumbled (15:24), resented having left Egypt (16:3) and doubted the Lord's presence and power (17:2–3, 7) without any qualm of conscience, and all the while the Lord had seemed graciously to overlook their resentment and unbelief and stepped in to meet their needs. No longer! Once the law came, sin sprang to life, and Israel saw all too vividly that the wages of sin is death and faced 'the wrath of a sin-hating God' (32:28, 35).

This was, however, the only thing that had changed. Moses expressed dismay when the Lord said that he would not go among them but that the angel would be their leader (32:34; 33:2–3). With the book of Exodus in our hands, we can only ask, 'So what's new?' From the start (3:2), and throughout their journey to date, the angel had been their divine leader (cf. 13:21–22, further explained in 14:19), and he would now still lead and conquer. What *was* new, however, was that the law had come and they themselves had been brought face to face with the dire reality of sin and its consequences. At last they realized that even though they were the Lord's people – and his redeemed people at that – they were still sinners before him, and that the angel, even though he was the true and real Presence of the Lord, was, nevertheless, an 'adjusted' Presence whereby the Holy One could dwell amid a sinful and unworthy people. In other words, nothing new had happened, but they had learned the meaning of what hitherto they had not properly grasped: the real significance of the holiness announced in 3:5 and enforced on them in 19:10–13, 23–24.

No wonder, then, that even Moses was taken aback (33:15) and that *stiff-necked* Israel was brought to a new place of contrition (33:5–6)[21] and reverential awe (33:8–10). But God had not changed: the angel was still their divine companion (cf. 23:20), and Canaan was still their destination (32:34). The Holy One had revealed the holiness which is his unchanging

---

[21] Coates (p. 283) says, 'If God's people find He is not with them it is well to mourn . . . it is the first step to blessing . . . All around us Christendom is putting on . . . ornaments . . . but the wisdom of faith is to take them off . . . [Thus] He opens up a path for those that love Him.' In 33:4 *began to mourn* is the hithpael of √*'ābal*, possibly here better represented by 'bemoaned themselves'. They did so, not, as many commentators claim, because the Lord had left them, but because they realized for the first time the true understanding of his presence and of their position before him.

nature, and he had also shown that what he has promised he will never fail to perform.[22] It is true that he 'adjusts' his Presence, so as to come in all his holiness and glory among sinners, but nothing will make him adjust his purposes – neither Israel's unworthiness (32:34)[23] nor all the power of the enemy (33:2). He is God, unchanged and unchanging.

Additional notes

32 – 34 Durham (pp. 417–419) sees the narrative of chapters 32–34 as 'a labyrinth of seams and separate paths ... sometimes mutually contradictory detail' but 'a unity, transcending a patchwork that is ultimately irrecoverable and in some cases purely imaginary'. He gives brief details of the divergent views of the source critics, whom he holds to provide 'valuable data', but to him it is 'a marvellous literary unity' of which 'any part must be understood in a specific connection with the entire composite ... a dramatic and tight-knit narrative' (p. 426). His treatment is valuable for bringing out the 'terrifying jeopardy' into which Israel brought themselves by their sin. 'An Israel from whom Yahweh's Presence has departed is far worse than an Israel that had not known that Presence.'

32:13 Most often (132 times) the verb 'to remember' ($\sqrt{z\bar{a}kar}$) takes a direct object of the person or thing remembered. Once (Jer. 3:16) it governs its object indirectly by the preposition *bĕ*, in the general sense of 'regarding'. Here and on fourteen other occasions, the governing preposition is *lĕ*, 'remember for'. This can be quite general in meaning (e.g. Jer. 31:34, [lit.] 'with reference to their sins'). Sometimes this preposition expresses 'to the disadvantage of' (e.g. Ps. 137:7, [lit.] 'to the detriment of the sons of Edom'), but here it means 'to Abraham's advantage' (cf. Ps. 132:1, [lit.] 'for David's good').

32:25 The verb 'to indulge in revelry' ($\sqrt{s\bar{a}haq}$) is for the most part used in a good sense of expressing or finding pleasure, of laughter (Gen. 17:17; 18:12–15; 21:6) and enjoyment, having a happy time, being free and easy with, and making love (Gen. 26:8). But it also has its unacceptable side too, that of mocking, providing crude and cruel entertainment (Judg. 16:25) or indulging in illicit sex (Gen. 39:14, 17). Thus, the word is non-specific and

---

[22] In 32:34 Canaan is not mentioned by name. It is simply referred to as *the place I spoke of*. Geographical identification is not the point, but only the fact of the divine word of promise. The word of God is never halted, changed or adapted.

[23] Note 32:34 where, as Mackintosh says (p. 335), the Lord 'asserted his rights, in moral government'.

must be dealt with as the context suggests. In verse 25 *running wild* (√*pāraʿ*) is 'to free from restraint', treating the Lord's regulations as though they did not matter any more. The example in Num. 5:18 of a woman unpinning her hair points us in the right direction. In Prov. 1:25 the NIV has 'disregard' (lit. 'threw off the restraint of my advice'), cf. 'avoid' (Prov. 4:15), 'ignores', 'lifts all the restraints of' (Prov. 13:18; 15:32).

33:7–11 Cassuto (p. 429) rightly disputes the view that the *tent of meeting* represents an alternative tradition to that of the tabernacle (cf. Durham, pp. 439–443), but urges that the 'tent' was a temporary expedient because 'for the present the Lord would not permit the building of the Tabernacle in accordance with his original plan, because of the unworthiness of the children of Israel'. Apart from the fact that this is a strange view of the sovereign and all-knowing God, it overlooks the fact that the tabernacle was specifically a place of sacrifice, that is, *a place where the holy God could dwell among sinners*. Why, then, should he need to alter or postpone his plan? Cf. also Mackay (p. 551): 'When the Tabernacle was later completed, this tent was no longer needed.' There is always need for a tent appropriately pitched where as individuals, and without liturgy or form, we can enjoy the Lord's fellowship. Nor can we say, with Cole, that the tent shows that though the Lord will not go in the midst of Israel (33:3), yet he will not withdraw his presence altogether. We would have to ask why the tabernacle was pitched (by divine command) in their midst. No, tabernacle and tent represent the two proper sides of true religion: the public, ordered ordinances of God, and the private place of secret prayer, worship and fellowship.

33:17 To 'know by name' is to enjoy the personal intimacy of friendship, person to person. For just as the Lord's name is the summary of what he has revealed himself to be, so Moses' name is the essential reality of who Moses is. Coates (p. 288) recalls the calling by name in 3:4 (cf. 31:2; Isa. 43:1). In the expression *you have found favour* (33:12; cf. *pleased with you*, 33:17), *favour* translates *ḥēn* ('grace'), the Old Testament equivalent of the New Testament *charis*, the unmerited, undeserved blessing of God. To 'find' grace does not mean to earn it or work for it but only to acknowledge one's need of it. Ruth, talking to Boaz (Ruth 2:10, 13), says, 'Why have I found such favour . . . ?', 'May I continue to find . . .', and thus acknowledges herself as one to whom Boaz owes no obligation and who has no means of obligating him. Likewise, Noah is said to have 'found favour [grace]' with God (Gen. 6:8), that is to say, in a world of universal offence from which no-one was exempt (Gen. 6:5–7), one man was singled out as the recipient of 'grace'. Indeed, the truth of the matter is that grace found Noah, and because of that grace, he became the distinctive man of Gen. 6:9 (see Motyer, *Look to the Rock*, pp. 42–43). In summary, the Lord, who knew all there was to be known about Moses (his *name*), pledged to extend to him all sufficiency. 33:13 touches on the free gift of grace (lit. 'if I have found'; NIV, *if you are pleased*), progress in the life which grace prompts (*your ways*), and the double objective of those to whom grace is given – to know the God of grace and to receive grace ever more abundantly (*continue to find*).

Exodus 35 – 40

23. The glory cloud

Bible repetitions underline Bible priorities. Important things get said twice! In this case, it is the awesome reality encapsulated in the tabernacle – that the Lord, the Holy One, the Redeemer, the ruler of the world, the sovereign God of grace and power, actually intends to come and live among his people. And it is not only a reality of indwelling but also a reality of identification: while they were a people living in tents, he would have his tent among theirs; while they were a people on the move, he too would live in a mobile home, so that whether they stopped just for the night or for a longer period, or whether they were on the march, the Lord himself was at the centre of their lives.[1] So, what Exodus anticipates, Ephesians 2:11–22 fulfils and Revelation 21:1 – 22:5 describes in its eternal consummation (cf. John 2:13–22; 1 Cor. 3:9, 16–17; 6:19–20; 2 Cor. 6:16; 1 Pet. 2:5).

1. The whole picture

Chapters 35–40 fall into four sections in a balanced presentation of how, under Moses, the tabernacle was completed according to exact divine specifications and how the Lord came in glory to take possession of his tent.

a. The Lord's Day (35:1–3)

The section opens (1) with a general introduction to the whole conclusion of the book of Exodus, not just as preface to the Sabbath law of verses 2–3.

---

[1] Num. 2:1 – 3:39 reveals that Israel's camp was set out in four tribal groups surrounding the tabernacle. The most telling representation would be to think of a cruciform pattern, with each group of three stretching out in line, east, north, west and south, but with the tabernacle positioned at the 'crossing'.

It heralds what throughout these chapters amounts to a refrain – that everything that was done was done according to divine command. This refrain occurs seven times with regard to individual articles made (39:1, 5, 7, 21, 26, 29, 32), seven times with regard to tabernacle articles in the course of completion (40:19, 21, 23, 25, 27, 29, 32), and three times with regard to the work as a whole (39:32, 42–43; 40:16). Mackintosh (p. 343) notes, 'We are too prone to regard the Word of God as insufficient for the most minute details [of] His worship and service.' Indeed, it seems to be one of the hardest things to bring modes of worship – especially those that are 'hallowed' by long tradition – under scrutiny, and to ask seriously whether they have any sanction from the Bible. It is, however, a plain derivative of this concluding section of Exodus that the Lord is to be worshipped only as he directs and allows.[2]

The general command to worship and serve under the authority of the word of God leads into the one supreme command that is to govern all the people's work: the observation of the Sabbath (2–3).[3] There could so easily have been a tendency to reason that 'holy' work was surely permissible on the 'holy' day or, at a lower level of thinking, to allow enthusiasm for this great and God-given task to sweep his word aside, to 'feel right' about working for seven days out of seven (as, indeed, many Christian ministers foolishly do today).[4]

But this was not allowed to be so. In verses 2–3 the Lord returned to what he commanded in 31:12–18. The sin of the golden calf was hugely important in Israel's spiritual life and development, but it was not even a hiccough in the Lord's purposes. He picked up again at the point reached before the incident of the calf, as if to say, 'As I was saying before I was so rudely interrupted . . .'! The Lord's Day matters to the Lord. Come what may, it is to dominate his people's programme.[5] This applies not only to the public work of tabernacle furnishing and building but also to domestic life, as the prohibition of lighting *fire in any of your dwellings* (3) shows. The Sabbath has to be the subject of thoughtful planning, publicly and

---

[2] What has only a human validation is 'in vain', says Isaiah (Isa. 29:13, NIV mg.), and this was endorsed by the Lord Jesus (Mark 7:6–7).

[3] 'The Sabbath command was to structure their response to all the Lord required' (Mackay, p. 579).

[4] Cf. Cole, p. 234.

[5] In 16:23–30 the Sabbath law governs the enjoyment of the manna; in 16:29 the Sabbath is the Lord's gift; in 20:8 it is the likeness of the Creator in his creatures; in 23:12 it is a day for no work, only rest and refreshment; in 31:13 it is a sign between the Lord and his redeemed, and our keeping of it is a recognition that he has set us apart; in 31:16 it is to be a perpetual obligation.

privately, so as to safeguard its work-free restfulness.[6] The prohibition of lighting a fire ruled out doing at home on the Sabbath what should have been done earlier in preparation for the Sabbath.[7] The Lord takes rest seriously, even if we may be inclined not to, and Coates beautifully observes, 'We shall not work with God if we have not known what it is to rest with him' (p. 303).

b. Materials and artisans for the work (35:4 – 36:7)

Within this section 35:4–29 deals with the great season of gifts for the tabernacle.

A¹ The Lord's command published (4)
   B¹ The offerings of the willing-hearted (5–9)
      C¹ Skills sought (mainly masculine) (10–19)
   B² The offerings of the willing-hearted (20–24)
      C² Skills sought (feminine) (25–26)
   B³ The gifts of the willing-hearted (27–28)
A² The Lord's command accomplished (29)

Notes

35:4 Childs (p. 635) tries to make 'documentary capital' out of the distinction between *what the* LORD *has commanded* (4) and what *the* LORD *through Moses had commanded* (29). The 'older form', he says, has been adjusted to the new pattern which characterizes chapters 35–39, and 'there is no parallel to 25:8–9, which speaks of the heavenly pattern'. Why should there be? Any differences there are reflect changes in place and intention. To Moses the revelation given on the mountain was the primary datum: the direct command of Yahweh. But what Israel needed for obedience was the Lord's word through Moses. The narrative as such is completely self-consistent.

35:20–24 In 35:22 *ornaments* (*kûmāz*) is of uncertain meaning. KB offers a cognate, 'to clench one's fist', and a Talmudic use of 'bodice'. In Num. 31:50 it refers to a spoil of war.

---

[6] 35:1–3 is balanced by 40:34–38 and therefore the prohibition of fire here and the perpetual fire of the Lord in 40:38 should be noted as part of the *inclusio*.

[7] Hyatt (p. 329) absurdly links this fire with the fire needed for the metal-working which the tabernacle would have required. But such fire would hardly have been *in any of your dwellings*.

These verses develop the position and principle laid down in 25:1–9 and drive home its lesson. In our church situations it is often the case that special 'gift days' are designed to plug holes in the ordinary finances of a church, but is there any evidence in the Bible for such a gift day? We can draw some conclusions from David's call for giving in 1 Chronicles 29:5. First, the purpose of any such 'gift day' should be not church maintenance but church extension and development. Second, there should be no making of gifts without a consecration of heart. In 1 Chronicles David appealed to those who were, that day, making a freewill offering of themselves by 'filling their hands', consecrating themselves, to/for the Lord. When Paul sought to stimulate giving (and, again, it was not to remedy a shortfall in church accounts but to extend Christian ministry), his model was the Macedonian church, which, out of deep poverty, not only gave lavishly, but 'gave themselves first of all to the Lord' (2 Cor. 8:5). Moses was instructed along the same lines. An *offering* is called for in 35:5. The word is *tĕrûmâ*, which, while non-specific, has the root idea of what is 'taken up' or 'raised' from an existing whole. Each person, therefore, was called to explore what he or she already possessed and to set aside from it what was to be the Lord's.

The passage concludes by noting how Israel obeyed the Lord's command through Moses by bringing a *freewill offering* (*nĕdābâ*) to the Lord (35:29). The stress here is on willingness and choice, on giving out of the sheer will and wish to give. In chapter 35 there are in all seven verses referring to the engagement of the heart in the exercise of consecrating possessions and talents to the Lord, most of which are not apparent from the NIV's translation. We have 'freely disposed in his heart' (*willing*, 5), 'wise of/in heart' (*skilled*, 10), 'whose heart lifted him and whose spirit made him willing' (*who was willing and whose heart moved them*, 21),[8] 'freely disposed in heart' (*willing*, 22), 'wise of/in heart' (*skilled*, 25), 'whose heart lifted them up in wisdom' (*who were willing and had the skill*, 26) and 'whose heart made them willing/so disposed them' (*who were willing*, 29).

Where the heart is right and motives of personal consecration are at work, the purse strings get relaxed and problems of finance and supply are at an end (cf. 36:4–7). The wealth that the people lavished must, for the most part, have come to them when the Lord touched Egyptian hearts to respond to the desires of departing Israel (12:36). It is always thus: that we

---

[8] In a combination like this, the 'heart' stands for the unseen reality of a person, the inner constitution and disposition; the 'spirit' is personal energy, 'gusto', the mobilization and direction of vital forces.

give only what the Lord has already given to us. Everything ultimately is traceable to his grace (cf. 1 Chr. 29:14). But the message of the great season of gifts in Exodus presses home another lesson too: that by the Lord's will our primary use of the fruits of redemption is to engage in those acts which secure his presence among us. When the Lord willed to come and live at the centre of his people's lives in the tabernacle, he imposed on them the obligation to provide the wherewithal and to devote their choicest and best to the enterprise. This no doubt involved sacrifice on their part, but they were called to make the decision to hold nothing back in order to secure the Lord's indwelling presence. To put it simply, no tabernacle, no indwelling – and so they had to decide if they wanted the Lord among them or not. On the divine side, it is all of grace; on the human side, it is a decision and desire of the heart.

The remainder of this section, 35:30 – 36:7, deals with workers and materials for the tabernacle and the sufficiency of what was freely given. Bezalel and Oholiab were called to lead the construction work. They were to engage in the work themselves and also teach others. When the time came to start the work, they discovered that notwithstanding the costliness of the work that lay ahead, they already had more than enough to complete the task.

The 'shape' of each of these little subsections is instructive. In 35:30 – 36:1, their God-given tasks (32–34) and God-given skills (35) are bracketed about by the Spirit of God to enable (31) and the word of God to obey (36:1). The enabling of the Spirit must flow along the channel of the word. In 36:2–7 the inward prompting of the individual heart (2b) and the willing gifts (3–6) are bracketed by the Lord's gift of wisdom (2a) and the people's gift of sufficient resources for all the work (7). Human wisdom is not enough for the work of God; there has to be an outpouring of heavenly wisdom. And yet without consecrated giving the work would remain undone and the awesome reality of the indwelling of God would be unrealized.

The purpose of the whole exercise – to secure and provide the dwelling place of God among his people – should still be the ambition of every group of Christians, living out their true reality as the temple of God, indwelt by the Spirit of God (1 Cor. 3:16; 6:19). If we take this passage in Exodus as a pattern, there is a principle of leadership for those so called and endowed: they should exercise their God-given gifts (35:32–33), teaching others (35:34b) and working in a fellowship of leaders (35:34a), under the word of

God (36:1). For those under such leadership there is a principle of committed following, involving responsiveness (36:2) and the willing giving of goods (36:3) and time (36:4), all again under the word of God (36:5).[9]

c. The detailed work: the tabernacle and its furnishings completed, approved (36:8 – 39:32), assembled and erected (39:33 – 40:33)

Exodus 36:8 – 39:32 lies at the centre of this final part of the book, and this is what we would expect. A 'theology' of the tabernacle was laid down in 29:42–46 by the revelation that the Lord's direct purpose in redemption was that he might dwell among his people. *His* work secured their redemption; and now *their* dedicated gifts and work secure his indwelling. Exodus 39:33 – 40:33 matches 35:4 – 36:7.

There are four 'lists' connected with the tabernacle in chapters 25 – 40. The first (25 – 31) is the list of specification, where the tabernacle was commanded in detail; the second (36 – 39) is the list of manufacture, how and in what order the various artefacts were made; the third (40:1–16) is the list of erection, when the Lord himself directed what was to be done to create his dwelling place; and the fourth (40:17–33) is the list of construction, the completion of the tabernacle ready for the great indwelling. Any differences in the order within the lists arise from the purpose for which that list is designed. For example, the first list concentrates on doctrinal priorities, and therefore the ark comes first of all. As we noted earlier, everything else followed from what the ark represented and what it was for. On the other hand, the second list (36 – 39) is much more like a builder's specification and is written in the order in which a practical craftsman would approach such a multiplex task. Thus, the tent itself comes first. The same applies to the list of erection, where the tent had to be there first before the ark could be put into it. All of this shows, according to Cole (p. 239), 'a careful and systematic rearrangement, not thoughtless repetition'.

The question has to be asked why so much space is taken up in such a repetitive way, for, notwithstanding differences in order and suchlike, chapters 35–40 broadly reiterate what has been said already. The tabernacle was erected as it was described. But this, precisely, is the point. The Lord does not change. That strange man Balaam was right when he said,

---

[9] Coates gently challenges our complacency by asking, 'Have we made anything for the tabernacle? The things *have to be made*.' In 36:2–7, 'work' (*mĕlā'kâ*) occurs seven times (2, 3, 4 [twice], 5, 6, 7); the verb 'to do' (√*'āśâ*) six times (2, 3, 4, 5, 6, 7); and 'service, work' (*'ăbōdâ*) twice (3 [NIV 'constructing']; 5).

'God is not human, that he should lie, nor a human being, that he should change his mind. Does he speak and then not act? Does he promise and not fulfil?' (Num. 23:19). Nothing, of course, justifies our sin, but not even the grossest rebellions of his people can deflect the Lord from his purposes. Such is God's overruling sovereignty in power and mercy that, without besmirching his holiness or condoning or in any way accommodating himself to the moral calamity of what Israel did, the disaster of the golden calf became the occasion when Israel learned the sinfulness of sin, the exceeding graciousness of grace, *and* the inflexible determination of the Lord to fulfil his stated purposes. Therefore, the Lord still intended to indwell his people, and, therefore too, the tabernacle specifications are repeated without alteration or adjustment. 'I the Lord do not change. So you, the descendants of Jacob, are not destroyed' (Mal. 3:6).

d. The cloud and the glory: the Lord comes home (40:34–38)

With these five verses, Exodus reaches a fitting and indeed beautiful climax. The form and language are virtually poetic, as if the grandeur of the theme lifted the literary presentation to its own sublime level.[10] The theme is made plain by the repetition of key words. The *cloud* is mentioned in each verse. At the beginning (34) it is paralleled by *the glory* and in the last verse (38) by *fire*. In each subsection of the verses (see below) there is a reference to *the tabernacle* ('dwelling', *miškān*; cf. √*šākan*; niv, *settled*, 35), and, in addition, the description of the *tent of meeting* occurs in verses 34 and 35. It was the Lord's 'dwelling', to which he came in all his *glory*, the reality of his divine nature, and in all his *fire*, his positive holiness. His presence was demonstrated by the settling of the *cloud*, typical of Exodus. The 'dwelling' was a tent, for the Lord came close, identifying himself with his people's circumstances and taking up his residence at the heart of their nomadic life. It was called the 'tent of meeting' for its declared purpose was that 'there also I will meet with the Israelites' (29:43).

The verses fall into four parts:

The advent cloud (34). This heralded the coming of the Lord into his home. Durham (p. 500) notes the sense of promptness, to say the least – maybe even of impatience and urgency – with which verse 33 is followed by verse 34: 'Moses finished the work, and the cloud covered the tent.' (The otherwise reasonably allowable *Then* of the niv somewhat obscures this

---

10 See Durham, p. 500; Cassuto, p. 484.

eager sequence.) It is as though the Lord 'can't wait' to come and live with his people. The covering cloud is distinctly reminiscent of 24:15–16, where (lit.) 'the cloud covered the mountain, and the glory of Yahweh dwelt [√šākan] on Mount Sinai'. This has led a number of commentators to speak, correctly, of the tabernacle as a 'portable Sinai'.[11]

The barrier cloud (35). Strange as it must have seemed, the tent designed for meeting was the very place where even Moses found he could not meet with the Lord. The title belied the reality. The Lord had come home but was not 'at home' to callers. Was Moses surprised? Reading between the lines, the text seems to hint that he was, that he tried to go in but found he could not. Yet, in reality, nothing had changed. On Sinai, while Moses did indeed enter the divine presence, he never did so without invitation, and in 24:15–16 he even waited six days to be called. The Lord is sovereignly in charge of his own front door. He makes what arrangements he chooses as the conditions of entrance (cf. 3:5). But by the time the tabernacle had been erected and the golden calf had been made, sin and its dire consequences had been exposed, the wrath of God had been revealed from heaven against all ungodliness, and the Israelites knew themselves to be sinners and the Lord to be holy. Once more Moses must await the divine invitation. This time, however, it takes virtually the whole book of Leviticus to spell out the conditions for this to happen – the way of the shed blood and of the life of the innocent being laid down in place of the guilty. The invitation to 'draw near' was not long in coming (Lev. 1:1). The tabernacle was specifically a place where sinners could live in fellowship with the Holy One, and he with them, on the basis of the atonement.

The guiding cloud (36–37). These verses are an intended contrast with verse 35. The 'barrier' might have suggested an ambivalence in the Lord's presence, that he was here and yet not here, in his dwelling but remote. Any such suggestions are at once contradicted. The Lord was effectively among his people and present as the living God, not as though at their disposal, but as the Sovereign One. In active control, care and leadership, he was the same God who had led his people in the tricky and testing days between Egypt and Sinai. They are to be at his disposal, not him at theirs.

---

[11] See Cassuto, p. 484. The actual words 'portable Sinai' are used by Mackay (p. 604), who adds, 'The Lord's presence with his people is not confined to a single site, but may now be with them wherever they go.' Currid (vol. 2, p. 369) speaks of 'the Immanuel principle'. Fretheim (p. 315) insists that the tabernacle 'is not simply a symbol of the divine presence. It is an actual vehicle for divine immanence . . . God actually takes up space in Israel's world.' And Davies (p. 252) adds that 'the Dwelling [was] made out of freewill offerings, constructed in absolute obedience, and so made worthy of the tabernacling Presence'.

They are his to command. It is not for them to find a comfortable campsite and then decide to stay longer, or to chafe at discomfort and decide to move on. They are his people; he is their God, coming to them always as 'commander of the army of the LORD' (Josh. 5:14). Furthermore, if the whole building of the tabernacle indicated the Lord's unchanged purpose to dwell among his people, then verses 36–37 underline his unchanged purpose to bring them into their promised inheritance.

> His love in time past forbids them to think
> He'll leave them at last in trouble to sink.[12]

But there was a clear discipline of guidance, and the people were to set out, stop, stay and go only as directed. And we should be careful to note that guidance was not something they 'looked for' but something they waited for. It was the Lord's business and not a matter of anxious care on their part to get their guidance right. All they had to do was to rest, wait and watch, keeping their eyes turned upward and fixed on their presiding God. Guidance was just one aspect of their daily life lived in the presence of God (cf. Isa. 50:4–5).

The faithful cloud (38). Verses 36–37 contrast with verse 35, correcting any misapprehension. Verse 38 amplifies verse 34, stressing that the advent cloud was to be a permanent reality at the centre of the life of the Lord's people, all the time, for *all the Israelites*, and throughout *all their travels.*

2. The Exodus *inclusio*

The ending of Exodus looks back significantly to earlier scriptures. Stephen Dray (p. 204) notes perceptively how 39:42–43 'seems to re-echo Genesis 1:1 – 2:4', thus making the people of God his new creation, in whom 'the original purpose of God for the world was to be displayed', and showing how the divine presence lost by Adam and Eve was restored in the indwelling Lord. In the same way, we might note with Bentley (p. 345) how the stress on obedience to the word of God (40:16, 19, 21, 23, 25, 27, 29, 32) is reminiscent of Genesis 6:22 and 7:5, 9. Obedience is ever the key to our enjoyment of the Lord's salvation (cf. Acts 5:32).

---

[12] From John Newton's hymn 'Begone, Unbelief'.

Coming, however, more closely to the actual ending of Exodus, we note that 40:34–38 forms a significant link with 25:1–9, especially 'let them make a sanctuary for me, and I will dwell [√šākan] among them' (25:8). In this way, the start and end of the tabernacle sequence are bound together, and we see again that the Lord did not change course. Golden calf or no golden calf, his plans of grace needed no adjustment.[13] The incident of the golden calf had its place and purpose. Through it, Israel's eyes were opened to their sin, its seriousness and its awful consequences, and they were made to face the divine holiness, not as a reality in heaven but as a force on earth. It also revealed the grace on which their whole standing before the Lord depended. But the Lord's purposes of grace, now seen in their true light, moved forward unchanged.

An even more significant *inclusio* looks back to the first chapters of Exodus. There is no verbal reference to a 'cloud' in 1:1 – 2:10, yet we could not expound that passage without reference to 'days of darkness' and to 'living in the shadows'. It was indeed such a time. The dark shadow of enslavement lay upon the people of God, the bitter cry of bereavement as their sons were snatched from them for the river, the blows of the taskmaster, a future without hope, and the relentless, uncaring policy of genocide. They were at that time a people under a cloud, even if the text does not expressly say so. Now, at the end of the book, they were again a people under a cloud, this time the cloud of the Lord, the signal of his presence in glory, holiness and grace. Between these two clouds the Sovereign Lord of the whole earth had routed all the power of the enemy, granted his people deliverance, brought them to himself by the blood of the lamb, graced them with his directive law and come, in the fullness of his person, to take up residence in their midst as their indwelling God. This is the whole story of the book of Exodus.

Additional notes

35:29 √*Nādab* (which occurs twenty-one times in the Old Testament) is mostly found in the hithpael mode of the verb, which is basically reflexive, meaning either 'offered freely of themselves' (i.e. of their own volition; e.g.

---

[13] Cf. 2 Tim. 1:9–10: the grace that 'was given us *in Christ Jesus* before the beginning of time . . . has now been revealed through the appearing of our Saviour, *Christ Jesus*', i.e. without any alteration or adjustment of the eternal plan.

1 Chr. 29:6, 9) or 'offered themselves' (e.g. Judg. 5:2, 9; 1 Chr. 29:5). Cf. its use for the Lord's 'freewill' gifts (Ps. 68:9[10]) and free love (Hos. 14:4[9]).

38:8 The allusion here to the women and their *mirrors* is given without explanation, but it is, of course, appropriate in what is simply a construction list. In the phrase *women who served*, √ṣābā' is used twice. The verb is used of military service (e.g. Num. 31:7, 42; Isa. 29:7–8), levitical service (e.g. Num. 4:23) and of 'mustering/enrolling' an army (2 Kgs 25:19). Maybe it had a base meaning of 'enlisted service', and the bands of women were officially 'enrolled' as levitical assistants? The text refers to (lit.) 'the enlisted women who gave enlisted service'. They are mentioned again in the hideous events of 1 Sam. 2:22 (see Mackay, p. 591; Cole, p. 236). Hyatt (p. 330) amazingly countenances the idea that even in Israel 'shrine girls' (whom he calls 'cult prostitutes') operated, but, as Cole acutely notices, why then was blame laid so squarely on Eli's sons? The reference to rotas of women here in Exodus can easily be provided with an explanation as teams of caterers supporting Bezalel, Oholiab and their men. We ought also to notice the unexpected reference to *Levites* in 38:21. It is the only time, other than 4:14, that Levites are referred to. This is inexplicable if (as the supporters of the documentary theory allege) the tabernacle legislation is 'late', but in its context it is correct. The golden calf incident brought out the Levites as a consecrated tribe, and surely their particular work as functionaries in the tabernacle was settled in principle during this period. They are not mentioned in the tabernacle forecast (chapters 25 – 31) because this took place before the episode of the calf.

40:35 To Hyatt (p. 332), the exclusion of Moses in 40:35 is inconsistent with the entrance of Moses into the Lord's presence elsewhere in Exodus. He 'solves' it by allocating verse 35 to the 'source' P[B] and verse 34 to P[A]. On the link between Exod. 40:35 and Lev. 1:1, see Mackay (p. 605).

Listen to God's Word
speaking to the world today

The complete NIV text, with over 2,300 notes from the Bible Speaks Today series, in beautiful fine leather- and clothbound editions. Ideal for devotional reading, studying and teaching the Bible.

Leatherbound edition with slipcase
£50.00 • 978 1 78974 139 1

Clothbound edition
£34.99 • 978 1 78359 613 3

The Bible Speaks Today:
Old Testament series

The Bible Speaks Today:
New Testament series

The Message of Matthew
The kingdom of heaven
Michael Green

The Message of Mark
The mystery of faith
Donald English

The Message of Luke
The Saviour of the world
Michael Wilcock

The Message of John
Here is your King!
Bruce Milne

The Message of the Sermon on the Mount (Matthew 5 – 7)
Christian counter-culture
John Stott

The Message of Acts
To the ends of the earth
John Stott

The Message of Romans
God's good news for the world
John Stott

The Message of 1 Corinthians
Life in the local church
David Prior

The Message of 2 Corinthians
Power in weakness
Paul Barnett

The Message of Galatians
Only one way
John Stott

The Message of Ephesians
God's new society
John Stott

The Message of Philippians
Jesus our joy
Alec Motyer

The Message of Colossians and Philemon
Fullness and freedom
Dick Lucas

The Message of 1 and 2 Thessalonians
Preparing for the coming King
John Stott

The Message of 1 Timothy and Titus

The life of the local church

John Stott

The Message of 2 Timothy

Guard the gospel

John Stott

The Message of Hebrews

Christ above all

Raymond Brown

The Message of James

The tests of faith

Alec Motyer

The Message of 1 Peter

The way of the cross

Edmund Clowney

The Message of 2 Peter and Jude

The promise of his coming

Dick Lucas and Chris Green

The Message of John's Letters

Living in the love of God

David Jackman

The Message of Revelation

I saw heaven opened

Michael Wilcock

The Bible Speaks Today:
Bible Themes series

The Message of the Living God
His glory, his people, his world
Peter Lewis

The Message of the Resurrection
Christ is risen!
Paul Beasley-Murray

The Message of the Cross
Wisdom unsearchable, love indestructible
Derek Tidball

The Message of Salvation
By God's grace, for God's glory
Philip Graham Ryken

The Message of Creation
Encountering the Lord of the universe
David Wilkinson

The Message of Heaven and Hell
Grace and destiny
Bruce Milne

The Message of Mission
The glory of Christ in all time and space
Howard Peskett and Vinoth Ramachandra

The Message of Prayer
Approaching the throne of grace
Tim Chester

The Message of the Trinity
Life in God
Brian Edgar

The Message of Evil and Suffering
Light into darkness
Peter Hicks

The Message of the Holy Spirit
The Spirit of encounter
Keith Warrington

The Message of Holiness
Restoring God's masterpiece
Derek Tidball

The Message of Sonship
At home in God's household
Trevor Burke

The Message of the Word of God
The glory of God made known
Tim Meadowcroft

The Message of Women
Creation, grace and gender
Derek and Dianne Tidball

The Message of the Church
Assemble the people before me
Chris Green

The Message of the Person of Christ
The Word made flesh
Robert Letham

The Message of Worship
Celebrating the glory of God in the whole of life
John Risbridger

The Message of Spiritual Warfare
The Lord is a warrior; the Lord is his name
Keith Ferdinando

The Message of Discipleship
Authentic followers of Jesus in today's world
Peter Morden

The Message of Love
The only thing that counts
Patrick Mitchel

The Message of Wisdom
Learning and living the way of the Lord
Daniel J. Estes